W9-BFC-264

LEWISTON PUBLIC LIBRARY
200 LISBON STREET
LEWISTON, MAINE 04240
(207) 784-0135
www.lplonline.org

WITHDRAWN

Humana Festival 2001
The Complete Plays

Humana Inc. is one of the nation's largest
managed health care companies
with approximately 6 million members in its health care plans.

The Humana Foundation was established in 1981
to support the educational, social, medical and cultural development
of communities in ways that reflect
Humana's commitment to social responsibility
and an improved quality of life.

SMITH AND KRAUS PUBLISHERS
Contemporary Playwrights / Collections

Act One Festival '95

Act One Festival '95

EST Marathon '94: The One-Act Plays

EST Marathon '95: The One-Act Plays

EST Marathon '96: The One-Act Plays

EST Marathon '97: The One-Act Plays

EST Marathon '98: The One-Act Plays

Humana Festival: 20 One-Acts Plays 1976–1996

Humana Festival '93: The Complete Plays

Humana Festival '94: The Complete Plays

Humana Festival '95: The Complete Plays

Humana Festival '96: The Complete Plays

Humana Festival '97: The Complete Plays

Humana Festival '98: The Complete Plays

Humana Festival '99: The Complete Plays

Humana Festival 2000: The Complete Plays

New Dramatists 2000: Best Plays from the Graduating Class

New Playwrights: The Best Plays of 1998

New Playwrights: The Best Plays of 1999

New Playwrights: The Best Plays of 2000

Women Playwrights: The Best Plays of 1992

Women Playwrights: The Best Plays of 1993

Women Playwrights: The Best Plays of 1994

Women Playwrights: The Best Plays of 1995

Women Playwrights: The Best Plays of 1996

Women Playwrights: The Best Plays of 1997

Women Playwrights: The Best Plays of 1998

Women Playwrights: The Best Plays of 1999

Women Playwrights: The Best Plays of 2000

If you require pre-publication information about upcoming Smith and Kraus books, you may receive our semi-annual catalogue free of charge, by sending your name and address to *Smith and Kraus Catalogue, 4 Lower Mill Road, North Stratford, NH 03590. Or call us at (800) 895-4331, fax (603) 643-1831. www.SmithKraus.com.*

Humana Festival 2001
The Complete Plays

Edited by
Tanya Palmer and Amy Wegener

Contemporary Playwrights Series

SK
A Smith and Kraus Book

812.54
H918f
2001

6-02

A Smith and Kraus Book
Published by Smith and Kraus, Inc.
PO Box 127, Lyme, NH 03768
www.SmithKraus.com

Copyright © 2001 by Smith and Kraus
All rights reserved

Manufactured in the United States of America

Cover and Text Design by Julia Hill Gignoux
Layout by Jennifer McMaster
Cover artwork © Tim Hussey

CAUTION: Professionals and amateurs are hereby warned that the plays represented in this book are subject to a royalty. They are fully protected under the copyright laws of the United States of America and of all countries covered by the International Copyright Union (including the Dominion of Canada and the rest of the British Commonwealth), the Berne Convention, as well as all countries with which the United States has reciprocal copyright relations. All rights, including professional, amateur stage rights, motion picture, recitation, lecturing, public reading, radio broadcasting, television, video or sound recording, all other forms of mechanical or electronic reproduction, such as CD-ROM, CD-I, information storage and retrieval systems and photocopying, and the rights of translation into foreign languages, are strictly reserved. Particular emphasis is laid upon the matter of readings, permission for which must be secured from the Author's agent in writing. See individual plays for contact information.

ISBN 0-7394-2532-3

Contents

Acknowledgments

The editors wish to thank the following persons for their invaluable assistance in compiling this volume:

Andrew Crocker
Claire Darby
Michael Bigelow Dixon
Tsue French
Jon Harrod
Brendan Healy
Marc Masterson
Jennifer McMaster
Stephen Moulds
Liz Nofziger
Carrie Nutt
Karen C. Petruska
Jeff Rodgers
Jimmy Seacat
Kyle Shepherd
Alexander Speer
Nancy Maria Vitale
Victoria Zyp

John Buzzetti
Sam Cohn
Mitch Douglas
Charmaine Ferenczi
Peter Franklin
Robert Freedman
Tony Kelly
Joyce Ketay
George Lane
Barbara Ligeti
Bruce Ostler
John Santoianni
Maria Striar
Wendy Streeter

Foreword

Every play in some fashion marks the passage of time. In the transitory world of theatre, these manuscripts are all that remain of those intense experiences that marked the twenty-fifth anniversary of the Humana Festival of New American Plays. We offer them here for your eyes and imagination so that they may be reborn again in other incarnations. Decades from now, someone else will judge how well they serve as an expression of our age, but in this instance they also serve to mark another point in time, the final year of the Festival's artistic founder, Jon Jory, and his longtime collaborator, Michael Dixon. Their contributions to the American playwright are considerable. With this publication we honor their passionate and courageous legacy.

Of course, these plays also mark a new beginning. Another set of arms is embracing the writers and artists who come each year to make new work in Louisville. The entrances and exits could have been orchestrated by Jane Martin herself—both Jon and I had a hand in selecting these plays and bringing them to life. We will leave it to you to decipher. The true focus of the Humana Festival will remain where it belongs—on the playwright who is engaged in a collaboration that is both intimate and public. We thank them for their gift.

To witness the abundance of creative spirit in these plays gives one hope for the future. The sheer variety leaves plenty of room for different likes and dislikes, and sometimes…personal discovery. We hope that in reading these texts you make some strong connections and return next year for more.

Marc Masterson
Artistic Director
Actors Theatre of Louisville

Editors' Note

The Humana Festival of New American Plays is a conversation. One that, like all the most lively and informative dialogues, begins with a few questions, then picks up steam, taking on more richness and complexity, sometimes erupting in hilarious laughter, occasionally shifting toward heated debate—but invariably leaving us with a more complete understanding of ourselves and the world we live in. For more than twenty-five years, Actors Theatre of Louisville has invited hundreds of voices to participate in this conversation, resulting in some of the most exciting and provocative plays to come out of the American theatre.

Some of the voices who've sparked and energized this discussion over the years have changed, though. Most recently, the 2001 Humana Festival marked the end of Michael Bigelow Dixon's impressive sixteen-season tenure as Literary Manager and (for his final season) Associate Artistic Director of Actors Theatre. A tireless advocate for playwrights, dramaturgical guru, and discerning and inventive force in determining the Festival's lineup—not to mention the longtime editor of this series of published collections—Michael has moved up north to Minneapolis, where he is continuing the dialogue at the Guthrie Theater. His dedication, intelligence, and vision continue to reverberate as a new artistic team begins to think about the next twenty-five years of conversation with the Humana Festival's local, national, and international audiences.

Because the Humana Festival is a conversation between so many voices—between plays, between playwrights, between audiences and actors, designers, directors, and dramaturgs—a remarkable number of different perspectives are heard. It is this scope and diversity that makes the discourse such an exciting one. The plays, performed in fast and furious sequence and in close proximity, collide and resonate with one another in ways that are endlessly illuminating. And the echoes can be heard throughout the building, springing to life in Actors Theatre's lobbies, the bar, and even the line for the washroom. This animated exchange—and sometimes passionate argument—arises naturally out of the energy of live performance. But we think you'll still hear the whispers when you open this book. So keep your ears open: these remarkable, funny and daring playwrights are telling you how they see things from their corner of the world. Whether that corner is a vast, metaphysical Rhode Island or a Wyoming bungalow, an American highway or a street in Havana, this is a conversation you won't soon forget.

Tanya Palmer & Amy Wegener

Humana Festival 2001
The Complete Plays

Wonderful World
by Richard Dresser

Copyright © 2000 by Richard Dresser. All rights reserved. CAUTION: Professionals and amateurs are hereby warned that *Wonderful World* is subject to a royalty. It is fully protected under the copyright laws of the United States of America and of all countries covered by the International Copyright Union (including the Dominion of Canada and the rest of the British Commonwealth), the Berne Convention, the Pan-American Copyright Convention and the Universal Copyright Convention, as well as all countries with which the United States has reciprocal copyright relations. All rights, including professional, amateur stage rights, motion picture, recitation, lecturing, public reading, radio broadcasting, television, video or sound recording, all other forms of mechanical or electronic reproduction, such as CD-ROM, CD-I, information storage and retrieval systems and photocopying, and the rights of translation into foreign languages, are strictly reserved. Particular emphasis is laid upon the matter of readings, permission for which must be secured from the Author's agent in writing.

ALL INQUIRIES CONCERNING RIGHTS, INCLUDING AMATEUR RIGHTS, SHOULD BE ADDRESSED TO: JOYCE KETAY. THE JOYCE KETAY AGENCY. 1501 BROADWAY, SUITE 1908, NEW YORK, NY 10036.

BIOGRAPHY

Richard Dresser premiered the car play *What Are You Afraid Of?* at the 23rd Humana Festival. His plays include *Below the Belt* (1995), and *Gun-Shy* (1997), both of which premiered in the Humana Festival and were subsequently produced Off-Broadway, at a number of regional theatres and in Europe. Also, *Something in the Air, Alone At The Beach* (ATL 1988), *The Downside, Better Days, Bait & Switch, The Road to Ruin, Bed & Breakfast, At Home* and *Splitsville*, all of which are published by Samuel French. He has twice attended the O'Neill National Playwrights Conference, is a former member of New Dramatists and a current member of the HB Playwrights Unit.

HUMANA FESTIVAL PRODUCTION

Wonderful World premiered at the Humana Festival of New American Plays in March 2001. It was directed by Marc Masterson with the following cast:

Jennifer	Babo Harrison
Max	Chris Hietikko
Barry	Jim Saltouros
Patty	Barbara Gulan
Lydia	Rosemary Prinz

and the following production cast:

Scenic Designer	Paul Owen
Costume Designer	Linda Roethke
Lighting Designer	Amy Appleyard
Sound Designer	Kurt Kellenberger
Properties Designer	Mark R. Walston
Stage Manager	Alyssa Hoggatt
Assistant Stage Manager	Erin Wenzel
Dramaturg	Tanya Palmer
Assistant Dramaturg	Karen C. Petruska
Casting	Stephanie Klapper, C.S.A.
Casting in Chicago	Janet Louer

CHARACTERS

MAX...a man

JENNIFER...Max's girlfriend

BARRY...Max's brother

PATTY...Barry's wife

LYDIA...Max and Barry's mother

TIME
The Present

SETTING
Various locations throughout New England.

Barbara Gulan and Chris Hietikko in
Wonderful World

25th Annual Humana Festival of New American Plays
Actors Theatre of Louisville, 2001
photo by Richard Trigg

Wonderful World

ACT ONE

SCENE ONE

Rolling thunder, then lights up on Max and Jennifer's apartment. Jennifer's putting flowers in a vase, fussing to get them just right. She moves plates of hors d'oeuvres, critically examining the effect. She fluffs up the sofa pillows. Max enters with an ice bucket.

JENNIFER: What do you think?

MAX: About what?

JENNIFER: This.

MAX: Oh, fine. Perfect.

JENNIFER: I didn't know what kind of cheese they like. I got Stilton and Gouda and Brie and Camembert and Velveeta.

MAX: That should cover it. What's this, paté?

JENNIFER: We've never had them over before. Which is unforgiveable.

MAX: For what this cost you could have bought cocaine.

JENNIFER: Pate is less trouble. And olives. I don't personally care for olives, but others might. I hate company.

MAX: I know, sweetie.

JENNIFER: Where are they? They should be here right now. You told them six-thirty, right?

MAX: Around six-thirty. Seven. Whatever.

JENNIFER: So what you're saying is we don't have a clue when they might blow in. Thank you very much. This is a disaster already.

MAX: Jennifer.

JENNIFER: I think during cocktails I'll sit over here so I can see into the kitchen if there's smoke or a fire breaks out. Where do we keep the fire extinguiser? *(Max makes himself a drink.)*

MAX: Life would be so much easier if you drank.

JENNIFER: That's your department, Max. I'm going to change my clothes.

MAX: Again? Why would you do that?

JENNIFER: I don't know. This just feels generally inadequate to the occasion.

> *(Jennifer starts out.)*

MAX: Hey, stop.

JENNIFER: Why?

MAX: Because you're beautiful. Just exactly the way you are right now.

JENNIFER: Oh, Max. *(They hug.)* How do you put up with me?

MAX: It's quite a nasty chore, believe me. *(Kisses her.)* Tonight is really going to be okay.

JENNIFER: Maybe.

MAX: It might even be fun.

JENNIFER: Now you're dreaming. You always make me feel better.

MAX: I love that about myself.

JENNIFER: Did you ever think you'd be this happy?

MAX: Honestly? I never thought is was possible to be this happy.

JENNIFER: Me either.

MAX: It frankly surprises me. How happy I am.

JENNIFER: Really? Why?

MAX: Well, you remember what a hard time I had. Before we agreed I'd ask you to marry me.

JENNIFER: I know, honey. I was worried. You were so deeply unhappy all the time.

MAX: I was miserable. I was lost. I was forlorn.

JENNIFER: I could tell. Poor sweetie.

MAX: To be honest, I wanted out. Big-time.

JENNIFER: You had cold feet. That's perfectly normal.

MAX: It's so crazy when I think of it now. And there was no one I could talk to.

JENNIFER: Why didn't you talk to me?

MAX: How could I? You were counting on me. You were the problem. And frankly, you were kind of fragile.

JENNIFER: Oh, I'm not all that fragile.

MAX: You mean I *could* have told you?

JENNIFER: I'm not saying I wouldn't have been utterly devastated. But you can tell me anything.

MAX: I'd have these incredibly violent dreams where I was chasing people through the woods shooting at them. But when I finally caught up with them I'd realize *they* were actually chasing *me*. So I'd have to run away through the woods as fast as I could, dodging their bullets. I'd wake up in a cold sweat—which I thought was blood—and there'd be this wonderful moment when I realized it was just a dream. And then I'd think about us and that's when the real nightmare began.

JENNIFER: I'm so glad we're past all that.

MAX: I know. But at the time, I didn't know what to do. It seemed like the only way out was if you died.

JENNIFER: Oh, Max. You're so silly sometimes.

MAX: I'm serious. I needed closure, something final. So I could move on.

JENNIFER: Why are you telling me this?

MAX: I love you and I trust you. Do you remember last fall, that rainy night, running to catch a bus?

JENNIFER: No...

MAX: Viveca's party, the night the car got stolen.

JENNIFER: Oh, right.

MAX: And just before we got to the bus I stopped and you got mad—

JENNIFER: Irritated. Because we missed it—

MAX: I stopped because I thought I might push you under the bus.

JENNIFER: You were trying to kill me, Max?

MAX: God, do I hate that tone of voice.

JENNIFER: *(Another tone of voice.)* You were trying to kill me, Max?

MAX: It was just a brief, tiny stage I was going through. I felt trapped. But I'm finally secure enough to be honest about my fears. Now that we're both so happy.

JENNIFER: I'm not so happy right now.

MAX: Jennifer, that was *last fall.* So much has happened since then. I had to personally overcome the miserable example of marriage presented by my parents so that I could make a commitment to you.

JENNIFER: Were there any other times, Max?

MAX: No...

JENNIFER: That's not a very convincing no.

MAX: No! I swear!

JENNIFER: Tell me about the other times.

MAX: It's not like there were *all these times!* *(Beat.)* Are you going to jump down my throat again? Because I really don't need that.

JENNIFER: No, I promise. I'm glad you feel safe enough to tell me.

MAX: Do you remember that night someone stole my wallet at the circus?

JENNIFER: The hashish night?

MAX: You were taking a bath and I was making strudel and the power suddenly went off and I got a flashlight and went into the bathroom.

JENNIFER: I remember.

MAX: My flashlight caught you sitting in the bathtub just so shockingly beautiful and vulnerable. I think I loved you more in that moment than in the whole time we've been together.

JENNIFER: You were going to toss the flashlight in the bathtub, weren't you?

MAX: What's important is that I love you, honey. I can't imagine my life without you.

JENNIFER: I have to leave, Max.

MAX: You said you wouldn't get mad. You promised.

JENNIFER: I'm not mad. I'm leaving.

MAX: I thought we were happy.

JENNIFER: So did I. You tried to kill me. Repeatedly.

MAX: I just thought there was room for honesty in our relationship. Now that we're planning our lives together I want you to know everything.

JENNIFER: I didn't need to know that. I was very happy not knowing that. *(Gets her coat.)* I've got to walk walk walk. Get some air.

MAX: I don't like the idea of you all alone. There are lots of sickos out there.

JENNIFER: I'll take my chances.

MAX: You can't go.

JENNIFER: Why not?

MAX: You bought all this cheese.

JENNIFER: What do you want, Max?

MAX: We have people coming over. Remember?

JENNIFER: They're not people. They're family.

MAX: My family. I'll bet it would be different if it were your family.

JENNIFER: Yes, they wouldn't be coming.

MAX: You're the one who wanted to try the soft shell crabs. I was never in favor of that.

JENNIFER: You actually want me to cook before I leave?

MAX: How long a walk are you planning?

JENNIFER: I honestly don't know if I'll ever come back.

MAX: I suppose you've never had even an innocent passing thought of wanting me dead?

JENNIFER: If I wanted to end things I'd just leave.

MAX: I couldn't face doing that to you. I know how much it would have hurt.

JENNIFER: Goodbye, Max.

(A moment between them. Then Jennifer opens the door to leave. Barry is standing there in a trench coat with an umbrella.)

JENNIFER: *(Continuing.)* Barry? How long have you been standing there?
(Barry enters.)

MAX: Barry. Didn't even hear you knock.

BARRY: I didn't knock.

MAX: Why not? Were you waiting for us to just arbitrarily open the door?

BARRY: I was turning things over in my mind.

MAX: Where's Patricia?

BARRY: Who?

MAX: Patty?

BARRY: Who?

MAX: Your wife?

BARRY: Oh, were you expecting her, too?

JENNIFER: Of course! Where is she?

BARRY: If you wanted to see Patty then you should have invited her.

MAX: We did.

JENNIFER: That's why *you're* here. Right?

BARRY: Exactly. *I'm* here because *I* was invited.

MAX: I don't understand.

BARRY: You left an endless message on the machine with a lot of inane bullcrap directed at me. Then you said, "Could *you* come to dinner?"

MAX: Yes, could you and Patty come to dinner.

BARRY: That isn't what you said. In that whole senseless, moronic message you never once mentioned her name.

MAX: Yes I did. I asked you both.

BARRY: *(Gets out tape.)* Do you want to listen to the tape, Max? Do you?

MAX: What, you brought evidence? Exhibit A?

BARRY: She just wanted to feel included. She wanted to feel that this wasn't the brothers getting together and she'd be some kind of a third wheel.

JENNIFER: If she's a third wheel then what kind of a wheel am I?

MAX: You're a very big important wheel, Jennifer, but this isn't about you.

JENNIFER: You're right, it's about you. You left the message, Max. Call Patty and invite her over.

BARRY: I wouldn't advise that. Patty's sunk into a hideous funk. She's taken to her bed.

JENNIFER: We have to do something. It's just not a party without Patty. I'll call her.

BARRY: That would be a first.

JENNIFER: Excuse me?

BARRY: Do you know how many times you've called Patty? Does the number "zero" ring a bell?

JENNIFER: Well I'd like to call her now.

BARRY: Patty doesn't need your pity.

JENNIFER: It's not pity, it's polite.

BARRY: You don't love Patty.

JENNIFER: Of course I do. But as Max said, this isn't about me. It's about Patty. And Max.

BARRY: I'm talking to you, Jennifer. Do you love my Patty?

JENNIFER: Yes. I love your Patty. I find her a very interesting person.

BARRY: My Patty doesn't think you love her. My Patty wonders why the two of you have never once gotten together on your own. To go on a hike or have a picnic by a stream. Not once have you called my Patty.

JENNIFER: Your Patty's never called me. Never. We live twelve blocks away. I'm the newcomer. Let's be frank, your Patty hasn't exactly gone out of her way to make me feel welcome.

BARRY: Boy oh boy. You're not talking like someone who loves my Patty.

JENNIFER: I do! But the truth is, your Patty can be very…

BARRY: Very what?

MAX: Careful, hon. This could be a trap.

BARRY: Very *what*, Jennifer? Very *what*? Very *what*?

(Jennifer starts to cry.)

BARRY: *(Continuing.)* What did I do?

MAX: Jennifer's upset about something else. She doesn't mean what she said about Patty.

JENNIFER: Yes, I do! I mean every damn word of it! Your Patty is a very scary intimidating woman who expects the world to wait on her hand and foot!

MAX: Stop it, Jennifer.

JENNIFER: Aren't you the one who wants to tell the truth, Max? Why don't you tell Barry what *you* think of darling Patty?

BARRY: What do you think of darling Patty, Max?

MAX: I love Patty.

JENNIFER: Max says the biggest mistake you ever made was marrying Patty.

MAX: Please, this is so wrong.

BARRY: That isn't what you said in your wedding toast, Max. As I remember, you were pretty effusive.

MAX: Yes, and I stand behind my toast one hundred percent.

JENNIFER: Max thinks Patty has stolen the joy from your life. He thinks you've become nothing but a helpless twitching caretaker for a selfish woman.

BARRY: Interesting.

MAX: This is pure fabrication, Barry. Jennifer is trying to get back at me because...

BARRY: Because why?

MAX: We had a little bit of a tiff-type situation here.

JENNIFER: In Max's defense, he probably says these things because he's jealous of all the money you two have.

MAX: This is where it stops. I won't have money bandied about in my home. You've gotta just try to shut up, Jennifer!

JENNIFER: I know what you'll do if I don't shut up. You'll push me under a bus. *(Jennifer exits to the other room.)*

MAX: *(Calls after her.)* Hey. That's personal.

BARRY: I spent hours trying to convince Patty she was imagining things. That she was welcome in your home. But now I find out she's absolutely right.

MAX: No, Patty's not right. Patty *convinced* you she's right. Which she does all the time.

BARRY: Oh, so you think Patty controls me?

MAX: I'm not saying that.

BARRY: If Patty controlled me would I be here right now? Would I, Max?

MAX: Patty wanted you to stay home?

BARRY: Well, no, she actually wanted me to come here.

MAX: So you're doing exactly what Patty wanted.

BARRY: She wants the best for me. If she's controlling, it's good control. *(Jennifer comes in wearing her coat.)*

MAX: What are you doing, Jennifer?

JENNIFER: I told you, Max. I'm leaving.

MAX: You're really going to embarrass me like this in front of my brother?

JENNIFER: Yes, I am. *(Tosses her ring at Max.)* Oh, and you can keep your engagement ring. *(Jennifer leaves.)*

BARRY: I didn't know you two were getting married.

MAX: Yes, we were going to tell you tonight. We're very excited.

BARRY: Well...congratulations.

MAX: Thanks. *(Goes to bar.)* We should celebrate.

BARRY: Are you serious?

MAX: About drinking? Absolutely.

BARRY: I'm afraid a drink is not possible. Now that I've heard what you two think about my Patty, I can't in good conscience stay. Her honor has been violated.

(A clap of thunder.)

MAX: *(Looks out the window.)* It's really coming down out there.

BARRY: What the hell. A quick drink isn't going to kill anyone. *(Gets a drink and joins Max at the window.)* Too bad Jennifer forgot her umbrella. Where do you think she's going in such a hurry?

MAX: Probably trying to get out of the rain, poor thing. Do you want anything? Perhaps a selection from The World of Cheese?

BARRY: Excellent. Bring it on.

(The brothers eat and drink.)

BARRY: *(Continuing.)* To tell you the truth, we were kind of dreading getting together tonight.

MAX: Us too.

BARRY: But it's actually working out fine.

(They eat and drink. Blackout.)

SCENE TWO

Lights up on a bar. Barry is sitting morosely at a little table with two huge empty mugs. Max enters with a small pitcher of beer, which he pours into the two mugs. The brothers watch like hawks to make sure it's equal. Neither gets much.

BARRY: Jennifer came back?

MAX: Thank God for that freezing rain. She stumbled back in, drenched and sobbing.

BARRY: Good. Marriage is everything.

(They drink.)

MAX: Are you two okay?

BARRY: Basically. Except Patty keeps leaving these mean little Post-its around the house for me to find. See?

(Barry shows Max a few of the Post-its.)

MAX: Wow. That *is* mean.

BARRY: I'll find these stuck on the refrigerator, the bathroom mirror, on my shoes in the morning. Gets the day off to a roaring start, let me tell you. I guess I shouldn't have told her what you and Jennifer said about her.

MAX: You told her? Why would you tell her?

BARRY: Patty has this power. She looks at me and I just panic. Do you know what a curse it is to suddenly find yourself telling the truth? Turns out on top of everything else she was mad I went to your house.

MAX: She wanted you to go. Didn't she?

BARRY: True. But she changed her mind after I left. I guess I should have seen that coming.

MAX: You should have known Patty was going to change her mind after you left?

BARRY: That's what she thinks. And the way she explains it, I believe her. The situation is worse than I thought, Max. I need your help.

MAX: You got it, Barry. Whatever you want.

BARRY: She's making slow but steady progress out of her funk. As a matter of fact, she was well enough to put pen to paper. This is a statement she released.

MAX: She released a statement?

BARRY: *(Gets out paper.)* She writes, "My rage at your appalling cruelty in excluding me from dinner is slowly running its course. According to Barry, it was an 'oversight' rather than the craven act of heartless malice it would appear to be. Taking Barry at his word, I suppose I should feel encouraged to learn that you are simply stunningly selfish rather than aggressively evil."

MAX: She thinks I'm evil?

BARRY: No, she did but now she thinks you're just "stunningly selfish." See, if we analyze this, I think there's real cause for hope. I believe she's almost ready to receive your apology.

MAX: What exactly am I apologizing for?

BARRY: For excluding her from your dinner party. And for the terrible things you and Jennifer said about her.

MAX: I didn't exclude her. And I didn't even say anything bad. Jennifer, on the other hand, was on a senseless bloody rampage.

BARRY: But Patty knows what was said. She can't stop thinking about it. The pain goes on and on, Max. And it's your fault.

MAX: Why are you doing this? You don't have to do this.

BARRY: It's my duty to defend Patty's honor. Which you and Jennifer have besmirched. Although, frankly, we don't hold Jennifer as responsible as you.

MAX: Why not? She said much worse stuff than I did!

BARRY: Yes, but, well, with Jennifer it's understandable.

MAX: Why?

BARRY: You know. Jennifer's a little flighty. Self-esteem issues. It's no wonder Patty intimidates her.

MAX: That's pretty insulting.

BARRY: Please. I love Jennifer. But, as Patty says, Jennifer blends right in with the furniture. One of these days someone's liable to just sit on her.

MAX: Patty said that?

BARRY: You know Patty. She's nothing if not honest. Bless her heart.

MAX: Maybe Jennifer was being honest about Patty. Just the way Patty was being honest about Jennifer.

BARRY: Forget Jennifer. Jennifer's not the man. You're the man. So be the man and apologize and get it over with.

MAX: Do you know what I think? I think Patty should apologize to me for ruining our party.

BARRY: Are you serious?

MAX: Dead.

BARRY: Get real. It doesn't work that way.

MAX: What way?

BARRY: Can I trust you, Max?

MAX: Totally.

BARRY: Patty doesn't apologize.

MAX: Why not?

BARRY: She has many wonderful qualities, but in all the years we've been together, she's never once admitted she was wrong. I don't think she'll start now.

MAX: So you always have to be the one to apologize?

BARRY: If I didn't our fights would never end.

MAX: Jesus Christ. How do you stand it?

BARRY: Because she's so great in every other way. It's just this one thing she can't do. We all have stuff we can't do. I can't fly an airplane, for example.

MAX: That shouldn't cripple your marriage.

BARRY: For example! That's why you've got to help me. You've got to reach out to Patty.

MAX: Or what?

BARRY: Or you and I are through.

MAX: We're not going to be brothers anymore? How will we do that? Travel back in time and kill our parents?

BARRY: I can't fraternize with you and then go home to Patty. She considers you the enemy.

MAX: Do you think I'm the enemy, Barry?

BARRY: I took vows. Big scary vows. My marriage depends on this. Don't make me choose between you and Patty, because Patty will frankly kick your ass.

MAX: You're not giving me any wiggle room, Barry.

BARRY: Look at me, Max. Does it look as if I have any wiggle room? I know for a fact that Patty doesn't have any wiggle room either. Nobody has any wiggle room because you have insulted her honor. Until you apologize to Patty, you aren't my brother.

(Barry downs his beer and leaves. Blackout.)

SCENE THREE

Lights up on Jennifer's work station. Jennifer is wearing a head-set. Barry enters.

JENNIFER: *(On phone.)* Customer service, please hold. *(Beat.)* Customer service, please hold. *(Beat)* Customer service, please hold. *(Sees Barry, records new outgoing message.)* Due to the large volume of calls, you may experience a brief delay. All of our representatives are currently assisting other customers who called before you did. Please stay on the line. Your satisfaction is vitally important to us. You, the customer, are the most valued member of our company. *(Finishes.)* There. Let the idiots talk to a machine. Hi, Barry!

(Barry looks around the place.)

BARRY: *This* is where you work?

JENNIFER: Is it that bad?

BARRY: Oh, no, I didn't mean that. It looks fine.

JENNIFER: Cooped up in a tiny little cell listening to endless whining? I could stay home with your brother if I wanted that. Coffee? Cruller? Advil?

BARRY: Oh, no thanks. I can't stay.

JENNIFER: The only thing I like about this job is putting people on hold. Look, I am so totally sorry about the other night. I can't believe the horrible things I said.

BARRY: It's okay. Really.

(Jennifer shows Barry her arm.)

JENNIFER: See that?

BARRY: What?

JENNIFER: The red marks? I hit myself over and over with a metal ruler as punishment.

BARRY: Well, for God sakes, stop it. Give yourself a break.

JENNIFER: There's absolutely no excuse for it. Except there kind of is.

BARRY: What?

JENNIFER: Well, this doesn't justify my behavior, but I got this weird upsetting jolt from Max just before you showed up. Oh, God, I never should have mentioned it. Sorry.

BARRY: What kind of a weird upsetting jolt? It's none of my business. Sorry.

JENNIFER: I couldn't possibly tell you what happened. Sorry.

BARRY: No, I'm sorry. You're stuck listening to jerks complain all day and here I am, a jerk with a complaint. About Max.

JENNIFER: What's he done?

BARRY: Patty's choking on her own venom. Every day it gets worse and worse. She thinks Max is Satan. I just know if Max could find it in his heart to go to Patty, we could get through this difficult time. But Max refuses.

JENNIFER: It's really not Max's fault. I'm the bad person. I'm the one who said all that mean stuff! Where's my ruler?

BARRY: Stop. Jennifer. I know you said mean things, it was appalling, but we don't hold you responsible.

JENNIFER: Why not?

BARRY: Well, we just don't.

JENNIFER: Why, Barry? Are you saying you don't expect any more from me than appalling behavior? Because that's hurtful.

BARRY: No! You said Max did something…and that's why you behaved so miserably. Right?

JENNIFER: I mean it, Barry, there's absolutely no way in the world I can tell you what Max did.

BARRY: Why not?

JENNIFER: Alright! If you'll stop badgering me I'll tell you. But this can't leave my work station.

BARRY: You have my solemn word.

JENNIFER: He admitted things.

BARRY: Oh God, not the IHOP waitress thing?

JENNIFER: What IHOP waitress thing?

BARRY: Nothing! Misunderstanding over a questionable tip.

JENNIFER: He admitted he's thought of, you know…

BARRY: Bringing another woman into your bed?

JENNIFER: Killing me.

BARRY: Killing you? That doesn't sound like Max.

JENNIFER: It wasn't anything personal. It had to do with his own fears of getting married and having a family and dying. He didn't actually do anything. They were just thoughts. We talked about it and I think I understand. How these horrible things can live inside a decent person. Maybe inside every person. Max says it's part of loving someone. Thinking about them being dead.

BARRY: Huh.

JENNIFER: Which means you probably even feel that way about Patty sometimes.

BARRY: Huh.

JENNIFER: I think he was really trusting me. Just as I'm trusting you, Barry.

BARRY: You've got a great big heart, Jennifer.

JENNIFER: I try. But then I screw up and have to get out the ruler.

BARRY: Do you know what I think? I think you're the only one who can save our family.

JENNIFER: Really? Me? You should know I get very nervous when people show any faith in me at all.

BARRY: Max won't talk to Patty, ergo, I won't talk to Max. So I'm hoping you can talk to Patty.

JENNIFER: Oh, boy. Frying pan into the fire. Just Patty and I? Alone?

BARRY: Is it that bad?

JENNIFER: No! I love Patty!

BARRY: You're my last hope, Jennifer. Someone has to be big enough to bring our family together again.

(Blackout.)

SCENE FOUR

Lights up on an office reception area. Two chairs: one straight and severe, the other large and soft. Jennifer is in the soft chair, sunk down deep into it. She's been waiting a long time. Patty appears, dressed for business. Jennifer doesn't see her.

PATTY: Jennifer? There you are!

JENNIFER: Patty! Hi. I think I fell asleep.

(Jennifer struggles out of the chair, dazed. She starts to hug Patty, who stops her with a firm handshake.)

JENNIFER: *(Continuing.)* I often fall asleep when I'm nervous. Once I heard a burglar in the house and I was going to call 911 and my heart was pounding in terror and then I woke up and it was morning.

PATTY: So there was really nothing to worry about.

JENNIFER: Except everything I owned was gone. Shoes, pills, thongs, dolls.

PATTY: Are you nervous now?

JENNIFER: Not now. Not really. No.

PATTY: I'm not late, am I?

JENNIFER: No. Well, maybe a teensy little bit…

PATTY: We said twelve-thirty, right?

JENNIFER: Actually, not that it matters, we said twelve, so I got here fifteen minutes early but it's really okay.

PATTY: Did you tell anyone you were here?

JENNIFER: No. Not yet. I thought you were busy.

PATTY: I am. I had to let my assistant go this morning.

JENNIFER: Oh, dear. That must be very hard.

PATTY: Yes, the paper-work is endless.

JENNIFER: I can imagine. *(Beat.)* What did he or she do?

PATTY: Do?

JENNIFER: To get let go.

PATTY: Is this just a polite question or do you really want to know?

JENNIFER: Well, I hope it's polite…but I really want to know.

PATTY: Very well. I had to let my assistant go because he or she wasted my time.

JENNIFER: Oh, dear! That's awful. Well. Shall we…go?

PATTY: Where?

JENNIFER: I made a reservation at Connolly's. I'm starved and I only get an hour. Actually now it's half an hour.

PATTY: Was this for lunch?

JENNIFER: Yes. I'm taking you out to lunch!

PATTY: That's very sweet, Jennifer, but you didn't tell me.

JENNIFER: Yes I did! I mean I think I did. I said I wanted to see you and how was twelve on Thursday?

PATTY: And I said I was delighted to see you at twelve-thirty?

JENNIFER: Or twelve and I asked if you liked Connolly's?

PATTY: And I said I did?

JENNIFER: Therefore…

PATTY: Is it me? I still don't hear the word "lunch."

JENNIFER: It's lunchtime. I wanted to talk. I mentioned Connolly's. I assumed you'd know.

PATTY: You and Max make a lot of assumptions.

JENNIFER: Oh, God. This is the last thing I wanted. A misunderstanding. After all that's happened. Look, if we go right now…

PATTY: Do you honestly think I could just go? Please! Jennifer, my lunches are sacred. That's when I solicit contributions and build alliances and defend myself against the relentless attacks of my adversaries. That's just the way it is in the not-for-profit world. As much as I might like to, I don't think I can waste a lunch on you.

JENNIFER: I'm sorry I wasn't clear.

PATTY: Well, I've got a minute or two before I have to run. Certainly enough time to hear what's on your mind. Sit.

(Jennifer sinks deeply into the soft chair. Patty takes the straight chair.)

PATTY: *(Continuing.)* Well?

JENNIFER: I just thought, you and I, we're both involved with brothers who are close and we haven't ever really spent time together. The two of us. Together.

PATTY: No. We haven't. Do you think maybe there's a reason for that?

JENNIFER: I guess there probably is. What's the reason?

PATTY: Go on, please.

JENNIFER: Oh. Well, now that Max and I are getting married—

PATTY: You and Max are getting married?

JENNIFER: Yes. Didn't Barry tell you?

PATTY: No, he didn't.

JENNIFER: Oh. Well, the big news is, we are.

PATTY: Interesting.

JENNIFER: Thanks so much, that's very sweet, we're both just thrilled. Anyway, Patty, I really want to be friends.

PATTY: That's very nice, Jennifer.

JENNIFER: Oh, good! I've always respected you, my God, you're so important and successful—even though I don't know exactly what it is you do—and I've never felt very close to you—and that's not a criticism—but you have to admit there's been a gulf between us which now we can bridge if we're good friends.

PATTY: Jennifer?

JENNIFER: Or Jenny. Yes?

PATTY: Barry has his little circle of friends and I have quite a number of friends of my own, professional and personal, some dating back to childhood. And of course we've made lots of friends as a couple.

JENNIFER: Of course. Nice going.

PATTY: Thanks. What I'm saying is, friendship is important to me. And my time is at a premium. For me to take you on as a friend means someone else gets bumped.

JENNIFER: Oh, dear, I didn't mean for anyone to get bumped.

PATTY: Hey, that's just the way it is, but before I bring the hammer down on a good friend, which I'm happy to do, I need to know: What is it you offer me as a friend? *(Pause.)* That's not a rhetorical question.

JENNIFER: You want me to tell you what I offer you as a friend?

PATTY: If you're serious about it, yes. I'd like to know so I can make an informed decision.

JENNIFER: Well, I think I'm loyal and compassionate. Whenever a friend gets robbed or loses a parent or a pet, you can bet I'm there with cards and candy and handholding, whatever they need. Once I even soul-kissed a girl-friend who was going through a transitional phase. You could talk to my friends, they'd give me the highest recommendations. I can be lots of fun.

PATTY: I'd certainly welcome discovering that side of you.

JENNIFER: Patty, we really don't know each other. There were traumatic events that shaped me. Did I ever tell you about the fire?

PATTY: Oh, my God.

JENNIFER: Thanks for your sympathy, it was just awful—

PATTY: No. I'm just very concerned about the invitations to our benefit. I need to think this through.

(Long pause as Patty thinks.)

JENNIFER: Should I...?

PATTY: Please, Jennifer. I need to think.

(Jennifer waits as Patty thinks. Blackout.)

SCENE FIVE

Lights up on Lydia's condo. Lydia is sitting in a chair, perfectly still. Max enters. A clock chimes. He watches her, concerned.

MAX: Mother?

(No response. Max puts his hand in front of her to see if she's breathing. Lydia suddenly emits an explosive sneeze, terrifying Max.)

MAX: *(Continuing; recoiling.)* Aah!

LYDIA: *(Awakening, frightened at seeing Max.)* Aah!

MAX: Hello, Mother.

LYDIA: What were you doing, all bent over me like that?

MAX: I was concerned. You were so still.

LYDIA: I was making a mental list of everyone who has ever disappointed me.

MAX: Sorry to interrupt.

LYDIA: I was still in the nineteen-seventies. The early nineteen-seventies. How are you?

MAX: A bit shaken, but fine, overall.

LYDIA: Well, as long as you're here, would you get me a glass of ice water?

(Max goes to the bar. A second clock chimes. He works through the following, responding to his mother's requests.)

LYDIA: *(Continuing.)* You can skip the water, dear, just ice in a glass would be enchanting. *(Pause.)* And you might liven it up with a hint of vermouth, if it's not a bother? Thank you. *(Pause.)* You know, just a tiny little splash of gin with the vermouth would be delightful. *(Pause.)* Oh, let's just forget the silly vermouth. And the ice. If it's no trouble.

(Max brings his mother a glass of straight gin.)

MAX: No trouble at all, Mother. Here's your ice water.

LYDIA: Thank you, dear. Sure you won't join me, as long as you dropped by at cocktail hour?

MAX: It's two o'clock. I have to get back to school.

LYDIA: You're in trouble. A student has made some terrible, sickening accusation.

MAX: Please. Everything's fine.

LYDIA: No it isn't. You have that look. You came into the world with that look and I have no doubt you'll stare up at me out of your coffin with that look.

MAX: What look? And I find it interesting you're planning to outlive me.

LYDIA: It's that girl.

MAX: You know her name, Mother.

LYDIA: Oh, I adore her. She acts so much younger than she really is. Which is just marvelous.

MAX: What's her name, Mother?

LYDIA: I'm sorry, they all run together for me. I promise I'll remember the next one.

MAX: Maybe there won't be a next one.

LYDIA: Did she leave you, dear?

MAX: As a matter of fact, we're getting married.

LYDIA: Oh. Well that's very nice, too. Very nice indeed.

MAX: We think so.

LYDIA: Remember when Barry and Patricia got married? That was one of the happiest days of my life. I knew she would always make Barry happy.

MAX: I think Jennifer will make me happy.

(Max makes himself a drink. A third clock chimes.)

LYDIA: Patricia has such a powerful grip on life. She keeps Barry on course. I don't know how she does it. And she runs that wonderful organization all by herself..

MAX: That would certainly be news to the fifty other people who work there.

(Lydia has opened a photo album of Barry and Patty's wedding.)

LYDIA: My God, Patricia was so beautiful on her wedding day. Just radiant!

MAX: Of course. But Jennifer and I are the ones getting married.

LYDIA: Come look, dear! Isn't she grand?

(Max comes over with his drink and glances over his mother's shoulder.)

MAX: *(Raises his glass.)* To Patty! On this special day of my engagement to Jennifer.

LYDIA: I thought you had to go back to school.

MAX: In a minute. *(Drinks deeply.)* I just have to teach a freshman archery class.

LYDIA: Did you ever notice, when Barry is with Patricia, he even *looks* better. *(Looks at album.)* Here he is with you, looking rather sallow. Actually, both of you look rather sallow.

MAX: Sallow? I'm not sallow.

LYDIA: But over here, when he's with Patricia, he looks so vibrant and alive. Oh, I think she's a marvel!

MAX: Mother? I'm going to be honest with you.

LYDIA: Oh, dear. Why?

MAX: We're having a little problem with Patty.

LYDIA: I can't imagine what that could be.

MAX: I love Patty, but she has single-handedly created a bit of a brouhaha.

LYDIA: What did she do?

MAX: I invited her and Barry to dinner and she simply wouldn't come. She claimed I had excluded her. Which is just silly. Now Barry wants me to apologize to her.

LYDIA: I'm sorry, dear. I was only half-listening.

MAX: I love Patty, but she is making our lives hellish. She claims I didn't invite her to dinner when I did.

LYDIA: I was under the impression you *didn't* invite her.

MAX: Yes, I did! Of course I did! Why would you think I didn't?

LYDIA: It seemed quite clear that you didn't on the tape.

MAX: The tape? Barry played the tape for you? I can't believe this.

LYDIA: He was very upset. He needed succor.

MAX: Well maybe I need succor! What about that?

LYDIA: He got here first.

MAX: How could Barry possibly drag you, of all people, into the middle of this snakepit?

LYDIA: I'm his mother. And isn't that what *you're* trying to do?

MAX: I don't get this. How can you be so partial to Patty—whom I love—but who is distant and cold, like the moon? And Jennifer always tries so hard.

LYDIA: I adore poor Jennifer. I really do. And nothing would make me happier than if you went through with your threat to marry her.

(*Max downs his drink in preparation for archery. A fourth and fifth clock chime. Blackout.*)

SCENE SIX

Lights up on Max's apartment. Jennifer is face down on the sofa, her body shaking, as Max looks on.

MAX: Maybe I shouldn't have told you all the details.

JENNIFER: I cannot believe how your family treats me! What have I ever done to them? They're all a bunch of bastards.

MAX: Mother too?

JENNIFER: She's the biggest bastard of all!

MAX: In Mother's defense, she repeatedly said she adored you.

JENNIFER: My family would never treat you like this. Never!

MAX: I know they wouldn't. Because I've never met them.

JENNIFER: If you did meet them they wouldn't treat you like this.

MAX: There isn't much chance I'll meet them since they're mainly dead and the ones that aren't you've surgically removed from your life.

JENNIFER: I mean if they were still alive and I were on speaking terms with them and they met you they would never treat you like this. Barry totally set me up with Patty. It was an ambush. Do you know what I had to do? I had to audition to be her friend.

MAX: How did it go?

JENNIFER: Excuse me?

MAX: How did your audition go? *(Beat.)* Have you heard back?

JENNIFER: Would you listen to yourself, Max?

MAX: I don't have to listen to myself.

JENNIFER: Lucky you. I just never thought your brother would be so mean, putting me in that position.

MAX: Don't blame Barry.

JENNIFER: I do blame Barry. Barry is just who I blame.

MAX: This crisis has torn him to pieces. He's trying to please everyone. And his job is very stressful. Do you have any idea how terrified he gets before he delivers his motivational talks?

JENNIFER: Do you really think he's unhappy because of his job?

MAX: You don't?

JENNIFER: Hah!

MAX: Good point. So you think it's Patty?

JENNIFER: Could *you* be happy living with Patty?

MAX: No, of course not! But I'm different than Barry. Less materialistic, a bit deeper, perhaps.

JENNIFER: True, he's emotionally shut down and crippled, but he still has feelings. And Patty stomps on those tender feelings with her cruel feet.

MAX: Why do you think she does this? Do you think she has some kind of plan?

JENNIFER: I hate to say this, because I love Patty, but I think Patty has a little secret.

MAX: What do you mean?

JENNIFER: When I can't figure out why someone's acting a certain way and I think about their motives and agendas and nothing fits, sometimes a little light goes on and I realize, "Oh, that person is stupid!"

MAX: Are you saying Patty is stupid?

JENNIFER: I know it sounds awful, but think about it.

MAX: Boy, I don't know. Patty's many things—arrogant, selfish, hostile, demanding, mean, vicious, possibly evil—but I honestly don't think she's stupid.

JENNIFER: It's just a theory, Max. God. The point is, we know that Barry's a drowning man. And still, we're not doing anything about it.

MAX: What could we possibly do?

JENNIFER: He's your brother. You love him. Throw him a life preserver.

MAX: You mean interfere?

JENNIFER: Do you have a choice?

MAX: We don't do that in our family. Interfere. That's one of those things we don't do.

JENNIFER: I know. Because it's hard. And it takes guts.

MAX: I wouldn't even know where to begin.

JENNIFER: You'd know what to do if you saw Barry eating a big bowl of steaming poison. And here he is, eating a big bowl of emotional poison that Patty is feeding him and you say you don't want to "interfere."

MAX: What if we're wrong? What if, beneath his gloom, he's happy?

JENNIFER: Barry has forgotten what happiness is. I love Patty, but he's under the thumb of a ruthless, troubled, vindictive woman who might also be stupid.

MAX: Maybe you're right. There are things I haven't even told you about. Like the mean Post-its.

JENNIFER: Barry doesn't have what we have. Sure, we have our moments, I mean frankly, your death threats were kind of upsetting—

MAX: Boy, that is really putting a negative spin on it—

JENNIFER: The point is, we have a pretty wonderful life.

MAX: We're lucky, I guess.

JENNIFER: A lot luckier than Barry and Patty. I hate to criticize them, but come on. I almost have to.

MAX: I have a confession to make. Whenever we talk about Barry and Patty's problems, I feel so close to you.

JENNIFER: Really? I do too, honey.

MAX: I shouldn't tell you this.

JENNIFER: Tell me.

MAX: It's about Patty.

JENNIFER: Oh, goody.

MAX: Jennifer, this is Top Secret. She's never apologized to Barry. About anything.

JENNIFER: Ever?

MAX: Ever. She can't apologize.

JENNIFER: That's incredible. I don't know what I'd do if I couldn't apologize. It would certainly open up a few more hours in the day.

MAX: You do apologize a lot.

JENNIFER: Too much?

MAX: Sometimes.

JENNIFER: Sorry.

MAX: It's okay. It's better than not apologizing at all. Barry always has to be the bad guy. Even pro wrestler bad guys sometimes get to be the good guy.

JENNIFER: And think of poor Patty. So tough on the outside and such a frightened little child inside.

MAX: They're in very bad shape, aren't they?

JENNIFER: It's so sad. There they are, living together, but all alone. Terrified.

MAX: It's scary what happens to people.

(Max and Jennifer kiss. Blackout.)

SCENE SEVEN

In darkness, a group of voices is heard loudly chanting, "Yes, I can! Yes, I can!" Lights up on an area outside a restaurant as Barry comes out of the restaurant flushed, on a high. Max and Jennifer suddenly appear.

MAX: Nice work, Barry.

BARRY: Hey! They just needed to feel good about themselves. Self-doubt can be crippling for a doctor.

JENNIFER: Sounds as if you got 'em back on track.

MAX: Feeling like gods again. So, can we buy you a drink?

BARRY: Wait. I'm not talking to you, Max. What are you doing here?

JENNIFER: We just happened to be passing by.

BARRY: That's a damn lie!

MAX: Okay, cards on the table, we need to talk.

BARRY: *(To Jennifer.)* Tell Max that will be difficult, since I'm not talking to him.

JENNIFER: Come on, Barry, let's all go sit in the bar.

MAX: Excellent idea. Three or four drinks, we can start making sense of this.

BARRY: I can't do that. If Patty found out we were meeting without her, it would crush her spirit.

JENNIFER: What if we sat on a bench outside so it was more like a chance meeting?

BARRY: I think we'd better stay on our feet. You never know who's going to see what and report back.

MAX: This is what we have to talk about. I love Patty, but she's inside your head like a selfish microchip, controlling everything you do.

BARRY: *(To Jennifer.)* Tell him I'm very happy.

MAX: How can you be happy when you're afraid to sit down and have a drink with your own brother?

BARRY: *(To Max.)* I could do that. But factor in Jennifer—no offense, Jennifer—and it starts to seem like a group activity that excludes Patty.

MAX: But this is just a chance meeting.

BARRY: No it isn't.

MAX: I know it isn't, but it could be.

BARRY: No, it couldn't be because it isn't. It's a planned event, and Patty wasn't included. History repeating itself, and we can't let that happen. Second time around, I would definitely stop the Nazis before they came to power, for example. But that's just me.

MAX: There's no need to drag the Nazis into this.

BARRY: For example!

JENNIFER: I could leave. Then it's just the two of you.

MAX: That won't solve Barry's problem.

BARRY: What's my problem?

MAX: I love Patty, but she holds you back.

JENNIFER: I love Patty, too, but I think she's so afraid of losing you she gets insanely jealous and sort of sick and crazy, not that it's her fault. But you have to pay the price.

MAX: Obviously, we both love Patty, but we don't love what she's doing to you. You wake up to nasty Post-its and bizarre rules and you live in constant round-the-clock fear, like a P.O.W.

JENNIFER: And it's written all over your face. It's heartbreaking for those few of us who still care.

MAX: I don't mean to compare Patty with Jennifer, but Jennifer wants me to be true to myself. I don't face a lot of hostile questions if I come home late—

JENNIFER: Or if you don't come home at all, which happens. A whole weekend, I guess I would have questions—

MAX: The point is, Jennifer and I are equals, communicating through love, not fear.

JENNIFER: But in fairness, we work at it. We're tough on ourselves. Because relationships aren't always easy.

BARRY: That's what I hear. Are you saying I should leave Patty?

MAX: Whoa, I'm not sure I'm ready to go that route.

JENNIFER: That's a big decision, Barry. Max and I would have to really mull that one over.

BARRY: But you two have kind of figured out how to make a relationship work?

MAX: Hey, I'm not perfect. And believe me, Jennifer's far from perfect. But you could sure as hell do worse than end up like us.

BARRY: Interesting.

MAX: So what do you think?

BARRY: I think if I had your life, in about one week I'd collapse from hopeless despair.

JENNIFER: That's not very nice.

BARRY: It's not just you, Jennifer. Max is one jealous guy. You look at me and see a guy who never finished college and makes more money than you'll ever make.

MAX: Do you honestly think a price can be put on the work I do with children?

BARRY: Yes, a very very low price. And it eats you up every day of your life.

MAX: I didn't become a Guidance Counselor for the money.

BARRY: Obviously. But it destroys you to watch me cheer up a bunch of pouting doctors for twenty-five grand.

MAX: Twenty-five—Jesus! What's wrong with our society? Everyone is so materialistic!

BARRY: Plus, Patty just approved a huge retroactive pay raise for herself. Our biggest problem is finding time to spend together. Because we're both so busy doing things we love and getting richly compensated.

MAX: You know, Barry, there's more to life than all this money and all these "things" you accumulate.

BARRY: Yeah? What else is there? Can't think of anything?

MAX: All your money and all your "things" just get in the way. What matters is what you're doing to make this a better world, what your life means to other people, what's in your heart.

BARRY: You talk like someone who lives in a small apartment.

MAX: Look, I love Patty, but she has changed you. The joy, the spontaneity, it's all gone. Barry, for the love of God, do you remember how drunk we used to get? Jesus, I miss that.

BARRY: Why are you so angry, Max? Is it just the money?

MAX: Know what I'm angry about? You and Patty—and I do love her—have turned this family into two armed camps and you enlisted Mother on your side.

BARRY: You're just sorry you didn't get to Mother first.

MAX: I would never stoop to that, wielding our poor shriveled mother like a deadly weapon. Never! And if I did, I would *never* play her that tape.

BARRY: Because the tape proves that you excluded Patty from your party. It took the gun out of your hands.

MAX: The gun? This is a family. Now I love Patty, but she is ripping our family apart. And I can't let her do this. As much as I love her.

BARRY: Do you know who the real culprit is, Max? It isn't Patty. It isn't me. It isn't even poor Jennifer. It's you. All Patty wants is a crumb from you, and you won't give her that, you're so sure you're right.

MAX: I am right. I've thought it through from everyone's point of view, it all checks out. Right?

JENNIFER: Right.

MAX: So I'm right.

BARRY: Does it feel good to be right?

MAX: It would feel a whole lot better to make things right with our family. I'd do anything for that.

BARRY: Then you know what you have to do.

MAX: What?

BARRY: Until you find it in your heart to face Patty, the blood is on your hands, Max.

MAX: Oh, you want me to just go and face Patty alone? With no back-up?

BARRY: Are you afraid?

MAX: *(Laughs without humor.)* Of Patty?

BARRY: My marriage is in crisis right now. And it's all because of you. You have hurt Patty and she's taking it out on me. You're slowly killing me, Max.

JENNIFER: Your marriage isn't Max's fault.

BARRY: I'm fighting for my life and the best you can do is to tell me to leave my wife. I guess I shouldn't be surprised.

MAX: What are you saying?

BARRY: Well, let's face it. I'm getting advice from two people who think it's perfectly normal to want to kill your loved one.

JENNIFER: Barry, you promised you wouldn't tell! *(To Max.)* I didn't tell him, Max! And you said it was normal!

BARRY: I guess the only thing that's keeping you two together is joining forces against Patty. Holding hands on a thrill ride through my marriage. I think that's a bit sad.

JENNIFER: There's something sadder than that, Barry. Living with a woman who has to be right, so you spend your whole life apologizing—

MAX: Jennifer!

(Blackout.)

In darkness, a doorbell. Lights up on Patty and Barry's house as Max enters with flowers. Music is playing.

MAX: Patty? Hello? *(He turns off the music.)* Patty? It's Max.

PATTY: *(Offstage.)* I never dreamed you cared enough to make this kind of effort.

MAX: Hey, I care a lot. That's why I'm here.

(Patty enters. She's wearing a robe and carrying a glass of champagne.)

PATTY: Just the sound of your voice gets me excited, gets me thinking of everything that could happen for us.

MAX: Well, good. I'm glad.

PATTY: I don't want to rush through the foreplay, but when can you start?

MAX: Oh…any time.

PATTY: I have the feeling you're the spark we need. Bye! *(She takes off the headset Max didn't see.)* New board member, but it's nice to know you're available. You got me flowers?

MAX: I hope you like them.

(Patty closely examines the flowers.)

PATTY: From the convenience store on the corner?

MAX: Beautiful, aren't they?

PATTY: You got them outside on the street?

MAX: Right.

PATTY: That's nice.

MAX: Thanks.

PATTY: They also have flowers inside. They cost just a little more but they still show signs of life.

(Patty throws the flowers away.)

MAX: I didn't know about the flowers inside.

PATTY: Do you ever tell the truth?

MAX: All the time!

PATTY: I'd offer you champagne but I don't want to open another bottle unless you're staying a while. How long are you planning to stay?

MAX: I don't really know. I thought it was important for me to come here and…talk.

PATTY: What did you say to your brother the other night?

MAX: About what?

PATTY: If I knew "about what" I wouldn't have to ask. Would I? He's been crying. I see enough men cry during a normal working day, I don't need to come home to another one.

MAX: Patty, I feel there's been a misunderstanding.

PATTY: Oh, I think I understand things pretty well. You and Barry don't want anything to come between you. You want to be little boys forever and ever. Your whole lives are just a big game. Well, I won't put up with it. That's why I called you on your phantom dinner invitation.

MAX: Honestly, I was really looking forward to breaking bread with you, Patty.

PATTY: You'll have to do better than that with me, Max. I demand it of Barry and I demand it of his family. When I met Barry he was going nowhere, dating every pretty girl he could find, working his own hours, surrounded by family and friends, having the time of his life.

MAX: I remember those days.

PATTY: I made it clear he had to pull himself together or else I was off limits. Without a five-year plan he didn't stand a beggar's chance of getting into my kimono.

MAX: Barry's on a five-year plan?

PATTY: I helped him. Do you honestly think he'd have come up with motivational speaking on his own? He's not a self-starter, you know. If it weren't for me he'd still be selling that hideous china over the phone.

MAX: Some of the patterns were quite festive and he was top salesman in the district. He seemed happy.

PATTY: To you he did. Fortunately, I knew better. But the battle isn't over. Barry needs to get his priorities straight and you need to accept me.

MAX: Patty, I accept you totally and completely.

PATTY: No, you endure me. Like chronic pain.

MAX: That's not fair. Haven't I been nice to you?

PATTY: "Nice" is what you do best. Do you know what I dislike the very most about you? Your likeability.

MAX: Oh, I should be less likeable?

PATTY: You should be real. What do you really think of me?

MAX: I really think you're...really great.

PATTY: How about you're angry that I've spirited Barry away? That I won't let him drift aimlessly through life in some half-cocked adolescent daydream?

MAX: Okay, to be perfectly honest, no hard feelings, I think you've got him on a pretty short leash.

PATTY: And I should lighten up?

MAX: No offense, but you do seem overly serious at times.

PATTY: And Barry was happier before I came along?

MAX: I'm not going that route.

PATTY: Scared?

MAX: No.

PATTY: Then admit it.

MAX: Okay, it was a different kind of happy. Barry used to be fun happy. Now he's more…morose happy.

PATTY: So you think I'm rigid, controlling and have made your brother miserable.

MAX: Don't put those words in my mouth.

PATTY: Why not? It's what you think.

MAX: How do you know what I think?

PATTY: Because jealousy is so easy to spot.

MAX: I'm jealous? Of what?

PATTY: You wish there was someone who cared about you the way I care about Barry.

MAX: Jennifer cares about me.

PATTY: I suppose she does, in her own small, frightened way, like a timid little robin perched on the feeder, hoping to escape with scraps.

MAX: She gets more than scraps, believe me.

PATTY: I don't care about Jennifer. I care about you. And you're not happy, you want more.

MAX: True, I've had to personally overcome the miserable example of marriage presented by my parents.

PATTY: Is that why you run around?

MAX: I don't run around.

PATTY: Oh, Max, just because you haven't gotten caught. The way you've acted from the time you came here tonight, I can tell one hundred percent, you run around. And you'd love nothing more than to run around with me.

MAX: Good God!

PATTY: Don't you think there's a reason you and I have never been close? Don't you think there's a reason the temperature changes when we're together? It's easier if you act as if you don't like me, isn't it? In most families hostility plays better than lust.

MAX: I don't like where this is going.

PATTY: I can only judge by your behavior, Max. Attraction and revulsion, flip sides of the same coin. The fact is, you either hate me or lust after me. Which is it?

MAX: You're my sister-in-law. How could I lust after you?

PATTY: Oh, come on, there's no limit to what men lust after. I'll bet there are days when nothing's safe: left-over yams, your old baseball mitt, the neighbor's Golden.

MAX: Granted. But I don't lust after you.

PATTY: Then you hate me. And I want you to leave. We'll all muddle along in this family the best we can, with seriously diminished expectations. But for the life of me, I don't know why you should hate me for trying to make a decent life with your brother.

MAX: Patty, listen to me. I don't hate you.

PATTY: Then what is it between us, Max? From the time we first saw each other, there's been something.

MAX: Has there?

PATTY: You think there's been nothing? No feelings at all?

MAX: There have been feelings, yes, but…entirely respectful, appropriate, in-law-type feelings.

PATTY: Since when have feelings ever been "appropriate?" The truth is, there are borderline homicidal feelings between us. Or am I crazy?

MAX: Homicidal feelings? Patty, I like you!

PATTY: Max. You either lust after me or you hate me or you think I'm crazy. Which is it?

MAX: I need time to think.

PATTY: Have you ever seriously considered what it's like for me in this family?

MAX: Yes, I have.

PATTY: Honestly?

MAX: No, I haven't.

PATTY: Nothing fills me with dread like your family parties. I always seem to get there late from work and I see you all in a cluster, drinks in hand, glowing with gin, just so happy to be together. The way Barry laughs with you is different from the way he laughs with me, full-bodied, carefree, practically sexual. I hear that laugh and my blood freezes. And then his eyes find me standing on the periphery and I see the look, from all of you. You fall all over yourselves to make me welcome, the hugs, the kisses, the pointless hilarity and you're all still laughing but now it's work. Have to be careful, now that Patty's here. And I feel so utterly hopeless I just want to crawl off into some cave where people aren't trying so hard to prove they want me around.

MAX: Patty, it's not like that—

PATTY: Don't pretend you know what it's like, because you don't. You've never felt that for one moment in your entire life. It's all been just so easy for you. I'm probably the first person in your whole life who hasn't been glad to see you.

MAX: It's a shame we got off on the wrong foot.

PATTY: I remember meeting you. I know I felt something powerful and it scared the hell out of me. I was in love with Barry but it was something else with you. You're so different from Barry.

MAX: Less materialistic, maybe a little deeper, perhaps…

PATTY: I've wasted so many hours trying to figure out what it all meant. Maybe we'll never know. But I do know it's not easy, being the scapegoat.

MAX: Nobody's scapegoating you.

PATTY: You are. Jennifer is. Your mother is.

MAX: Mother adores you.

PATTY: She treats me like I'm the ambassador from a terrorist nation.

MAX: She talks you up all the time.

PATTY: And she talks up poor Jennifer to me.

MAX: No. Really? Jennifer?

PATTY: Haven't you figured it out, Max? Your mother adores whoever isn't there.

MAX: *Mother* does this?

PATTY: Of course she does! But who cares, your mother can rot in hell.

MAX: Patty! That's my mother!

PATTY: I know, I love her, but please. What concerns me is that everyone thinks I'm the problem. Even Barry. Have you talked to him about me?

MAX: Of course not! Your personal life is sacrosanct.

PATTY: You're such a liar. You're working against me, and that's not smart. Because I will fight like a mad ferret to defend my turf.

MAX: You've got this all wrong. I'm a healer.

PATTY: I feel it from all of you, the blame, and Jesus Christ, it makes me feel so alone. What have I done? What the hell have I done? Would you please tell me so I can stop torturing myself?

(Patty sits on the sofa. She looks as if she might cry. Max sits next to her, try-ing to comfort her.)

MAX: Patty. You didn't do anything wrong. I don't hate you. And I don't think you're crazy.

PATTY: That only leaves one thing.

MAX: Oh. Right.

PATTY: The rules of attraction are so unfair, just like every other stupid rule. Why do we have to be drawn to each other? It'd be so much easier if we weren't.

(Patty turns to Max. He kisses her. They kiss, then Patty starts laughing.)

MAX: What's wrong?

PATTY: God, it's unbelievable, the male ego. You actually think this whole problem in the family is because I'm in love with you?

MAX: Well...you seemed to be saying that. Didn't you?

PATTY: And you believed it!

MAX: I'm sorry. Total misunderstanding. I'll go.

PATTY: No. Max, I'm so confused. I care so much for you and I know it's wrong and I started laughing because I'm scared of how I feel. I wish there was something I could do about it.

MAX: That's alright, Patty.

PATTY: Tell me, how wrong would it be...?

MAX: Very wrong.

PATTY: Still...

(They kiss. Patty erupts in laughter.)

MAX: *What?*

PATTY: It's just so amazing, I mean even when I tell you that I'm making fun of you you still want to believe I'm in love with you.

MAX: I don't think you're in love with me, okay? I'm just trying to do the right thing.

PATTY: And the right thing is to fall into your brother's wife's arms because you want to believe I'm in love with you? I mean how could any woman *not* be in love with you? Is that what you think?

MAX: I think the right thing is to leave.

(Max goes to the door.)

PATTY: Max? Don't go.

MAX: Why?

PATTY: It's just so hard, feeling like everything's my fault. I don't know what to do. So I do something stupid, like make fun of you. Yes, you drive me crazy, but you're the only one who understands me.

MAX: I haven't understood a single thing since I bought those flowers.

PATTY: Neither have I. Because the big things are impossible to understand. I don't know what it is that pulls people together against all reason. Careers end, families are destroyed, empires fall, all because two people have to have each other… *(Leaning against Max.)* Will you kiss me, Max?

MAX: No.

PATTY: I understand.

MAX: I just can't.

PATTY: It's alright.

MAX: After what's happened, I'd feel pretty stupid.

PATTY: Of course. *(Beat.)* Sometimes I feel like I wreck everything I touch.

MAX: Come on. You didn't wreck anything.

PATTY: I wrecked any chance you'll ever kiss me again. And that makes me very sad.

(Max looks at her. Then they start to kiss. Patty starts to laugh. Then she kisses him again. Blackout.)

ACT TWO

SCENE ONE

Jennifer and Max are waiting in Lydia's living room. A clock chimes.

MAX: Nervous?

JENNIFER: No, I'm fine. Why?

MAX: You just seem nervous.

JENNIFER: I'm not nervous. At least I wasn't till you brought it up.

MAX: I know it isn't easy for you. Being around my family.

JENNIFER: I'll survive. Anyway, it isn't just your family. I've always hated Thanksgiving.

MAX: Really? Why?

JENNIFER: Oh, you know. The food, the people, the whole idea of giving thanks. Spare me.

MAX: I feel bad. About Barry and Patty. There must be so much pain and remorse.

JENNIFER: Max, it's heartbreaking we couldn't make their marriage work. But they're better off apart.

MAX: Yes, but who are we to intervene? We're not perfect.

JENNIFER: You're letting your brother get under your skin. Just because he thinks we're sad. Do you think we're sad?

MAX: I think we're sensational, Jen.

JENNIFER: Sometimes I wonder.

(A crash from the kitchen.)

JENNIFER: *(Continuing.)* God, what's she doing in there?

MAX: *(Calls.)* Mother? Can Jennifer help?

LYDIA: *(Offstage.)* No!

JENNIFER: Is she angry?

MAX: She always sounds like that cooking. The kitchen makes her short and testy.

JENNIFER: I think we should put Barry together with one of my friends. Maybe Mona. Then this family might be bearable.

MAX: Which one is Mona?

JENNIFER: Haverford? Real estate? Vegan? Incest survivor?

MAX: I don't think Barry's ready for dating.

JENNIFER: We'll give him another week to grieve, then get him out dancing. Mona's a great girl when she gets her meds right.

(Barry enters wearing a cape and carrying an aspic. A second clock chimes.)

MAX: Barry. You're wearing a cape.

BARRY: I thought it would make me feel better.

JENNIFER: What have you got there?

BARRY: Aspic. It was one tough son of a bitch to make, so I hope everyone enjoys it.

(Lydia enters from the kitchen, lost.)

LYDIA: I fear I've done something ghastly to the turkey.

JENNIFER: Can I help you, Lydia?

LYDIA: Would you?

JENNIFER: I'll take your aspic, Barry.

(Jennifer and Lydia go to the kitchen. Barry and Max are alone.)

BARRY: Why aren't you drinking?

MAX: I was waiting so we could all celebrate together.

BARRY: Are you insane?

(Barry and Max make drinks. A third clock chimes.)

MAX: So. Cheers! Working hard?

BARRY: Jesus, Max, look at me. I can't work.

MAX: I can't imagine the cape is helping.

BARRY: I'm very very depressed. How can I motivate others if I can't get out of bed?

MAX: I'm sure things will get better.

BARRY: Really? Why do you think that?

MAX: Through the passage of time. Things will get better.

BARRY: That's very helpful, Max. Thank you. I'm going to write that down. You know, you guys were right. My life is pretty stupid. I'm bouncing up and down like a pom-pom girl getting everyone fired up, and I'm really just a withered husk of a man, surrounded by the sad trappings of a wasted life.

MAX: I'm not going to argue with you.

BARRY: Why not?

MAX: You want me to argue with you?

BARRY: I want you to do something.

MAX: I think you need to hit bottom before anyone can help.

BARRY: Maybe this is the bottom. Did you ever think of that?

MAX: Maybe. But I don't think so.

BARRY: So if this isn't the bottom then that means things are going to get worse. And yet you just told me things are going to get better. Which is it?

MAX: I don't know. I just know you're my brother and I want things to be the way they used to be with us.

BARRY: I guess I should thank you for trying to talk to Patty.

MAX: What did she say?

BARRY: She said you were "sweet".

MAX: Really?

BARRY: That's not necessarily a compliment, coming from Patty.

MAX: Have you seen her?

BARRY: I haven't actually *seen* her, but I feel her presence. Coming over here, a car swerved to go through a puddle and splash me. That sure felt like Patty.

MAX: Your cape *is* a little damp.

BARRY: Lately stuff just comes flying out of nowhere and hits me. More stuff than usual.

MAX: You think Patty's throwing stuff at you?

BARRY: I'm just telling you what's happening to me. After church I picked up a hooker.

MAX: No you didn't.

BARRY: Yes I did.

MAX: No you didn't.

BARRY: Yes I did.

MAX: Barry, do you know what you've done?

BARRY: I picked up a hooker.

MAX: That's bad.

BARRY: Do you think I don't know that? I know that.

MAX: Where did you find one?

BARRY: A hooker? Well, they're out there, my friend.

MAX: Yes, but where?

BARRY: This was at Barnes & Noble.

MAX: Jesus Christ. You just went up to her?

BARRY: We were browsing in new non-fiction, we both picked up the same book on maritime disasters and she smiled at me.

MAX: That was it? A smile? How'd you know she was a hooker?

BARRY: The only women who smile at me anymore work at Starbucks. This wasn't Starbucks, she smiled, hence, hooker. We went to her apartment and I had a glass of seltzer and she said she'd do anything for one hundred bucks.

MAX: Congratulations. Mother would be so proud.

BARRY: Do you want to know what we did?

MAX: No.

BARRY: I read the paper. Start to finish, even the car ads. I never get a chance to do that at home.

MAX: I don't understand.

BARRY: I paid her to leave me alone. To let me read the damn paper in peace. Don't you think that's pretty significant?

MAX: For one hundred bucks? It sounds like a rip-off.

BARRY: That was the little kick I needed. I went home and split up with Patty. I got my freedom back.

MAX: You just told her you wanted out?

(Barry nods. They drink in silence. A fourth clock chimes.)

BARRY: Actually, it was mutual. Probably more her, sixty-forty. Maybe eighty-twenty. She wanted out, Max. I couldn't stop her. She said she caught a glimpse of a different life.

MAX: What does that mean?

BARRY: Code for a fling with some jerk who's totally unavailable.

MAX: Oh, boy.

BARRY: I'm concerned about her. I mean I would be if I still cared.

(The doorbell sounds. Jennifer enters and sees Max and Barry not responding.)

JENNIFER: I'll get it.

(Jennifer opens the door and Patty enters. She has a small package.)

JENNIFER: *(Continuing.)* Oh, hi, Patty. What a wonderful surprise! I'll rush off and set another place.

PATTY: I can't stay. I'm on my way to another function.

JENNIFER: Then I'll rush off and tell Lydia you're here.

PATTY: Before you rush off, would you take this?

(Jennifer rushes off with the package.)

PATTY: *(Continuing.)* Hello, Max.

MAX: Nice to see you, Patty.

PATTY: You don't *ever* tell the truth, do you? How are you, Barry?

BARRY: Perfect.

PATTY: You've been crying.

BARRY: You're crazy.

PATTY: Barry, honey, I can always tell. Boo-hoo-hoo.

BARRY: Max, have I been crying?

MAX: Not since you were about eight.

PATTY: That's a reliable source.

(Lydia and Jennifer enter. Jennifer has the nuts that Patty brought. A fifth clock chimes.)

JENNIFER: Patty brought nuts for our party!

(Jennifer passes the nuts. Lydia kisses Patty.)

LYDIA: Well well. I'm so glad you didn't wait for an invitation, my dear!

PATTY: Thanks, Lydia. It's nice to be here.

LYDIA: Have these big lugs offered you a drink?

MAX: What'll it be?

PATTY: Half of whatever you're having, Max.

MAX: A child's portion of gin, coming up. Mother? Drink?

LYDIA: Nothing for me. I had a dressing drink and I'm still working on my cooking drink.

PATTY: Happy Thanksgiving, everyone.

(They all drink, except Jennifer.)

LYDIA: Sure you won't have a drink, Jennifer?

JENNIFER: Oh, thanks so much, but I never have a drink.

BARRY: We've all observed that. Exactly why do you keep throwing that in our faces?

JENNIFER: I have my reasons. Others in my family chose to drink. In the past.

BARRY: That explains it. Good story, Jen. Cheers.

(They drink.)

JENNIFER: Alright, I'll tell you. When I was fourteen we lived in a big drafty house where we kept warm around the fire and we used these very dry pieces of kindling which would explode in the fireplace and shoot against the screen but one night there was an enormous amount of drinking and people suddenly raced outside to play croquet in the moonlight and forgot about the screen and all during croquet these pieces of burning wood shot out into the living room and when I was sent inside to get the ice bucket the house was in flames and we had no choice but to stand in the yard with our croquet mallets and watch our house burn to the ground. So we moved in with relatives. One night I'm at a sleep-over with my friends, giggling in the dark about boyfriends and then suddenly I'm in a different school and my old friends are gone forever and that's when my childhood ended and I never really quite got over having my life just savagely ripped away from me. All because of alcohol.

LYDIA: We have sherry.

JENNIFER: No, thank you.

(Max and Barry are trying to open the nuts that Patty brought.)

BARRY: Patty? It's impossible to open these stupid nuts.

PATTY: *(Opening and eating a nut.)* Oh, these are good!

(Max and Barry still can't open them. A sixth clock chimes.)

BARRY: Why are you here?

PATTY: Our retreat ended sooner than expected. It seems our new board member doesn't play well with others. So I just wanted to make sure you were alright before I went to the other party.

BARRY: Is "he" going to be at the other party?

PATTY: Who?

BARRY: Your rotten jerk bastard boyfriend.

LYDIA: You're in love with someone else, Patricia?

PATTY: Can we please not discuss this now?

BARRY: Patty always says we just stand around talking about nothing. Now I want to talk about something that matters and she doesn't want any part of it.

MAX: This isn't the time, Barry.

BARRY: Are you siding with her? She hates you, Max. She hates everything about you. And you too, Jennifer.

PATTY: Stop it.

BARRY: She tried to cut you out of my life.

MAX: I don't care what she did.

PATTY: I always dreaded coming here for Thanksgiving—no offense, Lydia— but I was all alone this morning and I realized I missed it.

MAX: Why don't you stay, Patty? You're still technically family.

BARRY: She has a party to go to. A party with her lover.

PATTY: Barry. Shut up.

BARRY: You shut up.

LYDIA: I expect better behavior than this in my home. Can we please talk about something else?

BARRY: Mother means we should talk about nothing. Maybe venture some bold opinions about the weather. Getting a bit chilly, Patty?

LYDIA: I hope you're all going to join me at the shore. Do any of you know your vacation dates?

BARRY: Isn't Thanksgiving a little early to be making summer plans, Mother?

LYDIA: Lately I can't stop thinking about it. Everyone just seems happier there. I want us all to be together this year...

JENNIFER: Oh, I love it there! But last summer, the first night I kept hearing this owl. It really spooked me. *(She makes an owl sound.)* Remember, Max?

PATTY: That wasn't an owl you heard.

JENNIFER: Yes, it was. Wasn't it, Max?

MAX: I thought so.

PATTY: Owls don't sound anything like that.

JENNIFER: Oh, really? What do you think owls sound like?

PATTY: More like... *(She makes an owl sound.)*

JENNIFER: Please, that is so not an owl, Patty.

PATTY: It's exactly an owl, Jennifer.

JENNIFER: Owls sound like this... *(Makes an owl sound.)* Right, Max?

PATTY: I think you mean... *(Makes an owl sound, then, to Max.)* Well? Which is the owl?

(They both look at Max.)

MAX: They're both owls. They're just different owls.

JENNIFER: That's Max, boldly withholding his opinion.

PATTY: She's right, just say what you think, Max.

BARRY: Frankly, I didn't buy either owl.

PATTY: Shut up, Barry.

BARRY: You shut up.

PATTY: Well? Which is it, Max?

(Patty and then Jennifer make their owl sounds. They wait for Max.)

MAX: Okay, gun to my head, I'd have to say the more authentic owl is probably...Patty.

JENNIFER: Thanks for your support.

(A seventh clock chimes. Then the first and second clocks chime.)

BARRY: Mother, you have to get these clocks fixed!

(The third and fourth clocks chime.)

LYDIA: *(Listens.)* They seem to be working perfectly, dear.

BARRY: Get them synchronized. Get the clockman here!

LYDIA: I'm sorry to report that the clockman died.

BARRY: And there are no more clockmen in the land? God help us!

(The fifth, sixth, and seventh clocks chime.)

BARRY: *(Continuing.)* I can't take it! I feel like I'm having a breakdown.

PATTY: It's entirely possible you *are* having a breakdown.

BARRY: You don't belong here. Why don't you go to that party with the jerk you love?

PATTY: Darling, I'm at that party with the jerk I love.

(Barry goes to Patty.)

BARRY: Oh, honey. I'm sorry. I love you too. *(Uncomfortable pause, then, confused.)* What? You're saying you love me...aren't you? *(Barry turns from Patty to Max.)* You hate Max. You've always had a problem with him. From the time you met.

PATTY: That's right, Barry. I have a problem with Max. I think Max has a problem with me, too.

BARRY: *(Putting it together.)* Not a problem of hating him. A problem of...so what you're saying is that you and Max...

MAX: Nothing happened! Let's be clear about that.

JENNIFER: Why is everyone so upset if nothing happened?

BARRY: They're in love, Jennifer. That's what happened.

JENNIFER: Oh.

MAX: Jennifer, you and Barry wanted me to go talk to Patty. When two people talk—

PATTY: There's the odd chance they might even tell the truth. That's when things get sticky.

BARRY: Here I was, thinking my life couldn't get any worse.

JENNIFER: Patty, I wish you'd have just come to dinner at our house. We could have had a nice time and eaten soft shell crabs and none of this would be happening.

PATTY: Maybe this was fated to happen.

BARRY: Fate is just an excuse for bad behavior.

LYDIA: I don't like this. This is a national holiday.

(Lydia exits to the kitchen.)

BARRY: Yes, I have so much to be thankful for. A wife who deserts me and a brother who betrays me.

MAX: I didn't betray you. I was trying to help you.

PATTY: Oh, Max. You never do anything wrong, do you? You want to be all things to all people.

MAX: Barry, I went to see her for you. You know I didn't want to go. I was sickened by the idea—

PATTY: Excuse me?

BARRY: And now you're telling me nothing happened.

MAX: Right. Nothing happened!

PATTY: Did you kiss me, Max? Did you hold me in your arms? Or was that someone else?

(Clocks one and three chime.)

MAX: I'm sorry, Barry.

JENNIFER: What about me, Max? Did you ever think about me?

MAX: Jennifer, honey, of course I thought about you.

JENNIFER: Did you remember we were getting married?

MAX: Yes, and I'm very excited, but…

JENNIFER: But what?

MAX: Barry feels strongly that we have problems. If I care about us—

JENNIFER: Why are you listening to Barry about our relationship? You and Barry are totally different!

MAX: True, I'm less materialistic, a bit deeper…

PATTY: *(To Jennifer.)* Sweetie, you and Max didn't hesitate to interfere in my marriage. I know all about your intervention.

JENNIFER: We were trying to help. You both seemed so unhappy. I didn't know Barry was undermining us.

BARRY: Great. It's all my fault. *(To Max.)* You steal my wife and blame me. Perfect.

MAX: I didn't steal your wife. *(To Jennifer.)* It's obvious we have problems.

PATTY: Yes, there were little hints along the way, like your desire to kill Jennifer.

MAX: Can't anyone in this family keep a secret? I didn't want to kill Jennifer.

PATTY: No, honestly, you probably didn't.

MAX: Thank you.

(Lydia returns from the kitchen with the aspic.)

PATTY: You expressed it that way to hide your more primitive desire to kill your mother.

LYDIA What?

PATTY: *(Aside.)* And who can blame you… *(To Max.)* It's quite obvious that you and Jennifer aren't right for each other. Any more than Barry and I are right for each other.

BARRY: And I suppose you and Max are right for each other?

PATTY: Why don't you ask Max?

(They all look at Max.)

MAX: Patty, you know I like you, I respect you…

PATTY: Do you love me, Max?

MAX: I love you as a valued member of the family.

BARRY: Do you love her more than you love Jennifer?

MAX: Don't drag Jennifer into the middle of this!

LEWISTON PUBLIC LIBRARY WITHDRAWN

JENNIFER: I'm your fiancée, Max, I've already been dragged into the middle of this.

PATTY: It takes courage. To stand up and say how you feel. Are you ready to do that, Max?

MAX: Yes. I feel very concerned about what is happening in this family. I think it's time to put these painful events behind us and move forward.

PATTY: My God. What was I thinking?

JENNIFER: I can't believe you'd do this, Max. It's just so hurtful.

PATTY: I'll be alright.

JENNIFER: No, I meant hurtful for me.

MAX: I'm sorry. I will admit, it's been a struggle—and I hate to say this in front of Mother—trying to overcome the miserable example of marriage presented by our parents.

BARRY: What the hell are you talking about? They had a wonderful marriage.

JENNIFER: Really? They did?

MAX: No.

BARRY: Yes.

JENNIFER: You always said your parents' rotten marriage was why you didn't want to get married.

MAX: It was rotten to the core and it affected me deeply. I mean, look at me.

BARRY: I was there. It was a very good marriage. And we were happy.

MAX: Maybe you were there, but you weren't paying attention. We were miserable.

BARRY: I think you're confusing us with another family, Max.

MAX: Mother?

LYDIA: Excuse me, dear?

BARRY: Would you say you had a good marriage?

LYDIA: Do we have to talk about this now?

MAX: Yes, it's very important. My credibility is at stake. And Barry needs to know if he had a happy childhood.

BARRY: Go on, tell him it was happy.

LYDIA: Oh, dear, it's just so hard to think.

MAX: Mother, you must know what was in your heart.

LYDIA: Not really. As a matter of fact, it's always been quite puzzling to me.

MAX: Come on! You're not going to tell us you were happy, are you? That there was any passion in your life?

LYDIA: Oh, yes. There was passion. *(Beat.)* Is anyone else cold?

JENNIFER: I'll get you a blanket.

LYDIA: It was so cold then, March it was, an endless awful March, one blizzard after another… *(Jennifer puts a blanket on Lydia.)* Thank you, my dear. You're so very kind. Jennifer saved my turkey and now she's saving me. We were coming home from a party, late, and it felt as though the snow would never stop. The car was skidding wildly over the icy road—you remember that old Plymouth—and we were laughing like children, we weren't a bit scared even though the headlights barely made a dent in the driving snow and suddenly we lurched to a dead stop in a snowdrift and we sat there in the dark laughing and he put his arm around me and the radio was playing, what was that song? I never thought I'd forget, that was the moment when everything changed and we were so happy together. I believe it saved my life. Oh, dear, I know the song, I know I know it…
(Clocks two, four and six chime.)
PATTY: It doesn't matter, Lydia. Go on.
BARRY: Don't interrupt Mother! What was the song, Mother?
JENNIFER: Something's wrong.
MAX: Nothing's wrong. She's thinking.
JENNIFER: Where's the phone?
BARRY: Let her think. Why is everyone interrupting Mother?
(Jennifer carefully puts the blanket around Lydia, then calmly goes to the phone. All seven clocks chime as Lydia sits motionless. Blackout.)

SCENE TWO

Lights up on a hospital waiting room. Max is alone, looking at a magazine. Barry comes in.

BARRY: How is she?
MAX: Much better.
BARRY: Really? How is she better?
MAX: Actually, I haven't seen her yet.
BARRY: So you have no reason to say she's better.
MAX: I guess I feel that being here, with doctors, she's probably better.
BARRY: And I feel that this tendency of yours to look on the bright side against all evidence to the contrary is a bit pathological.
(Barry looks at the magazines on the table, then at the one Max is reading.)
BARRY: *(Continuing.)* How long are you going to be reading that?
MAX: Until I'm done.

BARRY: Could I possibly see it?

MAX: Yes. Just as soon as I'm finished.

BARRY: You're reading it just so I can't.

MAX: There are other magazines.

BARRY: I don't want other magazines. I want *that* magazine.

MAX: In a minute.

BARRY: You know, there are other people who live on this planet, Max. It isn't just you. You get my wife, you get the magazine. Where does it end?

MAX: I'm sorry. You can have the magazine. *(Hands Barry the magazine.)* Are you worried?

BARRY: About what?

MAX: About what? Our Mother is going through God-knows-what at this very moment.

BARRY: Yes, I'm worried about Mother. *(Beat.)* If you're worried about Patty, she's in the car.

MAX: I'm not worried about Patty.

BARRY: I thought there might be some aspect of your relationship you hadn't fully explored yet.

MAX: Hey, I didn't want to go see her. I went because of my love and respect for you, Barry. To make things right. It was a very dangerous and difficult situation you put me in.

BARRY: And you handled it beautifully.

MAX: I did almost nothing I regret. It's not my fault she can't face me.

BARRY: Don't get a big head. She doesn't like hospitals.

MAX: Oh, like the rest of us come with balloons and party hats?

BARRY: She has bad associations.

MAX: Who doesn't have bad associations with hospitals? *(Beat.)* All I can think about is being a little kid waiting to see Dad after his heart attack. I remember every horrible minute as if it was yesterday.

BARRY: You weren't a little kid. You were eighteen.

MAX: I was a little kid and I was scared. Just like I'm scared now.

BARRY: How old do you think you were?

MAX: About…seven.

BARRY: Fine. You were seven and I was twenty-three.

MAX: I was a small helpless child.

BARRY: We were all helpless but we weren't children. Why can't we get in to see Mother?

MAX: They're doing tests.

BARRY: What the hell am I going to do? I've got no job, no marriage, now this.

MAX: I've been thinking, we should take Mother to the shore.

BARRY: What, and just leave her there? You heartless bastard.

MAX: No, we'd stay with her. It's the place she loves most.

BARRY: It's November, Max. It's very very cold.

MAX: She wanted us all to be there with her at the shore.

(Jennifer comes out, composed.)

JENNIFER: Oh, good, you're finally here.

MAX: I would have been in the ambulance with you but it left so quickly.

BARRY: Isn't that kind of the point of an ambulance? To go quickly? If you don't care when you get here you could take a bus or a pony.

MAX: Give it a rest, Barry. *(To Jennifer.)* How is she?

JENNIFER: I've been talking to her and she's holding her own. You can go in and see her. *(Beat.)* You should know she can't talk.

BARRY: Can't or won't?

JENNIFER: Can't.

MAX: Why can't she talk?

JENNIFER: She just can't.

BARRY: Good explanation. These doctors sound top-notch.

MAX: You said you were talking to her.

JENNIFER: I was talking. She wasn't.

MAX: How do you know she could even hear you?

JENNIFER: I don't.

MAX: What's the point of talking if no one's listening?

BARRY: I don't listen to you and you keep talking.

JENNIFER: The point is, *maybe* she could hear me. It seemed to calm her down.

BARRY: Sounds like tree-falling-in-the-woods time.

MAX: What exactly did you say to her?

JENNIFER: I just talked. I mean, I never really had the opportunity of talking to your mother before.

MAX: I don't know what to say if she can't say something back. What should I say?

JENNIFER: She's your mother. Tell her whatever you want.

MAX: Aren't you coming in with us?

JENNIFER: I was just in there, Max.

MAX: Great. We're on our own. Jennifer? If you wait I'll take you home.

JENNIFER: That's alright. Go see your mother.

MAX: This obviously is not going to be a long conversation.

JENNIFER: I'm not going home with you, Max.

MAX: What? Why?

JENNIFER: I don't know where to begin.

MAX: Is it Patty? Because Patty is nothing to me. Zero. Zilch. Nada.

BARRY: Interesting.

MAX: Stay out of this, Barry. *(To Jennifer.)* We'll talk at home.

JENNIFER: I can't count on you, Max.

MAX: Yes, you can! I'm there for you one hundred percent!

JENNIFER: You're hardly there at all.

MAX: When have I ever let you down?

JENNIFER: You wouldn't even say I was the better owl!

MAX: Jennifer, you were a great owl, an inspired owl, but in fairness, Patty nailed it. She *was* an owl.

JENNIFER: Patty made you think she was an owl but I was a real owl. I was the owl I heard.

MAX: Fine. You're a better owl, Jennifer.

JENNIFER: Too bad you didn't notice sooner.

BARRY: Are you coming with me, Max?

(Max is torn between Jennifer, who's leaving, and Barry, who's about to go in to see Lydia.)

JENNIFER: Go see your mother, Max.

(Max follows Barry. Patty comes in, anxious, drinking coffee from a styrofoam cup. Jennifer is calm.)

PATTY: This place is creeping me out. Have you seen her?

JENNIFER: Yes.

PATTY: Dann, damn, damn! That means I have to go see her!

JENNIFER: No, you don't.

PATTY: I don't? *(Beat.)* Yes, I do. *(Beat.)* No, I don't. *(Beat.)* Do I?

JENNIFER: Would you like me to go in with you?

PATTY: I'd like you to go in *for* me.

JENNIFER: If you want, I'll tell her you were here. I have to talk to the doctor again. It's really important to monitor her treatment over the next few days.

PATTY: You have nerves of steel. How do you do it?

JENNIFER: I always know exactly what to do with sick people. The only time I run into problems with people is when they're well.

PATTY: I'm at my absolute worst with sick people. They make me mad. I actually haven't been doing so great with well people either. Jennifer, the thing with Max...I'm...you now, it was just very...

JENNIFER: Are you saying you're sorry?

PATTY: No, it's so unfortunate…I wish it hadn't happened.

JENNIFER: It's better this way. You just made me see things I didn't want to see.

PATTY: What I'm saying is, you don't need to worry about me. I don't know what came over me. I think it was some perverse fantasy I felt compelled to live out.

JENNIFER: I'm through with Max. So whatever you do is fine.

PATTY: Jennifer, listen to me, you're getting married.

JENNIFER: No, I'm not.

PATTY: Yes, you are! I insist.

JENNIFER: You can't make me.

PATTY: I won't be the reason you're not getting married.

JENNIFER: It's not about you, Patty. It's about me and Max. And we're through. No matter what you say.

(Jennifer starts to leave.)

PATTY: Jennifer? What should I do about Barry?

JENNIFER: You're asking my advice?

PATTY: You're just so calm. It's eerie. What should I do?

JENNIFER: Well…Barry's really in a lot of pain.

PATTY: So you think I should steer clear of him? For my own good?

JENNIFER: That isn't what I'd do. But it's really up to you.

PATTY: I'm going to leave. I've caused quite enough havoc in this family.

JENNIFER: You don't want to see Lydia?

PATTY: I do. But I don't want to see *him*.

JENNIFER: Barry?

PATTY: Yes. Or Max. Both of them. How do I get out of here?

JENNIFER: Come on, Patty, I'll walk with you.

(Jennifer and Patty leave. Blackout.)

SCENE THREE

The deck of a summer home. December. It's very cold. A phone rings and is answered inside. Barry is at a barbecue grilling many hamburgers. Max comes out of the house, agitated.

MAX: Hey, Barry. How about we go into town, have dinner?

BARRY: We have plenty of food here.

MAX: So I see. Nice work. We need a night to drink beer, play darts, get in touch with our feelings.

BARRY: I'm not done cooking.

MAX: The thing is, we should leave right now.

BARRY: Who was that on the phone, Max?

MAX: Come on, we'll talk about it on the way.

BARRY: It was Patty. Wasn't it?

MAX: I won't lie to you, this is a crisis. She called from her car. She's almost here.

BARRY: What did she want?

MAX: What she always wants. To suck the joy out of human life as we know it.

BARRY: She wants to see me?

MAX: It's not about what she wants. It's about what's best for you.

BARRY: What do you think is best for me?

MAX: You're in no shape for to see her, that's for sure. With my help you've made excellent progress, but you'd be putty in Patty's hands. Let's go.

BARRY: I'm not going.

MAX: Barry, stand up and be a man and run away with me.

BARRY: She wrecked my life, Max. So it's payback time. I want to face her, man to man.

MAX: And I want to hold on to the wonderful thing we've got here. I'm going to watch out for you, because that's what brothers do.

(Patty enters in a winter coat.)

PATTY: Hello, Barry. Max.

BARRY: Hi, Patty.

PATTY: So, we're barbecuing, are we? That's a good wintertime activity.

MAX: We'd have tossed on a few more burgers if we knew you were coming.

PATTY: I just came by to see how Lydia's doing.

MAX: She's mute.

BARRY: Totally mute. If you hear someone talking, it isn't Mother.

MAX: But I would have to say we've risen to the challenge. I think it's brought us all closer together.

PATTY: That's good. I feel terrible I didn't see her at the hospital, so I'd like to see her now. If it's alright.

BARRY: She's off with Jennifer.

MAX: Jennifer takes her around to all of her favorite places on the island.

BARRY: She gets upset if she isn't around. I don't know what we're going to do when Jennifer leaves.

PATTY: Why would she have to leave?

MAX: She has a job, a life, things like that. And maybe it's not important, but I think she hates me. *(Wrapping up the visit.)* So, we'll be sure to tell Mother you were here. Right, Barry?

BARRY: Okay.

PATTY: How are you holding up, Barry?

BARRY: Excellently.I just don't know what I'm going to do. I can't motivate people anymore. Would *you* listen to what I say?

PATTY: *I* would, but I'm not sure anyone else would.

BARRY: It's the only thing I can do and I can't do it anymore.

PATTY: Maybe you could go back to selling that china. You were top salesman, as I recall.

BARRY: You always detested that china.

PATTY: Oh, I still do. It's perfectly hideous. But I think I liked you more before you improved yourself into someone I could marry.

BARRY: Wait. Patty. That was all your idea. You were the one with the five-year plan to change my life.

PATTY: Maybe I…

BARRY: What?

PATTY: *Maybe…I…was…*

BARRY: Maybe you were what?

PATTY: Maybe I…you know…shouldn't have…

BARRY: Say it.

PATTY: Maybe I was wrong, Barry.

BARRY: Hey. It's a long drive back. You want to stay?

PATTY: For dinner?

BARRY: Yes. And if it goes okay maybe we could build on it at breakfast. And then, if that's a positive experience, we consider lunch. Take this one meal at a time so it doesn't kill us.

PATTY: I'd love to have dinner with you, Barry.

MAX: This is payback time?

BARRY: Do you have a problem with Patty staying for dinner?

MAX: I love Patty. I just want you to be happy.

BARRY: I am happy.

MAX: Not happy like last week, when it was just the two of us hanging out like the old days.

BARRY: Max? I wasn't actually happy. No offense.

MAX: You sure seemed happy. You were drinking a lot and sleeping late and not doing very much.

BARRY: I barely said a word all week. Neither one of us said a word.

MAX: There wasn't any need. We were both happy.

BARRY: Except for me.

MAX: If this is what you want, there's nothing I can do.

PATTY: Max, if you don't want me to stay…

MAX: Are you kidding? Please. The last thing I'd ever do is interfere. *(Beat.)* Goodbye, Barry.

BARRY: I'm not going anywhere. It'll be just like before.

MAX: I know. That's the worst part of it.

(Jennifer pushes Lydia in her wheelchair onto the deck.)

PATTY: *(Continuing.)* Hello, Jennifer.

JENNIFER: Oh, Patty. Hi. Welcome. Isn't it beautiful here? We found this spot looking out at a lighthouse on the very tip of a point. While we were watching the fog just rolled in till we couldn't see a thing.

(Lydia stares off. Patty and Barry go to her. They both speak loudly.)

BARRY: Hello, Mother!

PATTY: Nice to see you, Lydia. It's Patty.

JENNIFER: She can hear perfectly.

PATTY: So, Lydia. Here we all are at the shore. Just the way you wanted.

BARRY: Well…

PATTY: Well, no, of course it isn't exactly the way you wanted it.

BARRY: Still…

PATTY: Still, it's nice we could all be here. Together. At the shore. *(Beat.)* Barry, honey, shouldn't you be setting the table?

BARRY: Why should I set the table?

PATTY: Because I'm a guest in your home. I'm not about to set the table.

BARRY: That's typical.

PATTY: Yes, and it's typical you wouldn't stop and think how exhausted I am after all that time in the car.

BARRY: And it's typical you wouldn't stop and think that I did the cooking.

PATTY: Before you even knew I was coming. That hardly counts.

BARRY: Patty. This is our first meal. Let's take it slow so maybe there'll be another one.

PATTY: I'm sorry, honey. *(Starting inside.)* But I'm not setting the table.

(Patty and Barry go inside.)

JENNIFER: *(To Lydia.)* They're made for each other, aren't they?

(Max comes over to Jennifer.)

MAX: I can't believe how good you are with Mother.

JENNIFER: I'm really getting to know her. Much better than when she could talk.

MAX: We were just discussing whether you might possibly be able to stay on and take care of her.

JENNIFER: I have a job, Max. And I sort of need to get going with my life.

MAX: Well, maybe you'll think about it. The problems we had, I was so convinced my parents had this terrible marriage and it paralyzed me. But Mother's last words were a gift, telling me everything I knew was wrong. They actually were happy.

JENNIFER: You're lucky. Most people never find out the truth about their parents.

MAX: This has real repercussions. For how I'm going to live my life.

JENNIFER: You can go into another relationship with more hope.

MAX: I want this to work out. You and me. I want to ram into snowbanks with you and be consumed by wild passion. I want what other people have, what my parents had, what Barry and Patty have...

(Barry sticks his head out.)

BARRY: Max? Would you get in here and set the table?

MAX: I'm right in the middle of something.

BARRY: I need your help. It's getting very tense in here.

MAX: What a baby.

(Max goes inside. Jennifer takes a thermos of tea from Lydia's wheelchair and pours a cup for Lydia. Lydia sips the tea and stares off at the ocean.)

LYDIA: "Wonderful World."

JENNIFER: What? What did you say?

LYDIA: "What a Wonderful World." That was the song that was playing. I knew I'd remember it. We were stuck in the snowbank and of course the sad old Plymouth belonged to my husband, so I probably should have felt guilty sitting in it kissing another man. But my husband had chosen to stay at the party and I'd been alone for so long and I was just exhausted by the tedious terminal dance of the marriage. Here was a man who was holding me as if *his* life depended on it, too. The snow kept piling up and burying us in the car and I thought, my God, how are we ever going to get out and then I stopped caring. We were alive that night and that's all any of us can ever hope for, isn't it?

MAX: *(Sticks his head out.)* Aren't you freezing out here? I'm building a fire.

JENNIFER: A few more minutes. She loves the end of the day.

(Max comes out and joins them.)

MAX: There's some kind of hope for us, isn't there, Jennifer?

JENNIFER: I don't know, Max.

MAX: Everything's going to be different now. Now that I know the truth I can start my life over again and do it right. I never thought I'd be this happy.

(Lydia reaches back and takes Jennifer's hand. The two women squeeze hands tightly. Max shivers, hands jammed in his pockets. Fade to black.)

END OF PLAY

Chad Curtiss, Lost Again
3 Ten-Minute Plays in Serial Form
by Arthur Kopit

Copyright © 2001 by Arthur Kopit. All rights reserved. CAUTION: Professionals and amateurs are hereby warned that *Chad Curtiss, Lost Again* is subject to a royalty. It is fully protected under the copyright laws of the United States of America and of all countries covered by the International Copyright Union (including the Dominion of Canada and the rest of the British Commonwealth), the Berne Convention, the Pan-American Copyright Convention and the Universal Copyright Convention, as well as all countries with which the United States has reciprocal copyright relations. All rights, including professional, amateur stage rights, motion picture, recitation, lecturing, public reading, radio broadcasting, television, video or sound recording, all other forms of mechanical or electronic reproduction, such as CD-ROM, CD-I, information storage and retrieval systems and photocopying, and the rights of translation into foreign languages, are strictly reserved. Particular emphasis is laid upon the matter of readings, permission for which must be secured from the Author's agent in writing.

ALL INQUIRIES CONCERNING RIGHTS, INCLUDING AMATEUR RIGHTS, SHOULD BE ADDRESSED TO: ABRAMS ARTISTS AGENCY, 275 7TH AVE., 26TH FLOOR, NEW YORK, NY 10001, ATTN: CHARMAINE FERENCZI.

Chad Curtiss, Lost Again

For centuries, readers and theatregoers have enjoyed the myriad pleasures of serials, those episodic sagas with cliffhanger endings. Early examples of serialized literature include Dickens' *Pickwick Papers* and Melville's *Bartleby*. More recently, the miniseries *Roots*, TV's *Twin Peaks*, Stephen King's novel *The Plant* (released one chapter at a time over the Internet) and, of course, soap operas reveal that the serial remains a significant part of our information and entertainment culture.

The heyday of "America's continuing story," however, lasted only 30 years, from the 1910s to the 1940s, when at least 350 serial films kept audiences returning weekly to movie houses—and when hundreds of radio serials were broadcast daily to listeners young and old. Those action-packed capers took hold of the American imagination in 1914 with *The Perils of Pauline*, a title that's characteristic of the short and snappy banners of the genre: *The Exploits of Elaine*, *Tailspin Tommy*, *Elmo the Mighty*, *Daredevil Jack* and *Ruth of the Rockies*.

The essential elements required for serials to succeed in any society, writes cultural critic Roger Hagedorn, are "a market economy, a communications technology sufficiently developed to be commercially exploited, and...recognition of narrative as a commodity." Since all of those are, in fact, operative in America today, ATL commissioned Arthur Kopit to bring serials into the theatre for the new millennium. Using ten-minute plays as his medium, Kopit has created a three-part serial titled *Chad Curtiss, Lost Again*, which features an intrepid young man on a quest to discover the last four words spoken by God. But because Chad was born with a dreadful sense of direction—guess what!—he loses his way and ends up in dire predicaments that are worthy of Pauline, Elaine, Tommy, Elmo, Jack, Ruth and the rest of yesteryear's serial heroes and heroines.

In this new series, Kopit samples the mystery, melodrama, exotica and thrills of serials past in order to rescue Chad from—oh no!—we've run out of time and space...until next week...

To be continued...on a stage...near you.

—*Michael Bigelow Dixon*

BIOGRAPHY

Arthur Kopit is the author of *Y2K* (23rd Humana Festival); *Oh Dad, Poor Dad, Mamma's Hung You in the Closet and I'm Feelin' So Sad*; *Indians*; *Wings*; *End of the World with Symposium to Follow*; *Road to Nirvana* (13th Humana Festival, under the title *Bone-the-Fish*); and the books for the musicals *Nine*, *Phantom* and *High Society*. His current projects include a new play, *Discovery of America*, an original musical, *Tom Swift and the Secrets of the Universe* (score by Maury Yeston), and a film version of his play, *Y2K*, entitled *BecauseHeCan*.

HUMANA FESTIVAL PRODUCTION

Chad Curtiss, Lost Again premiered at the Humana Festival of New American Plays in March 2001. It was directed by Constance Grappo with the following cast:

Narrator/Uncle Ben	Fred Major
Chad's Mother/Clonella	Sharon Murray
Young Chad	Luke Craven Glaser
Evelyn Evangeline Rue, as a Mysterious Young Girl	Sarah Keyes
General Zoltan Zarko	Mark Mineart
Lieutenant Hatchet	David New
Chad Curtiss	Leo Kittay
Hammerhead	David Wilson-Barnes
Woman in Cocoon a.k.a. Engsinflaggnn	Lusia Strus
Evelyn Evangeline Rue	Rebecca Brooksher
K-3	James Saltouros
K-4	Chris Hietikko

and the following production staff:

Scenic Designer	Paul Owen
Costume Designer	Kevin McLeod
Lighting Designer	Paul Werner
Sound Designer	Jason A Tratta
Properties Designer	Mark Walston
Movement Consultant	Jennifer Hubbard
Fight Consultant	Drew Fracher
Stage Manager	Charles M. Turner III
Assistant Stage Manager	Erin Wenzel
Dramaturg	Michael Bigelow Dixon
Assistant Dramaturg	Stephen Moulds

CHARACTERS

NARRATOR/UNCLE BEN
CHAD'S MOTHER/CLONELLA
YOUNG CHAD
EVELYN EVANGELINE RUE, AS A MYSTERIOUS YOUNG GIRL
GENERAL ZOLTAN ZARKO
LIEUTENANT HATCHET
CHAD CURTISS
HAMMERHEAD
WOMAN IN COCOON A.K.A. ENGSINFLAGGNN
EVELYN EVANGELINE RUE
K-3
K-4

TIME AND PLACE

Episode One: A forest, and twenty years later General Zarko's torture chamber.

Episode Five: An operating room and other areas of General Zarko's fortress. Also, an incubator from hell.

Episode Fourteen: Purgatorio, then a seemingly abandoned mine shaft at the edge of a supposedly extinct volcano (but in actuality a cavern measureless to man).

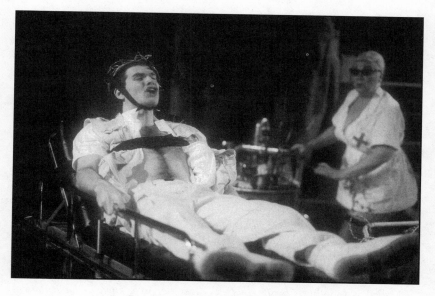

Leo Kittay and Sharon Murray in
Chad Curtiss, Lost Again

25th Annual Humana Festival of New American Plays
Actors Theatre of Louisville, 2001
photo by Richard Trigg

Chad Curtiss, Lost Again

Episode One: "The Mysterious Message"

Stage dark. Music: majestic and mysterious.

A VOICE IN THE DARK: *(Deep voice, imposing, authoritative.)* Not so many years ago, in a forest not too far away, a young boy discovered that he was lost. *(Lights up on Chad's Mother, running on, desperate.)*

CHAD'S MOTHER: Chad! ***Chad!***

A VOICE IN THE DARK: And yet, the boy was not scared.

CHAD'S MOTHER: *Chad!*

UNCLE BEN: *(From somewhere offstage.)* ***Chad!***

CHAD'S MOTHER: *(Calling to her brother.)* I can't find him anywhere! *(Enter Uncle Ben, a man of the cloth.)*

UNCLE BEN: Edna, I don't mean to criticize, but clearly somewhere you have failed as a mother. *"By thy children's deeds shall ye be known." Lamentations 2:23.* Edna, if you don't want your son getting lost all the time, either create a happier home, or buy him a compass.

CHAD'S MOTHER: He doesn't want a compass. ***CHAAAAAAAAD!!!***

A VOICE IN THE DARK: This is that boy's story.

YOUNG CHAD: *(From the distance.)* Over here, Mama!

CHAD'S MOTHER: *(Clutching her heart with relief.)* Oh Chad, Chad… *(Chad, six years old, emerges from the woods.)*

YOUNG CHAD: Have you been looking for me long?

UNCLE BEN: Just the past two days.

YOUNG CHAD: *Two days!*

CHAD'S MOTHER: Don't you *like* it at home?

YOUNG CHAD: Mother! I *love* it at home!

UNCLE BEN: Then why do you keep leaving?

YOUNG CHAD: But I *don't!*

CHAD'S MOTHER: Then how is it we never seem to find you at home?

YOUNG CHAD: Because I've gone *out*. They're very different concepts. "Leaving" suggests finality, whereas "going out" does not.

CHAD'S MOTHER: So then why do you keep going out?

YOUNG CHAD: Why, to see what's *there* of course.

UNCLE BEN: …See what's *where*?

YOUNG CHAD: **Everywhere!** And that's what takes so long. Today, you won't believe what I saw. AND! *Who I met*. Wait. Let me see if I can find it again.

(He races off.)

CHAD'S MOTHER: Chad!

YOUNG CHAD: *(Stopping.)* Yes, mother?

CHAD'S MOTHER: You came from the *other* direction, dear.

YOUNG CHAD: Ah!

(He turns and runs off in the direction she's pointing.)

CHAD'S MOTHER: *(Staring after her son, frightened.)* This can only lead to disaster.

YOUNG CHAD: *(Offstage.)* FOUND IT!

UNCLE BEN: At times like this, all we can do is trust in God…

(Chad runs back on, holding a red, eerily-glowing disk, about two feet in diameter, slightly thick in the middle. Uncle Ben and Chad's Mother stare at it, startled.)

YOUNG CHAD: What do you think of *this!*

UNCLE BEN: What is it?

YOUNG CHAD: A tablet of some sort. *With four words written on it*. Oh, you won't be able to see them. Apparently, no one can except me! Unfortunately, I can't make them out. They're in some odd language. At first I thought it was Aramaic! But it's not. He said not to worry. I'll be able to read it when the time is right.

CHAD'S MOTHER: *He?*

YOUNG CHAD: God.

UNCLE BEN: **God?**

YOUNG CHAD: Yes, Uncle Ben. That's who I met today.

CHAD'S MOTHER: *(Growing increasingly nervous.)* In the woods…

YOUNG CHAD: Yes, mother. And boy was I surprised!

(Chad's Mother and Uncle Ben exchange uneasy glances. She turns to Chad.)

CHAD'S MOTHER: And how exactly did you…*find* Him, dear?

YOUNG CHAD: Very pleasant.

CHAD'S MOTHER: …Ah.

YOUNG CHAD: And *very large.*

(Chad's Mother looks at her brother, scared.)

UNCLE BEN: *(Just trying to hold on.)* Well that seems about right.

YOUNG CHAD: I told Him you were a preacher man, Uncle Ben, but that He prob'ly knew that already, 'cause you talk to Him just about every day. That's right, isn't it?

UNCLE BEN: Uhhh, yes.

YOUNG CHAD: But God said He couldn't recall any such conversations. But that you sounded fascinating, and maybe He'd visit your church some time. But I told Him that wouldn't work. 'Cause it was a *small* church, and He'd never fit through the door. Unless of course He stooped. And that somehow didn't seem appropriate.

(Stunned silence.)

CHAD'S MOTHER: *(Hardest conversation she's ever had.)* And how did you... *discover* Him, darling?

YOUNG CHAD: Oh! This lovely little girl brought me to see Him. Evelyn, she said her name was! *Evelyn Evangeline Rue!* What amazing eyes! It was as if they could see right *through* you! She said God had been observing me for some time now, and was very pleased by what He'd seen. And had something important to give me.

UNCLE BEN: *This?*

YOUNG CHAD: Yes. At first, I thought it was a Frisbee. But it's not.

CHAD'S MOTHER: And why is this... "thing" so important.

YOUNG CHAD: I'm not sure. He just said, the four inscribed words were from Him, and constituted the last official statement He would make, He wasn't sure for how long, but possibly forever.

And these four words would change the future of the world, probably not for the better, but possibly they would. But that was not His concern. And that I should hide the tablet till the time was right. Which I would recognize because a Beast would appear, a *strange* Beast, unlike any the world had ever seen, and this beast would let me know.

And though I would not be able to remember exactly where I had *hidden* the tablet—in fact, would remember *none* of this!—nonetheless, if I still was brave and true, I would somehow find it again. At which point I would be able to read the four words. And then I could decide.

CHAD'S MOTHER: Decide what?

(Chad, aware of the enormity of the task, hesitates.)

YOUNG CHAD: ...Whether to let the world know what the four words say. He said, Whatever you decide will be fine with me. I have faith in you.

UNCLE BEN: *God* has faith in *you?*

YOUNG CHAD: That's what He said. Then He kissed me on the cheek, and left. I think He was crying.

(*His mother and uncle stare at him, stunned.*)

UNCLE BEN: Let me see this thing.

YOUNG CHAD: No.

UNCLE BEN: I said *let me see it!*

YOUNG CHAD: No! Uncle Ben! *No!*

(*His uncle grabs it away. The instant he does, he screams in pain and tries to drop it, but it's charred his hands already, and is stuck to them. In fact, his hands are* **smoking!** *Chad takes it from him.* **To Chad, it is not hot at all.** *His uncle races off, screaming in agony, hands smoking. Chad's Mother stares at Chad in disbelief.*)

CHAD'S MOTHER: I think maybe you'd better let me see this.

YOUNG CHAD: No, mother, *please!*

CHAD'S MOTHER: I'll be careful. I promise.

(*Reluctantly, Chad holds it out. She touches it* **very** *cautiously. And feels no pain. She and Chad look back in the direction Uncle Ben took, puzzled. Pause.*)

YOUNG CHAD: Well, guess I'd better go and hide it now... Oh! Look! *There's the girl!*

(*In the shadows, one can see a girl of Chad's age, wearing a dress of absolute sweetness. The way the shadows fall, one can't see her face. Chad's mother stares at the girl, startled. The girl waves to Chad and walks off.*)

YOUNG CHAD: He said it'll be a while till I see her again. Which saddens me. Because I think I'm in love with her. The way she looked at me. It was so *wonderful...*

(*He starts to leave with the disk.*)

CHAD'S MOTHER: Chad?

YOUNG CHAD: Yes, mother?

CHAD'S MOTHER: Can I tell anyone about all this?

YOUNG CHAD: No. Not even if you want to. He said you wouldn't remember it either.

CHAD'S MOTHER: What about your Uncle Ben?

YOUNG CHAD: Not sure. But I have a feeling the pain in his hands may prevent him from forgetting.

(Chad walks into the woods, his mother staring after him, stunned. Lights off on Chad's Mother and up on Uncle Ben, shaking his still-smoking hands at the heavens.)

UNCLE BEN: I've always believed in you! Why have you turned against me like this? **WHY?**

(Lights to black.)

A VOICE IN THE DARK: Now, twenty years later, Chad's time has finally come, for the Beast is loose upon the land, and chaos reigns.

(Lights up on Chad's Mother, strapped in a fiendish electric torture chair. She does not look well. Standing before her is the imposing figure of General Zoltan Zarko, arrogant commander-in-chief of WIF (Worldwide Industrial Forces), a privately subsidized military force, the mightiest army man has ever known (women as well), and whose uniforms bear an uncanny resemblance to those of the Knights Templar. At the moment, things are not going well for WIF. In the distance, monks can be heard, chanting—a deep, very strange sound.)

GENERAL ZARKO: We don't have much time left, Mrs. Curtiss. Do you understand what that means?

CHAD'S MOTHER: …Not much time left?

GENERAL ZARKO: Exactly. Now where is your son?

CHAD'S MOTHER: What son?

(He slaps her rapidly—whamp! whamp!)

GENERAL ZARKO: So, once again: Where is your son?

CHAD'S MOTHER: I've no idea and wouldn't tell you even if I did. *(This time he kicks her, once in each leg.)* Ooh! Agh! Eeek! I *still* wouldn't tell you, even if you were the last fiend on earth. *(He tries tickling her. For Chad's Mother, this is **real** torture. As the general tickles her, a trapdoor opens and someone's eyes peer out.)* No! No! Please! Anything but this! *Anything!*…All right! I'll tell you!

(He stops tickling her.)

GENERAL ZARKO: So where is he?

CHAD'S MOTHER: *(Beat.)* Up your ass? *(Slap.)* No, I mean it. *(Slap.)* I bet you'll find all *sorts* of things up there…mortar shells, land mines— *(Slap, slap.)* Maybe even a few tanks.

(He slaps her again. Music for the approach of a Terrible Beast. General Zarko looks up, scared. The earth trembles. Lieutenant Hatchet, General Zarko's aide-de-camp, peers in through a hole in the wall, terrified.)

HATCHET: General Zarko! The Beast approaches. Our defenses seem useless. Our men are being devoured left and right.

GENERAL ZARKO: What about the women?

HATCHET: Not so many women.

GENERAL ZARKO: I'll be back.

(The General starts out, past the slightly open trapdoor, which closes as he approaches, and which he does not notice.)

CHAD'S MOTHER: General Zarko!

GENERAL ZARKO: What?

CHAD'S MOTHER: Why do you need to find my son?

GENERAL ZARKO: Because reliable sources have informed us that God may have communicated with him directly. And that's not how things are done around here. And God knows it.

*(Exit General Zarko. The moment he's gone, the trapdoor opens again and Chad, age 25, peers out. **Note: his mother cannot see him, because the trapdoor is behind her.**)*

CHAD: Mother?

CHAD'S MOTHER: Chad?

CHAD: *Sssh!*

*(He gets out, wearing white. Chad **only** wears white. **Somehow, it never gets dirty.** He rushes to her chair and starts trying to undo her shackles.)*

CHAD'S MOTHER: How did you find me?

CHAD: Not really sure. Ever since those men kidnapped you, I've been searching for you everywhere. Somehow, I just ended up here. *(As he works on the shackles.)* What did that man mean, God spoke to me?

CHAD'S MOTHER: You don't remember?

CHAD: No. You'd think I'd remember a thing like that, wouldn't you? *(From the sound of things, the Beast seems to be getting closer. Chad, still struggling to free his mother, notices the sound for the first time.)* What's that sound?

CHAD'S MOTHER: They say it's a Beast.

CHAD: Hope it's a good one.

CHAD'S MOTHER: I didn't realize there *were* good ones.

CHAD: Oh yes! Some beasts are really nice. Just last week, I met one that even seemed to know me! But then someone came, I think he was a hunter, and it went away. *(She stares at him, oddly.)* Funny. I can't seem to get you out of this.

UNCLE BEN: *(Offstage.)* You won't need to. *We* can get her out.

(Enter Uncle Ben in high priest's robes, his hands inside baggies filled with ice water.)

CHAD: Uncle Ben! What are you doing here? And why are you wearing those strange clothes?

UNCLE BEN: I have become General Zarko's spiritual counselor.

CHAD: General Zarko! But he's an *awful* man! Just look what he's done to Mother!

UNCLE BEN: In order to protect the free world, General Zarko is often forced to take steps lesser men would not. This is why he sought my spiritual advice.

CHAD: Uncle Ben. Why are your hands in ice water?

UNCLE BEN: Because they still hurt, you son-of-a-bitch!

CHAD: *Uncle Ben!*

UNCLE BEN: Do you know what it's like to be the only spiritual leader in the Western World who cannot open the Good Book because his hands have to be in ice-filled baggies?

CHAD: That's awful!

UNCLE BEN: And did you ever once apologize? NEVER!

CHAD: What did *I* have to do with this?

CHAD'S MOTHER: He still doesn't remember.

UNCLE BEN: He will soon enough. GUARDS! GRAB HIM!

(Chad stares at him in astonishment.)

CHAD'S MOTHER: I think everyone's off fighting the Beast, dear. Don't worry, I can help.

(To Chad's amazement, his mother releases her shackles by pressing a button on one of the chair's arms. She gets up.)

CHAD: *Mother!*

CHAD'S MOTHER: *(Startling new tone.)* Sorry, sweetie. But someday you'll understand.

(Reaching under the chair, she pulls out a huge hypodermic.)

CHAD: *Mother?*

UNCLE BEN: We knew you'd try to rescue her.

"CHAD'S MOTHER": I'm just a simple clone.

(The clone—called Clonella—injects him.)

CHAD: Aaaaagh!

(Chad grows dizzy. Clonella catches him and guides him into the torture chair, then bolts the shackles.)

UNCLE BEN: We can't let control of the free world fall into the wrong hands, can we now?

CHAD: *(His last feeble words before he goes completely under.)* **Where is my real mother!?**

GENERAL ZARKO: *(Appearing in the doorway as he speaks.)* In the cellar. With the rats. And doing *very well.* *(To the others.)* Now we'll make him talk.

(General Zarko gives a signal and thousands of volts of electricity surge through Chad's body, which—needless to say—goes into amazing convulsions. As he does, a large, strange-looking animal's head peers in through the window. **IT'S THE BEAST!** *Seeing Chad in convulsions, it* **growls** *with displeasure. The lights fade,* **on Chad and the Beast last of all.***)*

A VOICE IN THE DARK: Will Chad survive? Will his poor mother, down in the cellar with God-knows-what crawling all over her? In fact, come to think of it, will the **world** survive? It's hard to know. At least, until we discover what those four words say. But perhaps we shall discover it when the lovely and mysterious Evelyn Evangeline Rue returns, all grown up. **Be there!** Or the Beast may come after you.

(The Voice laughs. As the music fades, the words "TO BE CONTINUED..." appear briefly in the dark.)

END OF EPISODE ONE

Episode Five: "Terror Incognita"

Stage dark. Eerie, subterranean music.

A VOICE IN THE DARK: At the end of Episode Four, Chad Curtiss, having escaped from General Zarko's Mountain Fortress by holding onto a giant condor, climbed back up to save his mother, only to find himself buried by an avalanche set loose by the General in a fit of rage.

And now, Episode Five: **"Terror Incognita!"**

(Lights up on a gloomy, subterranean operating room, hygiene clearly not a high priority. Voices approach.)

GENERAL ZARKO & OTHERS: *(Offstage, overlapping.)* Hurry! / In here! / Clear the way! / Pulse is weak! Pulse is weak! / Is he still breathing? / Think so! Not sure! / Let's go! / Out of the way! / We're losing him! / Move it! Move it! I said move it!

(The door to the operating room flies open. Harsh white light streams in, revealing a bizarre machine of uncertain but clearly sinister intent, called the Memotrode. Hammerhead—a mutant—and Hatchet rush in pushing a gurney holding Chad, apparently unconscious, and Clonella, in a blood-splattered nurse's uniform, mini-skirt variety, pushing a cart with surgical instruments. In charge of all is General Zarko, slipping into hospital scrubs.)

GENERAL ZARKO: Hurry! Hurry! I can sense the bastard slipping away. HURRY!

(Clonella starts prepping Chad for resuscitation.)

HAMMERHEAD: General Zarko, with all due respect, sir, if you don't want the bastard to die, why'd you try to kill him before?

GENERAL ZARKO: I didn't! I was only trying to *scare* him!—so he'd tell us where he hid the sacred tablet. But the son-of-a-bitch knows no fear!

CLONELLA: *(Hands on his chest, eyes on his groin.)* Doctor, Doctor, he's not responding!

(General Zarko starts pounding furiously on Chad's chest.)

GENERAL ZARKO: Bastard! Don't you die on me!

(The pounding does the trick, and Chad's eyes open.)

HATCHET: Well done, sir!

GENERAL ZARKO: Who needs medical school? *(To Chad.)* Okay, shitbag. Now listen to me. *(Re: the mysterious machine.)* Clonella darling, let me know when the Memotrode is ready.

CLONELLA: It's ready.

GENERAL ZARKO: Curtiss, I am here to help you *remember* things. Why? Because I am your "friend." *(To Clonella.)* Try 'm at five.

CLONELLA: *Five!*

GENERAL ZARKO: You think that's too low?

CLONELLA: No, no!

(She twists a dial on the Memotrode. Chad screams in agony.)

HAMMERHEAD: Should I get him some aspirin?

GENERAL ZARKO: Good idea. *(Hammerhead gets down on his hands and knees and starts searching for loose aspirin tablets. To Chad.)* Okay. Now once and for all, tell us where you hid this thing.

CHAD: *(Fighting through the pain.)* How can I tell you when I don't know what you are talking about?

HAMMERHEAD: Found one!

GENERAL ZARKO: Give it to 'm. *(Hammerhead blows dust off the aspirin, opens Chad's mouth, pops it in, shuts Chad's mouth, then strokes him under the chin the way one would a dog. Chad swallows. During the above.)* Curtiss, personally, I don't care whether God spoke to you or not. God speaks to *many* people, and at all hours. In fact, before major battles, He even speaks to me.

HAMMERHEAD, HATCHET & CLONELLA: *(In unison.)* Amen!

GENERAL ZARKO: Which is how I got this job.

HAMMERHEAD, HATCHET & CLONELLA: *(In unison.)* Hallelujah!

GENERAL ZARKO: So the fact that you *also* talk to Him is of no concern. You understand what I'm saying here?

CHAD: Strange, I just can't remember if I did.

GENERAL ZARKO: It doesn't fucking MATTER! What *does* matter is this *thing* that He apparently gave to you, because *that* is **very** odd.

CHAD: What thing?

GENERAL ZARKO: Push it to six.

CLONELLA: *Six!*

GENERAL ZARKO: Six.

CLONELLA: But General Zarko—

GENERAL ZARKO: I said six!

(Clonella does as bid. Chad screams in even greater pain. Instantly, Hammerhead starts searching the floor for more aspirins.)

CHAD: *(Through his pain.)* ...Oh my God... *I'm beginning to remember!*

GENERAL ZARKO: Good.

CLONELLA: Should I set him on "Simmer"?

GENERAL ZARKO: I would think so. *Yes. (To Chad.)* We're going to let you rest now, Mr. Curtiss. You're going to need all the strength you have.

*(General Zarko, Clonella, Hammerhead and Hatchet leave. Chad, barely conscious, writhes in pain. The lights shift. Strange music is heard. Under the music, almost as if a **part** of the music, one can hear a terrible distant moaning. Hard to know if it's a woman, or a child.)*

CHAD: Mother! Is that you? *(More moaning heard.)* ...Mother? *(The moaning is getting worse.)* **Mother!** *(Now the moaning seems to come from all around.)* Mother, where are you? *(Now, from somewhere below, he hears a slow banging.)* Mother? *(Then the moaning gives way to a sound of distant wind.)* ...**Mother!**

*(And then the wind dies, and a **new** music is heard, slightly demonic. Chad looks up, ready for...he's not sure what. He hears it before he can see it— A large dark ball of fur rolling down a slide and across the floor toward the operating table. He stares at it. **What the hell is that?** It appears to be some strange kind of egg! Even more astonishing, the shell starts to stretch in odd places. **Something alive is inside! And it's struggling to get out.** Then the "shell" cracks open and a long dark **tube-like** thing glides out **and just keeps on coming.** Seems to be some kind of... **COCOON!** One with an odd **hump** in the middle. As if the cocoon had swallowed something large, but not all the way. And now the cocoon starts to twitch. Some inner convulsion. It's giving BIRTH! **SOMETHING IS EMERGING**... It's a woman!—wearing an identical dress—except of course in size—to the one that little girl wore in the woods.)*

CHAD: ...Evelyn?

WOMAN IN COCOON: *(As Evelyn Evangeline Rue.)* Yes, Chad. *(Smiling warmly, she steps gracefully out of her cocoon like Venus from Botticelli's clam shell.)* I've grown up.

(Blackout.)

A VOICE IN THE DARK: Later that same day, General Zarko receives some unexpectedly disturbing news...

(Lights up on a deeply agitated General Zarko and an extremely nervous Uncle Ben.)

GENERAL ZARKO: What do you mean, he's *gone?*

UNCLE BEN: *(Waving his arms about as he talks.)* He's gone! He's gone! *Oh my God, I'm leaking!*

GENERAL ZARKO: **Clonella!**

(Clonella appears in a window.)

CLONELLA: At your service!

GENERAL ZARKO: The Reverend's hands need re-bagging. And tell Hatchet to bring me the boy's mother! Assuming she's still alive.

CLONELLA: Consider it done!

(Exit Clonella.)

GENERAL ZARKO: Now how did he escape?

UNCLE BEN: We've no idea, except… there seems to be a very large *caterpillar* skin lying nearby.

GENERAL ZARKO: Damn! Probably got in through an air vent. HAMMER-HEAD! I thought we had more time.

(Enter Hammerhead.)

HAMMERHEAD: You screamed?

GENERAL ZARKO: The Dark Forces have invaded our fortress.

HAMMERHEAD: I thought *we* were the Dark Forces!

GENERAL ZARKO: Only on earth.

HAMMERHEAD: So where are *these* guys from?

GENERAL ZARKO: Someplace else. Okay: first thing, I want you to seal off all the air vents.

HAMMERHEAD: How will we breathe?

GENERAL ZARKO: You're right. I need to think. *(Uncle Ben starts moaning. The baggie is empty!)* Will you stop that!? How's a person supposed to think?

(Enter Hatchet, dragging a long chain.)

HATCHET: Here she is.

(Moments later, at the end of the chain, a woman in a bondage suit enters.)

GENERAL ZARKO: Mrs. Curtiss, your son has been kidnapped by certain fiendish and nefarious forces of evil.

CHAD'S MOTHER: *(Barely audible.)* Idoncare.

GENERAL ZARKO: Wha'd she say?

(Hatchet unzips the mouthpiece.)

CHAD'S MOTHER: I don't care.

HATCHET: I think she's lost the will to live.

GENERAL ZARKO: Mrs. Curtiss, clearly this has not been an easy time for you. But if these particular forces find out where your son hid God's message, mankind could be in even greater peril than if *we* find it first. You understand what I'm saying here?

CHAD'S MOTHER: Yes. That God has more regard for my son than *you* do! *(To her traitorous brother, venomously.)* Or you—*you traitor!*

UNCLE BEN: If you knew the kind of pain I am suffering, you wouldn't say a thing like that!

GENERAL ZARKO: You and your stupid hands!

*(General Zarko pulls off a medal and jabs his "good" baggie with its pin. Now **both** of Uncle Ben's hands are in trouble! Uncle Ben stares at the General in shock. Lights to black.)*

A VOICE IN THE DARK: Meanwhile, far below, in a secret grotto accessed through an unsuspected fault line in the earth's crust...

(Lights up on a cave filled with cocoons similar to the one the woman emerged from. Chad and "Evelyn" enter.)

CHAD: Really, I had no idea this is what you meant when you said... *(Looking about, spooked.)* "I want you to meet the family."

EVELYN EVANGALINE RUE: "When they *emerge*."

CHAD: Yes. Right. Guess I forgot that part. *(Trying to act as if none of this was odd.)* And how often does that occur?

EVELYN EVANGALINE RUE: Every six hundred years.

CHAD: Wow!

EVELYN EVANGALINE RUE: Unless something unusual occurs which demands a speedier return.

CHAD: Does that happen often?

EVELYN EVANGALINE RUE: It's just happened.

CHAD: Ah-hah.

EVELYN EVANGALINE RUE: Chad, we need to know where you hid that tablet.

CHAD: The... "tablet"...

EVELYN EVANGALINE RUE: You do remember it, don't you?

CHAD: Well,...*sort of*... *(Beat.)* But...if I'm *right*... I believe I'm not supposed to say anything about it till the Beast arrives.

EVELYN EVANGALINE RUE: I am the Beast. *(Chad stares at her, stunned.)* ...Only joking. Sorry. Didn't mean to scare you.

CHAD: Oh. No, you didn't. I was just, you know, surprised.

EVELYN EVANGALINE RUE: I know. However, I really do need to find out where it is.

CHAD: Why?

EVELYN EVANGALINE RUE: God wants me to make sure it's still in good condition.

CHAD: Oh. Well, unfortunately I don't fully remember. But it is getting clearer! I'm sure I'll remember soon!

EVELYN EVANGALINE RUE: I'm afraid you need to remember *now*. *(She checks one of his ears.)* Good. It's wide enough.

CHAD: *Wide* enough?

EVELYN EVANGALINE RUE: Your ear. For me to get in and out of.

CHAD: **What!!!!**

EVELYN EVANGALINE RUE: Don't worry, dear. I can make myself *extremely* small. Relax.

CHAD: You're about to climb into my head through my ear and you want me to *relax?*

EVELYN EVANGALINE RUE: Trust me darling, you won't feel a thing.

(Music—possibly "Danse Macabre" from George Crumb's demonic Black Angels. *"Evelyn" starts to dance—for a dance of seduction, a strangely frightening dance, all sharp angles. As Chad watches his ability to resist "Evelyn" slowly fades; the dance is hypnotizing him. As she dances, the pods begin to stir,* **as if her dance were bringing them to life as Chad is being drawn into sleep.***)*

(Suddenly, a door opens and a blinding light pours in, silhouetting the figure of a woman in a dress. Just from her stance—legs slightly spread, well-balanced, arms down, body poised—we know: **this is a fighter.** *"Evelyn" turns toward the light. The newcomer walks in, slowly.* **It's ANOTHER Evelyn Evangeline Rue!***)*

(Chad sees her with shock and confusion. The **new** *Evelyn—in the same dress as the* **dancing** *Evelyn's—walks slowly forward, unafraid. The dancing Evelyn breaks into a violent dance, a dance that she expects will cast a lethal spell. But her spell doesn't work on the new Evelyn. She holds out her hand for Chad.)*

THE NEW EVELYN: *(Warm, loving, comforting.)* Come.

THE DANCING EVELYN: Leave him alone! **He is OURS!**

THE NEW EVELYN: No, he is God's.

THE DANCING EVELYN: Then let God come and claim him!

THE NEW EVELYN: He sent me in His stead.

THE DANCING EVELYN: Then He's a fool.

THE NEW EVELYN: *(To Chad, calmly, hand out.)* Come, Chad. Give me your hand.

THE DANCING EVELYN: *Do not touch her!*

THE NEW EVELYN: Chad, give me your hand and they will have no power over you.

THE DANCING EVELYN: Give her your hand and you DIE!

THE NEW EVELYN: Chad, listen to me. Her name is Engsinflaggnn, and she actually looks nothing like this. We have met many times before.

THE DANCING EVELYN: Don't listen to her!

THE NEW EVELYN: Chad, if I'm to help you, you have to give me your hand. But you have to give it of your own free will.

THE DANCING EVELYN: *(To the new Evelyn.)* Yes. And then you will die as well!

THE NEW EVELYN: *(Reaching out for him.)* Chad!

(He reaches for her hand. But just as he's about to take it, the dancing Evelyn charges—a mad, whirling dervish. The new Evelyn takes a fighting stance. The dancing Evelyn strikes, but the new Evelyn, in her utter calm, is clearly the superior fighter. Seeing she is losing the fight, the dancing Evelyn turns into a kind of beast. **And the pods are starting to open.***)*

THE NEW EVELYN: *(To Chad, with sudden urgency.)* Chad, quick, give me your hand!

(He does. The "Beast" growls.)

CHAD: *It's the Beast!*

THE NEW EVELYN: Yes, but not the one God spoke of. That beast is good, and awaits us in the woods.

THE DANCING EVELYN: *(Staring down, as if toward Hell.)* **HELP ME! YOU SONS-OF-BITCHES!**

(Thunder! Lightning! It's the signal the dancing Evelyn wanted. She aims her fingers at Chad. Sparks fly from her fingers. Fire surges from her mouth! Chad is so startled he drops the new Evelyn's hand.)

THE NEW EVELYN: *Chad!* **No!**

(She reaches out for him. But before he can grab her hand, the new Evelyn freezes and her body starts to convulse. Chad runs to her aid, fights his way past the dancing Evelyn, leaps over a writhing mound of pods, scoops the good Evelyn into his arms and starts out, fighting off the dancing Evelyn and some quickly growing pods as he goes. Suddenly, one of the pods breaks open and a man in a long black cloak rises out of the pod and enfolds Chad and the new Evelyn in his cloak. Chad fights his way out of the cloak. **BUT THE NEW EVELYN IS GONE.***)*

CHAD: Evelyn! *Evelyn!*

(As the dancing Evelyn laughs triumphantly, claw-like hands reach out of another pod, grab Chad's legs and pull him down into the terrible, writhing pod. A dreadful chewing sound is heard. Blackout.)

A VOICE IN THE DARK: Amazing, when you think of it—all this, just to learn one four-word message. *(Beat.)* Well, see you soon… **God willing.** *(As the music begins to fade, the words "TO BE CONTINUED…" appear briefly in the dark.)*

END OF EPISODE FIVE

Episode Fourteen: "Revelations"

In the dark, a man's deeply sonorous voice begins to intone Canto I of Dante's Inferno. *Let us call him The Reader. His voice is not one we've heard before.*

THE READER: Nel mezzo del cammin di nostra vita
mi ritrovai per una selva oscura
ché la diritta via era smarrita.
(Now we hear music: something majestic and calm, like the second theme in Verdi's overture to La Forza del Destino.*)*
Ahi quanto a dir qual era è cosa dura
esta selva selvaggia e aspra e forte
che nel pensier rinova la paura!
(And now the lights rise. Corpses lie everywhere, many dismembered savagely, and rotted beyond recognition. Some of the bodies, perhaps to preserve their flesh for leaner times, hang down on hooks, like racks of beef.)
Tant'è amara che poco è più morte;
ma per trattar del ben ch'i' vi trovai,
dirò de l'altre cose ch'i' v'ho scorte.

Io non so ben ridir com'i' v'intrai,
tant'era pien di sonno a quel punto
che la verace via abbandonai.
(Beat. Our Reader, having come to the end of the first twelve lines of Canto I, begins again. **For the remainder of this scene, he will never get past those twelve lines.** *After The Reader repeats the first four lines, other Readers join in.)*
SECOND READER: Midway upon the journey of our life
I found myself within a forest dark,
For the straightforward pathway had been lost.

Ah me! how hard a thing it is to say
What was this forest savage, rough, and stern,
Which in the very thought renews the fear.
(The Second Reader repeats the above.)
THIRD READER: Midway on our life's journey,
I found myself in dark woods,
the right path lost.

To tell about these woods is hard—
so tangled, rough and savage—
that thinking of it now, I feel
the old fears stirring.

(The Third Reader repeats the above.)

*(As the voices fade, a **familiar** voice is heard.)*

A VOICE IN THE DARK: Years have passed. General Zarko's forces have been routed by infidels searching for the same sacred tablet that by now *everyone* seems to be looking for. *(Enter the **real** Evelyn Evangeline Rue, bruised, filthy dirty, her sweet dress in tatters, and so weak she can hardly walk.)* Everyone who's still alive, that is. *(Yet, like some young Mother Courage, Evelyn forges on, undaunted, a dusty, once-elegant hatbox clutched in her right hand, a large sack held in her left.)* The General's terrible doomsday machine—code-name "Iron Chef"—which chopped off Chad's head just as he was about to remember where the sacred tablet was hidden, has self-destructed. A world of desolation lies everywhere. And now, Episode Fourteen, "**Revelations**."

(Heaving a weary sigh, Evelyn sits and stares out glumly.)

CHAD'S VOICE: *(Muffled.)* Dongivvup.

(She opens the hatbox cover and peers in.)

EVELYN EVANGALINE RUE: What?

CHAD'S VOICE: *(**From inside the hatbox!**)* Don't give up.

EVELYN EVANGALINE RUE: I'm not.

CHAD'S VOICE: Well, it doesn't feel that way.

EVELYN EVANGALINE RUE: What are you talking about?

CHAD'S VOICE: I sense a defeatist attitude coming over you.

EVELYN EVANGALINE RUE: Chad, let me tell you something. As far as I'm concerned, you are in no position to talk, 'cause you can't see what *I* see.

CHAD'S VOICE: What's there to see—a few palm trees, a pretty beach?

EVELYN EVANGALINE RUE: Chad, we are not in Florida.

CHAD'S VOICE: You told me we were in Florida!

EVELYN EVANGALINE RUE: I was lying.

CHAD'S VOICE: *Lying?*

(Evelyn opens the hatbox and peers in.)

EVELYN EVANGALINE RUE: Chad?

CHAD'S VOICE: I'm not talking to you ever again!

EVELYN EVANGALINE RUE: Chad, I'm sorry I lied. It's the only time in my life I ever have.

CHAD'S VOICE: *(Sudden hope.)* Is that true?

EVELYN EVANGALINE RUE: No. Oh Chad, what's to become of us? I've just lost my moral center, you've lost your body.

(Enter a large mutant spider—actually, not a spider at all, but Engsinflaggnn, the shape-shifter from Hell. Evelyn stares at it, disgusted.)

CHAD'S VOICE: Well I love you anyway.

EVELYN EVANGALINE RUE: *(Eyes on the spider, slowly making its way towards her.)* Thank you.

CHAD'S VOICE: When I find God's tablet and fulfill my destiny, do you think you'd maybe like to marry me?

EVELYN EVANGALINE RUE: *(Focused on the spider.)* Sure.

CHAD'S VOICE: Even if we don't find any more body parts for me?

EVELYN EVANGALINE RUE: *(Paying more attention to the spider than Chad.)* We'll find more.

CHAD'S VOICE: What's the count so far?

(That snaps her back, and she checks inside her sack.)

EVELYN EVANGALINE RUE: Four arms, three legs (one of them missing a foot), five—no, sorry… *(She digs around.)* …six penises…

CHAD'S VOICE: We'll need something to attach them to.

EVELYN EVANGALINE RUE: *Them?*

CHAD'S VOICE: Why not?

EVELYN EVANGALINE RUE: You'll look funny with six penises.

CHAD'S VOICE: No funnier than I look now. *(The spider stops a short distance away, hunkers down and just watches them.)* But if it's at all possible, I'd rather have them as part of my groin than my head.

EVELYN EVANGALINE RUE: Wait! I think I see a groin!

(Leaving the hatbox hidden as best she can, she rushes off toward a mound of dead bodies, looking for a spare groin. The moment her back is turned, the spider rushes, spider-like, to the hatbox, grabs it with her beak, pincers, whatever, and waddles off with it, chortling as only mutant spiders can.)

CHAD'S VOICE: *(As he's being carried away.)* Evelyn?… *(First signs of worry.)* Evelyn?

(Exit Engsinflaggnn with hatbox. Meanwhile, Evelyn is tugging at something buried in the mound of bodies.)

EVELYN EVANGALINE RUE: *(To the hatbox, not realizing it isn't there anymore.)* If this is what I think, you may not need those other six. *(She pulls… It GIVES!—the lower portion of a man's multi-tattooed torso, which she has yanked out of its enclosure by a penis any horse would be proud of. Still holding it by its penis, she turns triumphantly. Which is when she realizes the hatbox and spider are gone.)* Shit! *(To the heavens.) Sorry!*

(Evelyn, still holding the penis, races off after the spider and Chad. In so doing, Evelyn practically runs into someone we cannot see—at least, **not yet.***)*

EVELYN EVANGALINE RUE: *(Offstage, to the unseen person.)* Woops! Sorry!

(The unseen person, a man, mutters some incomprehensible but clearly surly reply. We sense he's in great pain. Two other voices, also men's, can be heard.)

K-3: *(Offstage.)* Don't worry, we've got you!

K-4: *(Offstage, overlapping.)* If you could maybe just lift this leg a little bit more...

K-3: *(Offstage.)* ...And this *arm*...

(Enter General Zarko, looking shockingly terrible, and unable to walk on his own for reasons related to his new physical state, which I will presently explain. Assisting him—by propping him up under the armpits and pretty much dragging him—are two albino soldiers, K-3 and K-4, the last two men he feels he can still trust.)

GENERAL ZARKO: Hurry! Hurry! They can't be far behind! *Goddam tanks! Don't get me the first time, they want to try again!* My own men! It's enough to make you weep. How many tanks ran over me?

K-3: Ten.

GENERAL ZARKO: Ten fucking tanks!

K-4: Plus one amphibious landing vehicle.

GENERAL ZARKO: Twelve fucking tanks plus three amphibious landing vehicles run over me and am I deterred? No. But as a leader of men, I am finished.

K-4: You can always teach.

GENERAL ZARKO: Yes, but what?

K-3: Moral philosophy?

GENERAL ZARKO: Oooh. I like the sound of that.

(A shot rings out.)

K-4: We have to go now.

(Another gunshot.)

K-3: Sorry.

(They prop him up against some corpses, and exit.)

GENERAL ZARKO: Wait-a-minute! Where are you going? I said wait-a-minute. WAIT-A-MINUTE! *(Suddenly he sees something that gives him hope.)* Oh, thank you Lord. Nurse! NURSE!

(Enter Chad's Mother, still in her S/M outfit, but with a saucy nurse's uniform over it. Gunshots continue.)

CHAD'S MOTHER: *(Hand cupped to ear—sweetness itself.)* Did someone cry for help?

GENERAL ZARKO: Yes! Over here! Quick! Before they kill me!

CHAD'S MOTHER: *(As she approaches—merrily.)* Well, we certainly wouldn't want that, would we?

GENERAL ZARKO: Oh my God! *Mrs. Curtiss!*

(She pulls out a giant hypodermic.)

CHAD'S MOTHER: This may hurt a bit.

*(She plunges the huge hypodermic into the area she's just swabbed. He screams. **Blackout**.)*

A VOICE IN THE DARK: Later that night, in a seemingly abandoned mine shaft at the edge of a supposedly extinct volcano (but in reality a cavern measureless to man), Engsinflaggnn, the shape-shifter from Hell, forms an unholy alliance with the Reverend Ben.

(Lights up on "The Reverend Ben's Chamber of Horrors." In the gloomy vault, along with the Reverend—his hands still in baggies—and Engsinflaggnn, still a spider, but now, due to her strange skills, able to stand upright, is Chad—or rather, Chad's head, which is set on a marble pedestal, and well-lit, the open hatbox sitting nearby.)

UNCLE BEN: So! My favorite nephew!—headstrong as usual.

ENGSINFLAGGNN: Show him the sacred disk.

UNCLE BEN: The sacred disk! Coming up!

ENGSINFLAGGNN: I love the sacred disk! It's so *beautiful!*

CHAD: How did you find it?

UNCLE BEN: Remember when you were trapped in Antarctica by the Boxer Gang?

CHAD: No.

ENGSINFLAGGNN: What about, trapped in Latvia by the Beadle Group?

CHAD: That I remember.

UNCLE BEN: That's when we found it.

ENGSINFLAGGNN: And I helped him find it! *(To the Reverend.)* Didn't I, didn't I?

UNCLE BEN: *(Annoyed—**all she seems to want is credit.**)* Yes!

(The Reverend Ben opens a hidden cabinet. Inside, the sacred red disk glows eerily.)

CHAD: But *how?*

ENGSINFLAGGNN: It would take too long to explain.

UNCLE BEN: BOX!

ENGSINFLAGGNN: *Box!*

(Engsinflaggnn, using whatever part of her anatomy she can, brings an insulated box to Uncle Ben, who, using insulated tongs, slides the disk out of the cabinet and into the box.)

UNCLE BEN: And now my young friend, you are going to tell me what the message says.

CHAD: Never! Those four words were meant for my eyes only. So *I* could decide whether they should be revealed to the *rest* of the world—which includes *you.*

UNCLE BEN: *(Shouts into the darkness.)* Bring in You-Know-Who!

ENGSINFLAGGNN: Yes! The "You-Know-Who!"

(Enter K-3, in monk's robes, leading the still-disheveled Evelyn by a chain.)

CHAD: *Evelyn!*

EVELYN EVANGALINE RUE: I've decided. I *will* marry you, Chad!

CHAD: Oh Evelyn! That makes me so happy!

(Enter K-4, also in monk's robes, leading Chad's Mother, still in her combo bondage suit and nurse's outfit, by chains.)

CHAD: **Mother?**

CHAD'S MOTHER: Imhereforyouson.

CHAD: *(To his uncle.)* What?

(K-4 unzips her mouth.)

CHAD'S MOTHER: I'm here for you, son.

UNCLE BEN: *(To Engsinflaggnn.)* Now show him the sacred disk!

ENGSINFLAGGNN: *"The sacred disk!"*

(Music swells. Engsinflaggnn walks over to Chad and opens the box. An eerie red light glows on Chad's face.)

UNCLE BEN: Tell us what the message says.

CHAD: *(Eyes averted.)* No! No! You can't make me!

ENGSINFLAGGNN: LOOK, DAMN YOU! LOOK!

CHAD: *Noooo!*

*(Suddenly, a strangely cold light falls on Uncle Ben. Without willing it, a remarkable transformation is coming over him. A new and terrible strength has seized him, which seems to startle him as much as it does us. When Uncle Ben next speaks to Chad, it is in a voice of dreadful authority. **SATAN HAS BECOME UNCLE BEN!**)*

UNCLE BEN: *(A true Mephistopheles.)* Funny, I would have thought your curiosity was *stronger* than this.

CHAD: *(Stunned by the malevolent transformation.)* Uncle Ben!

UNCLE BEN: Not anymore.

CHAD: But... you were a man of *God!*

UNCLE BEN: *(Pulling off his baggies.)* And still am. At our core, we are *all* men of God. *(Looking up—with fury.)* ARE WE NOT!? *(Sound of thunder, as if in response.)* Now read!

CHAD: No! God has put His faith in me, and I will not betray His faith.

UNCLE BEN: *(To Chad.)* So which of these two should I kill first?

CHAD: *(A cry to the heavens.)* **LORD, HELP ME!**

UNCLE BEN: Fine. Then I will choose.

CHAD: *(To himself, eyes shut, like a mantra.)* I will not betray His trust, I will not betray His trust, I will not betray—

(While Chad chants, Uncle Ben points at Chad's Mother.)

CHAD'S MOTHER: *Chaaaad...*

(Chad looks just as thunder crashes, electricity flies, and Chad's Mother screams, mortally done in by some fiendish power in the tips of Uncle Ben's fingers.)

CHAD: *(Utter horror.)* Mother!

CHAD'S MOTHER: *(Weakening fast.)* You made... the right... choice,... son. *(And with that, she collapses, dead. Uncle Ben turns his malevolent gaze upon Evelyn.)*

UNCLE BEN: And now the girl...

CHAD: No!

EVELYN EVANGALINE RUE: I love you, Chad Curtiss.

CHAD: And I love you, Evelyn Evangeline Rue.

EVELYN EVANGALINE RUE: I will *always* love you, Chad Curtiss.

CHAD: And I will always love you, Evelyn Evangeline Rue.

UNCLE BEN: Is that it, then?

CHAD: I will not betray His trust, I will not betray His trust, I will not— *(Thunder! Flashes of demonic light! And Evelyn Evangeline Rue crumples to the ground. Chad, overwhelmed with despair, looks up.)* Lord! Help me to understand! *(And with that, he looks down into the sacred box, hoping for words of comfort. Whatever Chad sees horrifies him beyond measure.)* ...Oh my God... This cannot be...

UNCLE BEN: *(Stunned by Chad's reaction.)* What! WHAT!

ENGSINFLAGGNN: *(The Beast's voice.)* TELL US! TELL US!

UNCLE BEN: *(Scared.)* ...What does it say?

ENGSINFLAGGNN: What does it say?

CHAD: It says... *(Incredulous.)* ..."Good-bye and good luck."

UNCLE BEN: "Good-bye and g—..." That's not possible.

CHAD: It's what it says!

UNCLE BEN: But He would never…

CHAD: I AM TELLING YOU WHAT IT SAYS!

UNCLE BEN: "Good-bye and good *luck*"?

CHAD: "Good-bye and good luck."

ENGSINFLAGGNN: *(She's been counting.)* That's five words, not four.

UNCLE BEN: "Good-bye" counts as one.

ENGSINFLAGGNN: Oh my God…

UNCLE BEN: *(Looking up.)* I thought we had a good relationship. I mean, who is there to oppose me now? THIS IS NOT FIGHTING FAIR!

(Uncle Ben wanders off, in shock. Engsinflaggnn, just as shocked, follows after him, forlorn.)

ENGSINFLAGGNN: Does it *always* count as one?

UNCLE BEN: Always. *Always!*

(They exit. Chad looks up to the heavens, terrified.)

CHAD: Mother… if you can hear me… *I am scared!*

(Lights fade to black.)

A VOICE IN THE DARK: Will Chad "get himself together"? Will God reconsider His decision and return? *Or…* Will something *else* occur, altogether unexpected? Be here next time…and, if you're very good, perhaps you will find out.

(He laughs. As the music fades, the words "TO BE CONTINUED…" appear briefly in the dark.)

END OF PLAY

When the Sea Drowns in Sand
by Eduardo Machado

Copyright © 2000 by Eduardo Machado. All rights reserved. CAUTION: Professionals and amateurs are hereby warned that *When the Sea Drowns in Sand* is subject to a royalty. It is fully protected under the copyright laws of the United States of America and of all countries covered by the International Copyright Union (including the Dominion of Canada and the rest of the British Commonwealth), the Berne Convention, the Pan-American Copyright Convention and the Universal Copyright Convention, as well as all countries with which the United States has reciprocal copyright relations. All rights, including professional, amateur stage rights, motion picture, recitation, lecturing, public reading, radio broadcasting, television, video or sound recording, all other forms of mechanical or electronic reproduction, such as CD-ROM, CD-I, information storage and retrieval systems and photocopying, and the rights of translation into foreign languages, are strictly reserved. Particular emphasis is laid upon the matter of readings, permission for which must be secured from the Author's agent in writing.

ALL INQUIRIES CONCERNING RIGHTS, INCLUDING AMATEUR RIGHTS, SHOULD BE ADDRESSED TO: BARBARA LIGETI, 910 WEST END AVE., APT. 6F, NEW YORK, NY 10025.

BIOGRAPHY

Eduardo Machado is the author of over 25 plays and several translations, including *In the Eye of the Hurricane, Cuba and the Night, Stevie Wants to Play the Blues, A Burning Beach, Why to Refuse* and *Broken Eggs*. His plays have been produced in regional theatres all over the country, New York City and London. Some of the theatres include the Williamstown Theatre Festival, the Long Wharf Theater, the Mark Taper Forum, Actors Theatre of Louisville, the Ensemble Studio Theatre, The American Place Theatre, El Repertorio Español, The Los Angeles Theater Center, and The New Mexico Repertory. Mr. Machado has recently completed writing and directing his first feature length film, *Exiles in New York*, which premiered at The Santa Barbara Film Festival, South by Southwest, AFI Film Festival, and Festival International Del Nuevo Cine Latino Americano. He just completed a screenplay of *Broken Eggs*. He is the head of playwriting at Columbia University and the Co-Artistic Director of the Cherry Lane Theatre.

HUMANA FESTIVAL PRODUCTION

When the Sea Drowns in Sand premiered at the Humana Festival of New American Plays in March 2001. It was directed by Michael John Garcés with the following cast:

Federico . . . . Joseph Urla
Fred . . . . Ed Vassallo
Ernesto . . . . Felix Solis
Percussionist . . . . Hugh "Fuma" Petersen

and the following production cast:

Scenic Designer . . . . Paul Owen
Costume Designer . . . . Lindsay W. Davis
Lighting Designer . . . . Tony Penna
Sound Designer . . . . Martin R. Desjardins
Properties Designer . . . . Amahl Lovato
Stage Manager . . . . Charles M. Turner III
Production Assistant . . . . Trudy L. Paxton
Dramaturg . . . . Michael Bigelow Dixon
Assistant Dramaturg . . . . Stephen Moulds
Casting . . . . Orpheus Group

CHARACTERS

FEDERICO

FRED

ERNESTO

TIME AND PLACE

Act One: December 1999. New York and Havana.
Act Two: Havana.

The set is a dark blue. The set pieces are minimal. When they are in a car or plane there are no seats. The drummer is on stage.

For my friend Ed Vassallo.

Ed Vassallo, Felix Solis, and Joseph Urla in
When the Sea Drowns in Sand

25th Annual Humana Festival of New American Plays
Actors Theatre of Louisville, 2001
photo by Richard Trigg

When the Sea Drowns in Sand

ACT ONE

SCENE ONE

Lights up. New York.

Federico, a man in his forties. He seems to be suspended in the air. All we see is his face. Drums play. He chants and talks.

FEDERICO: I land there I see it
The world
fills me sweetly.
Ah.
Ah.
Ah.

Enraptured
in such a precarious
dream
Can it be? Is this me?
Ah
ah
ah.
I'm loose now
I choose now
To be with you
darling.
Don't dangle the future
no meaning in that.

I'm captured
in a rapturous
rhapsody.
ah
ah
ah aah.
It's me.
I'm home now
I'm free now,
To be just
like me now.
Oh darling
in Spanish
don't speak more in English
no meaning in that,
ay
ay
ay aaay.
When you've reached your
promised land.
Where the people often dance.
Oh
oh,
Oh,
Hold on dear
Be sweet love
don't leave me
asleep here.
It's me dear.
I'm home.
Am I home?
I
I, Iii
It's a dream
after all
there's no one.
No home
No

ah
Oh Oooh.
It's all lost
my darling
you left me.
Like I always knew you would.
Why am I not
any good.
Why can't I hold
on to you
or it.
Or her
Or me.
Or dreams.
I'm beginning to awake now.
Like I always knew I would.
The sun shines
in bed now
alone.
Still so far away
from home
Oh
No
ay, aay.
My eyes clear
I focus
And I see
I'm, all alone.
Should I
just get up and
pee?
Why do good
things come in dreams.
Alone
now.
No
home now.
And for sure

I know you left me.

Like I always knew you would.

Like I always knew you would.

Like I always knew you would.

(Federico wakes up. Federico is in bed. He is wearing red pajamas. He holds his crotch.)

FEDERICO: *¿Qué pasa? ¿Qué pasa? ¿Qué pasa?*

(We hear his own voice echoing back to him.)

FEDERICO: *(Voice-over.)* What's going on? What's going on! What's going on?

FEDERICO: That's not how I would have translated it. I would have said, "What's doing?"—no that's not it. "How does it go!" No too casual. "How am I?" Too psychological. "How are you doing?" Too many words. Some things are impossible to translate. God, if two words are impossible to translate how do you translate an entire life? *Qué pasa.* "What's happening?" Too black, too street, too seventies. But that's the closest to my original meaning I think. "What's happening." Fred what's happening?

(Fred, an American Italian in his early thirties, is there with a video camera in his hand and a suitcase.)

FRED: The car is waiting.

FEDERICO: What?

FRED: We are going to Cuba, today.

FEDERICO: I got my visa?

FRED: They faxed it last night at the last moment. Remember?

FEDERICO: That wasn't a dream.

FRED: No.

FEDERICO: I thought it was a dream.

FRED: Come on, you got your passport and your visa. It only took five years.

FEDERICO: Right. You think they'll let me in.

FRED: Of course.

FEDERICO: I can go back.

FRED: Yes. I'm so glad I'm going with you. We are going to Cuba!

FEDERICO: When we are at the airport say we are going to Cancún.

FRED: Right.

FEDERICO: I got my Cuban passport, my visa. I got my heart in my stomach. I hope I don't vomit. I got my memories my past. I hope they're not all destroyed. What if they don't let me in? No!

FRED: The car is waiting.

FEDERICO: No.

FRED: What?

FEDERICO: No. I'm not going.

FRED: What do you mean? You've been waiting for this.

FEDERICO: No, I can't go, no I can't do it. It's too late. A year ago maybe not now.

FRED: Federico—

FEDERICO: Where's my dog?

FRED: I don't know. No, no.

FEDERICO: Stella? Baby come here! Stella! Come to daddy. Stella. Who's going to take care of my dog? Stella!

(Stella starts to bark. She is under the bed.)

FRED: We arranged for a student to take care of your dog.

FEDERICO: Stella, you're under the bed sweetie?

(Federico crawls under the bed.)

FEDERICO: Daddy's joining you. Come here bitch!

FRED: Federico come back here! "No" is not the answer I will accept.

FEDERICO: You're on your own.

FRED: You gotta do it. You gotta make that split you feel inside come together. I gotta make you do it!

FEDERICO: Underneath the bed with the dog that's the only home I know, need, want or can handle. Yes, Stella? You love me?

(Stella snarls.)

FRED: Jesus, you told me I was the only person…that without me you would not be able to go. To face it. That I was better than the rest. All the other guys who took advantage of you and used sex to learn and then leave you. That I meant something to you. That you relied on my strength.

FEDERICO: The panic the terror—

FRED: No!

FEDERICO: The terror. The warmth of a dog.

FRED: The love. I love you. You're my buddy. You can crawl under the bed with me when we get there. We can hold each other naked underneath the bed. We can scream into each other—

(Federico comes out from under the bed.)

FEDERICO: I don't know.

FRED: Why can't you do it?

FEDERICO: Fred, I've told this story too many times to too many people. So many that by now it should have lost all its meaning. But it hasn't; to be thrown out or did you walk out. That is the real question of us humans. Disoriented or unrequited? I do not know the answer to that. Was I thrown out or did I walk away from my country? Did I decide to leave or was I tricked?

FRED: Walk into me.

FEDERICO: There is an airport in Havana where I learned the meaning of impotence. I saw my mother on the other side of the glass. She let me go. She let me get on a plane without her. It could have been forever. I held my brother's hand. I handed over my blue aquamarine ring. My father did not reassure me. They searched my butthole for diamonds. You want me to get on a plane and go back and face that morning. You sadist!

FRED: It's what you need.

FEDERICO: Help me.

FRED: Get dressed.

FEDERICO: Someone will take care of my dog?

(Federico starts getting dressed.)

FRED: Your concern over your dog is highly hypocritical.

FEDERICO: I care about the dog. I mean she doesn't care about me. But I have a…I don't know, a need to be abused by her.

FRED: Who abuses who in that relationship is questionable.

FEDERICO: I feed her every day. I take care of her! But who takes care of me?

FRED: I will, bitch.

FEDERICO: I like it when you talk rough.

FRED: Trust me.

(Blackout.)

SCENE TWO

Lights up. Federico and Fred are flying. Fred is sleeping. Drums.

FEDERICO: Everyone seems to know I had to go. Wish you well.
    Now go! Go home.
    Home is that sentimental, abstract place.
    Home.
    Is that, yearning from the gut, feeling.
    Cut down at nine.
    A gulf more potent than any Berlin Wall. Separated.
    So now I sit on a plane.

I check my passport
My Cuban passport.
My birth certificate.
My identity?

I went into the bathroom and cried.

My identity?
Flamboyant writer, professor bla, bla, bla.
Darling to some a monster to others.
No doubt about his talent.
His talent is questionable.

Savior of people's creative life.
Horrible husband, lover and wife.
Good friend.
Abandons all his friends.
New Yorker from L.A.

My identity.

But on this plane
Back to home.
Home to where there is no home.
Or is the air home?
I cried in that bathroom.
Because I've begun to recall
Another person
That was me.

And my friend Fred sleeps
On a plane towards who knows.
Dec. 1, 1999. Nine fifteen P.M. Eastern Time.

(Blackout.)

Inside the car, Cuba. Federico leans his head against it. Ernesto, a Cuban man in his late thirties, wipes it with a rag. Fred is behind them; he lights a cigarette. Federico takes it from him. Fred lights another one.

FRED: God bless a country where you can smoke anywhere. Amen! Even in the elevators. Cuban cigarettes are heaven. Amen.
(Ernesto sweats nervously and wipes his brow with the rag.)
FEDERICO: Is it that one? Or that one?
FRED: You okay?
FEDERICO: Happiest day of my life.
FRED: Good.
(Fred opens a small pillbox filled with Valiums and downs a Valium.)
FEDERICO: You okay?
FRED: Happiest day of your life.
FEDERICO: Right, then why are you downing a Valium.
FRED: That's why we brought them.
FEDERICO: Right. Do you understand us Manny? Manny?
FRED: His name is Ernesto.
FEDERICO: Ernesto? Really?
FRED: Jesus.
FEDERICO: No?
FRED: You should remember.
FEDERICO: I have too many names inside my head.
FRED: Your head? Right.
FEDERICO: So Manny, Ernesto, so?
ERNESTO: You're happy, why shouldn't you be, you're home?
(Federico touches the glass.)
FEDERICO: Not real
    walking into
    What?
    The car is burgundy,
    my blood is blue.
    What am I to do!
    Oh god!
    The water is blue
    the sky is cloudy

it might rain,
like I always knew
it would.

The corner
the corner
is still here.
Is the house
in the distance?
you waited
Like I always knew you would.

ERNESTO: So you went on the Peter Pan flights?

(Federico does not answer.)

FRED: He was only nine, by himself with his six-year-old brother.

ERNESTO: What's his name?

FRED: I never met his brother and I don't know his name.

ERNESTO: And you two seem so close.

FRED: Oh we are...

ERNESTO: I thought so.

FRED: ...but his brother lives in another state. So does mine and he doesn't know my brother or my brother's name.

FEDERICO: Al. That's your brother's name.

FRED: So you know his name. But he doesn't know my brother.

FEDERICO: Jesus.

FRED: What?

FEDERICO: My brother's name is Jesus. He was born on Christmas Day.

ERNESTO: Tragedy.

FRED: Really?

ERNESTO: Shameful.

FRED: What.

ERNESTO: So many kids, thirteen thousand. Sent to the U.S. Like cattle, all because of a CIA plot and an English woman living here in Cuba. She was a spy, when she got old the CIA sent her a wheelchair. She died here.

FRED: In La Habana?

ERNESTO: Yes. Like she was one of us.

FEDERICO: Was her name Wendy?

ERNESTO: I don't know. But my friend made a documentary about it. The people in it, the children now grown up. Were broken by the experience.

You can tell when you watch the documentary. Fidel should have stopped their emigration. But he gave them a special kind of visa. Always trying to please, Fidel. Back then. He wanted to please.

FEDERICO: That's not what my parents thought.

ERNESTO: Gave you the visa didn't he?

FEDERICO: To get rid of us.

ERNESTO: No. When those thirteen thousand kids left. We cried.

FEDERICO: We all cried.

FRED: I'd like to see that documentary. Would you Federico.

FEDERICO: I lived it Fred.

FRED: Oh.

(Federico looks out.)

ERNESTO: So many children, CIA plot. Destroy the child corrupt the revolution. Pity.

FEDERICO: This one's not it. Fuck, I thought I could find it. Fuck.

ERNESTO: Maybe someone remembers your family here. What did they do?

FEDERICO: We owned the bus company.

ERNESTO: Then they got to remember. They rode the busses. Paid you a nickel everyday. People don't forget that.

FEDERICO: Really?

ERNESTO: I'll ask someone that looks old and they'll remember.

FRED: Yeah. We'll find it baby. We'll find it.

FEDERICO: Wait a minute. The address is on my birth certificate.

FRED: Really?

FEDERICO: I was born here Fred.

FRED: I know.

FEDERICO: And I've come back.

FRED: I'm so proud of you.

ERNESTO: I'm very happy that we started this period of "family reconciliation."

FRED: What?

ERNESTO: That's the period Fidel said we are in now. That's why he's letting you all come back.

FRED: Really?

ERNESTO: Yes.

FEDERICO: I think it should be called the period of "dollar reconciliation."

ERNESTO: That's true.

(They laugh.)

FRED: I'm proud of you.

FEDERICO: Why?

FRED: That you can laugh about it. Although it would be alright with me if you cried.

(Federico grabs the pillbox from Fred's hand and takes a Valium.)

FEDERICO: Want one?

ERNESTO: Valium, yes.

FRED: Valium yes, Yankee no!

(Ernesto laughs nervously. Takes the Valium with his hand. Ernesto takes out his wallet and very carefully stores the Valium in it. Then puts the wallet in his pocket.)

FEDERICO: You really do believe in saving for the future.

ERNESTO: We have to.

FEDERICO: So simple, "We have to."

FRED: You okay?

FEDERICO: Don't I look it!

FRED: Sure.

FEDERICO: Good.

FRED: Now take out your birth certificate.

FEDERICO: Why?

FRED: So we can find the address.

FEDERICO: Right.

(Federico searches through his pockets.)

FEDERICO: God!

FRED: You lost it.

FEDERICO: No...

FRED: Then where is it?

ERNESTO: It certainly is a beautiful little town. My wife and I used to come here.

FEDERICO: If you and your wife used to come here. Then why can't you find my goddamn house!

ERNESTO: ...We used to come here every...

FRED: Is it in your wallet?

ERNESTO: ...summer. We had big barbecues down on the beach...Perfect beach town only fifteen minutes from the center of La Habana... Barbecues by the beach, fish, sometimes lobster. I know a man who sells lobster for dollars. He's watched. Still does it, under the table. If you want to make a meal I can get you a good price on lobster, fresh fish, right out of the gulf. He sells them out of his garage. If you want to buy I'll get it for you. He also sells those antennas, which are against the law, because you can get stations from everywhere in the world! But people buy them hide them and use them. What are they called? They're round and...

FRED: Satellite dishes?

ERNESTO: Yes.

FRED: Satellite dishes, yes?

ERNESTO: I want to make enough money to buy a satellite dish.

FEDERICO: Name names.

ERNESTO: That's not funny.

FRED: People name names?

ERNESTO: Yes. Like with everything there's good and bad.

FRED: They do in America also.

ERNESTO: I know...Blacklisting...McCarthy...Black Panthers...Shame.

FRED: And other things.

ERNESTO: You have a right to be anything but a communist, in your country.

FRED: Among other things. Any radical's not so good either.

(Federico goes back to looking for his birth certificate. He has taken many pieces of paper out of his pocket.)

FEDERICO: Passport. List of people to contact. Airplane tickets. Mom's cousin's address...

FRED: You have a car.

FEDERICO: Picture of what the house looked like in 1959...Traveler's checks...Cash...

FRED: Keep the cash where it is.

FEDERICO: Fine. Where the fuck is the birth certificate?

FRED: You'll find it. Keep looking through that money belt.

ERNESTO: I made ten thousand dollars. Can you believe it ten thousand dollars.

FRED: You did?

FEDERICO: How?

ERNESTO: I sculpt.

FEDERICO: Ah.

ERNESTO: Special kind of sculpting from broken glass. Never been done the way I do it. I showed in Paris last year.

FRED: Great.

FEDERICO: Paris wow. You got to go to Paris.

ERNESTO: Sold this sculpting to an Italian restaurant that is opening in La Habana. That's how I bought this car.

FRED: Beauty.

ERNESTO: Nineteen forty-nine Chevy. I'll show you a picture of my sculpting when we get back to the house.

FRED: Can't wait. I'll take a picture with my camera. A picture of the picture so I can show it to my friends on the web. This camera is digital. Goes straight into my computer.

ERNESTO: You know anybody who owns restaurants?

FRED: My father knows people.

ERNESTO: There's a way that they can buy my fountains through a Paris gallery.

FEDERICO: Visa bill, Visa bill. Visa bill.

FRED: I'll help you in any way I can.

ERNESTO: Yes? Thank you, Fred. I made ten thousand dollars. That's how I bought the car. Great. The car is paying for itself. By driving friends like you around. Twenty dollars a day. Everybody wins. Right Fred?

FRED: Yeah. I'm Fred. He's Federico.

ERNESTO: Thank god you are not both called Federico.

FRED: Actually my name is Federico, people just call me Fred.

FEDERICO: And when I was first here. I mean over there. I was called Fred.

FRED: Maybe I should go back to Federico.

ERNESTO: No, you're not Cuban.

FRED: Federico is Italian also. And I am of Italian…my grandparents were Italian. Immigrants. But they called me Fred, 'cause that was the thing to do in Queens.

FEDERICO: I found it!

FRED: Good. I knew you would.

FEDERICO: 330 Maceo.

ERNESTO: 330 Maceo. I'll ask that man sitting on his porch for directions.

FEDERICO: Thank you Manny…

ERNESTO: Ernesto.

FEDERICO: Thank you Ernesto.

ERNESTO: Take care of your man.

FRED: What?

ERNESTO: It's hard to come back home.

(Ernesto walks away.)

FRED: Is it?

FEDERICO: I don't know.

FRED: I think he thinks I'm your boy.

FEDERICO: I'll set him straight.

FRED: I don't care Papi.

FEDERICO: Uh huh. I don't believe you.

FRED: I don't!

FEDERICO: Don't get defensive.

FRED: No?

FEDERICO: No. I'm not accusing you of anything.

FRED: Are you sure?

FEDERICO: Yes.

FRED: We're just friends?

FEDERICO: Yes.

FRED: Good.

FEDERICO: The sky is blue, the palm trees sway. I can taste salt on my lips. You'd think I've been crying. But it's because, we are surrounded by the sea.

FRED: It's okay with me if you cry.

FEDERICO: But not with.

FRED: He's talking to that man, for a long time.

FEDERICO: The man is black.

FRED: Handsome.

FEDERICO: You like black men. Don't you?

FRED: I don't like men.

FEDERICO: But, I've noticed, that you always notice black men.

FRED: Hey!

FEDERICO: I'm teasing you.

FRED: The only man I am interested in, is you. This. I need to see you through this.

FEDERICO: Thanks. Mama. The sky is blue. The mud is red. The palm trees still sway. What I dreamt of all my life. Coming back to "Never Land." The sand will be white. And there's a volcano inside of me. A volcano called regret. That I cannot let go of. Fred. I cannot…

FRED: Federico?

FEDERICO: What?

FRED: I had an impulse to do something cheap.

FEDERICO: What.

FRED: Repeating the volcano bit back to you as you said it.

FEDERICO: Don't quote me please.

FRED: Can I turn on the camera?

FEDERICO: Well.

FRED: Please.

FEDERICO: Sure.

(Fred turns on the camera. Federico imitates Blanche DuBois.)

FRED: "What's the matter honey are you lost?"

FEDERICO: "They told me to take a streetcar named Desire and then transfer to one called Cemetery, and ride six blocks and get off at Elysian Fields."

FRED: "That's where you are now."

FEDERICO: "At Elysian Fields?"

FRED: "This here is Elysian Fields."

FEDERICO: "They must have not understood what number I wanted."

FRED: "What number are you looking for?"

FEDERICO: "632."

FRED: "You don't have to look no further."

FEDERICO: "I'm looking for my sister Stella DuBoise. I mean Mrs. Stanley Kobualski."

(They laugh. Federico takes the camera and Fred imitates Blanche.)

FEDERICO: What's the matter are you lost honey?

FRED: I took a Mexican Airlines flight to Mexico City. And then transferred to one that took me to Cancún. Walked six blocks till I got to Air Caribe, got on that one, a plane with no windows. To land here.

FEDERICO: What number are you looking for?

FRED: 330 Maceo.

(They laugh. Fred takes the camera. Points it at Federico.)

FRED: So what does it feel like?

FEDERICO: Like having your pupils replaced and you can see again. Like walking into fiction, like being born again in the eyes of Fidel. There's a black hole inside of me...

FRED: I thought it was a volcano?

FEDERICO: It's dripping out little red drops of ink. Not of blood because my blood is blue. Little drops of ink. For all the ways that I betrayed my country with a pen.

FRED: Yeah.

FEDERICO: Yeah.

FRED: You didn't betray them.

FEDERICO: I did.

FRED: No.

FEDERICO: Really?

FRED: Yes.

FEDERICO: How would you know?

FRED: I know.

FEDERICO: How could you know what it's like?

FRED: Tell me.

FEDERICO: Shut the camera.

FRED: No.

FEDERICO: If you don't shut the camera I won't tell you.

FRED: Why?

FEDERICO: Because that's how things are.

FRED: Really.

FEDERICO: With me.

FRED: But...

FEDERICO: No. No buts. I won't.

FRED: Come on.

FEDERICO: Some things are private.

FRED: Alright.

FEDERICO: Some things are just for you and me.

FRED: Sorry baby, hurry I think he's coming back.

FEDERICO: When you taste the salt in the water again. And even that bitterness
is sweet. You wonder why they made you spend your life away from it...

FRED: Who.

FEDERICO: What?

FRED: Who made you spend your life away from it. Fidel Castro?

FEDERICO: No, my parents, the people of my class. The moneygrubbing sons
of bitches. No wonder they are so bitter. You saw La Habana. It's more
beautiful then in any of my dreams. Isn't it Fred?

FRED: I don't know what your dreams were like?

FEDERICO: Well it is. It's more alive than in any of my memories or pain, or
letters. Paragraphs or sentences. Or masochistic love. Or unrequited long-
ing. I don't know, it's dangerous Fred. I am beginning to feel like I am
someone. That I belong. That someone loves me.

FRED: People love you.

FEDERICO: That my people love me.

FRED: I'm your people. Aren't I your people?

FEDERICO: No.

FRED: Well, fuck you!

FEDERICO: You are a nice stranger that I met.

FRED: How can you!

FEDERICO: It's not the same.

FRED: That hurts.

FEDERICO: Sorry.

FRED: That hurts. I don't feel like you are a stranger to me. And believe me you are not nice. I'm...I'm putting it out here for you.

FEDERICO: Are you?

FRED: Yes. Yes I am.

FEDERICO: With me?

FRED: Yes.

FEDERICO: I can't trust that.

FRED: Why not?

FEDERICO: You usually run away.

FRED: What?

FEDERICO: We usually get close and then you run away.

FRED: That's not true.

FEDERICO: You know it's true Fred.

FRED: I won't this time.

FEDERICO: Why not? What's different?

FRED: Well...

FEDERICO: Tell me Fred. Hm?

FRED: Because I'm the one. That saw your face. When you went home.

FEDERICO: If we find it.

FRED: Home to Cuba. I've already seen it. So has my camera. So I have proof. Proof that Freddie did go home.

FEDERICO: We'll see.

FRED: You will.

FEDERICO: I hope he got directions.

(Ernesto enters.)

ERNESTO: I know the way.

FEDERICO: Is it still standing? Did he tell you.

ERNESTO: It's a school now.

FEDERICO: Of course it's still standing. My father's cousin was here last year. He said it was still standing.

(Ernesto looks upset.)

FRED: What's wrong, Ernesto?

ERNESTO: I'm so sorry.

FEDERICO: They tore it down?

ERNESTO: No that's not it.

FRED: What?

ERNESTO: The car.

FEDERICO: I didn't expect to find the cars, or the busses. Though the way people fix things around here. The busses are probably still running.

ERNESTO: No my car.

FEDERICO: I bet, this car was left by some family that went to Miami. I bet they have a picture of it. Up on their wall.

FRED: What's wrong with the car?

ERNESTO: Listen?

FRED: Oh, I hear it.

ERNESTO: You do hear that it's misfiring right? I have to clean the spark plugs or we won't get anywhere. Fucking Russian spark plugs.

FRED: Russian spark plugs in a 1940s Chevy. Next time I come. I'm bringing American spark plugs.

FEDERICO: You already decided that you are coming back.

FRED: Haven't you.

FEDERICO: No.

ERNESTO: Please bring us real spark plugs, Fred.

FRED: I will.

ERNESTO: I'm sorry.

FEDERICO: I like cars. We owned a fleet. Of cabs and busses. We ruled this land with our automobiles.

ERNESTO: You want to stretch your legs, outside. It's gonna take a few minutes.

FEDERICO: No.

ERNESTO: Take a walk. See your town.

FEDERICO: I'm not stepping out of this car till I see. *Mi casa.*

FRED: "*Mi casa,*" my home. Right?

FEDERICO: Right, Fred.

FRED: See, I am learning Spanish.

FEDERICO: Before you know it. You are going to be Cuban.

FRED: I know.

ERNESTO: Well, he is Cuban by injection.

FRED: What do you mean by that?

ERNESTO: Well, the rum you've been drinking. Dark, aged and 100 percent Cuban. Right, Federico?

FEDERICO: Right, Manny.

FRED: Ernesto.

FEDERICO: Ernesto, right.

FRED: Listen Ernesto…

ERNESTO: Federico and Fred. I still can't get over it.

FEDERICO: Our towels have F and F intertwining. F and F embroidered on them.

FRED: Stop it!

FEDERICO: I thought you didn't care.

FRED: I'm going to stretch my legs.

(Fred leaves.)

FEDERICO: I'm staying.

ERNESTO: It's going to be a few minutes.

FEDERICO: I need a few minutes.

(Ernesto leaves.)

FEDERICO: Roll down the windows and breathe, breathe it in.

(Fred walks by Federico and pats his shoulder. Federico holds onto his hand.)

FEDERICO: Don't go. Don't be mad.

FRED: I'm not. I don't care.

FEDERICO: My dad once betrayed my mother. Well, my dad always betrayed my mother.

FRED: So did mine.

FEDERICO: Yes?

FRED: Yes.

FEDERICO: We left our country. Betrayed it. This. Her.

FRED: You think this country is a woman?

FEDERICO: Yes. Then we betrayed each other. But once…the first time it became crystal clear, was on Valentine's Day. They had just gotten to the U.S. We were in L.A….We were poor. My mother made a heart-shaped cake. Not any regular kind. Not out of mix. But the kind that is mostly eggs and a little bit of flour.

FRED: Sponge cake.

FEDERICO: Yes from scratch. Then she poured syrup…drowned it in syrup. The kind that has a little bit of rum…

FRED: Dark rum or white rum?

FEDERICO: White, exiled Bacardi rum.

FRED: Yum.

FEDERICO: My mother made a heart-shaped cake and decorated it with white and pink meringues…little roses all around its edges. And in the middle she wrote Gilda and Othon. And waited for him. He came home with carnations, yellow and white. She presented him with the cake. He shoved it to the side of the table. Shoved it to the side of the table without even looking at it. Without a kiss. Without a thank you, just a half-embarrassed smile. And it confirmed to me that he did not love us. I suspected it because he took me away from this. This town. My town.

ERNESTO: Okay ready to go.

(He turns on the engine.)

ERNESTO: Listen?

FRED: Yeah.

ERNESTO: The sound is better.

FRED: Yeah.

FEDERICO: Let's go.

ERNESTO: To find your childhood.

FEDERICO: Yes.

(Federico starts to put things back into his money belt. He holds his birth certificate.)

FEDERICO: Fred.

FRED: Excited?

FEDERICO: Yes.

FRED: Good.

FEDERICO: I think you should have this?

FRED: What?

FEDERICO: You know where you are going right Manuel, Ernesto?

ERNESTO: 330 Maceo, a left in three blocks, then up and down the hill.

FEDERICO: So take it.

FRED: Your birth certificate?

FEDERICO: Yes.

FRED: Why don't you put it back in your money belt?

FEDERICO: Because I have too many things in it already.

(Federico stuffs things into it.)

FEDERICO: My glasses. Credit cards. Take it I have a feeling I'm going to lose something.

FRED: Your soul?

FEDERICO: I thought that's what I was going to find.

ERNESTO: Here's the hill.

FEDERICO: Here take my passport also.

FRED: Your entire identity?

ERNESTO: That's love.

FEDERICO: No I still have my credit cards.

FRED: Your entire Cuban identity?

ERNESTO: That's amore.

FEDERICO: And I'm keeping the traveler's checks and the cash and the credit cards.

ERNESTO: Are they American credit cards?

FEDERICO: Yes.

ERNESTO: They don't work here.

FEDERICO: Take the passport Fred and stop being a baby.

FRED: Aren't I your baby?

ERNESTO: European and Canadian and Latin American and Asian and Japanese and Australian credit cards work here. They don't have an embargo with us.

FRED: We know.

FEDERICO: Here.

ERNESTO: But they do in the U.S.A.

FRED: It's a big responsibility. A person's identity.

FEDERICO: I want it in your big capable hands.

FRED: Well.

(Fred takes the papers.)

FEDERICO: Thank you.

FRED: Reluctantly I take them.

(Fred focuses his camera and points it at Federico.)

ERNESTO: We are on top of the hill. Look down does anything look familiar?

FEDERICO: Yes and no?

FRED: Yes and no? Did you hear that folks.

FEDERICO: You're going to have that thing on! Are you!

FRED: You'll be glad I did later on.

ERNESTO: That's love.

FEDERICO: Yes.

FRED: Friendship.

FEDERICO: It's the dearest kind of love.

FRED: Yes it is.

FEDERICO: Absolutely.

ERNESTO: But not the most passionate.

(Fred brushes Federico's hair with his hand.)

FRED: Little boy lost.

FEDERICO: You're messing up my hair.

FRED: You don't care.

FEDERICO: No…little boy lost, looking for my own home. Should I fly in the window? And take away all the little schoolchildren? That have little desks in what used to be my bedroom. And tell them, "We are flying to Hialeah, then L.A., then New York. Your little selves will always be here but…"

FRED: Look out the window. Do you remember.

FEDERICO: I don't know. "Your little selves will always be here. But your voice will turn into something you won't recognize."

FRED: Walk into it.

FEDERICO: The past.

FRED: It's right in front of you.

FEDERICO: It's always been in front of me.

ERNESTO: Car sounding good.

FRED: Yeah. But now it exists. Still here. Waiting for you.

FEDERICO: No.

FRED: Yes.

FEDERICO: Breathe.

FRED: Yes.

ERNESTO: I hope I'm going the right way.

FRED: Take my hand.

FEDERICO: Your strong hand?

FRED: Yes.

FEDERICO: My mother's beige skirt it swayed in the breeze…My brother's red tricycle…his birthday cake that looked like a Christmas tree covered with snow, but the snow was really shredded coconut…my cousin's horses! Oh my god! I remember looking at this street corner from above. As I rode with my cousin on his horse…Held onto him I was five…on his horse. Oh my god!

FRED: You okay.

FEDERICO: Are we near it?

ERNESTO: Are we?

FEDERICO: I think so. Light me a cig. Will you, Fred?

FRED: Yeah.

(Fred lights cigarette. Federico doesn't take it.)

FEDERICO: Walking…marbles. We played marbles on this street corner. That's the house!

FRED: Where.

(Fred points his camera.)

FEDERICO: There.

ERNESTO: I'll park.

FEDERICO: No…That's the Marqueses' house. The one that always had a Rolls in the driveway. Oh my god if they saw it now. It's faded.

(Fred places the cigarette in Federico's hand.)

FRED: Here.

FEDERICO: Inhale, exhale.

(Federico smokes. Fred focuses his camera.)

ERNESTO: Exciting the period of "family reconciliation."

FEDERICO: Inhale, exhale. Look across the street.

FRED: Action.

FEDERICO: Let the smoke fill your lungs want to die, want to live.

FRED: Camera on!

FEDERICO: It's across the street.

ERNESTO: That is the one?

FEDERICO: I need to walk there.

ERNESTO: Okay.

FRED: He needs to walk there slowly.

FEDERICO: Yeah, let me have another cig.

FRED: Love this country you can smoke anywhere.

ERNESTO: Good. I'll go see if they'll let you in.

FRED: Good.

ERNESTO: Yeah. Can I have a cigarette?

FRED: Sure.

ERNESTO: I'll light it on my own thank you.

FRED: Sure.

(Ernesto starts to walk away.)

FRED: Can I film there?

ERNESTO: Keep the camera in the car use your zoom lens.

FRED: But…

ERNESTO: It'll be better.

FEDERICO: Why? It's my house!

ERNESTO: Was.

FEDERICO: Was my house, right.

ERNESTO: Federico and Fred…

FRED: Funny isn't it.

(Ernesto walks away.)

FRED: Can I film you.

FEDERICO: Yes. My mother will like it.

FRED: We'll make a little movie afterward.

FEDERICO: After I walk in, just follow me with the camera. Fuck them.

(Federico exits off stage. Fred points his camera.)

FRED: When they let you in. I'll follow. He walks slowly down the street he inhales one long deep drag. Ernesto is talking to a black woman. She has a mulatto baby, a girl with frizzy brown hair, lacy pink underwear, no shirt, and white dress shoes. The mulatto baby is playing on the steps like he did. Like you did, Federico. See that. He walks towards the entrance. His hand trembles a little. He looks towards what used to be the rose garden. He says, "That used to be…" Ernesto stops him and smiles. He's talking to the woman. She shakes her head no. He walks towards the door. She stops him. They argue. He's pleading. She shakes her head. No. Fuck they're not going to let him in. He goes to the big window he opens a shutter and looks in. Ernesto smiles at the woman. Gestures there's nothing I can do. She nods yes. The baby runs into his mother's arms. He, still looking inside. Are you finding it. What you're looking for? Your heart that's what you're looking for. I hope you find it 'cause then you can help me to find mine. I know it's in here somewhere inside my house, my body. He's moved away from the window. They smile at him, he smiles at them. He tells a joke. They all laugh. He tickles the baby's chin. The baby smiles. Now he is going to the left side of the house. The house. He points at me. Let me zoom in. He's looking inside a smaller window…He mouths to me, "My room." Fly in Freddie! Fly in. He looks away. There's a small tear in his eye. He wipes it away. He smiles at the camera. I'm panning back. He walks out the front gate. Slowly walking all around the house, like at a funeral. He talks to a man. They don't remember him. Let me leave him alone. Let's see what Ernesto is doing. Offering the woman a cig. So he does own a pack. She takes it. He lights it. They whisper something to each other. Federico is walking up to them. He shakes hands with the woman. They make some kind of deal. He walks to the other side of the yard, the right side. There's a big round white raised stage made out of concrete. Where he imagined his plays when he was young. He told me about it on the plane. On top of it there's a small statue of the head of Marti. The liberator of Cuba. He told me he used to pray to it. He goes up to the statue and does the sign of the cross. The woman follows him, she seems moved. They shake hands again. She leaves him alone. He is sitting there. His eyes are darting back and forth. Should I do a close-up of the eyes or is that too private. Why not. He looks like he is trying to take it all in. Take it all in. Take it all back. Breathe. That's good Papi. He lights a cigar he bites off the tip. Your cigar cutter is in your left pocket. I guess you've forgotten everything. Why not. He lights it slowly. He's having problems keeping the match lit. He always does. Should I go help you? You got it...pan back and let the camera see what he is seeing. A once grand house in ruin. But still there. A child playing in the rose garden in the past. He points to the upstairs room. The room he's always been afraid of. The room where he was conceived. So he said...his mother told him. Do a close-up. He's smiling at me. He does love me. I'm not a stranger. I make love to you with my camera. I'm smiling back we are together. And you are on your stage. Where you should have always been. You're back there. In your childhood. I hope you find what you are looking for. So I find what I'm looking for. My innocence. He's walking back. Pan back. Ernesto tells him he's going somewhere. He gestures fine. He gives the woman two dollars for the baby. He's walking towards me.

FEDERICO: Turn off the camera.

(Fred turns off the camera. Federico walks in.)

FRED: So...

FEDERICO: She wouldn't let me in.

FRED: I know.

FEDERICO: She said to come back on Monday when the principal is there.

FRED: Who is she?

FEDERICO: The janitor. Bitch.

FRED: What?

FEDERICO: She had the keys in her hands.

FRED: Bitch. But we'll come back on Monday.

FEDERICO: Maybe. I don't know.

FRED: It hurt you.

FEDERICO: You filmed it; you tell me.

FRED: Yes. Monday they'll let you in.

FEDERICO: I don't care.

FRED: Okay.

FEDERICO: I don't.

FRED: Fine.

FEDERICO: Give me a Valium.

FRED: You sure?

FEDERICO: That's why we brought them.

FRED: Why?

FEDERICO: So I don't have to reveal my anger in front of Ernesto.

FRED: Okay.

(Fred starts to take out Valiums.)

FRED: Where is he?

FEDERICO: He ran into a friend.

FRED: A spy.

FEDERICO: Who cares.

FRED: Where next?

FEDERICO: Lunch. The restaurant my father used to take me to. It's now a tourist trap.

FRED: Because of Hemingway.

FEDERICO: Yes. He ate there also.

FRED: This is the only country were Papa Hemingway is still a celeb.

FEDERICO: True.

FRED: In the rest of the world he's a hack.

FEDERICO: Not a hack. Forgotten.

FRED: Yes. Isn't that the same thing?

FEDERICO: No it's not. He used to eat there at La Terasa. When he wrote *The Old Man and the Sea*, he wrote it here.

FRED: Yes.

FEDERICO: We are going to have a *paella*. Like when I was six.

FRED: Good. Like Hemingway.

FEDERICO: The dollar will let me buy that bit of my past.

FRED: God bless the dollar.

FEDERICO: You get good footage?

FRED: Yes.

FEDERICO: I'm glad.

FRED: Here he comes.

FEDERICO: He is carrying a poster.

FRED: Of what?

FEDERICO: A little boy.

FRED: It looks like you.

FEDERICO: All little boys look alike.

(Fred gives him the Valium. Federico swallows it.)

FRED: Swallow it. Before he gets here. I don't want him to think we're drug addicts. Notice that he didn't take his.

FEDERICO: Well he's a spy.

FRED: Swallow.

FEDERICO: Yes sir. But it's so big!

FRED: Stop it.

FEDERICO: I already swallowed it.

FRED: When.

FEDERICO: As soon as you handed it to me.

(Ernesto enters with a large black-and-white poster of a little boy. Elian Gonzalez.)

ERNESTO: Maybe we should put this in the trunk.

FEDERICO: We want to see it.

(He shows them the poster.)

FEDERICO: Who is he?

ERNESTO: You haven't heard.

FEDERICO: No.

ERNESTO: Well.

FRED: Tell us.

ERNESTO: Well.

FEDERICO: Come on.

ERNESTO: I hope it doesn't insult you or your friend.

FRED: Why?

ERNESTO: You're Americans.

FEDERICO: I am not!

FRED: Come on…

ERNESTO: You look like one.

FEDERICO: *Pero no soy…*

ERNESTO: *Pareces.*

FEDERICO: *Vete al carajo!*

ERNESTO: *Que cono!*

FRED: Fight in English.

FEDERICO: We are not fighting.

ERNESTO: Debating.

FRED: Right.

FEDERICO: So tell us your story. Insult us.

FRED: We'll enjoy it.

FEDERICO: Absolutely.

ERNESTO: Okay.

FEDERICO: Now you sound American.

ERNESTO: Funny.

FRED: Who is this kid in the poster?

ERNESTO: A mother took a little boy in a raft. A raft that you had to pay five thousand a person to get on. So you had to be a capitalist already to go on it.

FRED: Right.

ERNESTO: Work in the tourist trade or be a whore.

FEDERICO: Both of which corrupt?

ERNESTO: Yes.

FEDERICO: I agree.

FRED: So we are corrupting you.

ERNESTO: Yes.

FEDERICO: The story.

ERNESTO: Everyone drowned but the little boy.

FRED: Where is he?

ERNESTO: In Miami.

FEDERICO: Poor boy.

ERNESTO: With his cousins.

FEDERICO: Doomed.

ERNESTO: The father is here. His grandparents. On both sides.

FEDERICO: And they want him back?

ERNESTO: Of course.

FEDERICO: My mother let me go and wasn't that interested in getting me back.

FRED: That's not true.

ERNESTO: We will never let Peter Pan happen again. Tragedy and shame.

FEDERICO: Shambles.

FRED: Why the rally?

ERNESTO: Because we are going to demand that he come back. Home.

FEDERICO: In the period of "family reconciliation."

ERNESTO: Yes.

FEDERICO: In the middle of this civil war that we live in?

ERNESTO: Revolution.

FEDERICO: Tinged with civil war. How many relatives do you have in Miami.

ERNESTO: Many.

FEDERICO: Which one hurt you when they left.

ERNESTO: She...

FRED: She.

ERNESTO: She left. My sister. They won't keep him.

FEDERICO: Who?

ERNESTO: Elian. The imperialist and that Miami Mafia, have him.

FEDERICO: I see...

FRED: Where to next?

ERNESTO: Right.

FRED: Lunch right. We'll get Hemingway's table.

ERNESTO: La Terasa.

FEDERICO: No, the rally.

ERNESTO: Are you sure?

FEDERICO: I am from here.

   (Ernesto hands Fred the poster.)

FRED: If I put this in my suitcase they'll know we've been to Cuba.

FEDERICO: Yes.

ERNESTO: It's not a souvenir.

FRED: Of course not.

ERNESTO: You are not insulted.

FEDERICO: I wish someone would have fought to get me back.

ERNESTO: Instead we let you go.

FEDERICO: Yes and thirteen thousand more just like me.

ERNESTO: I am sorry.

FEDERICO: Yes.

ERNESTO: Welcome home.

FRED: Where is it?

ERNESTO: Down the hill.

FRED: Let's walk down the hill.

ERNESTO: We won't let it happen again.

FRED: Look at that crowd.

ERNESTO: And in an hour they'll go to La Habana, to El Malecon. People from the entire island.

FRED: So this is the pre-rally.

ERNESTO: The rehearsal, yes.

FRED: I'm excited.

ERNESTO: Yes.

   (Ernesto leaves.)

FEDERICO: In high school. I had a girlfriend who made me burn the American flag, for the cameras.

FRED: During the Vietnam War?

FEDERICO: She told me if I loved her I'd set it on fire. Let's go.

FRED: Wait, I need to set the tape. Wait for me.

FEDERICO: Yes. NBC was there so I burned the flag. It made me feel guilty and excited. My parents were horrified. "We didn't take you away from communism so you could become a communist."

FRED: They said that?

FEDERICO: Yes.

FRED: I'm ready. Put on the hat.

FEDERICO: The straw hats we bought I think we should wear them.

(Fred takes two straw hats, places one on Federico's head, and the other on his own.)

FRED: The sun is scorching.

(They walk down stage.)

FRED: Look at him he's already down there with his poster. I wish we had a poster.

GIRL'S VOICE: *Feliz Cumpleaño Elian...*

(The crowd goes wild.)

FEDERICO: Who's speaking.

FRED: Let me find her with my lens. A young girl...maybe eighteen. She's very pregnant.

FEDERICO: Film her.

FRED: I am. She's dramatic like an actress.

FEDERICO: Except she means it.

FRED: So do actors.

FEDERICO: She means it for real.

(They walk towards the voice. To the tip of the stage. Ernesto runs towards them. He has two other posters.)

GIRL'S VOICE: *Porque queremos que esté aquí con nosotros.*

CROWD'S VOICE: *¡Sí! ¡Elian Sí!*

FRED: They are going wild.

ERNESTO: Here are posters, everybody has to have one. And put your camera away.

FRED: Fuck!

ERNESTO: See you down there.

FRED: I'm going to put it in my hat and leave it running. At least we'll have audio.

FEDERICO: Poke a hole in the hat.

(They poke a small hole in the hat. Fred puts it on. The camera lens sticks out.)

FRED: Can't see it?

FEDERICO: Only if I was looking for it.

FRED: See I told you.

FEDERICO: What?

FRED: That we needed the hats.

GIRL'S VOICE: *¡Elian te queremos!*

FRED: *Sí.* I look like a Cuban don't I.

(*He lifts up the poster.*)

FEDERICO: You do.

FRED: Hold up your banner.

FEDERICO: I don't know.

FRED: Why not.

FEDERICO: I feel guilty and excited.

FRED: Really?

FEDERICO: I'm not here on vacation.

FRED: Neither am I.

GIRL'S VOICE: *Porque el niño que yo tengo aquí en mi vientre nunca se lo daría a los imperialistas. Este niño va a vivir...*

FRED: Translate.

FEDERICO: Because this child that I have inside my uterus. I would never give to the imperialist. Because this child is going to live...

GIRL'S VOICE: *Conmigo aquì. En Cuba. Porque él es Cubano.*

FEDERICO: Is going to live with me. Here in Cuba, because he is Cuban.

CROWD'S VOICE: *Que devuelvan a Elian.*

FEDERICO: Return Elian!

GIRL'S VOICE: *Porque este niño no es mio! Ni de su padre! El es hijo de Fidel!*

FEDERICO: Because he is not my child! Or his father's child! He is Fidel's child!

FRED: That's scary.

FEDERICO: But true.

(*Federico lifts up his poster.*)

FRED: How does it feel.

FEDERICO: Guilty and free. Return Elian! Mother fuckers.

FRED: I wish I could take a picture.

FEDERICO: Take it.

ERNESTO: Take it.

FRED: They'll get angry.

FEDERICO: I don't care who gets angry!

Red.
Fire.
Flag.

I'm on fire.
Pour rum all over me.
Light the match
And I'll be free.
Ah.
I'm home.

Red.
Fire.
Elian come back.
Red.
Blood.
Fire.
All over me.
Bed.
Not alone.
Home.
(The crowd is chanting "Return Elian" in Spanish. Fred takes the camera and photographs Federico.)
FRED: Great shot.
FEDERICO: Return Elian.

END OF ACT ONE

ACT TWO

SCENE ONE

The stage. Cuba. Noon. Fred is filming. Ernesto walks in.

ERNESTO: He's not out?

FRED: He's not in how can he be out.

ERNESTO: What?

FRED: She didn't let him in again.

ERNESTO: I meant out of the yard.

FRED: They're arguing.

ERNESTO: Again?

FRED: Again.

ERNESTO: Oh well.

FRED: That's what happens, when two ideologies clash.

ERNESTO: His temper will get him nowhere. That's part of being from the ruling class.

FRED: I know.

ERNESTO: What an attitude your friend has. He acts superior. She can smell it she will not budge. Believe me.

FRED: Yeah.

ERNESTO: I have the pictures ready for you.

FRED: Good.

ERNESTO: Don't you want to see them?

FRED: In a minute.

(Ernesto takes pictures out of a manila envelope.)

ERNESTO: Special…beautiful…Taken with your digital camera. Of my sculpting…at sunrise. The light hit it like…

FRED: I'm sure.

ERNESTO: Take a look.

FRED: In a minute.

ERNESTO: You've got to watch his every move.

FRED: You need some money?

ERNESTO: No. Really no…well…how much?

FRED: How much do you need?

ERNESTO: I want to earn it.

FRED: You have putting up with him. Here's forty. Now let me film.

(Ernesto takes money.)

FRED: Good.

ERNESTO: How do you do it?

FRED: What?

ERNESTO: He's in love with you, isn't he?

FRED: No! You think so?

ERNESTO: He's always grabbing your arms your legs.

FRED: You Cubans are very touchy.

ERNESTO: I've never touched you.

FRED: True.

ERNESTO: And I would never—

FRED: He's needy.

ERNESTO: We all need.

FRED: Yes. You need dollars he needs—

ERNESTO: Your body?

FRED: No. My body? Maybe. No. Believe me, he falls in love with sadists. Believe me. I am too nice a guy for him.

ERNESTO: I try.

FRED: What?

ERNESTO: To understand people like you.

FRED: Americans?

ERNESTO: Sure, Americans.

FRED: Good. I understand your goals and ideals. And I will work to stop the embargo, for the rest of my life!

ERNESTO: Good. Sure you will...thank you.

(Fred points his camera.)

FRED: So go talk to the lady.

ERNESTO: The principal?

FRED: Yes. See if you can do something. He needs to get inside the house. For the journey to be complete.

ERNESTO: You bring him over here first.

FRED: But...

ERNESTO: Please.

FRED: Sure.

(Fred hands Ernesto the camera and exits. Ernesto turns it on himself.)

ERNESTO: I never thought I'd break the rules. The rules of Marxism. Catering to the frivolity of the bourgeoisie. The hard-on over a dollar. The lure of capital. Fred edit this out tonight please. As ever your comrade, Ernesto.

(Ernesto turns off the camera. Federico is there; Fred follows.)

FEDERICO: Okay.

ERNESTO: Okay?

FEDERICO: Talk some sense into her now.

FRED: Relax Baby. Papi.

FEDERICO: You don't know.

ERNESTO: Okay. I'll be right back.

(Ernesto exits.)

FRED: I'm, here. Fred is here. Everything is under control.

FEDERICO: Yeah?

FRED: I am in charge of this trip.

FEDERICO: Why do I care. There are only bad memories waiting for me in there.

FRED: It will work out.

FEDERICO: I don't think so.

FRED: You're upset.

FEDERICO: We should have gone to the beach.

FRED: We'll go to Varadero tomorrow.

FEDERICO: Why did they say that they would let me in on Monday?

FRED: I don't know.

FEDERICO: They want to fuck with me. That's why.

FRED: Maybe.

FEDERICO: They won't forgive us for leaving.

FRED: You might be right.

FEDERICO: They're so fucking self-righteous 'cause they stayed.

FRED: Calm down.

FEDERICO: Where are the pills?

FRED: Well…

FEDERICO: What?

FRED: I left them back in our room.

FEDERICO: And I'm supposed to trust you.

FRED: Sorry.

FEDERICO: Fuckers.

FRED: Take a deep breath.

FEDERICO: Take a deep breath?

FRED: Okay.

(Fred takes a deep breath.)

FEDERICO: I was asking you a question.

FRED: Okay.

FEDERICO: Not telling you to do it.

FRED: Okay.

FEDERICO: Stop agreeing with me.

FRED: Will you just fucking try to breathe!

(Federico tries to breathe.)

FEDERICO: Fucking bitch. I'm so fucking angry! Fucking country!

FRED: She's just a bureaucrat. She doesn't represent the revolution.

FEDERICO: The revolution?

FRED: Yes.

FEDERICO: What the fuck do you know about the revolution!

FRED: I've learned. Since I've been here. I've learned a thing or two!

FEDERICO: The bullshit that Ernesto talks about all day long. That guy contradicts himself. Every five minutes.

FRED: Just like you.

FEDERICO: You think I contradict myself.

FRED: Yes. Come on. One breath is better than a Valium.

FEDERICO: If I breathe. I'll scream.

FRED: That's okay.

(Federico tries to breathe.)

FEDERICO: Oh god!

FRED: Yes?

FEDERICO: Fuck!

FRED: Good.

FEDERICO: Yeah!

FRED: Yeah. That's it let it out.

FEDERICO: I don't want to start to shake.

FRED: You won't.

(Federico breathes.)

FEDERICO: Vomit. Assholes on both sides. A race full of fucking assholes. I hate my fucking father! And fucking Jorge Mascanosa, I don't care if he's dead! And the whole Cuban National Foundation. And Clinton and Jesse Helms! I hate fucking Fidel! And his brother Raul! I hate block committees! But most of all I hate that fucking bitch that won't let me inside my house!

FRED: Feel better?

FEDERICO: Yes.

FRED: Good.

FEDERICO: Are you becoming a revolutionary Fred?

FRED: Yes.

FEDERICO: Why?

FRED: Because I know they're right.

FEDERICO: How do you know that.

FRED: Because I'm privileged.

FEDERICO: Because you are rich?

FRED: Not rich, well-off.

FEDERICO: Admit it, rich.

FRED: Alright…rich. And I know people like my father run the world. And they're not generous. Believe me.

FEDERICO: And you feel guilty.

FRED: For the time being.

FEDERICO: So do I.

FRED: You do?

FEDERICO: I never felt so much what class I come from. This country makes you feel that. I hate myself.

FRED: Don't.

FEDERICO: Bourgeoisie through and through. That's you and me.

FRED: That we recognize it. That's the first step.

FEDERICO: I always recognized it. But now I feel it. I hate myself.

FRED: I hate myself.

FEDERICO: My petty concerns.

FRED: Mine.

FEDERICO: Got to get through it.

FRED: You'll become a proletariat yet.

FEDERICO: What's taking him so long?

FRED: Ernesto is trying to talk the principal into it. I gave him forty bucks.

(Fred takes out his camera and focuses it.)

FRED: Now I'm the spy.

FEDERICO: They know what you're doing.

FRED: So what.

FEDERICO: A spy is someone who goes undetected.

FRED: He's saying, "Why not. Please, come on." She shakes her head no. She points at some children. She's tough. But he hasn't given up. Keep going comrade.

(Ernesto runs in.)

FEDERICO: Am I walking in now to the house?

ERNESTO: She needs to make a call. The Writers' Union…They're sponsoring you right? Lizette Villa? If Lizette Villa says you can get in, you can get in.

FEDERICO: Lizette loves me.

ERNESTO: Then no problem.

FEDERICO: Maybe we should give Lizette the forty.

ERNESTO: What?

FEDERICO: I didn't decide to leave here. It was not my decision...

FRED: Any more than Elian.

FEDERICO: I was sent away. I was...my childhood was stolen. Is that self-pity?

ERNESTO: Maybe.

FRED: No.

FEDERICO: I was totally dependent on her my mother and she betrayed me.

ERNESTO: We've all been betrayed.

FEDERICO: I feel like a woman who flies up to the sky and then falls into the ocean. Every time I stand in front of this fucking house. I feel like a woman. Who wants her husband back no matter if the price is her pride.

ERNESTO: I'll go see if Lizette's called.

FEDERICO: Give the principal some money.

ERNESTO: No.

FEDERICO: I'll talk to her.

ERNESTO: No. No. You get too emotional. It won't do any good.

FEDERICO: Emotion?

ERNESTO: Yes.

FRED: Why?

ERNESTO: Because in Marxism. Logic is God.

FRED: Oh.

ERNESTO: You see.

FRED: Yes.

ERNESTO: And if he tells her he feels like a woman. We are in trouble.

FEDERICO: Jesus! Dollars, are God here! Who the fuck are we kidding. Here take...

ERNESTO: No this one is a real communist, she won't take money.

FEDERICO: Not like you.

ERNESTO: No. An Italian restaurant has corrupted me. I own a car. Tourists pay me to drive them around.

(Ernesto exits.)

FEDERICO: Son of a bitch called me a tourist.

FRED: You feel like a woman?

FEDERICO: What?

FRED: You said that you feel like a woman. You said she flew then fell. No pride...

FEDERICO: Yes, so what!

FRED: I feel like a woman. I'm not gay, but I feel like a woman.

FEDERICO: Two girls lost in La Habana?

FRED: What?

FEDERICO: You and I. Two girls lost in La Habana. *(Imitates Blanche.)* Did you take a car down El Malecon, through a tunnel, to a town called Cojimar...

FRED: Stop it!

FEDERICO: Come on, do Blanche for me. Are you Blanche inside that macho body? Does Blanche really dwell inside your soul?

FRED: Stop it! Don't make fun of me.

(Fred sulks.)

FEDERICO: Jesus, Fred?

FRED: I tell you something about myself...

FEDERICO: Oh.

FRED: Something fragile inside of me and you exploit it.

FEDERICO: Sorry, I don't like it when you talk that bullshit.

FRED: "Talk that bullshit"! My insides are bullshit to you!

FEDERICO: No... But that girl stuff...when you finger a dress, or put on a little lipstick... And that time you went through Natasha's closet and tried on her dresses and modeled.

FRED: Let me tell you something! I fucked Natasha good and hard that night. Yeah! Good and hard!

FEDERICO: Really?

FRED: Yeah gave it to her. Gave it...

FEDERICO: I believe you.

FRED: All night long baby. I left her begging for more. Yeah.

FEDERICO: Please stop talking like that!

FRED: Like what?

FEDERICO: Like a fifties man.

FRED: Fifties man and nineties chick. What a combination. What the fuck? Jesus, what a mess.

(Fred starts to cry.)

FEDERICO: Fred don't. Don't you dare fall apart on me.

FRED: I once looked in the mirror at my face and I saw a line going up and down, dividing my face...the line went all the way down my body one side masculine the other feminine. I could not move for hours it was all too clear, I felt so weak. Divided, I don't know where to run. Split. And it scares the shit out of me. Hold me!

FEDERICO: Hold you?

FRED: Yes. Hold me.

FEDERICO: Hold you?

FRED: Yes, please!

FEDERICO: Well...no...I don't want to hold you. I don't want to hold a man on the block where I come from. Not here.

FRED: Look beyond my manly body. See the girl that needs you.

(Fred cries.)

FEDERICO: I'm frozen.

FRED: Please.

FEDERICO: I'm angry!

FRED: That I need you?

FEDERICO: That you'll use me.

FRED: No, that I need you!

FEDERICO: That you'll ask me to open up every part of me. My heart, my brain, my nipples, my thighs, my testicles, my penis... And then you'll tell me... "What do you think I am?"

FRED: You know I'm straight.

FEDERICO: You are not at this moment.

FRED: What?

FEDERICO: You are not straight at this moment.

FRED: No. At this moment... I need a man... I need you. Please. Look at me I'm not hiding anything.

FEDERICO: No you're not.

FRED: No. This is me.

FEDERICO: I...am...walking towards you...

(They embrace. They touch each other. They kiss each other's necks. They look into each other's eyes.)

FRED: We just held each other.

FEDERICO: I know.

FRED: Yes.

FEDERICO: Yes.

FRED: Don't stop.

FEDERICO: Alright.

FRED: We are holding each other.

FEDERICO: Like lovers.

FRED: I kissed your neck.

FEDERICO: I kissed yours.

(*They kiss each other's necks again.*)

FEDERICO: You grabbed my ass.

FRED: Yeah!

FEDERICO: We are looking into each other's eyes.

FRED: Take me in.

FEDERICO: If I take you in…if I take you in…we'd be lovers.

FRED: Maybe. Maybe not.

FEDERICO: No.

(*Federico closes his eyes.*)

FRED: Open them. Open your eyes!

FEDERICO: I can't.

FRED: In them I feel whole.

(*Federico opens his eyes.*)

FRED: Thank you.

FEDERICO: Sure.

FRED: See everything?

FEDERICO: Yes.

FRED: You are a very needy person. So am I.

FEDERICO: Yes.

FRED: My friend.

FEDERICO: What?

(*Fred kisses Federico on the mouth. Federico pulls away.*)

FRED: No.

FEDERICO: My mouth opened.

FRED: I can forgive you.

FEDERICO: My bambino. My beautiful bambino.

FRED: My grandfather—

FEDERICO: Used to call you that.

FRED: Yes.

(*Fred buries his face on Federico's chest.*)

FEDERICO: If I had milk I'd suckle you.

FRED: You are suckling me.

FEDERICO: What a mess.

FRED: I'm not some nice stranger.

FEDERICO: You never were.

(*They hold each other.*)

FRED: Is anybody looking at us.

FEDERICO: Someone is always looking at us.

FRED: Who gives a fuck.

FEDERICO: *(Sings.)* "Hey there Georgy girl. There's another Georgy deep inside." "In-betweens we are just lonely in-betweens."

FRED: Not lonely. *(Sings.)* "Me and my shadow, all alone and feeling blue."

FEDERICO: "And when it's two o'clock, I climb the stairs,"
(They dance.)

FRED: "We never knock,"

FRED AND FEDERICO: " 'Cause nobody's there. Just me and my shadow, all alone."

FRED: Not alone.

FEDERICO: And feeling fine.

FRED: I want to be a man. But not a stereotype like my dad. "Where are the broads. She's got great tits but she's a little bottom-heavy. Want to get it in. You're getting too emotional honey. You gotta cut me loose." I hate it when I say shit like that. I sound just like him.

FEDERICO: Yes.

FRED: A man who can love like a woman. That's what I want to be. That's what this country is bringing out in me.

FEDERICO: Every girl's ideal.

FRED: You think?

FEDERICO: Get Ernesto. Let's get out of here. I've been inside of you. Emotionally, I mean.

FRED: You can get inside my emotions whenever you want.

FEDERICO: And inside of you, Fred, it's very warm and reassuring. I don't need to see the inside of that fucking house! Get him!
(Ernesto is there.)

FRED: It's like you can read our thoughts.

ERNESTO: Maybe your camera is bugged.

FRED: What!

ERNESTO: It was a joke.

FRED: Really?

ERNESTO: I'm an artist. I don't work for the state.

FEDERICO: But you believe in the state.

ERNESTO: That's different than working for it.

FRED: Is it?

ERNESTO: One is corrupt. The other is not.

FRED: Maybe you have a point.

FEDERICO: So?

ERNESTO: Not today. Lizette is shooting a documentary in Santiago. Couldn't get her on the phone.

FEDERICO: Not today. *Mañana.*

FRED: The story of bureaucrats.

ERNESTO: But there is the rally. Look they're in color.

FRED: It would look less organized...if people had different designs.

ERNESTO: Really.

FRED: It might look like this is all organized by the government. Maybe we've had enough of rallies.

ERNESTO: What.

FEDERICO: Maybe the mother did want him in Miami.

ERNESTO: The mother did. But we don't.

FEDERICO: Maybe you don't have the right. To decide. She died. You didn't.

ERNESTO: Just 'cause you don't get your way, you turn on us.

FEDERICO: You got a double standard. You know that?

ERNESTO: No. Tell me what you mean by that.

FEDERICO: I should try to help you get the boy back. But you don't even try to let me have a peek inside my house. My house. My house.

ERNESTO: You're just like the rest. Give me, give me. Give me.

FEDERICO: Well I'm a tourist aren't I.

ERNESTO: What?

FEDERICO: You're the one that called us tourists.

ERNESTO: Just like my sister, spoiled.

FEDERICO: Worms.

FRED: What?

FEDERICO: That's what they called us. When we left. Worms that were rotting the apple. Let the worms go. Now we're butterflies. Butterflies with dollars for wings.

ERNESTO: It's not just the dollars.

FEDERICO: No?

ERNESTO: In the period of "family reconciliation." You think it's easy for us here waiting.

FRED: Waiting?

ERNESTO: For all of you to return.

FEDERICO: Waiting for us to return. That's a little hypocritical.

ERNESTO: I haven't spoken to my sister in nineteen years. When I'm with you

I think of her. I miss her and I hate her. I think of the letter that I will write, that you will take to her. If I have the courage.

FEDERICO: Are you going to ask for forgiveness?

ERNESTO: Forgive what?

FEDERICO: Being a commie.

FRED: Wait! Can't you hear the sea?

FEDERICO: What?

FRED: I never noticed before that you can hear the sea from your house.

ERNESTO: The house! Not his house. Not his country. My country. I stayed! I own it!

FEDERICO: You stole it!

ERNESTO: You abandoned it!

FRED: I think I can hear your sister calling you.

ERNESTO: Fuck off you fag!

FRED: Who you calling a fag?

ERNESTO: You.

FRED: Well...gay is the proper term.

ERNESTO: In this country a fag is a fag. Not happy.

FEDERICO: And a bigot to boot.

ERNESTO: You fags! I should say. You limp-wristed...

FEDERICO: We don't fuck.

ERNESTO: Fags that don't fuck what's the point.

FEDERICO: What are you?

ERNESTO: I'm a man!

FEDERICO: A puppet. Begging for a dime. Kissing Italian and Spanish ass. For a dime.

ERNESTO: Survival.

FEDERICO: I've never kissed ass.

ERNESTO: No, you were too busy on your knees, kissing the feet of the Yankees.

FRED: I'm not kidding I hear her voice in the sea.

ERNESTO: What is she saying? Leave me alone. Don't speak to me. There's a wall between us that is a hundred thousand feet high it has embargo written on it. Don't cross it.

FEDERICO: I crossed it, already.

FRED: Listen please.

ERNESTO: I haven't spoken to my sister in nineteen years. The first five years, she made the calls once a month. The letters filled with pity, the gum inside. The razor blades so I could shave at fifteen….so I wouldn't look like Fidel. The assumptions.

(Drums play.)

FRED: loneliness

no matter how many cars.

loneliness ice is falling from the sky.

Alone

calling out to you.

endless

quiet messages

when I eat ham

is he eating ham?

ERNESTO: No I am not eating ham. I'm eating a drop of rice. Stop it!

FRED: When I used soap

Have you watched.

Mi hermano.

Mi unico hermano.

ERNESTO: I want to survive here. I don't want anything from the imperialist or the Miami Mafia.

FEDERICO: Your prized possession is an American car.

(The drums stop. Fred is out of breath.)

FRED: I can't hear the sea anymore. You guys ruined it.

ERNESTO: Yes, an American car that does not exist in the U.S. anymore. That we struggled for forty years to keep running.

FRED: You have.

ERNESTO: That we valued. That we did not throw away.

FEDERICO: I haven't thrown away anything.

ERNESTO: Except who you are.

FEDERICO: Go to hell!

ERNESTO: Look at you. You're here with a friend that you don't even make love to. Instead of a wife, or a mother, or at least a male lover. You hold onto him and he's not even aware of your desperation.

FEDERICO: My desperation. What desperation?

ERNESTO: To be something. To take care of someone. Even a stranger.

FRED: I am not a stranger.

ERNESTO: In the period of "family reconciliation," I have to try to make peace with you…anyone that reminds me of my sister. No matter how loathsome I find them to be.

FRED: Because she will not make peace with you.

ERNESTO: No she won't.

FEDERICO: I see why.

FRED: Look I'm sure I heard her in the waves. And then you started fighting and ruined it all.

ERNESTO: All you heard was the ocean hitting the sand.

FEDERICO: Fred, tomorrow we are renting a car.

FRED: He doesn't mean that.

FEDERICO: I won't pay somebody that thinks I'm loathsome.

ERNESTO: My sister stopped speaking to me nineteen years ago...because I refused to get on the boat she had sent for me to the port of Mariel.

FEDERICO: I see.

ERNESTO: I didn't ask her for the boat. I didn't ask to leave...and the fucking thing is that I still love her.

FRED: At least you two know what it is you're arguing about.

FEDERICO: And what is that.

FRED: The beauty of this land.

(Fred takes a poster and walks away.)

FEDERICO: We ruined it for him.

ERNESTO: Yes. He's a mystical Marxist.

FEDERICO: A clairvoyant comrade.

(They laugh.)

FEDERICO: He wants everything fast.

ERNESTO: He wants to think there's one right way. Make up. Compromise. No regret. Everybody from over there is like that.

FEDERICO: Over where?

ERNESTO: The U.S.A.

FEDERICO: Actually I am not like that. Actually I try to look at both sides.

ERNESTO: What if there are twenty-two sides?

FEDERICO: Then, that is chaos.

ERNESTO: Then that is what—

FEDERICO: What this is?

ERNESTO: No what your soul is.

FEDERICO: No you don't. Don't start again.

ERNESTO: The real meaning of not having a place in the world. A window that's never opened. Of being walled out. Of being that forbidden, exotic, sexy place... In the middle of the sea. Pandora's box. Demonized and tortured. But by you. By people like you.

FEDERICO: Peter Pan. Peter Pan. Tinker Bell. I believe. I believe in fairies. I believe in communists. I believe YOU. I believe you suffered. I believe we wanted to strangle the life out of you.

ERNESTO: You do?

FEDERICO: I believe your living in isolation, was worse than my living isolated from you. Ernesto.

ERNESTO: You remembered my name.

FEDERICO: I will never forget it, Ernesto. Ernesto, forgive me.

ERNESTO: I am trying.

FEDERICO: I want to be your family. I want to when I leave here...to know that you know my name. That someone in my country is thinking of me.

ERNESTO: You don't want to hurt me anymore?

FEDERICO: I will do everything I can to end the embargo.

ERNESTO: I need proof.

FEDERICO: I mean it.

ERNESTO: Peter Pan. What an odd name. We sent thirteen thousand children away from their bicycles, their dolls, their toy guns. The parents that loved them...even though they were misguided.

(The drums begin to play.)

ERNESTO: They used to use drums to talk to each other.

FEDERICO: To send different messages, from plantation to plantation.

ERNESTO: To announce, a birth, a beating, a death.

FEDERICO: A revolution.

ERNESTO: Listen.

FEDERICO: Yes.

(They listen.)

FEDERICO: What?

ERNESTO: They are saying the healing has begun.

(Blackout.)

SCENE TWO

We hear the sound of airplanes landing and taking off. La Habana airport. Blue panels surround Ernesto, Federico and Fred. They are all smoking cigars.

FEDERICO: Delicious.

FRED: Yeah.

ERNESTO: The real thing.

FRED: Thanks for taking us to the factory.

ERNESTO: Sure. You know even in La Habana they'll sell you fakes.

FEDERICO: But these are not fake, I can taste a fake. When we get to Cancún we have to take off the labels.

FRED: Yep. Fucking embargo.

ERNESTO: Yeah. Maybe the cigar smokers in the U.S. will be the ones that stop the embargo.

FRED: That would be a trip. I think we should also hide them...in chocolate boxes.

FEDERICO: You carry them. Because there is no doubt that they are going to check my bags.

ERNESTO: Good idea.

FRED: Yeah. *(He smokes.)* What a taste.

FEDERICO: I had a dream right before I woke up this morning. I was in a taxi in L.A. The taxi guy asked me where I lived and I couldn't remember. We went down one street and another but I couldn't remember where I lived. I was lost.

FRED: Did you ever get there.

FEDERICO: The only address I could remember was of a house in Hialeah. Funny. It's made me anxious.

FRED: Maybe, you were anxious and that's why you had the dream.

FEDERICO: No, the dream made me anxious.

(He takes a long drag from his cigar.)

FRED: You're smoking like a guy who's anxious.

FEDERICO: No, I'm not.

FRED: Fine.

(Fred takes a long drag from his cigar.)

FEDERICO: What do you call that?

FRED: I admit it. You've made me anxious.

FEDERICO: Of course we are anxious. We are leaving for god's sake! At least this time I know that I'm leaving.

FRED: Right.

FEDERICO: The first time...I didn't know.

FRED: I know.

ERNESTO: Are you ready to go?

FEDERICO: I don't know.

FRED: If you're not we will get off the plane.

FEDERICO: Sometimes this seems like home sometimes it doesn't.

ERNESTO: Sometimes you seem like family sometimes you don't.

FRED: Sometimes I feel like an outsider.

FEDERICO: Funny.

ERNESTO: I feel the same.

(They all three smoke.)

FRED: One thing I know for sure. Last time I'll be able to smoke without some uptight, righteous, bitch non-smoker staring at me.

FEDERICO: At least we don't live in L.A.

FRED: True. But New York is being immigrated by people who should live in L.A.

ERNESTO: They're worse in L.A.?

FRED: They live in one of the most polluted cities in the world. Each of them owns, "Like, three cars." No rapid transit. But they are antismoking fanatics. You can't even smoke outside in L.A.

FEDERICO: No smoking anywhere.

FRED: Just breathing their air is like having three packs a day. They are in deep denial.

FEDERICO: Denial is a concept that was invented in L.A.

ERNESTO: Here they let us smoke, but they don't let us watch American television.

FEDERICO: The world's not fair.

FRED: Nope.

ERNESTO: You are right about that. I am sorry that you never did get in.

FEDERICO: I feel like I did. Why long for a building? The buildings have crumbled. The past does not exist. Does not, will not ever come back. It only lives in photo books. Kept, maintained by both sides. For either one of us to flip through on any given afternoon on either side of the blockade. Block of ice. Block of cement. Where no semen can get through.

FRED: He means life.

ERNESTO: I understood that.

FRED: I didn't want you to get homophobic again.

FEDERICO: I came to my island. I met you. And I found what lives inside of you. I have stood in the courtyard of my school and wondered how a boy could have been anything but a writer. That walked down those hallways into that courtyard. How did my dad ever end up being an accountant?

FRED: He denied his past.

ERNESTO: He ran away.

FEDERICO: But. I came back, Cuba. I went to the church where he married my mother. Not the courtroom in L.A. where they were divorced. I have seen the sink outside my house, granite. A granite sink. Still intact after fifty years. Cuuuu Baaa!

FRED: Cuba!

ERNESTO: Cuba. We are friends.

FEDERICO: For lack of a better word.

ERNESTO: Yes.

FEDERICO: There should be something…another word that describes the state of human relations that lies somewhere, between lover and friend.

ERNESTO: But there isn't.

FRED: They are calling our flight.

ERNESTO: I better go.

(Federico has taken out a dictionary from his bag.)

FEDERICO: Fred look up "friend." See if it leads us to another word.

ERNESTO: Comrade.

FEDERICO: Overused. Not emotional enough.

ERNESTO: I should go.

FEDERICO: We got a minute.

FRED: Okay, "Friendship. One attached to another by affection or esteem. One not hostile. One that is of the same nation or group. One that favors something. Paramour. A member of a group that stresses Inner Light. Rejects ostentation. They opposed war."

FEDERICO: I think the last definition is about Quakers.

ERNESTO: Quakers?

FEDERICO: An American religion.

ERNESTO: Oh.

FEDERICO: But I was wrong. Even though "friend" is used too much to mean acquaintance nowadays. In its true definition. It does define us.

FRED: Even the bit about the Quakers.

ERNESTO: Yes.

FEDERICO: Good-bye.

ERNESTO: Come back.

FEDERICO: I'll try.

ERNESTO: Good-bye friend.

(He goes to Fred and kisses him quickly and sweetly on the lips.)

ERNESTO: God. I've kissed a man in the middle of La Habana airport.

FEDERICO: Your wife won't find out.

(Fred starts to cry.)

ERNESTO: Don't cry Fred. Please.

FRED: This is very hard. Leaving this country. Thank you.

ERNESTO: For what?

FRED: Being my friend.

ERNESTO: Federico?

FEDERICO: My humble handshake for a sincere friend?

(Ernesto and Federico shake hands.)

FEDERICO: The embargo is melting.

ERNESTO: Not really.

FEDERICO: Between us.

ERNESTO: Because of one little boy. One little boy that made us be together in protest.

FEDERICO: Yes.

(Ernesto starts to leave. Then he turns around.)

ERNESTO: I have a letter for my sister. It has on it her maiden name. Her married name and her last address.

FEDERICO: I'll find her.

(Ernesto hands Federico an envelope.)

FRED: We promise.

ERNESTO: *Ciao.*

(Ernesto runs out.)

FRED: I won't.

FEDERICO: What?

FRED: Forget him; like I do everything else in my life.

FEDERICO: I won't let you.

FRED: I won't run away. From either of you. Read the letter.

FEDERICO: I can't!

FRED: Come on!

FEDERICO: It's to his sister.

FRED: He won't care. And we might not ever find her.

(Fred takes the letter from Federico's hands and opens it.)

FEDERICO: Fred!

FRED: He didn't even seal the envelope.

FEDERICO: It's wrong.

FRED: Modesty does not become you.

(Fred looks at the letter.)

FRED: Hm?

FEDERICO: Well?

FRED: Interesting.

FEDERICO: Really?

FRED: Wow!

FEDERICO: What does it say?

FRED: I can't read it. It's in Spanish.

(Federico grabs the letter.)

FRED: Translate.

FEDERICO: Okay.

(Federico reads.)

FEDERICO: "My dearest Sister. Rosa it has been such a long time. So many years without a word, a note, a sentence, a postcard, a hello. I know why. I know that I disappointed you..."

FRED: You okay.

FEDERICO: Give me a minute.

FRED: It's okay.

FEDERICO: I've cried enough.

FRED: Take your time.

(Pause.)

FEDERICO: "I know that I have disappointed you. By not believing in what you believe. By betraying everything you hold dear... In your eyes I betrayed, our parents. Their store. The house which I still live in. The church, but the Pope has come back. Why can't you? I have not seen what you look like in almost twenty years. Have you aged? I bet you haven't. I bet you are still...still the most beautiful girl in La Habana, but you are not in La Habana anymore... Are you? Send me a picture please at least that... Here is a picture of my wife and our daughters and myself. They look like you don't they? My daughters...They look like you. If this man gets this letter to you it means he forgave us. All of us that wanted a revolution. If he forgave me why can't you? I'm still here. In our house. The same telephone number. Nothing's changed in twenty years. Time is still here... We are here...It is here...changed. But still recognizable... Everything... including my love... Your brother, Ernesto."

(A long pause.)

FEDERICO: I am going to deliver this letter.

FRED: Oh my god! We are taking off.

FEDERICO: Yes. I can hear the motors revving up.

FRED: I'm scared of flying.

FEDERICO: Think lovely thoughts.

FRED: Really?

FEDERICO: And we will fly.

FRED: Lovely thoughts?

FEDERICO: Yes. Listen. A world where cold wars are not fought over children.

FRED: Yes.

(They start to go up in the air.)

FEDERICO: Where their childhood is not stolen from them. So they can be happy and grow up.

FRED: Without being afraid of their fathers.

FEDERICO: Yes.

FRED: Where money is not the important thing.

FEDERICO: Where cultures value each other. Where ownership is not the bottom line. Free of Imperialism.

FRED: We're flying.

(They fly.)

FEDERICO: Yes.

FRED: But... Well... How?

FEDERICO: It's something to wish for. I don't know how.

(They start to slowly fall.)

FRED: I think the engine stopped. Oh god. We are going to crash into the island. I think this is it!

FEDERICO: Where a small little island is allowed to stand up for itself.

FRED: Where a person can be a man a woman a boy a little girl. Whatever feels right inside.

FEDERICO: Where a child can decide where he wants to live.

FRED: Where more than one ideology can exist.

FEDERICO: More than one superpower.

FRED: Where friendship is valued as much as marriage.

FEDERICO: Where love is not a fetish.

FRED: Yes.

FEDERICO: We are going up.

(They fly.)

FRED: The motor started! The motor started!

FEDERICO: We are going home.

FRED: Home?

FEDERICO: One of two.

FRED: Look. Look at it. The sea is drowning in the sand.

(They look down on the stage.)

FEDERICO: *"Mi coral en la tiniebla, ire a Santiago."*

FRED: *"Ire a Santiago."*

FEDERICO: *"El mar ahogado en la arena."*

FRED: *"Ire a Santiago."* Down there.

FEDERICO: Yes. *"Oh Cuba! Oh curva de suspiro y barro!"*

FRED: *"Ire a Santiago."* Where magic happens.

(They fly off. The lights come on Ernesto. He is holding up a poster of Elian.)

ERNESTO: Miami Mafia. Yankee politicians. Exxon and United Fruit Company. Meyer Lansky and all his disciples. Mother fuckers. You've kept us apart long enough. Return us. Mother fuckers! You've kept us apart long enough. Return us. Us. Elian. Peter Pan. Give them back. Give them back to us. Mother fuckers! Let us come together. End the embargo. Please. Fuck you. Mother fuckers! Give them back!

(Blackout.)

END OF PLAY

Quake
by Melanie Marnich

Copyright © 2001 by Melanie Marnich. All rights reserved. CAUTION: Professionals and amateurs are hereby warned that *Quake* is subject to a royalty. It is fully protected under the copyright laws of the United States of America and of all countries covered by the International Copyright Union (including the Dominion of Canada and the rest of the British Commonwealth), the Berne Convention, the Pan-American Copyright Convention and the Universal Copyright Convention, as well as all countries with which the United States has reciprocal copyright relations. All rights, including professional, amateur stage rights, motion picture, recitation, lecturing, public reading, radio broadcasting, television, video or sound recording, all other forms of mechanical or electronic reproduction, such as CD-ROM, CD-I, information storage and retrieval systems and photocopying, and the rights of translation into foreign languages, are strictly reserved. Particular emphasis is laid upon the matter of readings, permission for which must be secured from the Author's agent in writing.

ALL INQUIRIES CONCERNING RIGHTS, INCLUDING AMATEUR RIGHTS, SHOULD BE ADDRESSED TO: WENDY STREETER, THE JOYCE KETAY AGENCY, 1501 BROADWAY, SUITE 1908, NEW YORK, NY 10036.

BIOGRAPHY

Melanie Marnich is the author of the plays *Quake, Blur, Beautiful Again, Tallgrass Gothic,* and *Season. Blur* was included in New York's Public Theater's New Work Now Festival, the U.S. West Festival of New Plays, and premiered at the Manhattan Theatre Club in April 2001. *Quake* was selected for the Fall 2000 A.S.K. International Writers Exchange held at London's Royal Court Theatre. Major awards include two Samuel Goldwyn writing awards, two Jerome Fellowships, a McKnight Advancement Grant, inclusion in Lincoln Center's American Living Room Festival, and the Francesca Primus Prize. Ms. Marnich earned her M.F.A. in playwriting from the University of California, San Diego. She now lives in Minneapolis. She is a member of the Dramatists Guild and of the Playwrights' Center.

HUMANA FESTIVAL PRODUCTION

Quake premiered at the Humana Festival of New American Plays in February, 2001. It was directed by Susan Booth with the following cast:

Lucy . . . . Tracey Maloney
Guy/Jock/Roger/Angel Bruce. . . . . David New
Brian/Cooper Trooper/Auto Repair Man . . . . . David Wilson-Barnes
That Woman . . . . Lusia Strus
The Other Woman/Dr. Psychiatrist/
    Store Clerk/Pilot/Priest . . . . Allison Briner
Nice Man/Flight Attendant/Drilled Guy/
    Park Janitor. . . . . Joey Williamson

and the following production staff:

Scenic Designer . . . . Paul Owen
Costume Designer. . . . . Linda Roethke
Lighting Designer . . . . Tony Penna
Sound Designer. . . . . Martin R. Desjardins
Properties Designer . . . . Mark R. Walston
Stage Manager . . . . Elaine M. Randolph
Production Assistant . . . . John Armstrong
Dramaturg. . . . . Amy Wegener
Assistant Dramaturg . . . . Brendan Healy
Casting in Chicago. . . . . Janet Louer
Casting in New York . . . . Laura Richin

CHARACTERS

(This play can be done with 3 women and 2-3 men.)

    LUCY

    THAT WOMAN

    GUY

    BRIAN

    THE OTHER WOMAN (A non-speaking part. Just an arm, really.)

    JOCK

    COOPER TROOPER

    DR. PSYCHIATRIST

    NICE MAN

    STORE CLERK

    ROGER

    FLIGHT ATTENDANT/BRIDESMAID

    PILOT (CAPTAIN LARSON)/PRIEST

    DRILLED GUY (Non-speaking.)

    PARTY PEOPLE

    AUTO REPAIR MAN

    ANGEL BRUCE

    PARK JANITOR

TIME

The present.

LOCATIONS

Constant migration around the U.S., ending up in San Francisco.

Lusia Strus and Tracey Maloney in
Quake

25th Annual Humana Festival of New American Plays
Actors Theatre of Louisville, 2001
photo by Richard Trigg

Quake

ONE

LUCY: The day I was born I walked into the Great Lake.
   The cold drove my feet into my legs.
   My legs into my stomach.
   My stomach into my throat.
   My throat into my head and out the ends of my hair.
   And I tried to float but I sank.
   Like a rock.

   And I made a little rock sound that sounded like—
   "Help."
   And the voice bounced back—
   "Move," she said.
   "Move with the curve of the world.
   Wear yourself out against the road and air
   till you're dust on your arm,
   till you float like a leaf.
   It's a big love you're looking for," she said.

   Then I was on the bottom of the lake
   and I was crawling out.
   My eyes are open and my heart's on my sleeve.
   I am moving.
   Looking for the love of my life.

TWO

The woods of the upper Northeast.

A Guy in a flannel shirt and ear-flap hat grills a bunch of fish. He's cute in a Normal Guy sort of way. There are several fish on the grill, and buckets of fish on the ground. The grill smokes a little.

Lucy appears.

LUCY: Here you are.
> *(Guy looks around to see who else she could be talking to. He's nice—but no rocket scientist.)*
LUCY: You. I found you. I walked through the woods, followed your smoke. Followed it like a signal. For miles and miles and miles.
GUY: You must be hungry then.
LUCY: No.
GUY: You sure? 'Cause I can I grill ya somethin'.
LUCY: No thanks.
GUY: A pike or a walleye?
LUCY: No.
GUY: Woodchuck?
LUCY: No.
GUY: Rabbit?
LUCY: Nope.
GUY: How 'bout a squirrel or some venison then?
LUCY: I'm not here for your food.
GUY: *(Getting a little wary.)* Well then what *are* you here for?
LUCY: You.
> *(He stops, blinks. He's not quite equipped for this.)*
LUCY: Did you hear me?
GUY: Um...
LUCY: Did you understand me?
GUY: Listen, lady—
LUCY: Lucy.
GUY: Lucy.
LUCY: And your name is...
GUY: Guy.

LUCY: You're not married, are you Guy?

GUY: No. I live with my mom.

LUCY: Guy?

GUY: Yeah?

LUCY: I think you're incredible.

(Guy shuffles a foot at the flattery.)

GUY: *(Gesturing to the grill with his spatula.)* You sure you don't want one of these?

LUCY: They look a little boney.

GUY: I'll pick the bones out for you.

LUCY: You'd do that for me?

GUY: Sure.

LUCY: Will you cut the head off?

GUY: No problem.

LUCY: Scoop the guts out?

GUY: Yep.

LUCY: Would you carry my books, pull my hair, and carve my name in the tree?

GUY: Uh-huh.

LUCY: Would you drive me home, turn on all the lights, and check under the bed after the scary movies?

GUY: Easy.

LUCY: Would you slice the turkey, mash the potatoes, and pass the cranberries?

GUY: Yep.

LUCY: Would you hold the ladder while I put the star on the top of the tree?

GUY: Gotcha!

(A few red and orange and yellow leaves flutter to the ground.)

LUCY: What was that?

GUY: Autumn.

LUCY: Already?

(The wind starts to blow.)

LUCY: What's that?

GUY: Winter.

LUCY: You're kidding.

GUY: Time flies around here, Lucy. The world turns.

(Snow starts to fall. The wind starts to howl.)

LUCY: Hold me, Guy. I'm cold.

GUY: Just a sec.

(He pulls a tube out of his shirt and blows, inflating his belly and love handles. He pulls tufts of hair out of his head and plugs them into his ears.)

LUCY: What are you doing?!

GUY: Letting myself go. Ahhh... Life's short, Lucy. We'll make the most of it, you and me. We'll have kids. Lots of them. Two, three...nine. You'll breast-feed. I'll teach them to hunt.

(More snow. More wind.)

We'll live off the land. We'll go with the flow, mature with the seasons.

(Bigger snow. Bigger, louder wind.)

LUCY: *(Yelling above the wind.)* I think I'm getting frostbite!

GUY: And through the years your love for me will grow and deepen—

LUCY: I'm freezing to death!!!

GUY: —through all the years of my life!

(At this, Lucy collapses in the snow and tries to crawl out of the storm against the wind. It's tough.)

LUCY: I don't want to die like this! My snot is freezing! I'm growing weaker, weaker. Need food. Need food.

(She grabs a fish and starts gnawing on it as she resumes her crawl toward freedom.)

GUY: Wait! You can't walk out! You have responsibilities! People need you! It's laundry day! Where are you going? Hey!

LUCY: Must keep moving. Must keep moving.

(The blizzard is fierce and screaming. Nearly a white-out.)

GUY: *(Now also on his knees, crawling, struggling after her.)* Wait up! It will be perfect. You and me! Together! Forever! LUUUCCCEEEE...

(And he disappears in the storm.)

(Lucy looks back for a second. Hell with it. And keeps going. She crawls out of the blizzard of death and into a very cool urban coffee shop/café.)

(She spits out the fish. Pt-tooh. And sits down at a table.)

(She notices Brian, sitting at a table, reading a book. He's cute. She's interested. She tries to read a newspaper. She decides to start something.)

LUCY: Hi.

BRIAN: Hi.

(Silence.)

LUCY: So...*Hebe uber alles?*

BRIAN: What?

LUCY: Oh, nothing. Just a little spontaneous...Latin.

(Brian quickly returns to his book.)

LUCY: Would you...like to...dance?

BRIAN: Excuse me?

LUCY: Dance with me?

BRIAN: There's no music.

LUCY: Somewhere there is.

(He goes back to his book. She stares. Silence.)

LUCY: Fast or slow?

BRIAN: Excuse me?

LUCY: You prefer to dance fast or slow?

BRIAN: I prefer not to dance.

LUCY: I bet you wish I left you alone.

BRIAN: Well...

LUCY: And stop trying to flirt with you.

BRIAN: Yes.

LUCY: I'm not very good at this, am I?

BRIAN: No.

LUCY: I'm just learning. So bear with me.

BRIAN: I need to read this before class—

LUCY: And you seemed like you would be patient and kind and good to practice on and I'm harmless.

BRIAN: There's gonna be a test...

LUCY: What's it about?

BRIAN: Well. Pleistocene rock formations.

LUCY: That's my favorite epoch of the Quaternary Period.

BRIAN: Mine too.

(He smiles, goes back to his book. Silence.)

LUCY: I made you smile.

BRIAN: A little.

LUCY: Can I tell you that I love your name?

BRIAN: You don't know my name.

LUCY: Can I tell you a secret?

BRIAN: Think I should buy you a cup of coffee first?

LUCY: Cream. No sugar.

BRIAN: That's how you like your coffee?

LUCY: No. That's my secret. Can I come to your table?

(He smiles. She joins him.)

LUCY: Lucy. *(She extends her hand.)*

BRIAN: Brian. *(They shake.)*

LUCY: You know I—

BRIAN: You love my name?

LUCY: No. I was just going to say it's cold outside.

BRIAN: Yes. It is.

LUCY: Sometimes I get this chill, you know? This deep, deep chill.

BRIAN: So do I, Lucy.

LUCY: Do you think it would be okay if— Can I—?

> *(He nods.*
> *She kisses him.)*

BRIAN: Can I?

> *(She nods.*
> *He kisses her.)*

LUCY: *(About Brian.)*

> Then I loved a man who knew the
> difference between gravity and stone.
> He taught me to see that the lake bed was only aftermath.
> He put his hand up my shirt and said
> you know the glacier made the valley.
> And I said yeah.
> He slid his hand down my pants and said
> the continental divide goes both ways.
> And I said ooh.
> I'll show you the watershed, he said.
> What's hard can become molten.
> What's molten can become bedrock.
> I leaned my head back and opened my throat.
> Granite holds the heat, he said.
> I leaned my head back and looked this way.

(Lucy and Brian in bed watching TV. Brian channel-surfs.)

BRIAN: Channel 3, news at 10. Channel 7, news at 10. Channel 10, news at 10. Channel 37, channel 41, channel 53, channel 59—

LUCY: Stop. Go back one. There. There she is.

BRIAN: Who?

LUCY: That Woman. You know.

BRIAN: No.

LUCY: That Woman. The *America's Most Wanted* woman.

BRIAN: Rings a bell.

LUCY: Killed a couple boyfriends and now she's branching out. Killing total strangers.

BRIAN: Oh yeah.

LUCY: The Astrophysicist Gone Bad?

BRIAN: Her.

LUCY: Look at her. That shot from the ATM camera. She's amazing.

BRIAN: She's scary.

LUCY: She's beautiful.

BRIAN: She's a freak.

LUCY: She's a force.

BRIAN: She's horrible.

LUCY: She's intense.

BRIAN: She kind of has nice eyes.

LUCY: She's incredible. And she's out there. Somewhere.

BRIAN & LUCY: I think I love her.

BRIAN & LUCY: Are you jealous?

BRIAN & LUCY: *(Looking at each other.)* Of her?

BRIAN & LUCY: Of her.

LUCY: No.

BRIAN: No.

LUCY: Not really.

BRIAN: Good.

LUCY: Good.

BRIAN: Good.

   (They sleep.)

   (Lucy dreams.)

   (That Woman appears.)

THAT WOMAN: Like most scientific pioneers, I do my boldest work in near isolation. Like most scientific pioneers, I'm called a crackpot. Like most scientific pioneers, I'm out of a job. Unlike most scientific pioneers, I have to dispose of a body.

I am fucking brilliant. And that is pure energy. Energy doesn't disappear. Cannot disappear. Never ever. It's transferred. It's an undeniable force. It's nature. It's science. It's out of my hands.

I loved each one. Then there's that minute you look at him and wonder who? Why? Why don't you love me like you used to? Where did it go? It can't disappear. It's energy. It must be somewhere.

These guys... They were only human, and I knew what it was like to wish upon a supernova.

I just wanted more.

(The phone rings.)
LUCY: Hello? They hung up.
    (Ring.)
LUCY: Hello? Another hang-up.
    (Ring.)
LUCY: Hello?
    (No one's there. She hangs up.)
    (Ring.)
    (This time, Brian, who's been getting increasingly nervous, grabs the phone. He mutters "Don't call me at home," then hangs up.)
BRIAN: Wrong number.
LUCY: Weird.
BRIAN: Really weird.
LUCY: *(Reaching under the covers.)* Hey, what's this?
    (She pulls out a big dangly earring.)
BRIAN: Um. I dunno.
LUCY: And this?
    (She hold up a pair of panties.)
BRIAN: I dunno.
LUCY: And this?
    (She holds up a bra.)
BRIAN: I dunno.
    (The Other Woman's arm shoots out from under the covers, snatches it all back, and disappears under the bedding.)
LUCY: Are you seeing someone else?
BRIAN: No.
LUCY: Would you lie to me?
BRIAN: No.

LUCY: You're lying to me, aren't you?

BRIAN: I think you're really paranoid.

LUCY: You lied to me.

   (Silence.)

LUCY: No one's ever lied to me before.

BRIAN: Lucy—

LUCY: Brian?

BRIAN: *(As one word.)* It didn't mean anything It was only once No I don't love her It was a mistake I never saw her before I'll never do it again It didn't mean anything It was only once No I don't love her It was a mistake I never saw her before I'll never do it again It didn't mean anything It was only once I'll never do it again.

LUCY: But I thought you were perfect.

BRIAN: Give me another chance.

LUCY: You were supposed to be perfect.

BRIAN: I'll make it up to you. I swear. It didn't mean anything, ever.

LUCY: Then why did you do it?

BRIAN: I'll never do it again.

LUCY: Brian? Why don't you love me like you used to?

BRIAN: It was only once. Lucy?

LUCY: It's late.

BRIAN: Lucy?

LUCY: Go to sleep.

   (Brian sleeps. Lucy tries to sleep.)

THAT WOMAN: Velocity plus gravity equals:
   Locomotion plus mass equals:
   Escaping steam plus the light from a green eye equals:

   These are not equations.
   We're beyond the new math.
   Didn't you hear?
   There's been a revolution.
   The numbers were tired of adding up.
   Sparks ignite and there's an explosion.
   A speck becomes a mass that holds you back.
   Keep looking for mach one.
   Mach one million.
   Your body burns when you fall through atmosphere.

(Lucy crawls out of bed and leaves Brian.)

THAT WOMAN: Velocity of escape. The speed at which an object can leave another object behind—without being held by gravity.

End of scene.

THREE

Lucy and Jock ride (stationary) bikes. They're outfitted with all the latest/greatest/necessary gear and clothing. As they pedal side-by-side, slides are projected behind them as a backdrop that reflects the terrain through which they ride. As the scene progresses, slides change from nice fields, to small hills, to big hills.

They huff and puff. Jock can huff and puff and smile because he likes this. Lucy hates this—but she tries to fake it.

JOCK: You're a real sport, Lucy.

LUCY: Oh...I like...this.

JOCK: I mean, we just met last night. And when you said you wanted to do the whole tour with me, well...

LUCY: I said what?

JOCK: I thought it was just the rum, tequila, and vermouth talking. But when I saw you in the Drunken Splat Ball Games...

LUCY: I was in what?

JOCK: I said to myself, "This gal can really take a beating!"

LUCY: Oh God.

JOCK: Did I mention that my last girlfriend raced mountain bikes?

LUCY: *(She pedals even harder.)* You did.

JOCK: Cool, huh.

LUCY: Was she the triathlete?

JOCK: No. The triathlete was the med student. The mountain bike racer was the trilingual bush pilot.
(She pedals harder.)

LUCY: I can't keep them straight.

JOCK: Amazing women. Amazing. The bike racer could pee standing straight up. Which made her great to travel with.

LUCY: Really really incredible.

JOCK: Could ride eighty miles without breaking a sweat.

LUCY: Fascinating.

JOCK: Hasn't menstruated in seven years. Body like a machine. I think you two would hit it off.

LUCY: Great. How far've we gone? Thirty, forty—

JOCK: Six.

LUCY: Forty-six?!

JOCK: No. Six.

(Jock takes a deep breath and smiles.)

(Lucy copies him. She takes a big deep breath and—POP! HISSSS... We hear a noise like a tire exploding and the air hissing out.)

JOCK: You just blow a tire?

LUCY: *(Feeling her chest.)* My lung!

JOCK: Cool!

LUCY: Think we should stop?

JOCK: No, no. You're fine.

LUCY: I am?

JOCK: Sure. No pain, no gain.

LUCY: Right.

JOCK: Besides, it's just a lung. I mean, that's why we have two. Right?

LUCY: Right.

JOCK: Like my ex-girlfriend, the beach-volleyball-team-captain/trial lawyer used to say—

LUCY: *(Pedaling even harder.)* Yeah, yeah, yeah.

(Jock smiles and enjoys the pain of riding the hills.)

JOCK: *(Standing up, working hard.)* I really like it when sweat gets in my eyes. It burns. You know why it burns? Because there's salt in sweat and salt burns your eyes. Like it burns an open sore. Burning is good. Like it when it burns. Good burn. Good.

LUCY: *(Standing up, trying to work hard.)* Good, good, burn, burn.

JOCK: Oh yeah. Feel that burn.

LUCY: I feel it.

JOCK: Oh yeah.

LUCY: Jock?

JOCK: Yeah?

LUCY: Are we there yet?

JOCK: Depends where "there" is, Lucy. When you live the life of a jock, there is never here. There is always…out there.

(The slides change again. Now it's BIG HILLS. Another POP! HISS! Her other lung bursts.)

LUCY: Oh my God! I'm going to die, aren't I? Our Father who art in heaven, hallowed be thy name…

(He starts talking over her prayer. Not rude. Just clueless.)

JOCK: If you want to ride with me, Lucy, you'll keep riding. You'll learn to change a tire without slowing down. You'll learn to eat without chewing. You'll learn to sleep without closing your eyes. You'll learn to rest without stopping. It's a great way of life, Lucy. Like one of those commercials. Extreme gusto.

LUCY: Gusto. Right. Gusto.

JOCK: Keep riding, Lucy. Keep riding. Body is a machine. Oil chain. Shift gears. Burn is good. Good burn, good. You're slowing down, Lucy. Pick it up.

LUCY: I can't.

JOCK: Yes you can.

LUCY: No, I can't.

JOCK: But last night you said—

LUCY: I was drunk and I thought you were cute. I woulda said anything.

JOCK: You know, my last ex-girlfriend—

LUCY: Your ex-girlfriends are FREAKS! I don't want to ride eighty miles without sweating. I *want* to menstruate. I *like* menstruating. I like it more than bike riding. I'm pulling over. Don't take this personally, but this isn't working.

JOCK: I can't stop.

LUCY: It's okay. Go, go, burn, burn… Good, good…

JOCK: *(Overlapping her.)* Burn, burn, go, go, burn, burn is good…

(And he takes off, leaving Lucy behind.)

(That Woman appears in another area.)

THAT WOMAN: Two bodies coast in orbits set in stone
until a third throws them off.
X marks the spot where their chaos connects.
Any celestial mechanic worth her salt knows this
is the place to jump the tracks.

Do it well and you're a rocket.
Do it right and you're a star.

End of scene.

FOUR

Lucy is in a beauty contest. She wears a puffy tulle skirt with one of those banners draped across her body. It says "Sponsored by Memphis Meats." She stands in a line with the other contestants—all mannequins who are dressed like her.

She is being judged by Cooper Trooper, a rich southern guy. He sits at a table with the other judges—all mannequins who are dressed like him.

LUCY: Am I winning?

COOPER: *(In a Southern accent.)* We ask the questions.

LUCY: Sorry.

> *(Silence.)*
>
> Am I?

COOPER: Are you sorry?

LUCY: No. Am I winning.

COOPER: We think it's gonna be close.

LUCY: This is my first beauty contest, you know.

COOPER: Huh.

LUCY: I've never thought of myself as particularly, you know, *beautiful* before.

COOPER: Yup.

LUCY: But I guess there's a first time for everything.

> *(She waits for a response from him. Nothing.)*

LUCY: Actually, I'm here by accident on purpose. I keep moving. Following the curve of the world, looking for the love of my life, yadda, yadda, yadda. And something just told me to take a hard right out of Knoxville.

COOPER: Excuse me a second.

> *(He leans toward one of the judge mannequins as if it's whispering to him.)*
> *(To mannequin.)* Uh-huh. Yes. Yes. No. No. I'll say it.
> *(To Lucy.)* Can you stick your chest out?
> *(Lucy sort of adjusts her posture.)*

LUCY: So I guess this is the evening gown part.

COOPER: Yep.

LUCY: Am I a contender?

COOPER: I'd say it's a crap shoot right now.

LUCY: Long as I'm here, what could I do to tip the scales in my favor?

COOPER: I don't know. You can do that "one wish" part of the contest if you want.

LUCY: ?

COOPER: It's like, if you had one wish, what would it be?

LUCY: Okay. I get it.

COOPER: Go.

LUCY: I think I'm obsessed.

COOPER: That's not a wish.

LUCY: I know. But it seemed like the thing to say.

COOPER: Alright then.

LUCY: I might be. Obsessed.

COOPER: You little filly.

LUCY: With a serial killer who has a full tank, a good map, and a mean romantic streak. See, I keep going and going and going and going and going and going and going and going. I'm not even sure where I am.

COOPER: Memphis. Where you headed?

LUCY: Won't know till I get there. You ever think you're obsessed?

COOPER: I used to think about Lisa Marie Presley a lot.

LUCY: Hm. Who are you?

COOPER: Cooper Trooper the Third. I'm very rich. My wife used to be president of the Junior League.

LUCY: *(Obsessed.)* Leave her.

COOPER: *(Obsessed.)* Okay.

LUCY: For me.

COOPER: Okay.

LUCY: So. Did I win yet?

COOPER: You bet.

> *(Lucy pushes over the contestant mannequins and walks toward Cooper. She now feels "beautiful." There's a power in that.)*

LUCY: You know you're not my first.

COOPER: I don't mind.

LUCY: And I'll leave you. In a horrible mess.

COOPER: When?

LUCY: Got no idea. Can you live with that?

COOPER: Yeah. I am so fucking rich.

LUCY: You know, I don't want to wear diamonds. I just want to look like I'm wearing diamonds.

COOPER: You don't love me for my money?

LUCY: I don't love you.

COOPER: Like me?

LUCY: A little.

COOPER: Why?

LUCY: You tell me.

(He goes to her. They start kissing passionately and tumble to the floor. They become entangled with the mannequins and get so tangled that Cooper winds up making out with a dummy and Lucy slips out from under them. Cooper doesn't notice and continues kissing.)

LUCY: And because of him I learned to lay down in the full light of day.
Because it was too hot to do anything else.
Under the ceiling fan the white walls don't talk.
And the peach tree ripens
and the magnolia blooms and says here, smell this.

Till the time I drank too much down on Beale,
walked to the river, turned into paper and
folded myself into a boat.
I boarded myself and sailed away.

End of scene.

FIVE

Lucy is asleep and dreaming. That Woman is in the room.

LUCY: I picked these for you. *(She holds out flowers.)*

THAT WOMAN: Thanks.

LUCY: Like them?

THAT WOMAN: Yeah. Yeah, I— I'm allergic to some kinds, but not to these.

LUCY: Good.

THAT WOMAN: I don't want to be here.

LUCY: Where?

THAT WOMAN: In your sleep. In your dream. I can't stay here.

LUCY: How do you keep moving?

THAT WOMAN: By degree. By coordinates. By solar power. Sometimes by bicycle. Just for kicks. Just kidding. So tell me.

LUCY: What?

THAT WOMAN: Why I'm here.

LUCY: I honestly have no idea.

THAT WOMAN: When I dream, I dream that the phone is ringing and ringing and I can't get to it, or that I keep missing my plane, or that I'm stuck outside without any pants. I don't dream about killers. You must be having problems.

LUCY: You look like you've lost weight.

THAT WOMAN: Yeah, well, seems like I always have to eat and run lately.

LUCY: Why?

THAT WOMAN: 'Cause I see flashing red lights or a guy in uniform and I get a little jumpy.

LUCY: No. Why? The Big Why? Why do you do what you do?

THAT WOMAN: Because. Because sometimes I think I might be an animal or a monster. But I know I'm not. No matter what they say. Because I think about crying.

But sometimes, you know, the pipe breaks. And sometimes I'm sorry. I worry I'm an animal or a monster when I'd rather be astral. I'd rather be a laser beam or radioactive dust. Something stunning you don't dare mess with. Something you wonder at and leave alone. Something with a helluva half-life. Energy can't disappear, no matter what they tell you.

LUCY: Where are you?

THAT WOMAN: You know what a fractal is, Lucy?

LUCY: Where are you now?

THAT WOMAN: It's a geometric shape that gets repeated over and over and gets smaller and smaller till it's not geometric at all but sort of crazy and beautiful. The brain can do it. The body can do it. The land can do it. Break into pieces small enough to swallow.

LUCY: You're my hero, you know. My idol.

THAT WOMAN: You know why?

LUCY: You scare me.

THAT WOMAN: So. You scare me.

LUCY: I think you scare me more.

THAT WOMAN: Point taken.

LUCY: So now what?

THAT WOMAN: Like I always say, don't get scared. Get angry. And get going. And go and go and go and go and go and go and go. 'Cause we want better, we want bigger, we want more. It's got to be perfect and we won't stop till we find it.

LUCY: I'm following you.

THAT WOMAN: It's a dream, Lucy.

(She sings Lucy to sleep.)
Twinkle twinkle little star
how I wonder where you are.
Up above the world so high,
like a diamond in the sky.
Twinkle twinkle little star...
(Lucy snores, asleep.)

THAT WOMAN: Thanks for the flowers.

(That Woman slips away.)

End of scene.

SIX

Lucy in Dr. Psychiatrist's office. Lucy fidgets.
Dr. stares at her and takes notes.

DR: Mm-hmm.

(Silence, note-taking. Lucy wiggles her feet.)

DR: Ah-hah.

(Silence, note-taking. Lucy wiggles something else.)

DR: Ooooo.

(Silence. Lucy adjusts her underwear.)

LUCY: So, um, exactly what kind of psychiatrist are you?

DR: Jungian.

LUCY: Oh.

DR: Freudian.

LUCY: Really?

DR: Armenian.

LUCY: Wow.

DR: Okay. Get started. Let's. So…

LUCY: Yes?

DR: To help me build. Baseline. Psychology. Of your. Questions. A few. Mmm?

LUCY: Okay.

DR: Phone. Of it. Are you afraid?

LUCY: Am I afraid of the phone?

DR: Yes.

LUCY: No.

DR: Mmm. In head. Yours. Voices. Do you hear?

LUCY: Do I hear voices in my—?

DR: Yes.

LUCY: No.

DR: Mmm. Satan. Talk to. More than Thursdays. Wednesdays?

LUCY: No.

DR: Substances. Mood-altering. Addiction to?

LUCY: No.

DR: Caffeine?

LUCY: Yes.

DR: Mmm. Russian brick layer. Sex with. Fantasize?

LUCY: Who doesn't.

DR: Yepyepyepyepyep.

LUCY: Listen, Doctor, I'm here because I'm dreaming of a killer. She chews up my sleep. She injects me with ideas. She shows angry muscle. Is she invading—or am I calling? I do what she says and she says keep going. I'm obsessed but I don't want a cure. I want what she has. Power. Velocity. Ferocity. Light. Courage without compromise. Nothing scares her. Everything scares me. Maybe she's lost her mind. Maybe I found it. This is so new. Am I nuts? You've read the books.

DR: Clinical.

LUCY: You know the mind.

DR: Quantitative.

LUCY: Then tell me.

DR: Read the books. Know the mind. But the supplicant heart and the questing soul…

LUCY: Am I delusional?

DR: No.

LUCY: Depressed?

DR: No.

LUCY: I'm confused. I thought you could help me.

DR: Can I help you?

LUCY: I need something.

DR: What do you need?

LUCY: I don't know.

DR: What do you want?

LUCY: I don't know.

DR: What do you think?

LUCY: What I think is—

DR: What do you know?

LUCY: I'm not sure I know.

DR: Oh I know you know you know.

LUCY: You do not know I know I know!

DR: I know I know you know you know.

LUCY: I know I know you don't know I know!

DR: I know I know you know I know you know you know.

LUCY: You don't know I know I know—!

DR: You don't know I don't know you know you know—

LUCY: FUCK YOU!!

> (*Where the hell did that come from? Lucy blinks, a bit surprised at her own anger. Dr. is happy at the breakthrough.*)

DR: Ah. Good. Very. Progress.

End of scene.

SEVEN

Lucy and a Nice Man on a date.

The man is very animated—talking, laughing, sipping wine, nodding in agreement, etc.—but completely silent. Like his sound button is turned off.

Lucy, however, is audible. She goes through the motions of the date, interacting with him, but speaks her thoughts.

LUCY: Uh-huh. Uh-huh. Good sense of humor. Personal hygiene all right. Solid hairline. *(He laughs with his mouth open.)* Three fillings. One crown. Not bad. Nice hands. Masculine. Good sign. Note: Do laundry. Out of shampoo. Itch. *(She scratches.)* Focus, focus. *(She nods with him.)* Actually… Nice smile. Nice eyes. No. Wait. Great eyes. Dreamy eyes. Yeah. And smart. Really smart. Generous. Kind. Supportive. Sweet. Stable. Romantic. Good to me. Nice to me. Oooo. Likes me. Could like him. Could kiss him. French. Snuggle. Spoon. Sweet. Faithful. Dependable. Loyal. Irish setter. Cocker spaniel. Trapped. Stuck. Rut. Help. Panic. Escape. Move. Move. Move.
(Lucy leaves, while Nice Man continues to have a great conversation.)

End of scene.

EIGHT

An urban-blight convenience store. A female clerk sits behind the counter reading a magazine. She has a gunshot wound in her shoulder that's still smoking.

The door "dings" and Lucy enters.

CLERK: Hi.
LUCY: Hi. Ten dollars on pump four, please.
CLERK: Anything else?
LUCY: Yeah. That donut and a pack of gum.
CLERK: Comin' right up.
LUCY: Something's burning… Is that a gunshot wound?
CLERK: *(Suddenly remembering it.)* Damn kids. Hand me those Band-Aids, will you?
    (Clerk digs around in the wound, pulls out the bullet, and drops it on the counter with a "clink.")
CLERK: *(As she cleans the wound.)* You know, I got so busy I forgot all about this.
LUCY: Doesn't it hurt?
CLERK: Not like the first time.
LUCY: You get shot a lot?
CLERK: Here, here, here, here, here twice, here and here.

LUCY: Aren't you afraid?

CLERK: Of what?

LUCY: Dying.

CLERK: No. I am not afraid of Death. To accept this job is to look Death in the eye and say, "Fuck you. Either buy something or get outta my face, Death. No loitering. No shoes, no shirt, no service, Death. Restroom reserved for patrons only. Move your car—it's blocking the fire lane, Death. If you're gonna read the magazine, you gotta pay for it. No change without purchase, Death." Every day. That's what it's like.

LUCY: Have you ever actually seen a dead person?

CLERK: Other than in here?

LUCY: Yeah.

CLERK: My grandpa died when I was six. But that's different.

LUCY: Different from what?

CLERK: Different from when they die because you shot them between the chips and the Ho-Ho's.

LUCY: I suppose. Hey, can I have the key to the restroom?

CLERK: *(Handing it over.)* Knock yourself out.

LUCY: Thanks.

(Lucy exits.)

(The door dings and That Woman enters.)

CLERK: Hi.

THAT WOMAN: Hi. Um. Pack of Camel Lights. Matches. A Milky Way. And a state map. Ohio, right?

CLERK: Oklahoma.

THAT WOMAN: Birthplace of James Dean?

CLERK: You're thinking of Indiana.

THAT WOMAN: Yeah. Hey. Nice entrance wound.

CLERK: Thanks. Anything else?

THAT WOMAN: How 'bout a Pudding Pop and... Got any phosphorus?

(Clerk places a glowing jar on the counter.)

CLERK: Last jar.

THAT WOMAN: Great.

CLERK: Selling like hotcakes ever since...

(Clerk gives That Woman a very arch look.)

THAT WOMAN: What?

CLERK: Ever since...

(Clerk grabs a tabloid and flips through till she finds a picture.)

You're her, aren't you?

THAT WOMAN: Who?

CLERK: That Woman! That Woman! I thought so. You poisoned all those guys. Used phosphorus on a couple. You started a real trend with that one.

THAT WOMAN: I used freon a few times, too.

CLERK: But phosphorus is so much cooler.

THAT WOMAN: It's a fast but fantastical death.

CLERK: You're the first celebrity I've ever had in here. Oh God, my hair.

THAT WOMAN: You look fine.

CLERK: Oh, God, thanks.

(The door dings and Lucy returns and hands over the key.)

LUCY: Thanks. Hey. Is that…phosphorus?

(The Clerk directs Lucy's attention to That Woman with a cough or a look.)

LUCY: Is it really you?

CLERK: It's her!

LUCY: I can't believe it's you!

CLERK: Neither can I!

LUCY: The Pretty Poisoner!

CLERK: The Terminal Traveler!

LUCY: The Lethal Lover!

CLERK: The Kiss-n-Killer!

LUCY: The Dame of Death!

THAT WOMAN: That's me.

CLERK: That's her.

LUCY: Wow.

CLERK: Wow.

LUCY: Wow.

CLERK: Wow.

LUCY: I'm…overwhelmed. I think you are beautiful and incredible and brilliant.

THAT WOMAN: Why?

LUCY: Because you are…fearless.

THAT WOMAN: Just because I kill people with no regard for the consequences?

LUCY: But you don't *kill* people. You *avenge*. You *aspire*.

CLERK: Totally.

THAT WOMAN: I'm a walking tabloid. I'm an icon for the demented. I'm inhuman. I'm alone.

CLERK: I close in five minutes.

LUCY: But you're a genius.

CLERK: If you want anything else…

THAT WOMAN: Yes.

CLERK: You want something else?

LUCY: Yes.

CLERK: Help yourself…

THAT WOMAN: I want.

LUCY: I want.

(They can eventually start to overlap.)

THAT WOMAN: I want to lose five pounds.

LUCY: I want a dimple right here.

THAT WOMAN: I want night vision.

LUCY: I want blue eyes.

THAT WOMAN: I want altitude.

LUCY: I want fuel.

THAT WOMAN: I want to break the law of falling bodies.

LUCY: I want to spin on the axis.

THAT WOMAN: I want my own new moon.

LUCY: I want to shake across the fault lines.

THAT WOMAN: I want power to the nth.

LUCY: I want to solve you for me.

THAT WOMAN: Solve for x.

LUCY: Stop.

THAT WOMAN: Accelerate.

LUCY: Wait.

THAT WOMAN: A body in motion continues in motion unless—

LUCY: I want to follow you.

THAT WOMAN: —unless acted upon by another force.

LUCY: I want to follow you.

(Silence.)

LUCY: Let me follow you.

THAT WOMAN: I have to go.

LUCY: Let me go a little way with you.

THAT WOMAN: No.

LUCY: Please.

THAT WOMAN: Get lost, Gidget.

LUCY: I'll call the police.

THAT WOMAN: Fine.

LUCY: I'll tell them I saw you.

THAT WOMAN: Go ahead.

(That Woman exits. The door dings.)

CLERK: Nice try.

LUCY: Think i scared her?

CLERK: Think you could scare anyone?

LUCY: Good point.

CLERK: You in her fan club?

LUCY: No.

CLERK: *(Pulling out a clipboard.)* Wanna be?

LUCY: I'm not really a...fan. I don't think.

CLERK: Well, you're something.

LUCY: Just obsessed.

CLERK: People love her. They hang wreaths on what used to be her lab door.

LUCY: I heard that.

CLERK: You have to admit, she has a certain *je ne sais quoi.*

LUCY: Do you think she'd ever let love stop her?

CLERK: Nah.

LUCY: Think she'll settle down?

CLERK: She'd be too bored.

LUCY: Think so?

CLERK: I'm closing.

LUCY: What if she stops?

CLERK: She can't.

(Clerk exits.)

LUCY: Her life. My life. We wind around.
Double helix into each other. I'll see her again.
I'm learning her topography.
I'm learning her mother tongue.
We're in the land where want is a four-letter word.
So is love.
So is move.

End of scene.

NINE

A plane. Lucy stands there, confused. A Flight Attendant appears and speaks into the intercom.

FLIGHT ATTENDANT: Please take your seat. Please take your seat. Make sure your tray table is locked and that your seat is in the upright position. Please store all carry-on items below your seat or in the overhead compartment above. Please be careful opening the overhead compartment as items may shift during the flight.

(Lucy hasn't moved.)

FLIGHT ATTENDANT: Please take your seat. Please take your seat.

(Lucy sits down next to Roger. They stare straight ahead.)

(The Flight Attendant goes on to make increasingly elaborate and weird hand signals as she wordlessly demonstrates procedure. As she does so, we hear the pilot over the speaker...)

PILOT: Good evening, everyone. This is your pilot, Captain Larson. And on behalf of the crew of flight fifteen-sixteen, I'd like to thank you for flying Air Tel Aviv. Have a comfortable flight.

LUCY: *(To Roger.)* I thought this was a Delta flight to Denver?

ROGER: So did I.

(They both start pressing their assistance buttons like crazy. Ding ding ding. The Flight Attendant finally stops with her hand actions to help them.)

FLIGHT ATTENDANT: Can I help you?

LUCY: I thought this was the Delta flight to Denver?

FLIGHT ATTENDANT: It is.

LUCY: Then why did the pilot just say thanks for flying Air Tel Aviv?

FLIGHT ATTENDANT: Because he gets a little silly from all the fumes in the cockpit.

LUCY: Oh. Thanks.

FLIGHT ATTENDANT: You're welcome.

(She disappears.)

LUCY: *(To Roger.)* Doesn't that make you nervous?

ROGER: Not really.

LUCY: You're kidding?

ROGER: No. I'm Swedish. I can stay pretty calm through anything.

LUCY: That's kind of cool. I'm Lucy.

ROGER: I'm Roger.

LUCY: Hi, Roger.

ROGER: Hi, Lucy.

LUCY: Rog.

ROGER: Luce.

ROGER: Luce.

LUCY: Rog.

(They giggle like high school kids.)

(Lucy stares at his lap for a second.)

LUCY: Those nuts look good.

ROGER: *(Holding up a little bag of peanuts.)* Want 'em?

LUCY: Um. Okay. Sure. Thanks.

ROGER: You fly often?

LUCY: Not really. You?

ROGER: Not really. Why you going to Denver?

LUCY: I'm looking for something. You?

ROGER: Looking for a job.

LUCY: What kind of job?

ROGER: I'm a nurse. But I'd really like to be a cowboy.

LUCY: Either way you'd be providing a valuable service to society.

(Roger blushes.)

ROGER: Want my pretzels?

LUCY: Sure. Thanks.

(They smile at each other, settle in. He pulls out a book and starts to read.)

LUCY: Whatcha reading?

ROGER: I'm working my way through all the Louis L'Amour's. Just in case this whole Western thing works out.

LUCY: That's really smart.

ROGER: You don't think it's hokey?

LUCY: Not at all.

ROGER: Because I tend to be a little hokey.

LUCY: Hokey's fine.

ROGER: On a bad day, I'm corny.

LUCY: Corny's sweet.

ROGER: I'm also diabetic.

LUCY: That's cute.

ROGER: And dyslexic.

LUCY: I don't mind.

ROGER: You don't?

LUCY: No.

ROGER: Not in the least?

LUCY: Not at all.

(Hm. A nice "Hm." They look into each other's eyes. Magic.)

ROGER: Have we taken off yet?

LUCY: Oh, I think so.

ROGER: Do you like—

LUCY: Blue eyes?

ROGER: Yes.

LUCY: Oh yes.

ROGER: Do you like—

(She now touches his body parts as they name them. Increasingly steamy.)

LUCY: Broad shoulders?

ROGER: Yes.

LUCY: Oh yes.

ROGER: Do you like—

LUCY: A cleft chin?

ROGER: Yes.

LUCY: Oh yes.

ROGER: Do you like—

LUCY: A tight ass, powerful thighs, and hard nipples perched on dreamy pecs?

ROGER: Yes!

LUCY: Oh yes oh yes oh yes!

(From here, a rhythm builds.)

ROGER: And I say yes—

LUCY: To your lips.

ROGER: To your eyes.

LUCY: To your breath.

ROGER: To your cheeks.

LUCY: To your nipples.

ROGER: Dimples.

LUCY: Tendons, ankles, toes.

(Hotter rhythm.)

ROGER: And I say touch.

LUCY: And I say kiss.

ROGER: And I say teeth.

LUCY: And I say tongue.

ROGER: And I say start.

LUCY: And I say go.

ROGER: And I say now.

LUCY: And I say slow.

ROGER: And I say soft.

LUCY: And I say make—

ROGER: Me—

LUCY: Stay.

    (Everything sighs at this great altitude.)

    (BIG WEDDING MARCH.)

    (Flight Attendant, now Bridesmaid, places a veil on Lucy. Roger snaps on cummerbund and bow tie.)

    (The Pilot, now Priest, appears.)

PRIEST: We are gathered here today—

LUCY: I do.

PRIEST: Joined in—

LUCY: I do.

PRIEST: To have and to hold—

LUCY: I do, I do, I do.

PRIEST: Fine. And do you—?

ROGER: Roger.

PRIEST: —Roger, take Lucy as your lawfully wedded wife, from this day forward, in sickness and in health, for richer and for poorer, for better and for worse, for rides with the top down, for ice cream sundaes on Mondays, and never ever for granted?

    (Silence.)

LUCY: Roger?

PRIEST: Roger?

LUCY: Please say something, Roger.

    (Silence.)

ROGER: I—

LUCY: You?

ROGER: Don't.

LUCY: Don't?

ROGER: Yes.

LUCY: "Yes" you do?

ROGER: No. "Yes," I don't.

LUCY: But you have to! We're in love, we're in lust, we're in mutual respect and admiration! Aren't we?

(Silence.)

LUCY: We have a history! We're invested in this! You gave me your nuts! Remember that?!

ROGER: I'm not really crazy about nuts, so it wasn't a big deal.

LUCY: You mean you wouldn't have given me your nuts if you'd liked them?

ROGER: Maybe not.

LUCY: Oh my God.

ROGER: It's just—

LUCY: What?

ROGER: I don't know.

LUCY: How can you not know? We *flew* together. We crossed the great divide on wings. We cooled ourselves over alluvial fans and opened pink quartz veins. We saw where the rocks fold. We saw the plates slide and the continent smile. We passed time. And we did it all in the air. Isn't that a big love?

ROGER: I don't know.

LUCY: I have to take that as a "no."

ROGER: I know.

LUCY: *(Destroyed but trying to be decisive.)* Then you really leave me no choice. You really, really, really, really don't.

ROGER: I understand.

LUCY: Okay then. *(She takes off her veil.)* I'm leaving.

ROGER: I'll remember you.

LUCY: I'm starting to walk away.

ROGER: Take care of yourself.

(Lucy stops.)

LUCY: Remember to walk the dog twice a day, to water the plants three times a week, and to leave a card for the mailman at Christmas.

ROGER: I will.

LUCY: I'll stay if you ask me.

(Silence.)

ROGER: I'll miss you.

LUCY: That's it! You leave me no option! I'm going.

(Pilot/Priest leaves.)

Going.

(Flight Attendant/Bridesmaid leaves.)

Roger? Aren't I pretty enough?

ROGER: You're very pretty.

LUCY: Aren't I smart enough?

ROGER: You're very smart.

LUCY: Aren't I nice or fun or clever enough?

ROGER: You're very nice and fun and clever.

LUCY: Then can you tell me why?

ROGER: It's your heart.

LUCY: What about my heart?

ROGER: It has a murmur, it makes a sound. I put my ear to your heart when you were sleeping, and I heard it.

LUCY: What kind of sound?

ROGER: It says: "I boom-boom Want boom-boom More boom-boom."

(Roger exits.)

(Lucy is all alone.)

End of scene.

TEN

That Woman walks up to Lucy, carrying a box with stuff in it.

LUCY: Oh God.

THAT WOMAN: How ya doing?

LUCY: Been better.

THAT WOMAN: Guy trouble?

LUCY: Yeah.

THAT WOMAN: Can't live with 'em. Can't use 'em for mulch. Just kidding. Hey, look what I have.

(She pulls out a power drill, fires it up.)

LUCY: I'm not up for this.

THAT WOMAN: Got one for you, too.

(She hands Lucy a drill.)

LUCY: I've been thinking that I'm afraid you're going to be caught, then put on trial, and then killed. Then all of us who follow you and dream about you and think you're an incredible siren, a force of nature, a Lorelei, a storm, a phenomenon will be left hanging. Don't you care?

THAT WOMAN: *(Waving drill.)* Know what this is for?

LUCY: No.

THAT WOMAN: For trephining.

LUCY: ?

THAT WOMAN: It's what they used to do to women like us.

LUCY: Like us?

THAT WOMAN: Yeah.

LUCY: Like you and me? You're including *me*?

THAT WOMAN: You know, deviant women, possessed women, monstrous women, evil, crazy, violent women. Pissed off women—

LUCY: This is so cool.

THAT WOMAN: —Women on a mission. Hungry women, precise women. Bitches who know exactly where a ball peen hammer can do the most damage.

LUCY: *(Miming some ball peen hammer maneuver.)* Bonk!

THAT WOMAN: They'd drill holes in your head. To let the bad stuff out. The demons, the voices, the attitude. Let it out. To cure you. Just drill and drill and drill and drill.

(She revs up her drill.)

LUCY: Oh God.

THAT WOMAN: Like this!

(And That Woman starts drilling holes in her head, smiling, like she might as well be curling her hair.)

THAT WOMAN: This is great! Come on! Try it! Like this!

(Lucy starts up her drill and hesitatingly, wincingly drills a hole in her head. But wait! It doesn't hurt! She drills another hole. And another. Feels kind of good, actually.)

(Now she and That Woman are drilling like crazy.)

LUCY: Hey! This is fun!

THAT WOMAN: Not bad, huh?!

LUCY: Look at me go!

(Drill, drill, drill.)

(A Man appears next to That Woman. To her surprise, her hand gets a mind of its own and drills the guy in the head. He drops dead with a thud.)

THAT WOMAN: Shit.

LUCY: Another one?

THAT WOMAN: Yeah. I gotta go.

(She puts her and Lucy's drills back in the box, and puts the box on the dead guy's stomach.)

LUCY: Wait. Um...

THAT WOMAN: I really have to—

LUCY: Why.

THAT WOMAN: We've been through this.

LUCY: Why do you hate them so much?

THAT WOMAN: Who? The guys?

LUCY: Yeah.

THAT WOMAN: I don't hate them. I love them. I love them so much. Like crazy. That's the problem. I love them inside out, upside down, every which way and back again from head to toe. And I just can't take what love is really like compared to the love I want. But I keep trying. I keep looking.

LUCY: For what?

THAT WOMAN: I'll know it when I find it. I'll stop when I find it.

LUCY: What about me?

THAT WOMAN: What about you?

LUCY: Where do I go? What do I do?

THAT WOMAN: Figure it out. You're not a rookie anymore. You've picked up speed.

LUCY: I've picked up speed.

THAT WOMAN: But are you ready for lift-off?

LUCY: I'm ready for lift-off.

(That Woman drags the dead guy off by his feet.)

LUCY: I am ready.

End of scene.

ELEVEN

A club. It's dark.
Music starts to play. Pulsating, throbbing music. Music to screw to.

Lucy stands there, alone, not fitting in and wondering if she should try to fit in. Hm. Weird. She sips from a jumbo martini glass.

Dance lights come up in the middle of the floor. They beckon Lucy but she's not quite ready.

From the edges of the dance floor, voices rise up. They can be pre-recorded to add depth and variation.

PEOPLE: *(Overlapping and ad-libbing.)* Wanna dance?
    Wanna dance?
    Yeah.
    Dance with me?
    Yes.
    I love you.
    I love you.
    I love that you love me.
    Love me.
    I love you.
    Dance?
    Dance with me?
    Yes.
    I love you.
    I love you.
    I love you.
    Love me.
    I love that you love me.
    Love me.
    etc…
    (This is completely new for Lucy and she can't resist. She steps into the dance lights, glows for a brief instant, then lights snap to black.)

End of scene.

TWELVE

Somewhere in the West. Lucy enters an auto repair garage, fresh from her fairly recent visit to the sexy club. There is a dangerously good-looking man slouched there.

LUCY: Hello.

MAN: Hep.

LUCY: This is a…garage?

MAN: Yep.

LUCY: And you are a…mechanic?

MAN: Uhn.

LUCY: I like your…tools.

MAN: Mmn.

LUCY: When I was growing up, there was this neighbor-guy. He spent all his time in his garage with his car. He was either under the hood or under the whole thing, rolling around on his back on this little roly cart. And he never talked. Not a word. He was amazing and had great stomach muscles. He had a big black tool box. He was like a grease monkey James Dean. Or Dennis Quaid. You are just like he was. And he was so hot. I always wanted one like him. I can't believe I just said that. Pretend I didn't say that. Act like I didn't say that. I didn't say that. I didn't. Oh God. *(She pats her forehead and face with a handkerchief.)* Oh God. Can I start over? I'm starting over. Brand new. Okay. Um, hello.

MAN: Hep.

LUCY: This is a…garage?

MAN: Yep.

LUCY: And you are a…mechanic?

MAN: Uhn.

LUCY: My car's broken.

MAN: Hmph.

LUCY: It just petered out.
   (Man lights a cigarette.)

LUCY: At first I thought it was just me, but then the warning lights started coming on. And it smelled.
   (Man smokes.)

LUCY: Yeah, so I got it off the freeway because some of the dials were going into the red warning danger-danger zone. I thought it was gonna, you know, blow.
   (Man smokes.)

LUCY: Like, blow up.
   (Man smokes.)

LUCY: With me in it. So I got out. Got a tow. And here I am. So um. What do you think?

(Man thinks. And thinks.)

MAN: Sounds like a carburetor/crankshaft/hose/joint/nut/bolt/spark/fuel/bull-shit/crap thing.

LUCY: You talk!

MAN: Of course I talk.

LUCY: I didn't think guys like you talk!

MAN: Make too big a deal out of it, and I'll stop.

LUCY: Sorry.

MAN: Stick to car stuff, and we'll be fine.

LUCY: Okay. So. In terms of car stuff, when will it be ready? My car.

MAN: Won't get started on it till tomorrow.

LUCY: Oh.

MAN: Or the day after.

LUCY: I can't go anywhere till you fix it.

MAN: I know.

LUCY: I know you know. You're the expert.

MAN: You like that, don't you? That I'm the expert.

LUCY: Yes.

MAN: With cars.

LUCY: I guess so.

MAN: You do. You like that I know cars but don't know much else. And that you can think rings around me and talk circles around me and know big words and big books and big things and I have a tenth grade education. And that I look good in a pair of jeans.

LUCY: Just something about a guy with grease under his nails. Who smells like gasoline and cigarettes and who knows what to do with a belt sander.

MAN: You like that?

LUCY: Oh yeah.

(Man stares at her.)

LUCY: It's. Manly. Intensely. Manly.

MAN: And you like the way I hold my beer bottle by its neck. You like that I sit in the chair in the kitchen, quiet, because that's just me being strong. And silent. Because silence is sexy.

(Silence.)

MAN: Because silence is electricity. Because silence is intensity. Because you can fill the quiet with whatever you want me to be. Like they do in the pretty movies. Because isn't it great that a girl like you and a guy like me can— Well. Isn't it…romantic?

(But it's not romantic. It's sinister.)

LUCY: Are you ready to work on my—?

MAN: I'm just getting started.

LUCY: Could you…hurry?

MAN: No.

LUCY: Oh.

MAN: And you want one like me because…?

LUCY: Because…

MAN: And you want me why….?

LUCY: Well…

MAN: Because I scare you. And that's why you'll lay down for me. Because I'm rough, I won't play nice. And you want it that way, don't you?

You know I know how to kiss in a way that takes the air out of your joints. You know I'll put one finger inside you, then two, then five, then my fist, up to my elbow, my shoulder, my head is inside, I'm going upstream and pretty soon I'm doing the Australian crawl through your bloodstream.

And nobody's done that to you before.

You always wanted one like me. And I'm not nice.

(He's maneuvered her onto her back on the floor. He's crouched over her, on all fours.)

LUCY: Are you gonna hit me?

MAN: I'm gonna knock your socks off.

LUCY: You gonna hurt me?

MAN: Don't worry. After a while, it'll just make you smell different. And that's how I'll find you. How I'll always know where you are. By your smell.

LUCY: Bruises?

MAN: They're just the flowers your body gives you for taking the punch.

(He crawls around her.)

MAN: I'll bounce you off the side of the pickup truck, and you'll know I love you. I'll fuck you up the ass till you spit out your teeth and you'll know I'm crazy for you.

(He moves down to her feet and starts to smell her, still on all fours, working his way up her body as she starts to cry. He passes over her, a knee on each side of her body, so that he's like a cage over her.)

*(He's gone.
She lies there.*

Broken.
Crying.)

(Time passes.)

(A knock at the door. Another knock.)
LUCY: Who's there?
(A person approaches Lucy. It's Angel Bruce. A New Age Healer from Santa Fe.
He's decorated in New Age things: crystals, sage, pyramids, dream catchers, etc.)
ANGEL BRUCE: One Our Father, ten Hail Marys, one Glory Be to the Father.
Ponder the Ascension. Announce the Second Mystery.
(Lucy gets up. She's wobbly and sore.)
LUCY: Go to hell.
ANGEL BRUCE: One more Our Father, ten more Hail Marys, one more Glory
Be. Ponder the Resurrection. Announce the Third Mystery.
LUCY: I didn't do anything.
ANGEL BRUCE: Announce the Fourth Mystery.
LUCY: I can barely walk.
ANGEL BRUCE: *(Feeling her aura.)* Your chakras are clogged up. And your aura
is very angry.
LUCY: I'm gonna mace you. I'm not a victim. I've taken self-defense classes at
the Y. I could knee you in the groin and shove the bridge of your nose
into your brain. I could crush your windpipe. I could kill you with my
bare hands. You'll die like a pig.
ANGEL BRUCE: *(In a Godlike voice.)* I am Angel Bruce, an ordained healer-seer
from the Santa Fe Center for Enlightenment. Aum.
LUCY: Get the hell away from me!
ANGEL BRUCE: Behold!
LUCY: Stop it.
ANGEL BRUCE: Wooo oooo.
LUCY: Get out!
ANGEL BRUCE: I sense resistance. I don't understand this hostility.
LUCY: It's the only logical reaction.
ANGEL BRUCE: Let go of the tension…
LUCY: Please leave.
ANGEL BRUCE: But you called me.
LUCY: No I didn't.
ANGEL BRUCE: You sure?

(Lucy nods.)

(Angel Bruce is confused. He pulls out a piece of paper, scans it.)

ANGEL BRUCE: Is this 1459 Elm Street?

LUCY: No.

ANGEL BRUCE: Are you Babette Bowman?

LUCY: No.

ANGEL BRUCE: You sure?

LUCY: Yes.

ANGEL BRUCE: Shit. Shitshitshit.

LUCY: Sorry.

ANGEL BRUCE: No. My fault. My fault. Sorry to bother you. We've got this
new guy in dispatch...

LUCY: Dispatch?

ANGEL BRUCE: Yeah. The center sends me out for emergency aura adjustments.
You're not Babette...

LUCY: I'm Lucy.

ANGEL BRUCE: Bruce.

(They shake hands.)

LUCY: I'm sorry I yelled at you, Bruce.

ANGEL BRUCE: Forget about it.

LUCY: Can I ask you something?

ANGEL BRUCE: Shoot.

LUCY: Is it okay that I'm not Babette?

ANGEL BRUCE: Fine with me.

LUCY: I mean, your magic still works if—

ANGEL BRUCE: Healing energy. Not magic. *Energy.*

LUCY: Your energy still works if I'm just anyone?

ANGEL BRUCE: Of course.

LUCY: As long as you're here, then, could you do something for me?

ANGEL BRUCE: Name it.

LUCY: Can you do what you do?

ANGEL BRUCE: Can you be more specific?

LUCY: Well...

ANGEL BRUCE: You want money?

LUCY: No.

ANGEL BRUCE: Fame?

LUCY: No.

ANGEL BRUCE: Ageless timeless beauty?

LUCY: No.

ANGEL BRUCE: Work with me here.

LUCY: I think I am...broken. Can you fix me? I'm ashamed. Can you cover me? I went too far. Can you bring me back? I don't know what I'm doing. Can you teach me? I've seen something awful. Can you make it go away? I'm dirty. Can you clean me? I left skin on the road. Can you patch me up? I'm lost. Can you find me?

ANGEL BRUCE: In the name of the Holy Spirit, a Holy No.

LUCY: He hit me.

ANGEL BRUCE: Yes.

LUCY: He hurt me.

ANGEL BRUCE: Yes.

LUCY: He scared me.

ANGEL BRUCE: Yes.

LUCY: I can't breathe.

ANGEL BRUCE: Yes.

LUCY: It was my fault.

ANGEL BRUCE: It just feels that way.

LUCY: And I still can't stop. Sometimes my steps are so big, I can tell that the earth is round. I've covered miles, regions, states, mountain ranges, rivers, lakes and jet streams. I still haven't found it and I'm running out of room.

ANGEL BRUCE: And?

LUCY: I have vivid dreams of a killer. She moves and kills and I dream of her in black and white and in full color and in silence and in Dolby stereo. And I'm afraid.

ANGEL BRUCE: Of what?

LUCY: Of where she's taking me and what I'll find when I get there. I want to go backwards. I want to erase the tape. I can't do this anymore. Can you help me?

ANGEL BRUCE: I— I don't know.

LUCY: Try.

(Angel Bruce goes to her.)

ANGEL BRUCE: Oh, Lucy.

I bless your blue veins.

I bless your big steps.

I bless your lost compass.

I bless you for your brave mileage.

You're almost there.

Follow the curve to the right body.
To the big love.
I anoint, baptize and bless you.
Oh Lucy
Lucy
Lucy
Oh.
Can you move?
LUCY: Yes.
ANGEL BRUCE: Will you move?
LUCY: In the name of the Holy Spirit, a Holy Yes.
(Angel Bruce kisses her on the forehead. She is blessed.)

End of scene.

THIRTEEN

It's a deep blue night in San Francisco. Lucy finds her way to a park bench. She notices That Woman sitting next to her, knitting.

LUCY: It's you.
THAT WOMAN: Get lost.
LUCY: I know you.
THAT WOMAN: No you don't.
LUCY: Yes I do.
THAT WOMAN: No you don't.
LUCY: We met. A long time ago. In a different place.
THAT WOMAN: No we didn't.
LUCY: I know you.
THAT WOMAN: No you don't.
LUCY: I recognize you.
THAT WOMAN: Impossible. I've had complete reconstructive surgery.
LUCY: You're That Woman.
THAT WOMAN: My name is Peggy Papsi. I'm married to an insurance guy. I have two kids and a dog. I'm suburban. I'm fine. I'm normal. I'm on the PTA. I do bake sales. So don't fuck with me. Fuck off. You don't fucking know me. You never fucking saw me. And if you fucking keep insisting, I'll fuck with you.

I'm going to knit now.

I came here to relax. My husband's on the phone and the kids are on Ritalin. Dropped a stitch. Goddammit.

LUCY: You seem tense.

THAT WOMAN: I'm fine. Fuck off.

LUCY: You.

THAT WOMAN: Me what?

LUCY: You...you know.

THAT WOMAN: Me fuck off?

LUCY: Yeah. How could you go get married and all that?

THAT WOMAN: You're pushing my buttons, Bambi.

LUCY: But you're my hero, my idol. You never settled and you never slowed down. I love that. You swagger. Inside. I love that. You kept moving and you weren't afraid. I love that. You're everything I'm not. I love that.

You got under my skin, on my mind, in my sleep. And I kept moving, like you. Place to place, like you. Looking for the love of my life. And you said don't stop.

THAT WOMAN: I never said that. Prove I said that. I never said that.

LUCY: Liar. So I didn't. I didn't stop. And now look at me. Look at you.

THAT WOMAN: You got it all wrong. Everyone had it wrong. All I wanted to do was stop. But not here. I was going to build rockets, you know. I wanted to be the star of stellar phenomena, but I was a problem because I was a scientist who believed in magic.

I was furious. Furious by destiny. The day I taught myself to make a fist, they told me to sip my tea. When I beat my chest, they told me to cross my legs. Fuck. That.

Whoever the hell you are, know this. I am brilliant. And that is pure energy. Energy doesn't disappear. Can't disappear. No matter what the courts say. No matter what the doctors say. It's nature, it's science, it's out of my hands.

Then one day I was looking at the sky and Polaris said hello. Orion said it's nice up here. Scorpio said we saved a place for you. And I knew where I needed to be. Past the fifth sky is seventh heaven.

Is that Ursa Major or Ursa Minor?

LUCY: It's the Golden Gate, I think.

THAT WOMAN: I'm a little rusty.

LUCY: I needed to find you. I need to know. What did it take to stop you? A car chase? A fight? A knife? A bullet? Someone so magnificent?

THAT WOMAN: Thought it would take a rocket but it only took a rock, someone who'd hold my hand when we crossed the street.

LUCY: That's all?

THAT WOMAN: No.

LUCY: Is there such a thing as a perfect love?

THAT WOMAN: You're asking *me*?

LUCY: Yeah.

> *(That Woman thinks. Hard.)*

THAT WOMAN: Absolutely.

> *(Lucy sighs. Relief.)*

THAT WOMAN: Just depends on how many flaws you're willing to put up with.

> *(Lucy sighs.)*

THAT WOMAN: Before I was furious, I was afraid. Like an animal, like a baby.
That feeling. I hated it. Sometimes I miss it.

> *(She knits a few stitches.)*

THAT WOMAN: The earth spins a little slower now. The riot's gone.
It's almost quiet. But not quite. Some days when I'm driving I look in the
mirror and everything I've done is right behind me, screaming and gain-
ing. That's what it's like on a bad day. But I have good days, too. My best
days are nights when I sit on my porch and look at the sky. The people I
love are sleeping inside my house. I guard them and look at the stars.
I know I can still throw sparks. Still launch myself if I have to. Live up
there if I want. But not now. I'm gonna stay here for awhile. *(Noticing
Lucy staring at her.)* What are you looking at? Quit staring at me. Freak.

LUCY: You are just so different.

THAT WOMAN: What did you expect?

LUCY: Something else.

THAT WOMAN: Disappointed?

LUCY: Maybe. A little.

THAT WOMAN: Hey. Look. There. It's the Big Dipper.

LUCY: It's the lights from Alcatraz.

THAT WOMAN: Oh. Yeah. Guess it is.

> *(They sit.)*

THAT WOMAN: I'm not what you expected. I'm not what *I* expected.

> *(That Woman exits. Lucy is alone.)*

LUCY: I know.

(A Park Janitor comes by, picking up garbage with one of those long poles. He works his way over to Lucy and picks up all the garbage around her.

He gestures to the bench as if to ask "Mind if I sit there?"
She gestures "Go ahead."
He sits.

He pulls a handful of sunflower seeds out of his pocket. Eats a few. He's just enjoying the view, happy as a clam.
He offers her some seeds. She accepts.
They sit. And eat. And chew.

He starts to hum a song. He's just a happy guy.
After a bit, she starts to hum. But it's a different song.

They hum, each doing their own thing, and chewing on seeds.

Her mood starts to change, lift.
Somehow, their two songs blend into a third that they hum together.
It's not a romantic duet—simply a nice groove.

The tune ends.
He's still in a good mood—and now she is, too.

He wipes his hands and stands up to leave.
He shakes her hand and bows.
She smiles.
He smiles.
He walks away, picking up garbage, humming a song.)

LUCY: I am moving.
    I cross the fault line.
    Shock.
    Aftershock.
    I hit the beach and keep going.
    Water up my thighs
    up my belly.
    I try to float but I sink.

Like a rock.
And I make a little rock sound that sounds like:
"Now."
And the voice bounces back—
"Kick," she says.
"Stroke," she says.
"Swim."
The shock from my body makes waves in the ocean
because energy doesn't disappear.
It's transferred, it's a force, it's nature, it's science.
It's out of my hands.
I breathe.
I'm on my back on the surface.
Looking at the sky.

END OF PLAY

Flaming Guns of the Purple Sage
A "B"Western Horror Flick for the Stage
by Jane Martin

Copyright © 2001 by Jane Martin. All rights reserved. CAUTION: Professionals and amateurs are hereby warned that *Flaming Guns of the Purple Sage* is subject to a royalty. It is fully protected under the copyright laws of the United States of America and of all countries covered by the International Copyright Union (including the Dominion of Canada and the rest of the British Commonwealth), the Berne Convention, the Pan-American Copyright Convention and the Universal Copyright Convention, as well as all countries with which the United States has reciprocal copyright relations. All rights, including professional, amateur stage rights, motion picture, recitation, lecturing, public reading, radio broadcasting, television, video or sound recording, all other forms of mechanical or electronic reproduction, such as CD-ROM, CD-I, information storage and retrieval systems and photocopying, and the rights of translation into foreign languages, are strictly reserved. Particular emphasis is laid upon the matter of readings, permission for which must be secured from the Author's agent in writing.

ALL INQUIRIES CONCERNING RIGHTS, INCLUDING AMATEUR RIGHTS, SHOULD BE ADDRESSED TO: ALEXANDER SPEER, ACTORS THEATRE OF LOUISVILLE, 316 WEST MAIN ST., LOUISVILLE, KY 40202

BIOGRAPHY

Jane Martin returned to ATL with her latest play following her premiere of *Anton in Show Business*, winner of the American Theatre Critics Assocation Award for Best New Play in 2000, at the 2000 Humana Festival. Ms. Martin, a Kentuckian, first came to national attention for *Talking With*, a collection of monologues premiering in the 1982 Humana Festival. Since its New York premiere at the Manhattan Theatre Club in 1982, *Talking With* has been performed around the world, winning the Best Foreign Play of the Year award in Germany from *Theater Heute* magazine. Ms. Martin's *Keely and Du*, which premiered in the 1993 Humana Festival, was nominated for the Pulitzer Prize in drama and won the American Theatre Critics Association Award for Best New Play in 1996. Her other work includes: *Mr. Bundy* (1998 Humana Festival), *Middle-Aged White Guys* (1995 Humana Festival), *Cementville* (1991 Humana Festival) and *Vital Signs* (1990 Humana Festival). Ms. Martin's work has been translated into Spanish, French, German, Dutch, Russian and several other languages.

HUMANA FESTIVAL PRODUCTION

Flaming Guns of the Purple Sage premiered at the Humana Festival of New American Plays in March 2001. It was directed by Jon Jory with the following cast:

Big 8	Phyllis Somerville
Rob Bob	Leo Kittay
Shedevil	Monica Koskey
Shirl	Peggity Price
Black Dog	Mark Mineart
Baxter Blue	William McNulty
Memphis Donnie Pride	Atticus Rowe

and with the following production staff:

Scenic Designer	Paul Owen
Costume Designer	Lindsay W. Davis
Lighting Designer	Amy Appleyard
Sound Designer	Mark R. Walston
Fight Supervisor	Drew Fracher
Production Stage Manager	Paul Mills Holmes
Assistant Stage Manager	Amber D. Martin
Dramaturg	Michael Bigelow Dixon
Assistant Dramaturg	Brendan Healy
Casting	Laura Richin

CHARACTERS

BIG 8

ROB BOB

SHEDEVIL

SHIRL

BLACK DOG

BAXTER BLUE

MEMPHIS DONNIE PRIDE

Monica Koskey, Mark Mineart, William McNulty, Phyllis Somerville,
Leo Kittay, and Peggity Price in *Flaming Guns of the Purple Sage*

25th Annual Humana Festival of New American Plays
Actors Theatre of Louisville, 2001
photo by Richard Trigg

Flaming Guns of the Purple Sage

ACT I – Scene 1

A kitchen in a small $40,000 house built in the 50s, in Casper, Wyoming. There are two posters of early cowboy movies on the wall, and a stitched "Home Sweet Home." The only unusual feature is a butcher-block island in the middle of an otherwise working-class, run-down space. There are beer cans scattered about and a new six-pack (with two missing) on the island. It's 3:00AM, and Rob sits at the island chugging a beer and perusing the maga-zine Western Screen. *He is a good looking 26, and the youngest rodeo rider to have won the "World's Top Cowboy" silver buckle. He is recovering from back and leg injuries inflicted by a rodeo fall. Big 8, a substantial woman of 48, an ex-rodeo star and expansive personality, carries a beer and is cooking up bacon and eggs in a frying pan on the stove. She is, as usual, in the midst of a rodeo reminiscence. A storm, lightning and all, rages outside.*

BIG 8: Yeah, cowboy, the rodeo it's gone to hell in a hand basket. *(She chugs the rest of her beer, as does Rob. She has a spatula in her other hand. Thunder!)*
  All sold out to the corporations. Guy in a banker suit finally called me in, said, "Lurlene…" "Hold it," I said, "who's this Lurlene? Round here they call me Big 8."
ROB: Yeah, boy.
BIG 8: "Well, Big 8," says he, "my name's Wallace." "Well, that's a real sur-prise to me," I said, "'cause everybody here just calls you dumbass." My, he laughed real big, slapped his big ol' desk an' then he said I wasn't suit-able for the rodeo no more. Said they was lookin' for another type, some-thin' a little more in the showgirl line.
ROB: *(Digging into his breakfast.)* Yummy, yummy.

BIG 8: Ol' Wallace said ridin' an' ropin' wasn't the thing to him. Talked on about floats, costumes, chor-eog-aphy.

ROB: Oh, yeah!

BIG 8: ...Astro-dirt! Dust free. Artificial damn dirt, honey, Lord have mercy! If I was a man, I woulda pissed on his shoe. Said he'd give me a lifetime pass, though. Said I could come to his rodeo anytime I wanted. Pissed me off. From that day to this, I just stay pissed off all the time. *(He nods. He's heard it before. He picks up the* Western Screen.*)* You hear what I'm sayin'? *(She looks at him immersed in the magazine. She takes a slug of beer and then knocks the magazine out of his hands and across the room.)*

ROB: Hey!

BIG 8: Hey what?

ROB: I'm just checkin' facts, okay?

BIG 8: An' what facts would those be?

ROB: Facts on Gabby Hayes.

BIG 8: Good Lord, Rob Bob, we got that settled afore dinner.

ROB: I'm just sayin'...

BIG 8: You got your sidekicks ass-betwixt an' backwards.

ROB: *(Frustrated. Louder.)* Dude, Gabby Hayes didn't come on as Hoppy's sidekick 'til *Moon Over the Mojave.*

BIG 8: Big wrong.

ROB: Gollee, it was still Burt Smoot.

BIG 8: Burt Smoot? Burt Smoot?! Gabby was on three pictures before that.

ROB: Darn-a-doodle, Big 8, Smoot's finale was *Guns of Thunder.*

BIG 8: Smoot's last sidekick was *Hoppy Serves a Writ!* An' that picture wasn't worth heifer piss. *(Big thunder. He goes to the windows. A silence. She picks up.)* Whatcha lookin' at?

ROB: Just lookin'.

(He turns and stares out the window again.)

BIG 8: Gittin' antsy, huh?

ROB: Boy my age jest wants to be up and doin'.

BIG 8: Hey.

ROB: Hey what?

BIG 8: You wouldn't jes' walk off on me, would you? *(He doesn't answer.)* 'Cause, cowboy, I'd take that right unkindly. *(He looks back out the window.)* You hear me?

ROB: Yes, ma'am.

BIG 8: An' don't never, ever or forever call me ma'am.

(He nods.)

ROB: You my healin' angel, ladybird.

BIG 8: Walk on it full for me. *(He walks.)* 'Zat yer full weight?

ROB: *(Walking.)* I ain't comin' off 'er at all.

BIG 8: Got a little hip hitch in there still.

ROB: Shoot.

BIG 8: Six more weeks.

ROB: Six more weeks!? I got to get busy in my life. You show me where John Wayne spent six weeks sittin' himself around.

BIG 8: Hey, who's the number one rodeo healer on the circuit, Rob Bob?

ROB: You are.

BIG 8: *(Unbuttoning his shirt)* Don't need no x-ray machine when you got me. *(Kisses his chest.)*

ROB: Hey, that there tickles.

BIG 8: Now, it's s'posed to tickle, ain't it?
(She reaches for his belt buckle, undoes it.)

ROB: Come on, girlfrien', that ain't right in the kitchen.
(He steps back and turns to the window, buttoning himself up.)

BIG 8: 'Zat so?

ROB: Well, every room's got a purpose, don't it? Come on now. Rainin' frogs out there, man.

BIG 8: When it's sunny, I miss the rodeo.

ROB: *(Finishing buttoning.)* You in the hall of fame, babe.

BIG 8: Hall of damn fame ain't the rodeo.

ROB: Dude, you cain't ride rodeo all yer life. *(Turns her to him.)* You rode till you was forty years old!

BIG 8: Don't never say that number. I mean it now, Rob Bob, don't never.

ROB: Sorry, ma'am.

BIG 8: An' do not, damnit, call me ma'am! *(He moves away from her.)* Hey? *(He doesn't turn.)* Rob Bob Silverado, Top Cowboy, '98. Hand me over yer belt, boy. *(He does.)* Ain't no buckle has that heft, is there? *(Holds the belt up, looking at the buckle.)* Oooooo, baby, ain't you pretty. There's still ten thousand cowboys, but there's but one buckle looks like this. You jes' that little bit different that makes all the difference, ain't you? *(There is a knock at the door.)* Hell, it's 3:00 AM.

ROB: Three-thirty.
(Knock repeats.)

BIG 8: You git the door an' I'll get the shotgun.

(Knock repeats. Takes shotgun off the wall. Gets cartridges from a drawer.)

ROB: Say when, 8.

(Knock repeats. She chambers the cartridges.)

BIG 8: If that's State Land agents come to foreclose my property, they'll by God have to clean 'em up with a tweezers. *(Knock repeats. Closes the shotgun. Shoulders it.)* Okay, Rob Bob, let's git us a big look.

(Rob pulls the door open. A young girl, completely drenched, wearing Army fatigue pants and an odd leopard print blouse, wrapped in a sodden blanket, stands there. She has many piercings, a couple of tattoos, electric pink short hair, one long glove and carries a duffel bag.)

SHEDEVIL: *(She speaks a strange tongue.)* Ca-ching, eeeyow, kaboom!

BIG 8: *(A moment.)* You an American citizen, darlin'?

SHEDEVIL: I'm…kaboom, schwang…looking for Lucifer Lee. Thwang, splat?

ROB: Holy mackerel.

SHEDEVIL: Doing!

BIG 8: She got a little problem.

ROB: *(Admiringly.)* She does.

SHEDEVIL: Just, rat-tat-tat-tat-tat, happens when I'm nervous.

ROB: Oh, I get nervous, too.

BIG 8: Oh.

SHEDEVIL: Is this number 125 West Hacienda?

BIG 8: Child, do you wear a watch or carry a timepiece of any kind?

SHEDEVIL: I'm wet through.

ROB: She's wet through, Big 8.

BIG 8: *(Who has lowered the shotgun.)* All right, step in an' say your piece.

SHEDEVIL: You Lucifer Lee's mama? Big 8?

BIG 8: Could be.

SHEDEVIL: I met him…bam!…when he was singin' at the La Cienega Best Western Motel Sparkle Lounge. Let me crash in the suite they put him up in. He had a driftwood lamp by his bed carved to look just like Lucille Ball.

ROB: You know, you got a bunch of metal stuck in yer face.

SHEDEVIL: Yeah.

BIG 8: Looks like a junkyard.

(Her piercings.)

SHEDEVIL: Thanks.

ROB: You take off your blanket an' I'll git you a towel.

(He exits.)

SHEDEVIL: Waka-waka-waka-waka.

BIG 8: Jes' take 'er easy now.

SHEDEVIL: We stayed in the Best Western 14 weeks, then I told Lucifer I was knocked up, so we drove up to Vegas an' had a real nice ceremony at the Wee Chapel of Jesus Resurgent.

BIG 8: You kiddin', huh?

SHEDEVIL: *(Shaking her head.)* My daddy runs it.

BIG 8: Yeah, well, Lucifer always liked to git married.

SHEDEVIL: Three days later, I woke up. He'd packed up his Mel Tormé records and split.

BIG 8: Lucifer Lee has a dog's taste in music.

SHEDEVIL: You ever hear of Mel Tormé?

(Rob re-enters.)

ROB: Gotcha a towel.

SHEDEVIL: Ga-boing.

(He hands it to her, taking the wet blanket and hanging it on the stairs.)

ROB: I'm Rob Bob by the way.

(He holds out his hand; she takes it gingerly.)

SHEDEVIL: Go a little easy, I got a plastic hand.

ROB: *(Going really easy.)* Oh, sure.

BIG 8: How'd you get a plastic hand?

SHEDEVIL: Look, Lucifer's not the first guy split on me.

(Puts her hand to her forehead.)

ROB: You okay?

SHEDEVIL: *(Waves him off.)* So, one night while he was doing his lounge act, I got this address from his address book.

BIG 8: I haven't heard nothin' from Lucifer in three years, darlin'.

SHEDEVIL: You mean he's not here?

ROB: Not here.

SHEDEVIL: He has to be here, godamnit!

BIG 8: Well, darlin'…

SHEDEVIL: I hitchhiked 1500 miles.

BIG 8: Long gone.

(Shedevil stands staring at them and then, suddenly, collapses in a faint.)

ROB: Damn.

BIG 8: Well, this is real nice.

ROB: *(Goes to her.)* Littlebit? You okay girl?

BIG 8: Really needed this.

ROB: Lemme' get her up, over to a chair, Big 8.

BIG 8: Well, don't get no lice on you.

ROB: Stick her right by the kitchen table. I'll get her a wake-up call.

(Pours her a drink from a pint bottle of whiskey.)

BIG 8: What's all them noises she makes?

ROB: *(Shrugs.)* Maybe she's Catholic.

BIG 8: *(Not sold.)* Okay.

ROB: *(Regarding her.)* Now, what color would you call that hair?

BIG 8: Throwed-up strawberry milkshake.

ROB: Listen, you believe she's with child?

BIG 8: Question is, who put the roast in the oven?

ROB: Golly! Ol' Lucifer.

BIG 8: See, we don't know that.

ROB: Them two is married!

BIG 8: Baby, jes' cause you an angel on earth don't mean the devil ain't workin'.

(Shedevil opens her eyes.)

ROB: Looky there! Hello, li'l darlin'.

SHEDEVIL: Kerthunk. Boom.

ROB: Get you a glass a water.

BIG 8: You okay?

SHEDEVIL: How the hell would I know?

(Starts to rise. Big 8 puts a hand on her shoulder.)

BIG 8: Stay sit.

SHEDEVIL: Walked the last few miles.

(Rob re-enters with water.)

BIG 8: How far's that?

(Takes glass from Rob, puts it in the girl's hand.)

SHEDEVIL: Bison's Hole.

ROB: Bison's Hole!

BIG 8: Girl, that's twenty-seven mile.

(Gives her a drink.)

SHEDEVIL: *(Suddenly irate, aggressive and loud.)* Well, what the hell am I sup-posed to do?! I'm hitchhiking, okay! *(On her feet.)* Yo, twenty-two rides from L.A. to wherever the hell I was when I started walking. And hey, yo, excuse me, I'm pregnant!

ROB: Who

SHEDEVIL: Your baby boy owes me 17,000 bucks, okay! Plus, excuse me, he took my...gaboom...comic book collection, Disc Man, my charm bracelet, my ecstasy stash, an' hey, yo, I'm wet, okay!!

(She starts crying and sits.)

ROB: Well, gollee, darlin'.

BIG 8: *(To Rob, pointing to the stairs.)* Git.

ROB: Well, darn-a-doodle, Big 8…

BIG 8: You get up those stairs!

ROB: Okay, I'm goin'.

BIG 8: Move it or lose it!

ROB: *(Disappearing.)* Geez Louise.

BIG 8: *(To Shedevil.)* Y'see that whiskey on the table. *(Shedevil looks.)* Slug on it.

SHEDEVIL: You got any Kaluha?

BIG 8: I said drink it down! *(Shedevil does.)* Lord, I got me a headache. Strip off that sweatshirt.

SHEDEVIL: Doogie, doogie, kapow.

BIG 8: An' don't go makin' them noises.

SHEDEVIL: Eeeeeyow!

BIG 8: Looky here, I ain't your mama. I ain't into no "alternative lifestyles." I got problems of m'own, okay? I got mortgages, I got arthritis, got my cowboy lookin' at yer little pointy tits, it's 3:00 AM, an' why the hell should I believe you're carryin' Lucifer Lee's baby anyhow?!

SHEDEVIL: *(Holding out her glass.)* Can I have some more?

BIG 8: No, you can't! Now I got questions girl, and you prevaricate on me I'll drop-kick you out on the highway, let you get hit by lightnin'. There was a hitchhiker up here got hit by lightnin' they didn't find nothin' but his contact lenses an' his foreskin. *(Shedevil starts to blubber.)* Hell, here… *(Pours another hit in Shedevil's glass.)* Now. Numero uno: what shape is the mole on the inside of Lucifer Lee's thigh?

SHEDEVIL: Looks like a purple rose.

BIG 8: Middle initial?

SHEDEVIL: X for Xavier.

BIG 8: What's the signature tune in his lounge act?

SHEDEVIL: "I Did it My Way!"

BIG 8: Lord, I hate that song!

SHEDEVIL: *(On the attack.)* First thing he eats?

BIG 8: Snickers bar.

SHEDEVIL: Has he ever, ever, ever done it in anything but the missionary position?

BIG 8: How the hell would I know?

SHEDEVIL: Well, I lived it! An' the answer's no!!

(The two women stare at each other.)

BIG 8: I ain't takin' you in.

SHEDEVIL: You think I care?

BIG 8: Where's your wedding ring?

SHEDEVIL: Didn't buy me one.

BIG 8: What the hell'd you give him $17,000 for?

SHEDEVIL: 'Cause I'm a damned fool!

(She knocks back the whiskey.)

BIG 8: How'd you get $17,000?

SHEDEVIL: I screwed R.V. salesmen for an escort service.

BIG 8: *(Shocked.)* That ain't no all-American way.

SHEDEVIL: You asked me, Mama hick.

BIG 8: Don't be callin' me "hick," child. Rode me barrel races front of the Queen of England. You want a place to lay your head, you damn well respect me.

SHEDEVIL: Thwack!

(A standoff.)

BIG 8: You got a good size cut up in your hairline.

SHEDEVIL: Yeah.

BIG 8: Nasty lookin'; how'd you git it?

SHEDEVIL: Fell down walkin'.

BIG 8: Sit. *(Shedevil stares.)* When I say sit, you sit. *(She does.)* Rob Bob!

ROB: *(Offstage.)* Yeah?

BIG 8: Run me down a needle an' thread.

ROB: *(Offstage.)* Okay.

SHEDEVIL: "Rob Bob?"

BIG 8: Yeah. An' while we're on that subject, just who the hell are you?

SHEDEVIL: Shedevil.

BIG 8: Nah, I mean, what's your name?

SHEDEVIL: Shedevil.

BIG 8: What's yer daddy's name?

SHEDEVIL: Front Load.

BIG 8: What's yer mama's name?

SHEDEVIL: Meretorius.

BIG 8: We're just gonna move on past this, hon.

(Rob shows up with the needle and thread.)

ROB: Here you go.

BIG 8: Sit back, I'm just gonna sew up your head.

SHEDEVIL: Sew up my head?

BIG 8: Yeah.

SHEDEVIL: Nuh-uh.

BIG 8: Rob Bob, give her the chewin' stick.

SHEDEVIL: Look, it's just a little cut and...

BIG 8: Nine, ten stitches, we don't take care of it, yer like to get an infected brain.

SHEDEVIL: I don't want anybody stickin' needles...

(Big 8 sticks the "chewing stick" in her mouth, silencing her. Shedevil rises.)

BIG 8: Hold her still, Rob Bob. *(Rob Bob sits her down and holds her.)* When I'm cuttin' or sewin', there ain't nothin' like a chewin' stick. *(Shedevil makes sounds. Big 8 goes to work.)*

ROB: She's real good, Littlebit. Gonna fix you right up.

BIG 8: *(Big 8 sews. Shedevil makes muffled pain sounds.)* Now, you ain't should've got mixed up with Lucifer Lee. Hold still. Twenty-seven years old, an' been married four times I know of. *(Shedevil spits out the stick. Big 8 picks it up.)*

Now girl, we gonna put you out with a wooden mallet you don't suck it up. *(Sticks the chewing stick back in.)* Wipe that blood off, Rob Bob, so I can see where I'm at. *(He does.)* As to him stealin' your money, it wouldn't be the first time...steady now...not knockin' you up neither...hell, that's his damn hobby. Now, this might hurt some. *(She sews. Shedevil makes muffled sounds.)* Don't go messin' me up. *(Feeling pain, Shedevil wrenches to the right.)* Dang! Okay, smarty, now I got the needle stuck in your eyelid. Git aholt, will you Rob Bob?

SHEDEVIL: *(Big 8 removes it.)* Ow.

ROB: Had me aholt.

SHEDEVIL: Off me!

BIG 8: Well, git you a bigger holt! Damn, I hate sloppy work.

SHEDEVIL: Let go of me.

BIG 8: Girl, I'm a healer. Lay my hands on a fracture or break...

SHEDEVIL: Ow!

BIG 8: Sit still an' sit quiet! ...that break'll knit up maybe twice as fast as a doctor could do. Stop twitchin'. Healin' just come on me, I didn't no way go lookin' for it.

ROB: You gone be all right.

BIG 8: Now, Rob Bob here is defendin' his World's Top Cowboy title...look up now... an' he's broke up off a fall in nine pieces I can feel. Top a' that,

I'm a full-time cheese grater for Beatrice Foods down the road...last stitch...what I'm sayin' here...got it. *(She leans in and cuts the thread with her teeth and then steps back.)* How's that feel?

ROB: Feels good, huh?

SHEDEVIL: *(Amazed.)* It feels good.

ROB: Don't hurt, huh?

SHEDEVIL: Feels real good.

ROB: See?

BIG 8: What I'm sayin' here is I can't provide no surcease for your storm, girl.

ROB: Gol-lee...

BIG 8: Now the Rainbow Trail Motel down three mile got perpetual vacancies, an' ol' Rob can run you down there, end of story, amen.

ROB: That's pretty cold, Big 8.

BIG 8: You worry about your own self.

SHEDEVIL: Hey! I got $24, that's what I got.

BIG 8: Uh-huh.

> *(Turns back to Rob.)*

SHEDEVIL: $24! Stitched up head, walking to nowhere through nowhere, an' Black Dog's coming.

BIG 8: Girl...

SHEDEVIL: BLACK DOG!

ROB: Whazat?

SHEDEVIL: He's a Ukrainian, one-eyed Hells Angel's biker.

ROB: What's a Ukrainian?

SHEDEVIL: See, when Lucifer split, I met Black Dog in a Pep Boys. I don't know...fifteen minutes later, we were screwin' in a dumpster. Stayed with him awhile, an' he's got this dumb idea I took $ 9,000 of his stupid cocaine money.

ROB: But...

SHEDEVIL: He's the one chopped off my hand!

BIG 8: Doubly glad to have you for a houseguest.

ROB: So, he's bad?

SHEDEVIL: Bad what?

ROB: Okay, there's good guys an' bad guys, okay?

SHEDEVIL: I saw him bite the head off a cat.

ROB: Well, that's rough.

SHEDEVIL: Stabbed some cop who spit on his hog. Killed two bikers from the Idaho Skulls with a pool cue and a No. 6 power stapler.

ROB: Okay, that's a bad guy, see.

SHEDEVIL: Yeah, well, he'll be by here soon.

BIG 8: She's goin' to the Rainbow Trail.

ROB: You think Roy or Gene or Randolph or the Duke would leave her unaccompanied with this Black Dog comin' on? That ain't the Cowboy Code.

BIG 8: An' she ain't my deal.

ROB: Gollee, jes' look at her, with child, shiverin', wet, cut-up, degraded by life an' too much time in California. We got hearts as big as the west, Big 8.

BIG 8: Listen here, Shedevil.

SHEDEVIL: Yes, ma'am.

ROB: You got the majesty of the mountains lookin' at you.

BIG 8: Will you bite your tongue?! *(A moment.)* Okay, you can sleep out front in the hammock.

ROB: Yeah boy!

SHEDEVIL: Outside?

BIG 8: Don't keep no hammock in the house.

SHEDEVIL: It's pouring rain.

BIG 8: Got a nice view, though.

SHEDEVIL: I left my address book...Black Dog...

BIG 8: Ain't my problem, darlin'.

SHEDEVIL: An' if he rides in?

BIG 8: I was you, I'd run for the trees. *(To Rob.)* Go pull her off a blanket.

ROB: *(Fascinated.)* Why'd he cut off your hand?

SHEDEVIL: I was jerkin' off some rock star, and Black Dog cut it off with a hatchet.

ROB: Holy moley!

BIG 8: Well, I sure needed to hear that.

SHEDEVIL: Thwack!

(Lights fade.)

Scene 2

The next morning around 7:30. Big 8 making coffee and cleaning. Shirl, Big 8's sister, an attractively blowsy woman of forty, has just entered. She carries a somewhat bloody package of spare ribs.

SHIRL: An the Viagra just made his thumbs swell up.

BIG 8: Poor ol' Baxter.

SHIRL: Poor ol' Baxter? What about your poor ol' sister?

BIG 8: He's a good ol' boy.

SHIRL: He's a limp ol' boy, is what he is…

(Searches in her bag.)

BIG 8: Shirl, don't go drippin' blood on my linoleum.

SHIRL: *(Pulls out a couple of letters and hands them to Big 8.)* Sis, you didn't pick up your mail. Honeybunch, pour me a cupper, wil'ya? *(Runs a hand along the kitchen island.)* This turned out nice, didn't it? How much that old man charge?

BIG 8: Died before he could send a bill.

SHIRL: Well, there's bad luck an' good luck. Sis, I was thinkin', you get foreclosed on…'nother sugar…you just come on over, I can set you up with Daddy's ol' iron bed in the living room.

BIG 8: I ain't wakin' up with Baxter.

SHIRL: Don't you worry about Baxter.

BIG 8: Why you keep on with him's a mystery to me.

SHIRL: I don't like rattlin' around a house on my own. Oh-oh.

BIG 8: Oh-oh what?

SHIRL: I did drip a little blood.

BIG 8: Sponge's over by the toaster oven.

SHIRL: Bad ol' me. Say, you know, there's a young girl with stupid hair layin' in your hammock?

BIG 8: Uh-huh. *(Scans a letter brought by Shirl.)* I am not openin' another letter from that bank.

SHIRL: "Uh-huh?" What do you mean "uh-huh?" Who is she?

BIG 8: She woken up?

SHIRL: Said something like "ca-ching" when I walked by.

BIG 8: I don't want to hear about it.

SHIRL: Okey-dokey. *(The presentation.)* So, I brought you some spare ribs!

BIG 8: Shirl, you always bringin' me spare ribs. I got more spare ribs than a herd.

SHIRL: What's the use workin' down to the slaughterhouse I can't bring my sweet little sister spare ribs. Say, listen, you think I should go fer a breast reduction?

BIG 8: Break Baxter's heart.

SHIRL: Oh-oh, I'm still drippin'. Drip, drip, drip.

BIG 8: Will you stick them ribs in the freezer?

(Shirl goes to do it. Big 8 takes the sponge and cleans up.)

SHIRL: How's your little cowboy?

BIG 8: He ain't little an' I ain't little, will you stop callin' everbody little?

SHIRL: Well, I wish you'd send him over to me for about one night. Say, you know how ol' Mr. Dawson cut his finger off with the lawnmower?

BIG 8: *(Knowing what's coming.)* Shirl...

SHIRL: Well, I found it. *(Getting it out of her purse.)* Well, actually, my dog Rusty found it. *(Unwrapping a Kleenex.)* You think it's too late for it to get reattached?

BIG 8: Damn Shirl, that happened last month.

SHIRL: Yeah, it's lookin' a little ragged.

BIG 8: Get that thing away from me. *(Shirl moves to the freezer.)* Don't you go puttin' that in my freezer.

SHIRL: Should I take it over to him?

BIG 8: Put that thing down the disposal!

SHIRL: You think so?

BIG 8: Yes, I think so, do it!! *(Shirl pops it in her mouth.)* My God, Shirl, you gone crazy!

SHIRL: April Fool.

BIG 8: What??

SHIRL: It was just a Vienna sausage I bloodied up a little so we could have some fun!

BIG 8: Jesus, you made my cross too big.

SHIRL: April Fool. Now tell your little sister what that little girl's doin' out there? *(Big 8 explodes with laughter.)* What? What?

BIG 8: That was pretty damn funny, Shirl.

SHIRL: Well, all your troubles, I thought you needed a laugh.

BIG 8: Well, I did. Lord girl, you are stranger than dirt.

SHIRL: Well, you are so nice to say so.

(She jerks her thumb to the door.)

Now, for heavens sake, tell!

BIG 8: If I'm believin' what I'm hearin', that chile seems to be the pregnant fourth wife of Lucifer Lee.

SHIRL: No!

BIG 8: Yeah. It was, maybe, 3:00 AM and...

(Shedevil walks in. She's not in a good mood.)

SHEDEVIL: Okay I use your goddamned john to change my goddamned clothes? *(Shedevil exits to bathroom.)* See how you like bein' rained on all night!

SHIRL: *(Looking after her.)* Well, she's personable.

BIG 8: Sign on her forehead says, "I'm a world of trouble."

SHIRL: *(Pouring herself another cup.)* Oh, I read the sign.

BIG 8: She's bein' pursued across America by some Russian biker with an ax.

SHIRL: Well, you know young people.

BIG 8: All I needed. *(Picks some torn-off signs off the counter.)* Went around rippin' these off m'land. They gonna auction off my property, all but the house.

SHIRL: Well, little girl, you'll still have the house then.

BIG 8: I got horses, Shirl, I got stock.

SHIRL: How much you need?

BIG 8: Six damn thousand.

SHIRL: Lord, I don't have six thousand.

BIG 8: I know you don't have six thousand.

SHEDEVIL: *(Offstage.)* I can't see a damn thing in this mirror!

BIG 8: She can't see a damn thing in the mirror.

SHIRL: That child doesn't look pregnant.

BIG 8: Shirl, I know when a woman's pregnant.

SHEDEVIL: *(Still off.)* An' the toilet don't flush!

BIG 8: You put her brains in a bluebird, it'd fly backwards. Push in on the button!

SHIRL: Now, it's not your job takin' the child in, Sis.

BIG 8: I suppose not.

SHIRL: Time you look out for yourself. I mean it now.

BIG 8: I know you mean it.

SHIRL: Had you two husbands worthless as cat litter. Got you the head injury couldn't rodeo no more. Raised Lucifer Lee so stupid he couldn't roll rocks down a steep hill...

BIG 8: Shirl...

SHIRL: Workin' night shifts and half shifts try to keep this place together...

BIG 8: Okay, Shirl...

SHIRL: Got you a nice boy around the house now, don't go temptin' him with twenty-year-old flesh!

BIG 8: Shirl! Thank you, darlin', I got the point.

SHIRL: *(Going through cabinets.)* You got you any Goo-Goo Clusters?

BIG 8: Fried pie, maybe.

SHIRL: Lord girl, I can't be eatin' fried pie before I slaughter pigs. Now, you do or you don't know where Lucifer's at?

BIG 8: Playin' cocktail piano at some raggedy-ass Holiday Inn, I'd guess.

SHIRL: Little girl, that child should clean up his own damn mess. Where's Lucifer's daddy at?

BIG 8: Well, wherever he is, he's drunk.

SHIRL: *(Jerking her thumb towards the bathroom.)* This is not your deal.

BIG 8: What's she gonna do though?

SHIRL: You choose the pleasure, you pay the measure, babe.

BIG 8: Yeah, but…

SHIRL: No "yeah, buts," girl's rough as hog gristle, she'll keep on tickin'. Hey, you know what I wanna know.

BIG 8: What's that?

SHIRL: *(Pointing upstairs.)* Does that boy go as good as he looks?

BIG 8: *(Grinning.)* Well, he rides hard but fair.

SHIRL: There's many ride hard, but few ride long.

BIG 8: Sister, he can do a night's work.

SHIRL: Ooooo. You givin' me the shivers. *(Checks her watch.)* Whoa! We got to get goin'!

(Shows Big 8 the time.)

BIG 8: Oh my.

SHIRL: You give her some marchin' orders, you hear me? Go on now!

BIG 8: *(Calling.)* Shedevil?

SHEDEVIL: *(Offstage.)* Yeah?

BIG 8: We got to vamanos, me and Shirl. There's biscuits and spoon gravy, you hungry…

SHIRL: An' then out.

BIG 8: Then get you to goin'.

SHEDEVIL: *(Off.)* Can't hear you.

BIG 8: I'm leavin' twenty bucks on the butcher block…

SHIRL: *(Warningly.)* Sister?!

BIG 8: I got no line on Lucifer, sad to say.

SHIRL: Now don't you be 'round here when she gets back!

BIG 8: Shirl, I can do my own dirty work in my own dirty house. *(To the offstage Shedevil.)* Good luck travelin', an' don't be wakin' up Rob Bob, he's healin'.

SHIRL: An' don't be 'round here when she gets back!

BIG 8: *(Irritated, to Shirl.)* Will you fridge those ribs?

SHIRL: I fridged 'em. Don't be cleanin' up. Lord, my supervisor's goin' to fry eggs on his forehead.

BIG 8: Well, come on then.

(They are gone. A moment, and Shedevil enters from the bathroom in a little white dress she picked up in a consignment store. She looks, well, virginal. She looks around; then tries a half-hearted, experimental hail.)

SHEDEVIL: Yo? *(No answer. She walks over to the butcher block and picks up the $20 bill. She looks at it; then holds it up to the overhead light. She sticks it in her blouse. A little louder.)* Yo? *(Still no answer. She stands still, listening, then explodes into action. She opens the kitchen drawers, rummages, shuts them. She opens cabinets, throwing out food items. Nothing she can use. She pulls out a box of cereal, rips it open and pours it out on the butcher block. Nope. She stands thinking and looking at the stairs. She experimentally eats a handful of the cereal dry. She takes off her shoes and moves upstairs. All is quiet and still. She comes back down with a cheap jewelry box in one hand and a shoebox in the other. She opens the jewelry box and pours the contents on the butcher block in among the Cheerios. She picks up a silver ring, holds it up to the light and puts it on. She picks around in the rest of the jewelry, discontent. She picks up one more ring, starts to toss it down, stops, listens. She stands frozen for a moment; then puts the second ring on. She brushes the cereal and jewelry over to the corner of the butcher block to make a clear space. She dumps the shoebox out. It's all silver rodeo buckles, close to two dozen.)* Bingo! *(She picks several up and reads the backs.)* Sterling, sterling, sterling, sterling. Oh, yes.

(She leaves the buckles and goes over to the sink, opening the cabinet below it. She pulls out a box of Hefty tall garbage bags. She takes the bag over to the butcher block and in two or three swipes she gets all the buckles in the bag. She puts the garbage bag on the counter and goes back to the bathroom, emerging with the duffel bag and the clothes she changed out of. Hurriedly, she jams the dirty clothes in her duffel, grabs the garbage bag and heads for the door. Rob appears on the stairs with a silver-plated traditional cowboy six-shooter in his hand. He wears only a jock strap.)

ROB: Turn around real slow. I got you covered. *(She turns. She laughs.)* Excuse me, I was sleepin'. *(She continues to laugh.)* It's the way God made us, okay?

SHEDEVIL: Okay, nutcase, now what?

ROB: Damn, you look pretty. Whew. Lookin' like ice water on a hot day. Darn. I get this. I get what this is. Sure, I recognize it. Oh, man. I seen this in *Bells of Rosarita, Plainsman and the Lady.* By golly, straight out of *Cimarron Petticoats.*

SHEDEVIL: What the hell are you talking about?

ROB: Love at first sight.

SHEDEVIL: Kaboom, whack.

ROB: It happens between the hero and the schoolmarm, or sometimes it's the deceased kindly rancher's daughter an' the travelin' sheriff, has amnesia from the avalanche. *(He's still holding the gun on her.)* Put the bags down, okay? *(She does.)* Never thought it would come on me 'cause I ain't the hero. I'm sort of more the young man the hero befriends. See? 'Cept they usually got their clothes on.

SHEDEVIL: Hey, doofus, I got to find Lucifer Lee and, yo, I can't do it on $20.

ROB: Love at first sight. Boy, it's painful.

SHEDEVIL: What good's a bunch of silver buckles in a shoebox?

ROB: At's all the cowboys Big 8 has healed.

SHEDEVIL: Yeah?

ROB: What's love at first sight feel like to you?

SHEDEVIL: You're retarded, huh?

ROB: Beg your pardon?

(Sound of a motorcycle.)

SHEDEVIL: *(Holds out her hand for silence.)* Motorcycle. *(Rob Bob opens front door.)* No! *(They listen; it approaches; it roars by.)* Wasn't him.

ROB: How'd ya know!

SHEDEVIL: It's some two-bit Japanese bike. Okay, here's the deal. I'll go upstairs with you. Then I leave with the buckles.

ROB: Lord, I 'preciate that, but I'm savin' myself for marriage.

SHEDEVIL: What about Big whatsername?

ROB: Well, that don't count. That's customary.

SHEDEVIL: She screwed every one of these buckles?

ROB: Just a mark a' respect. Like when Gene or Roy tip their hat to the saloon lady when they ride off.

SHEDEVIL: Shazaam!

ROB: Beggin' your pardon, but what's them noises?

SHEDEVIL: Nuthin'.

ROB: Hey, they're somethin'.

SHEDEVIL: Just started when my daddy'd lock me in the basement.

ROB: My daddy locked me in the basement too!

SHEDEVIL: No way.

ROB: Yeah! Well, we didn't have a basement, kinda chained me under the house.

SHEDEVIL: Yeah? How come you sleep in a jock strap?

ROB: I don't like woolly pajamas. Say, I got mucho respect you're huntin' for your husband.

SHEDEVIL: Whatever.

ROB: Sounds like he's bad though.

SHEDEVIL: Like in those movies?

ROB: Yeah. See, there's good people an' bad people, an' funny sidekicks an' the love interests, an' the bystanders, which it don't matter what they are.

SHEDEVIL: *(Sort of charmed.)* Yeah?

ROB: Yeah. Now, the good people, no matter what happens, what they have to do...whatever...they are good people, an' the bad people, they're bad.

SHEDEVIL: So what am I in the movie?

ROB: Schoolmarm.

SHEDEVIL: I look like a schoolmarm?

ROB: You look real nice in that white dress.

SHEDEVIL: What about me takin' the buckles?

ROB: It's real sweet 'cause you're doin' it fer your unborn child. Now, if you were one of the bad people, it would be bad to do it.

SHEDEVIL: You're goofy as hell, huh?

ROB: I guess.

SHEDEVIL: Listen, can I ask you a question?

ROB: Yes, ma'am.

SHEDEVIL: Does it bother you talkin' to me bareass?

ROB: Guess I mainly forgot about it. *(Looks down at himself.)* Didn't mean no harm.

SHEDEVIL: It's okay. *(A pause; they look at each other.)* Cowboy, what the hell are we going to do now?

ROB: Well, in a love-at-first-sight deal, we could do a little kiss. Nothin' real involved.

SHEDEVIL: I don't have the love-at-first-sight deal.

ROB: Shore you do. 'Member back now. I came round the corner. Our eyes met like. It was real still.

SHEDEVIL: You scared me pissless.

ROB: It feels like that.

SHEDEVIL: You were pointing the gun!

ROB: That jes' gives the love scene a little pep. Little originality. It's still a damn love scene. Looky here...you go to the movie an' there's a boy an' a girl...you followin' me?

SHEDEVIL: You know, you're talking when we could be screwing.

ROB: Ummm, no, I didn't know that.

SHEDEVIL: You nervous or what?

ROB: Well, sort of am, yeah.

SHEDEVIL: Okay, kiss me then.

ROB: You don't mind I'm in the buff?

SHEDEVIL: I can deal with it.

ROB: I'm jus' gonna kiss the outside of yer lips now.

SHEDEVIL: Okay.

ROB: Real easy like.

SHEDEVIL: Okay.

ROB: Tilt your head up.

SHEDEVIL: Shut up, okay?

ROB: Okay. *(He moves toward her, putting the six-shooter on the butcher block as he comes. He stops a step from her.)* Close your eyes.

SHEDEVIL: I don't close my eyes.

ROB: You sure?

SHEDEVIL: I'm sure.

ROB: Well, people got to get used to each other.

SHEDEVIL: Smack!

(She puts her arms around his neck.)

ROB: Smack right back atcha.

(They kiss gently.)

(Lights fade.)

Scene 3

Rob is now wearing a pair of jeans but is still naked to the waist. Shedevil wears his western shirt, but her legs are bare. The two sit, legs crossed under them, on the butcher block island in the center of the kitchen. They are pass-ing a quart of orange juice back and forth and eating from a bag of Reeses Pieces. A motorcycle is heard coming closer.

SHEDEVIL: So, after he hit me, I waited till he was asleep an' then I tied him to the bed an' left my initials in his chest with pushpins. That's when they started calling me Shedevil. *(They stop. The motorcycle roars by.)* Naw, that wasn't his Harley. *(Looks at the walls.)* How come she got the guns?

ROB: Some's family. Use 'em huntin', puttin' down sick stock. Burglars, need 'em if the Chinese come, Democrats try to take over. Citizen got to be armed.

SHEDEVIL: *(Watches him carefully.)* Uh-huh.

ROB: What's your true life name?

SHEDEVIL: I don't tell my name.

ROB: Okay. Shoot, I like a good nickname. All the riders got nicknames. Only me, I don't got one.

SHEDEVIL: When your name's Rob Bob, you don't need one.

ROB: So you're a preacher's daughter, huh?

SHEDEVIL: *(Raises a warning finger.)* Don't go there, mister.

ROB: Okay. *(A brief pause.)* Hey, one thing I like about you is how real your plastic hand looks.

SHEDEVIL: One thing I like about you is you got a lazy eye.

ROB: I do. Left one.

SHEDEVIL: You'll be goin' bald, too.

ROB: Naw.

SHEDEVIL: Yeah. I can tell from the way a guy's hair comes together in front.

ROB: *(A moment.)* It's nice to notice things about each other.

SHEDEVIL: It's okay.

ROB: How come you took up with a biker?

SHEDEVIL: Well, sometimes guys is kind of contiguous. See, one leaves while you're in the 7-Eleven, so you just take another one that's in there.

ROB: Like a relay race.

SHEDEVIL: Yeah. The first night with Black Dog he took me to a Chinese restaurant that had this grandé fish tank, you know, an' he says, "I can catch those fish barehanded, an' swallow them raw."

ROB: Did he do it?

SHEDEVIL: Yeah. It started a hell of a fight. He finally broke the fish tank with a waiter.

ROB: *(Shedevil giggles.)* I once fought nine guys in a Best Western parking lot.

SHEDEVIL: Nine?!

ROB: Yeah. They beat the holy Toledo out of me. *(She laughs.)* You ain't gonna leave with the buckles, are ya?

SHEDEVIL: I can't spend my life sittin' on this butcher block.

ROB: All right then, I got to say my piece. *(He hops down.)* Listen, I don't feel comfortable callin' you Shedevil.

SHEDEVIL: Too bad.

ROB: Well, shoot, okay. Shedevil...I already tol' you I got love at first sight. I'm a aces high bronc rider, bulldogger and Brahma buster. Big 8 heals me up, be maybe the all-time best. See, Shedevil...you're the one, girl. A hero, he mates for life like a swan. He can't be contiguous. Now, I ain't a hero yet, but I'm a good guy…no holds barred on that, so I just got to take it to the next level. And to do that, Shedevil, I need the love of a good woman. I got to have it. Now, hells bells, we both got a ways to go. Listen here, I got to tell the truth an' shame the devil. You got to get rid of that pink pus colored hair…an' we probably got to tone down your lovemakin' some, but we kin git this right, girl. *(She gets off the butcher block and starts retrieving her clothes, which are scattered about.)* Now don't git nervous, I ain't callin' in the preacher, what I'm sayin' here is let's get in practice. See, my hip's healin' real good an' I'm thinkin' I could ask Big 8 could I have a few days off, follow my drift? Shedevil, I got my daddy's huntin' cabin up in the cottonwoods in the Greaser Mountains. Sits real pretty on a bluff. What I'm sayin' is, we could take off from here, ride up there. Big 8, she's got a mare handles soft as butter…hell, it's like ridin' in a Buick…I'm not kiddin'. We could go up there an' git used to each other, see? Go on up there an' practice!

(He is finished. A pause.)

SHEDEVIL: I hate love.

ROB: No you don't.

SHEDEVIL: Yes I do.

ROB: I'm sayin' you don't!

SHEDEVIL: An' I'm sayin' I do!! Hey, I always end up getting treated bad. An' I don't ask for it, okay? Yo, have I asked you to treat me bad?

ROB: No, ma'am. Did I treat you bad?

SHEDEVIL: You will.

ROB: Swear on the bible I won't.

SHEDEVIL: Hey, as soon as the sex wears off, a man's got no idea what to do with you. "What's this?," they say. "How did this get in the house?" "What's it for?" Only thing they can think of is to have you watch 'em do stuff. Black Dog wanted me to watch 'im sleep. Like his old grunts and moans was entertainment. An' when you won't watch 'em, hey, they start treatin' you bad.

ROB: I ain't like that.

SHEDEVIL: The hell you're not.

ROB: I ain't. What I would want is to have you explain things to me. 'Cause most of what goes on, I don't get it. Shoot, that would be paradise to me.

SHEDEVIL: Are you for real?

ROB: Far as I know.

SHEDEVIL: How in hell did you get this way?

ROB: Well, I'm just naturally kind of out of it.

(She considers this phenomenon.)

SHEDEVIL: Lemme show you somethin'.

ROB: You bet. *(She opens her mouth wide. He moves in close to look.)* Holy mackerel, you got a nail through your tongue! Holy mackerel, you want me to take you to the hospital?

SHEDEVIL: Look again.

ROB: It's real shiny and pretty.

SHEDEVIL: You sure it doesn't gross you out?

ROB: *(Working hard.)* You gimme a couple of minutes, I'll like it. *(Revelation.)* Hey, it's sorta like jewelry, huh?

SHEDEVIL: Yeah.

ROB: That's good.

SHEDEVIL: *(That was pretty good. She observes him.)* You notice I'm pregnant?

ROB: Hardly.

SHEDEVIL: I mean, yo, do you mind?

ROB: Why would I mind?

SHEDEVIL: It's nice at your cabin, huh?

ROB: There's antelope.

SHEDEVIL: Kiss me.

ROB: Did once.

SHEDEVIL: Again. *(He moves to her and kisses her gently, chastely, the way one might in an old western. Shedevil pulls back and roars at him.)* I said kiss me! *(She leaps up into his arms with her legs around his waist in a wild kiss. Just at that moment, Big 8 and Shirl enter, home from work. They carry grocery bags. Big 8 is dumbfounded. She watches. She looks at Shirl. She exits. Shirl looks after her, dumbfounded. The kiss continues. Big 8 re-enters, raging.)*

BIG 8: Sonufagunufabitch, curl my hair an' suck my toes! Let go of me, Shirl. Hey, far as I know, Hopalong Cassidy kept it in his pants.

ROB: Now, girl…

BIG 8: *(Riding over him.)* What in hell do you think would be the hardest thing on a hip, huh? How about screwin' in a rotary fashion, Rob Bob? You think maybe that's it?

(She throws her bag of groceries at him, and they fly all over the kitchen.)

ROB: Hey…

BIG 8: What the hell am I haulin' my ass on your behalf, huh? Get off me, Shirl. You just followin' yer li'l baby dick around in a circle!

(Grabs Shirl's groceries and throws them at Rob.)

SHIRL: Hey, I got mayonnaise in there!

BIG 8: *(To Shedevil.)* Did I tell you to git off my place? Well, I'm tellin' you, bitch!

SHIRL: *(Intervening. To Big 8.)* Now you think what Jesus would do in this situation?

BIG 8: Damn it, Shirl, there's a commandment on this. *(To Rob.)* What the hell do you have to say for yourself?

ROB: Love at first sight.

BIG 8: Dick at first chance is more like it.

ROB: One swan sees another swan an' that's it.

BIG 8: Don't start in on the swans.

ROB: Love is good!

BIG 8: An' jus' what the hell are you?

ROB: *(Truly riled.)* Don't start, Big 8!

SHEDEVIL: Hey!!!

BIG 8: What!!!?

SHEDEVIL: Yo!! Am I alive or am I dead!!?

SHIRL: *(Soothing the multitudes.)* How 'bout we all go out get us some ribs?

SHEDEVIL: *(Flashing a switchblade.)* I…am…with child…okay? Do I have to slice myself open to prove it? I dropped by Loony Tunes here, lookin' for my husband an' my $17,000. I'm lookin' for some place to rest! All this dilly-dally, shilly-shally…yo, you are in a world of trouble you can't even imagine, because Black Dog, the psychopath from Kiev, is out there on the road, headin' this way! I can smell him. Now, let's get down an' get some modus operandi worked out before we're roadkill! *(Sticks knife in butcher block.)*

ROB: Now, I am the man of the house…

SHIRL: *(Head in hands.)* Oh, my God.

ROB: (To Big 8.) Ma'am. Rodeo been my life. Shoot, you are the rodeo, Big 8, but a good man's got to have a good…

SHIRL: Will you just hush up!

SHEDEVIL: Hold it!

BIG 8: What? *(Shedevil puts a warning finger to her lips. There is a far-off hum.)* What is it?

SHEDEVIL: Too late.

ROB: Too late for what?

SHEDEVIL: He's comin'.

ROB: I can hear it.

SHEDEVIL: I know that bike.

ROB: Black Dog?

SHEDEVIL: You just wouldn't listen, would you?

ROB: You just come on over here.

SHEDEVIL: The bunch of us are toast.

ROB: *(Seating Shedevil.)* Sit yourself down.

SHEDEVIL: *(Head in hands.)* I can't believe this! Don't you get it? He's a walking time bomb! He's the Frankenstein freakin' monster. I've seen him suck the brains of a pet monkey out its nose!

SHIRL: Ohhhhhh my.

SHEDEVIL: I am dead meat.

ROB: *(Still to Shedevil, who has begun to cry.)* You kin blow on my neckerchief.

SHEDEVIL: Thwang, ka-boom!

SHIRL: I think I got to go to the bathroom. *(Goes to bathroom door. Closes herself in.)*

BIG 8: Ain't nobody, no-body, settin' foot in here with hostile intent. This is private property, buddy.

(Rob is strapping on his belt and holster.)

ROB: Yes, ma'am; yes, ma'am.

BIG 8: Rob Bob, what the hell are you doin'?

ROB: High noon, my damn favorite.

BIG 8: *(Goes for the wall.)* I'm gettin' my shotgun.

ROB: I believe everybody is born for one special moment. And this is, by God, mine!

BIG 8: Simmer down, Rob Bob.

ROB: Back off, Mama, give me room to roll.

SHEDEVIL: *(Rising.)* I'll just go with him.

ROB: Hell you will. Clear the floor now. By God, a man's got to do what a man's got to do.

(Rob takes the familiar ready-to-draw position. Big 8 appears on the stairs.)

BIG 8: You let me take care of this.

ROB: This is my town, and my time. Stay off me, Big 8, this is a man's fair fight.

(Suddenly, with a murderous kick, the door explodes inward, completely off its hinges. Into the room steps a monstrous, Harley-clad, mustachioed, eyepatched, tattooed, fierce, 45-year old Ukrainian biker; the dreaded Black Dog. He takes in the room and roars.)

BLACK DOG: I'm here to crush some goddamned skulls!!!

ROB: Go fer yer gun, Black Dog!

(Black Dog laughs a sharp croaking laugh.)

BLACK DOG: Eat excrement, little American idiot!

ROB: Bet 'em or fold 'em, cowboy!

BLACK DOG: *(Laughs, slaps his side with his bare hand in an imitation of a draw and points his finger-gun at Rob.)* Bing, bang! *(Rob draws right on top of this and fires three times. The bullets slam Black Dog back against the wall.)* What the hell is this? *(Rob fires three more times, and Black Dog slides down the wall, leaving a trail of blood. Shedevil screams. Big 8 runs downstairs with the shotgun. Black Dog lurches to his feet.)* You kill me! *(Blood pours out of his mouth. He pitches over stone dead. Shedevil runs to the body. Big 8 kneels down and tries his pulse. Shirl comes out of the bathroom. All three women turn and look at Rob. He blows on the end of the pistol, twirls it expertly and slides it coolly into the holster.)*

ROB: Man got what he came for.

BLACKOUT

The whole group is gathered silently around the body of Black Dog. They stare down at him, holding their beers.

SHEDEVIL: What kind of beer is this?

ROB: Local.

BIG 8: *(Nodding.)* Local beer. *(They look at the body.)* Shit. *(They all drink beer.)*

SHIRL: He's dead, huh?

BIG 8: Oh, yeah.

SHIRL: Broke your door.

BIG 8: Tore that sumbitch right off.

(Shedevil explodes in tears and throws herself in an embrace with Rob.)

ROB: It's okay, girl. Gonna be okay, little lady.

(She grabs him by the back of the hair and kisses him; then she pulls back and hits him square in the face.)

SHEDEVIL: Kaboom! *(She kicks him.)* Crunch! *(Hits him again.)* Skreek! *(Then she grabs him and kisses him again. Rob and Shedevil have let their passion drive them up on top of the butcher block, where they are making love.)*

SHIRL: *(Sitting on a stool at the island.)* Makes me feel old.

BIG 8: *(Still looking at the body.)* He just inhaled.

SHIRL: Huh-uh.

BIG 8: Seemed like it.

SHIRL: *(Peers at him.)* I kill things all day long an' this here is dead. We got some modified shock goin' on here.

BIG 8: Rob Bob, get offa that girl! Git offa her right now! *(He does.)* You don't think I have any feelings here? You can jes' rape an' pillage an' shoot an' it's all jes' part of the wallpaper?

ROB: Sorry, Big 8.

BIG 8: You should be sorry. Gollee! Did you never care for me or what?

ROB: Did, an' I do.

BIG 8: Well, you got one hell of a strange way of showin' it!

(A strange, low growl emanates from the body of Black Dog. Everybody shrinks back. It stops.)

SHIRL: I believe corpses let off gas.

SHEDEVIL: Was that gas?

ROB: You sure that was him?

BIG 8: Well, it sure as hell wasn't me.

SHEDEVIL: He used to growl; he used to growl in bars.

BIG 8: Used to growl?

SHEDEVIL: Yeah. It was a sign, you know, that you should back off. Yo, I would always tell whoever was on his case that they might, you know, want to drive to another state or whatever.

SHIRL: See, I'm pretty sure that was gas. Happens all the time with deceased pigs. *(Sees their concerned, incredulous faces.)* Cross my heart. It was nasty gas, too. Sometimes, one person would press on the belly and another one would hold a match, and the gas would catch fire an' shoot out.

BIG 8: No kiddin'.

SHIRL: Not with steers though. Wouldn't catch fire with steers.

BIG 8: Well, I'm glad to hear that.

(There is another ominous growl from Black Dog.)

SHEDEVIL: I don't think that's gas.

(Another growl and Black Dog rolls over on his side.)

SHIRL: Jesus.

SHEDEVIL: Look out.

(Black Dog, his bad eye a bloody hole, several bullet holes in his chest oozing, blood running down his arms, begins a monstrous, agonizing struggle to rise to his feet. He grabs hold of a stool by the butcher block and uses it to drag himself up.)

SHIRL: Oh my God, oh my God, oh my God, oh my God, oh my God, oh my God, oh my God.

(Simultaneously with that.)

SHEDEVIL: We ought to run. Everybody should really ought to. We shouldn't just stand here. It's a mistake just to stand here. Everybody run. Everybody run.

(Black Dog's growling becomes a kind of roaring. It's like a horror movie. He forces himself upright, using the butcher block for leverage. Rob goes for his gun, drops it on the floor. Picks it back up. Fires repeatedly. It is, of course, empty. Black Dog is now erect; across the butcher block from him is Shedevil.)

SHEDEVIL: Hi there, baby.

BLACK DOG: *(He swivels, looking at them around the room, speaks in tortured English.)* Give…me…beer!

SHIRL: *(To Big 8.)* He wants a beer, Sissy.

BIG 8: Uh-huh.

SHIRL: I'll get you a beer, darlin'. *(She goes to fridge. Black Dog moves around butcher block. Shedevil moves too, staying away from him.)* You bet I will. Nice cold beer. *(Pops top. Black Dog turns toward the sound.)* Here you are, Honeybunch, and I know you'll enjoy it. *(She hands it to him gingerly. He upends it and chugs it down. They watch, hypnotized. As he drinks, liquid stains his shirt. He feels it. He looks down. Shirl speaks, hysterically cheerful.)* It's leakin' out his chest, see there, it's leakin' out his chest.

BLACK DOG: What is this I am seeing with my eyes?

SHIRL: It's comin' out the bullet holes.

BLACK DOG: Can't even drink beer, you son-of-bitch! *(Throws the beer can through the window, shattering glass. A guttural roar.)* I eat you, kill you, crack your bones!

(He spins around and falls to the floor once more like a concrete block.)

BIG 8: I'm switchin' to bourbon. *(She goes to a kitchen cabinet and pulls out a bottle. At the same time, Shedevil, sickened, runs into the bathroom and slams the door.)* Shirl?

SHIRL: What?

BIG 8: How you feelin' over there?

SHIRL: Oh, well, I guess I'm good to go.

BIG 8: You think you could lean over, check around fer a pulse.

SHIRL: Well, it's sweet of you to think of me.

BIG 8: Shirl!

SHIRL: Yeah, I...I can do that.

ROB: What should I do?

BIG 8: You should stand there.

ROB: Okay.

BIG 8: *(Drinks.)* What's the verdict down there, Shirl?

SHIRL: He got but nothin' going on.

BIG 8: You sure now?

SHIRL: If he got a pulse, I got a hard-on.

BIG 8: We was doin' rodeo in Wisconsin, so they took us down fer some ice fishin' an' this bronc rider fell through the ice. Two hours later, he smashed up outta there like a damn Jack inna box.

SHIRL: I'm tellin' you, this dude is dead.

BIG 8: Rob Bob.

ROB: Yeah?

BIG 8: Walk yourself over there, kick that body real hard.

ROB: Do I have to?

BIG 8: Rob Bob, you have betrayed my trust. An' I'm not gonna lie to ya, I'm hurtin'. Hurtin' in the rain.

ROB: It stopped rainin'.

BIG 8: Damnation! I just want me an ordinary life. Is that too damn much to ask!? *(Shedevil comes wanly out of the bathroom.)* What is it?

SHEDEVIL: I'm shakin'. I'm shakin' bad.

BIG 8: Well, hell, Rob Bob, git over there an' hold her! You know, I blame every damned bit of this on Lucifer Lee. *(Sees Rob hugging Shedevil.)* An' that's enough of that. *(To Shirl.)* Shirl, walk over there an' kick that corpse.

SHIRL: My sneakers are bran' new.

BIG 8: Shirl.

SHIRL: All right.

(She does.)

BIG 8: I mean kick him!

(Shirl gives him a good one. Nothing.)

SHIRL: *(Looking down on Black Dog.)* Since he's layin' on his face, I'd haveta notice he ain't packin'.

ROB: He went for his gun.

SHIRL: In your dreams, Rob Bob.

ROB: Hey, this was a fair fight, okay? We was eyeball to eyeball, I tol' him to draw, an' y'all saw him reach.

BIG 8: Got him a sheathed huntin' knife.

ROB: See there, betcha he's an expert knife thrower.

SHIRL: *(Irritated.)* He can't throw it when it's sheathed.

ROB: Code a' the west is no shooting a unarmed man, okay... *(He unsheathes the knife.)* ...but he had him a razor sharp 10-inch bear gutter. He went for his an' I went for mine. This ain't shabby. This here passes muster.

SHIRL: What are we doin' here?

ROB: What are we doin'?

SHIRL: Have we lost our damn minds?

ROB: We are discussin' whether I'm the good guy or the bad guy.

SHIRL: This is the first of the month, right?

ROB: Yeah, but...

SHIRL: Does my boyfriend Baxter, without fail, propose to me ona first of the month?

ROB: Yeah, but...

SHIRL: What time does my honey pick me up at my sister's?

ROB: Around six o'clock, but...

SHIRL: An' is it six-fifteen?

ROB: Shirl, we got important issues, girl…

SHIRL: What does my honey do for a livin'?

ROB: He's a deputy sheriff, Shirl. *(They look at Black Dog. Rob looks heavenward in frustrated recognition.)* Oh-oh.

(The room explodes into action. Rob grabs hold of Black Dog's arms and tries to drag him around the island so he can get him out the back door. Moving Black Dog however is no simple task. Shirl is rushing around picking up the beer cans. Big 8 opens the mop closet, grabs a mop and heads for the sink to wet it. Shedevil closes her eyes and sings "Rock of Ages" in a small, clear soprano. Shirl now moves to the door, trying to set it back in the frame. Big 8 is mopping up the blood trail left as Rob drags the riddled Black Dog.)

BIG 8: Rob Bob. Rob Bob! Where the hell you takin' him?

ROB: *(Dragging.)* Out.

BIG 8: *(Mopping.)* Where? Out where?

ROB: Backyard.

BIG 8: You can't take him in the backyard. Backyard's flat. Backyard's empty. It's completely damn empty clear to the horizon. Rob Bob, goddamnit, hold it!

ROB: *(Finally in a fit.)* How the hell am I supposed to git anything done you yak-yak-yakking upside down an' backwards while I'm workin' here? *("Rock of Ages" finally irritates him.)* Shedevil, honey, will you jes' shut the hell up, sweetie? Will you, little darlin', for God's sake, stick a sock in it?

BIG 8: Rob Bob.

ROB: What?!

BIG 8: Out in the backyard he will be the only object of size in five miles.

ROB: There's cows out there, fer God's sake.

BIG 8: He don't look nothin' in the known universe like a cow.

ROB: I'm not jes' gonna leave him there! I ain't a complete moron, am I; I'm gonna bury him.

BIG 8: On'y a complete moron would think we got time to bury him!

SHIRL: Put him in the icebox!

(She rushes to the fridge and starts throwing stuff out.)

BIG 8: *(Rushing to help Shirl.)* See, put 'im in the icebox.

ROB: *(Leaving Black Dog.)* He's bigger than a damn steer, you cain't git him in the icebox!

BIG 8: *(Furious.)* See, that the deal, see. You always lookin' on the dark side. You got to accentuate the positive, damn it.

(Shedevil is down with dishtowels, mopping blood and singing again.)

ROB AND BIG 8: *(To Shedevil.)* Stop singing!

SHEDEVIL: *(Simply.)* Yo, you can't get him in the icebox!!

(There is the sound of a car driving in onto the gravel. Shirl whirls and runs to the empty door.)

BIG 8: Oh-oh.

SHIRL: It's Baxter in the cruiser. Baxter's comin' up the drive. Stick him in the broom closet!

ROB: In the broom closet.

SHIRL: *(Yelling and waving out the door hole.)* Hi, there, Baxter puddin'! How you doin', sweet thing?

(They reverse direction. Shirl pulls brooms, mops and buckets out of the broom closet and hurls them out the back door. Shedevil rushes about, mopping up blood fiendishly. The two older women and Rob exert superhuman strength and get Black Dog to his feet.)

BIG 8: One, two, three—lift.

ROB: Hold it, hold it...

SHIRL: Lemme help.

ROB: I got him now.

BIG 8: Ow!

ROB: Sorry, babe. Okay. Okay. Haul him, haul him.

SHIRL: Jesus, Mary and Joseph...

BIG 8: Git your arm back here. Now. Now! Now!!

(Amazingly enough, he is on his feet. They steady for their final assault on the broom closet.)

BLACK DOG: *(Gravelly and small but audible.)* Give me...beer.

(Shirl screams. They all step back; he falls. Rob leaps on him, hands on his throat. He exerts every muscle in the act of strangulation.)

ROB: Die, damn you. Die, die, die, die, die...

(Shirl screams. Big 8 slaps her. She stops.)

BIG 8: *(Speaks calmly and sweetly. Meanwhile, Rob has scrambled off Black Dog and gone to get the hunting knife left on the island.)* Shirl, darlin', why don't you go on out there an' give your sweetie pie a great big kiss. (At this point, Rob re-straddles Black Dog. Black Dog reaches up and grabs his knife hand, and they struggle.) Uh-huh, uh-huh, welcome him home from his work with a little damn affection.

(Black Dog and Rob roll across the floor.)

SHIRL: *(Panicked and horrified.)* Uh-huh.

BIG 8: Uh-huh. Little kisses and hugs. *(Rob, with a supreme effort, drives the knife into Black Dog's chest. A second time. A third time. Both Big 8 and Shirl scream. Black Dog goes limp. His arm drops. To Shirl.)* Go GO.

SHIRL: Well, uh-huh, sure, I'll just go right out there. *(Shedevil sits rocking in a chair, singing "What a Friend I Have in Jesus.")* I'll kill you if you don't shut up! *(Exhausted, Rob rolls off the body.)*

ROB: Well, he's dead now, by God.

SHIRL: *(To Big 8.)* Does it matter that I'm covered with blood?

BIG 8: *(Smiling both wildly and coquettishly. To Shirl.)* Ummm, well, let's see, I don't know, it just might.

ROB: See, I finished him off.

BIG 8: Shirl, you just sashay on over there to the faucet an' pretty up.

ROB: Dead as a possum on a highway interchange!

BIG 8: *(Shaking him by his shirtfront.)* Will…you…be quiet. *(She goes to the door and calls.)* Baxter, what are you doin' out there, darlin'?

BAXTER: *(Offstage.)* Been meanin' to check my oil.

BIG 8: *(Looking back in.)* Checkin' his oil.

SHIRL: *(Turning.)* How I look?

BIG 8: *(Going over.)* Well, honey…I could just…well…tidy you up. *(Maniacally cleans her.)*

ROB: *(To Shedevil.)* Sorry what I said. I'd like to hear the hymn you were singin'.

BIG 8: *(A murderous whisper.)* No, you wouldn't. You wouldn't like to hear that hymn. *(Out the door.)* I cain't think on a better thing in this worl' you should be doing, Baxter. *(Shirl, through washing, fights to bring order to her hair and demeanor.)* Now, Baxter, you stay put, 'cause Shirl, she's comin' out with a surprise.

BAXTER: *(From offstage.)* Surprise!

BIG 8: *(To Shirl.)* Git the hell out there, Shirl.

SHIRL: Do I look all right?

BIG 8: You jes' tell him you got a nosebleed.

SHIRL: My God, Big 8, what the hell are we into?

SHEDEVIL: Murder an' strangulations.

BIG 8: *(To Shirl.)* Go. Go on, baby. Shoo. Go.
(Shirl heads out. Big 8 heads over for where Rob is at work.)

BAXTER: *(From offstage.)* Hi, Honey, I can't hardly wait.
(Shirl pops back in.)

SHIRL: Surprise!
(Rob and Big 8 are getting Black Dog back on his feet.)

BIG 8: I cain't believe yer jokin' now, Shirl.

SHIRL: Surprise. Surprise, goddamnit.

BIG 8: Have you gone flat crazy?

SHIRL: You told Baxter I was bringing him out a surprise.

BIG 8: *(Irritated, straining every muscle.)* Well, bring him out a surprise, Shirl.

SHIRL: Well, what the hell am I s'posed to bring him?

BIG 8: Well, what the hell does the man like?

SHIRL: I don't know.

BIG 8: You been datin' him for nine years.

SHIRL: I just don't know.

BIG 8: You have to know!

SHIRL: Breasts.

BIG 8: Well, take off yer shirt an' go tell 'im hello. *(Shirl goes out unbuttoning her shirt.)* Shedevil, get over here.

SHEDEVIL: I can't touch him.

ROB: We ain't got the heft to git him in.

SHEDEVIL: Don't make me.

ROB: Baby, darlin' chickadee, I'm yer lovin' man, askin' for some help here. Give yer ol' baby jes' a little hand here, Sweetiecakes.

BIG 8: You don't git over here, you'll spend the rest of your miserable life in a maximum-security prison.

SHEDEVIL: Okay.

(She comes over.)

ROB: Grab on.

BIG 8: Git him up on his knees.

ROB: Dang.

BIG 8: Pull.

ROB: One, two, three…. Lift!

(They get Black Dog upright.)

BIG 8: Git the door.

(Shedevil opens the broom closet.)

Okay, we got 'er.

(To Shedevil.)

You clean.

SHEDEVIL: Do what?

BIG 8: Clean. Clean! My God, you musta cleaned up somethin' in yer miserable life. Clean up!

SHEDEVIL: Okay.

(She does.)

ROB: Gotta get him up.

BIG 8: Oh God, my hand went inside his chest!

ROB: Back him in.

BIG 8: Losin' my grip.

SHEDEVIL: I'm cleanin'.

ROB: Little more. Now. Gonna lift him up an' in.

BIG 8: On three.

BIG 8: One, two, three. *(They all roar with the effort, but they get Black Dog in and slam the door. They are exhausted and bloody and half-crazed with the effort.)* Hot damn! Whooee!

(They embrace.)

ROB: Ain't done nuthin' like that since your horse died in that horse trailer. *(Big 8 starts to laugh.)* You remember that horse trailer?

BIG 8: *(Laughing.)* Do I remember?

ROB: *(Starting to laugh.)* Started pullin' that horse out an' his leg come off.

SHEDEVIL: His leg came off?!

BIG 8: Right in his hand.

SHEDEVIL: That's horrible.

ROB: It was.

BIG 8: It was downright horrible.

(All three of them are laughing.)

ROB: I fainted.

BIG 8: He did.

ROB: Bam, right on the ground.

(They all rock with laughter.)

BIG 8: Wait a minute. Hold it! *(The laughter stops.)* Put the stuff in the fridge.

(Mayhem.)

ROB: Don't have time.

BIG 8: Throw it out the back then.

(More mayhem.)

ROB: You want these ribs?

BIG 8: No, I don't want the ribs! *(They finish. They look at each other. They're smeared with Black Dog's blood.)* We gotta change!

(The three of them rush upstairs just as Baxter comes in with Shirl, who is buttoning up her shirt. He has his arms affectionately around her.)

BAXTER: *(He is a small, balding cop, slightly overweight, maybe 45 years old.)* Honey-bunny, baby, you are the everlovin' best.

SHIRL: Thank you, Baxter bow-wow.

BAXTER: I've never, ever, never been welcomed home like that.

SHIRL: I just been thinkin' on you all day.

BAXTER: An' I been thinkin' about you.

SHIRL: You have?

BAXTER: An' now, I'm really thinkin' about you!

SHIRL: You naughty thing.

BAXTER: So I want you to sit right over here, an' I want you to listen to me good.

SHIRL: *(She sees drops of blood on the island.)* You bad ol' policeman, I got both my ears trained on yer mouth.

BAXTER: You a good ol', big ol' girl.

SHIRL: Baxter, you are makin' me giggle an' squirm!

(She turns and tries to wipe it off with her handkerchief.)

BAXTER: Bee-utiful Shirl, you see before you, in the uniform he is proud to wear…an' I want you to see the 'Merican flag on my breast… *(Shirl cleans up here and there.)* …on my breast, sweet land o' liberty, a man… *(Points to himself.)* …man standin' before you…little overweight…a man you know is crippled for procreation 'cause of wounds he received below the waist protectin' the bulk grocery store…this man givin' his life to two things: Shirl Bitahatcher an' justice. *(Shirl sees another drop and wipes.)* Hey, Shirl, don't move around too much or I goin' to forget this.

SHIRL: Sorry, Baxter.

BAXTER: Hardest thing I ever done.

SHIRL: I'm lovin' it.

BAXTER: *(Picking up the thread.)* …an' justice. You could ask a hunnert folks an' they would tell you Baxter Blue, he's a man who does right, couldn't do no wrong.

SHIRL: *(Taking every opportunity to remove blood spots.)* Amen.

BAXTER: Now, I'm standin' on the precipice of a big career, Shirl. Bein' a two-man de-partment, I'm already the number two man.

SHIRL: Uh-huh.

BAXTER: Chief Esperanza, at 300 pounds, he's on the edge of retirement, 'cause he can't make the stairs. That day comes, you wouldn't hafta slaughter cattle no more. A wife ain't meant to come home bloody… *(A pause.)* That ain't a joke on your nosebleed now.

SHIRL: Not taken as such.

BAXTER: You got a hesitancy on me, Shirl…

SHIRL: Now…

BAXTER: You do. You turned me down eighteen months running. *(Improvising.)* I will say I take yer welcome today as a turnin' point. Everbody knows I'm a breast man.

SHIRL: I'm jest gonna lean on the kitchen island here.

BAXTER: Sure thing. *(Looks down at some blood they didn't wipe up, also sees some blood on the broom closet door.)* You got the nosebleed pretty bad.

SHIRL: Get 'em sometime when I'm thinkin' about you.

BAXTER: You're kiddin'?

SHIRL: Huh-uh.

BAXTER: Damn, Shirl, you get a man hot. Listen… *(He pulls a letter out of his back pocket.)* This here's a letter from Big Fork…she's a job offer.

SHIRL: Police?

BAXTER: Cement. Used to work in cement. My daddy was in cement.

SHIRL: *(Glancing at the stairs.)* I remember you tol' me. *(A moment.)* Big Fork's pretty far off.

BAXTER: This here's the moment, girl. We poised on a knife edge. It's either you or cement.

(Big 8 re-enters. A new outfit, clean as a penny. She is followed by Rob, also spotless, and Shedevil, who is wearing a housedress of Big 8's, which is much too big.)

BIG 8: Well, hell, if it ain't Baxter Blue. Good on you.

BAXTER: Uh-huh.

BIG 8: How they hangin'?

(Baxter looks stricken.)

Hell, Baxter, I'm sorry, I jes' allus forget.

BAXTER: Ummm. 'Pology accepted. It ain't "how's a man hangin'," it's does he do right?

ROB: Now that's the damn truth, Baxter. There is good an' there's bad…

BIG 8: Don't git him started. *(Turns to Shedevil.)* Now, this little girl here…

SHEDEVIL: *(Definitely playing a role.)* Susie Pertman.

BAXTER: Perkman?

SHEDEVIL: Pert. Pertman. Some folks call me Perky.

BAXTER: Real pleasure, Perky.

(They shake hands.)

SHEDEVIL: *(Chipper.)* I got an artificial hand.

BAXTER: Aw shoot, I'm sorry.

SHEDEVIL: Don't you worry, it's Teflon.

SHIRL: Perky is just visitin'.

SHEDEVIL: Till my hair grows out.

(*Everyone laughs.*)

BIG 8: Her fiancé is...

(*Pause.*)

SHIRL: Well, he's just an ol'...

(*Pause.*)

ROB: Friend.

BAXTER: Would you be expectin'? I mean, sorta seems like a maternity frock.

SHEDEVIL: (*Perky.*) Well, I would.

BAXTER: Ain't nobody respects the miracle of birth like I do.

SHEDEVIL: (*Curtseying.*) Well, thank you a bunch.

BAXTER: That wouldn't be yer Harley hawg out there, would it, Perky?

SHEDEVIL: Ummmmm, well...

BAXTER: Couldn't help noticin' that big ol' thing when I come in.

BIG 8: B'longs to her fiancé.

ROB: No, it don't.

BIG 8: Yes, it does.

SHIRL: What they mean is...

ROB: In point of fact...

BIG 8: Not to cut it too fine...

SHEDEVIL: It's mine.

(*A pause.*)

BAXTER: But he's here, huh?

(*Black Dog's limp arm slides out of the closet into view.*)

SHEDEVIL: Ummmmmmmm...

BIG 8: He sure is an...

(*Pause.*)

SHIRL: An' he's just...

(*A pause.*)

ROB: Takin' a nap.

(*Shedevil pushes the arm back inside the closet.*)

BAXTER: Long ride?

SHEDEVIL: Oh, sure...

SHIRL: He's just...

BIG 8: Out lika light.

(*They chuckle courteously. They are out of conversation.*)

SHIRL: Cuppa?

BIG 8: Coffee?

BAXTER: I can pour me one.

(*Heads for the stove. Shirl, Big 8 and Rob all clean up telltale blood.*)

SHEDEVIL: It's so pretty out. Don't you think it's pretty out. I think it's so pretty out.

BAXTER: (*Stopping with the pot in his hand.*) Dang, Shirl, you nosebled on the stove, too.

SHEDEVIL: We could just all go for a walk!

BAXTER: (*Something is confusing him.*) Shirl?

SHIRL: (*Completely taking over.*) You know what, this here is a big day! Uh-huh, it is. Big, big, super big day.

(*A nod to Shedevil.*)

BIG 8: (*Picking up.*) Well, what kinda big day is this, Shirl?

SHIRL: (*Moving him away from the stove.*) Well, Baxter here... (*Slaps his shoulder coyly.*) ...he is such a cute thang!

BAXTER: What?

SHIRL: Well, he just...

(*She fans herself and giggles.*)

BIG 8: (*In the spirit.*) Baxter Blue, you dirty ol' thing, what're you up to?

BAXTER: What?

ROB: Hol' on here. Hol' on jest a dang minute. Shoot, Baxter, you didn't...

SHIRL: He did!

ROB: (*Slapping Baxter on the back.*) Well, you dirty ol' thing...

BIG 8: Did you go an' pop the question on my bes' friend?!

SHIRL: He did.

BIG 8: He did!

ROB: (*Slaps him again.*) You rowdy ol' breast man!

BAXTER: I do that every month.

SHIRL: But!!! (*Baxter is so startled he whirls around, almost losing his balance.*) But there's a big difference this time.

BIG 8: (*Keeping the ball in the air.*) What's the difference this time, Shirl?

SHIRL: The difference this time is...I'm gonna say "yes."

(*Big 8 lets out a scream, throws her hands up in the air and grabs Shirl in an embrace. Rob pounds Baxter on the back.*)

ROB: Ring-a-ding-ding, Mr. Baxter Blue!

BIG 8: (*To Shirl.*) Girl, you are on easy street!

ROB: Hot snookie, Baxter! What you got to say for yourself, son?

BAXTER: I'm just stunned.

BIG 8: (*To Baxter.*) Open me up a hug, you chunky li'l lawman you!

SHEDEVIL: Well, am I in the right place at the right time or what?

ROB: You done the right thang by that boy, Shirl.

SHIRL: I just thank you all potfulls.

ROB: Speech, Baxter, dagnabbit.

BIG 8: Speech, an' no kiddin'.

(Big 8, Rob and Shedevil chant "speech, speech, speech." Rob grabs Baxter and sets him up on the butcher block.)

BAXTER: *(When he's grabbed.)* Whoa, there, hoss!

ROB: I gotcha.

SHIRL: Now, you be careful there.

BAXTER: All right, fer heaven's sake.

(He's up.)

ROB: Let 'er rip, Blue-boy!

(They applaud.)

BAXTER: Well, shoot, I'm damn gratified. *(More applause; Rob whistles.)* Hells bells, I'll give a damn speech, damnit.

ROB: *(Quieting the applause.)* Give that man room ta let loose!

(Silence descends.)

BAXTER: *(Lets out a sort of rooster/coyote call. Waves his hat.)* Gonna be a hot time in the sagebrush tonight! *(Applause. Whistles.)* I love Shirl Bitahatcher, an' I love America! I am the by God wild man of the wild west. Rip-diddley-ay-do-ring-a-ding-day!

ROB: You tell 'em, wild man!

BAXTER: *(During this speech, Shedevil, taking advantage of the focus on Baxter, slips away, takes the silver buckles, which are still in the kitchen, and puts them in her bag. Shirl notices. Big 8 notices.)* I am tall as a tornado, noisy as a thunderstorm, hotter than any hell you got in Arizona! EEEYA! From my left hand to my right hand is a by God thousand miles. I'm half man, half mountain lion an' half alligator. I drink me a five gallon jug a' corn whiskey between the time my eyes open an' my feet hit the floor. I eat me Texas for breakfast with the Pacific Ocean for a chaser, an' dine on a thousand head of short horn steers roasted on a slow spit in hell come nightfall. Yowsa bowsa! You lookin' for trouble, I'm Beelzebub in a cotton nightshirt. Yippy-ay-ay-ay-yo, I'm an old cowhand with a wedding band, I'm a gonna do it for sure!

(Rob lets loose a rodeo yell. A pause.)

BIG 8: You gonna talk about Shirl?

BAXTER: *(Laughing embarrassedly.)* Ah hell, I forgot. *(Everybody laughs.)* I'm a family man, Shirl. Been lookin' fer my family ever since I was born.

When my sweet Ginny Sue threw herself front of the Amtrak, I didn't think I'd never find true love again.

SHIRL: You poor thang.

BAXTER: But the land a the bald eagle, it took care a me in good time. Brought Shirl down from Laramie an' I been goo-goo since the first day. Hell, I been double goo-goo. *(Laughter.)* She always overlooked my little disability…

SHIRL: Honey, that's nothin'.

BAXTER: Brought me back to the church, keeps me down to six-pack a day an' she allus drops some spare ribs by the station. *(He tears up.)* I'm gonna be a good husband, Shirl. Gonna stick with law enforcement. Gonna love, honor an' obey you, so help me God. *(Quiet.)* I guess tha's all. *(Wild applause.)*

ROB: Damn, that was fine! Y'all the man, Baxter Blue.

BAXTER: Well, I ain't one of your fancy talkers.

SHIRL: *(Really touched.)* You come on over here an' give me a smacker, Baxter.

BAXTER: *(Taking Rob's hand to get down.)* I would purely be honored to do that. *(Shirl is standing in front of the broom closet. Baxter comes around where she is.)*

BIG 8: All right, you get on in here, sweet thang. *(He is positioned where he can kiss her.)*

ROB: *(Dead serious.)* There ain't nothin' beats love. *(There is a tremendous roar and, simultaneously, Black Dog's fist pierces the broom closet door right between Shirl and Baxter. Shirl shrieks with terror and keeps shrieking as she flees.)*

BAXTER: Holy moley! *(He backs away, unsnapping his service pistol.)*

BIG 8: Take it easy, Baxter.

BAXTER: Son-of-a-bitch!

SHEDEVIL: Oh my God. *(Tremendous shattering and the door of the broom closet falls into the room, revealing…)*

BLACK DOG: I kill you and eat your hearts!! *(Baxter empties his pistol into this gory Frankenstein amidst the shrieks and yells of the others. Black Dog continues in Russian as the bullets strike home.)* Animals! Vultures! Capitalist whores!

ROB: *(The following lines also overlap during the firing.)* Git out, Big 8!

SHEDEVIL: Oh my God, he's comin'.

BIG 8: Git back, critter! *(When the gun is emptied, Black Dog takes one more step and falls to the floor. Silence descends, except for hard breathing and minor whimpering. We see Big 8's mind work. She takes a step forward.)* Baxter Blue, what the hell have you done?

BAXTER: What?

BIG 8: I jes' cain't believe this.

BAXTER: What?!

SHIRL: *(Pointing at the fallen Black Dog.)* He was jokin'!

ROB: But...

BAXTER: Jokin'?

BIG 8: You goddamned fool, that's her fiancé. *(She points at Shedevil.)*

ROB: But...

SHEDEVIL: *(On it. She breaks down in piteous sobs.)* My poor...

SHIRL: Billy.

SHEDEVIL: ...Jimmy.

BAXTER: *(Appalled.)* That's Jimmy?

BIG 8: They came down here on the Harley to git married.

BAXTER: Oh my God.

SHIRL: *(Coming to him.)* Baxter, honey, you went crazy.

BAXTER: But he came blastin' outa that closet. Yellin', sayin' he was gonna eat us.

BIG 8: Completely unarmed, darlin'.

BAXTER: He had an accent!

SHIRL: Baby, ain't you s'posed to give a warnin'?

BAXTER: Well, I...

SHEDEVIL: *(Kneeling by Black Dog.)* Jimmy, Jimmy, my darling Jimmy.

BAXTER: But he...

BIG 8: He's a joker, honey. We'd been talkin' on you an' here you come pullin' in, an' Jimmy says "how 'bout I give him a little scare," an' we said, "okay," 'cause how you love a li'l jokin'.

(Shedevil, crying, runs into the bathroom and closes the door. Shirl goes after her.)

BAXTER: He's unarmed?

BIG 8: *(Gently.)* Look at him.

ROB: Jeminy crickets, what are we gonna do?

BAXTER: I killed him.

BIG 8: Shot him twelve times.

SHIRL: Six times.

BIG 8: Yeah, it was six.

ROB: Hell, that'd kill an elephant.

BAXTER: *(Disoriented.)* I shot an unarmed man playin' a joke.

SHIRL: *(To the bathroom door.)* Please come out, Patti.

SHEDEVIL: *(From inside.)* Perky.

SHIRL: *(To the door.)* Perky, damnit.

BIG 8: We got to do some quick thinkin' here, boy.

BAXTER: *(It hits him.)* I'm a rogue cop.

BIG 8: Wadn't yer fault, Baxter.

SHIRL: *(A murderous whisper.)* Git out here, Perky.

BAXTER: *(Pointing at the body.)* That isn't right. I didn't do right.

> *(He puts his hands over his face. Shedevil walks out of the bathroom and over to Baxter.)*

SHEDEVIL: Mr. Blue?

BAXTER: It's a blot on my badge.

SHEDEVIL: Mr. Blue?

BAXTER: *(Looking at her.)* Perky?

SHEDEVIL: You have to listen to me.

BAXTER: I have to turn myself in.

SHEDEVIL: Hold my hand. *(He does.)* Hold hard. Vladimir was doomed.

BAXTER: His name was Vladimir?

SHEDEVIL: No, but he let me call him that. His family in Kiev used to take him to the basement…

ROB: *(Pleased.)* The basement…

SHEDEVIL: You don't even want to know what they did there. Jimmy had been an alcoholic…

BAXTER: His name was Jimmy but he let you call him Vladimir?

SHEDEVIL: Yes. He was drug addicted, had an eating disorder, he had terrible, terrible problems with depression; it's what made him a jokester. He killed a man, by mistake, on peyote.

BAXTER: As a joke?

SHEDEVIL: Hold my other hand. *(He does.)* He served his time and found his God. Then he disappeared, left everybody, me included, an' was gone for five years.

BAXTER: But…

SHEDEVIL: Vaporized from the face of the earth. I wanted to help him. He wanted to marry me.

BAXTER: So, you're not carryin' his baby?

SHEDEVIL: I am.

BAXTER: He's been gone five years.

SHEDEVIL: He popped in once before.

BAXTER: I see.

SHEDEVIL: The last two weeks have been hell. Every night, he'd beat me…

BAXTER: *(Horrified.)* Beat you?

SHEDEVIL: Then he'd want me to cook home fries.

BAXTER: No?

SHEDEVIL: Then he'd beg me to kill him. Then he'd pull a few jokes.

BAXTER: Holy moley.

SHEDEVIL: Tonight, he'da made me cook home fries again.

BAXTER: Lordy…

SHEDEVIL: I just want to thank you, sir; you give him the peace he'd searched the world for.

BAXTER: I can hardly believe it.

SHEDEVIL: I can only say you did right.

SHIRL: You did right, honey.

ROB: More than that, you did good.

(Baxter breaks down crying. Shirl holds him; the others applaud him.)

BAXTER: Perky.

(He embraces her. Big 8 steps forward.)

BIG 8: I got to point out we got a sichy-ation here. *(People listen up.)* To the world, we got a lawman who's a brutal killer. They gonna rip off his badge…

SHIRL: Rip it off…

BIG 8: Whap him in the banger fifteen to twenty years.

SHIRL: A policeman in prison?

BIG 8: That man will never be able to take a damn shower.

SHIRL: Why can't he take a shower?

BIG 8: I'll explain it to you later.

SHIRL: Okay.

BIG 8: However, seen the other way, it's a act a' compassion.

SHEDEVIL: It is.

BIG 8: Somethin' every one of us in this room shoulda' done.

ROB: 'At's right.

SHIRL: Oh, I see about the shower.

BIG 8: We should have tried an' we didn't.

SHEDEVIL: Should have.

BIG 8: On'y Baxter did right.

ROB: Damn straight.

BIG 8: Now, we know it was Baxter did it… *(A chorus of "He did," "Did it right here," "Did it in cold blood.")* ...but we will never, never, never say. *("Never, never.")* You shot him down, but it's family business now. *(She hugs him.)*

BAXTER: By God, I'm honored...I am honored just to be in this home.

ROB: *(Raising one arm, fist closed, to the sky.)* For Baxter.

SHIRL: For Baxter.

(The others raise their arms and then, finally, Baxter. They are bound in blood. They look at each other.)

ROB: Now, how we gonna do this?

SHIRL: Well, one good thing, he ain't been seen in five years.

SHEDEVIL: That's right.

ROB: That's right.

BIG 8: His last wish was just to...disappear.

(A pause. They look at each other.)

SHIRL: Well, I can give him some help on that.

BAXTER: How's that, Honeybee?

SHIRL: I got my tools and aprons in the truck.

(She strides out.)

(Lights go down on the scene.)

Scene 2

The music between scenes should be Dolly Parton's "Working 9 to 5."

The lights come up on pure Breughel. Blood is everywhere. What's left of Black Dog is under a tarp on top of the butcher block island. Everyone wears bloody slaughterhouse aprons. They are equipped with well used hatchets and saws, dripping gore. There are several garbage bags already filled. It is night; the room is full of shadows. A hanging lamp over the island swings back and forth. Shirl, Big 8 and Shedevil are on top of the butcher block, working. Shedevil is standing with an open bag to receive the parts. As the lights come up, Shirl throws something into Shedevil's bag. We don't see exactly, but it reminds us of a foot. Rob is stacking bags and cleaning. Baxter sits away from this scene, his head in his hands. Everyone's face and hands are smeared with blood, except Baxter's. Shirl is sawing. Big 8 is hacking right through the tarp with an ax. A radio on the counter is tuned to a country station.

BIG 8: Hell, I like a little music while I work.

SHIRL: On the last leg now.

SHEDEVIL: Thwack!

ROB: I'm stackin' 'em up over here.

SHIRL: How you doin', Baxter honey?

BAXTER: Lord, dear Lord, give me strength.

SHIRL: Lemme finish up here, Big 8.

BIG 8: *(Rolling off the butcher block.)* Hard on the sciatica. I got to get me some Tylenol.

SHIRL: Shoot. *(Whack!)* I can do this. *(Whack!)* Twelve hours at a go. *(Whack, whack, whack!)* I believe that should just about do 'er. First one of those I ever butchered. *(Getting off the island. To Shedevil.)* Bring that bag around here, will you, sweetie? *(Shedevil brings a black bag to the other side. Shirl pulls the tarp off, leans forward and, with her forearms, sweeps the last of the remains into Shedevil's bag.)* Okey-dokey hokey-pokey.

ROB: Here we go.

SHIRL: *(She looks around at her companions.)* Hey, I could use me some snacks. *(Baxter runs out the front door.)* Shoulda give him a Dramamine.

BIG 8: Work up a damn thirst.

SHIRL: Shedevil, whack us out a couple of ice waters, will ya? *(Shedevil goes to the fridge.)* I did a couple more of these, I'd be nie onto gettin' it right. *(Baxter appears in the door.)* How you doin', Sweetpea?

BAXTER: Little mite queasy.

SHIRL: *(Reassuring.)* I was every bit of that when I started in slaughterin'. You just got to realize the nation's got to eat.

BIG 8: Or somethin'.

SHIRL: *(Gets it.)* Or somethin'.

BAXTER: I just...

BIG 8: Speak up, Baxter boy.

BAXTER: I just...see, I'm just wantin' to thank everybody.

BIG 8: Like they say on TV, "It takes a village." *(Gives Baxter a pat.)* Now, we got to have a little pow-wow here.
(Shedevil passes around ice water.)

SHIRL: *(Having checked the cupboards.)* Chex-Mix anybody's peckish.
(Rob leans on the island. Shedevil hops up and sits. The overhead lamp creates an odd spectacle. All except Baxter are in the slaughter aprons provided by Shirl.)

ROB: Got a couple root beers left.
(It has the atmosphere of a lunch-break at an abattoir.)

SHIRL: *(To Big 8.)* Little Thing, you still got my ol' cover-up from our pajama party? *(Touches Baxter's arm.)* A boy don't like to see his honey in her work things.

BIG 8: Top of the stairs. *(Shirl goes.)* Now, you listen up here, Baxter. We done our part, now it's up to you.

BAXTER: Yes, ma'am.

BIG 8: Don't call me ma'am. Time to take the garbage out, Baxter. Stick those bags in yer cruiser, honor poor ol' Jimmy's desire to disappear.

ROB: Got to stick him where the sun don't shine, boy.

BAXTER: I don't know...

SHEDEVIL: You can do it, Mr. Blue.

BAXTER: City dump's out.

ROB: How come?

BAXTER: Dogs.

SHIRL: How 'bout your attic?

(Shirl reappears in a robe. She also brings one for Big 8.)

BAXTER: Mama goes through my things. There is an old cistern in the basement of the police station.

ROB: See there.

BAXTER: Nobody goes down there.

BIG 8: Hey!

BAXTER: What?

SHIRL: Big 8's sayin' we don't want to know, baby.

BAXTER: Oh. But nobody does go down...

BIG 8: *(Finger to her lips.)* Shhh.

BAXTER: I git it.

SHIRL: *(Pecks him on the cheek.)* Snuggle bunny, you might want to load up.

BAXTER: Okey-dokey. *(Goes for a load of bags.)* I think it's gonna work out. *(Heads for door.)* I'll tell you one thing. *(Turns to face them.)* I got friends.

ROB: You do.

SHIRL: That's right.

BAXTER: Gonna take me a couple of loads.

SHIRL: Don't drop nothin'.

(He exits.)

BIG 8: Well, it's been real interestin' for a Monday. Did pretty good, though.

SHIRL: *(Offers Big 8 a cover-up.)* Sis, we did real good.

(Big 8, Rob and Shedevil take off the slaughterhouse aprons. They get piled

with the trash bags for Baxter to take out. Big 8 puts on the cover-up, taking off soiled clothes, if necessary.)

BIG 8: *(To Shedevil.)* Your real name Perky?

SHEDEVIL: Yeah, right.

BIG 8: Plus you ain't got an artificial hand, huh?

SHEDEVIL: Hell no.

ROB: So Black Dog didn't cut if off.

SHEDEVIL: Duh.

BIG 8: You got you a real talent for deception.

SHEDEVIL: Like you don't?

ROB: Well, it worked out, didn't it? Worked out for the best. See, the good guys...

BIG 8: *(Baxter re-enters for more bags.)* Rob Bob?

ROB: Well, it did.

BIG 8: Put a plug in it, would ya?

SHIRL: *(Pointing.)* You got a little finger stickin' out the bag there.

BAXTER: Oh my God.

SHIRL: *(Pushing the finger back in with her finger.)* This little piggy went to market.

BAXTER: Oh my God.

(She pecks him on the cheek.)

SHIRL: All set now, sugar pie?

BAXTER: *(As he exits.)* What am I doin'?

ROB: *(To Big 8, who is washing up. He puts on his shirt.)* Hey, Big 8?

BIG 8: *(A little cranky.)* What?

ROB: You know there's eleven Hoppy pitchers where the hero an' the girl ride out, you know, end of the pitcher?

BIG 8: Nine.

ROB: No, there's eleven.

SHIRL: *(Warningly.)* Rob Bob.

ROB: I wondered could I borry the loan of a couple of horses.

BIG 8: Where you headed, Rob Bob?

ROB: Well...

BIG 8: Go on, I ain't gonna be mad.

ROB: Figgered we'd go up to the cabin. No offense meant.

BIG 8: No offense taken.

ROB: Practice up, an' we might git hitched 'fore rodeo season.

SHIRL: *(Looks at Big 8.)* Oh my.

BIG 8: You up for that, Shedevil?

SHEDEVIL: Whatever.

BIG 8: What the hell's your name, girl?

SHEDEVIL: *(Staring directly at her.)* My name is get-outta-my-face, yo.

(A moment, then Big 8 looks over at Rob.)

BIG 8: You still goin' for "Top Cowboy," right?

ROB: Girl, I'm bringin' you back the buckle.

BIG 8: *(Looking at Shedevil.)* Yeah, I got me some fine buckles.

SHIRL: Speakin' of buckles...

BIG 8: Put a sock in it, Shirl.

ROB: *(To Big 8.)* That's a solemn promise.

BIG 8: Well, that's all right then.

SHIRL: It is?

BIG 8: It's all right.

ROB: Gollee! Give me a hug, 8.

BIG 8: Not in front of your fiancée.

ROB: Oh yeah. Say now, end of the pitcher it's usual the hero would pick out a little somethin' on the guitar.

BIG 8: It's pretty late, Rob Bob.

ROB: Couple of choruses of "Tumblin' Tumbleweeds"?

SHIRL: We got work real early.

ROB: *(Disappointed.)* Well, okay then.

BIG 8: *(To Shirl.)* Girlfrien', tomorrow mornin' I can skip the spare ribs. *(Shirl chuckles.)* Shedevil, seems like a pretty girl allus gits good luck, don't it? Got a good man fer yer hubby, got a bad man off yer trail, an' you don't have to listen to Lucifer Lee singin' "I Did it My Way." My hat's off to you, darlin'. *(Baxter is taking another load out.)* Git outta here, youngun's, I got housework to do.

ROB: We got to do the kiss.

SHIRL: We might could skip the kiss.

ROB: Dude, you can't skip the final kiss.

BIG 8: *(Shirl starts to speak; Big 8 stops her with a gesture.)* Cowboy, you the most traditional sumbitch I ever saw.

(Baxter returns. They all look at Rob and Shedevil.)

ROB: Stand up straight, Shedevil. We gonna ride the trails together.

(He kisses her sweetly on the lips.)

BAXTER: What's goin' on?

SHIRL: Don't even start to think.

BAXTER: But, she's affianced.

BIG 8: He's kinda dead, Baxter.

BAXTER: *(Looks at the bag he's picked up.)* Well, that's true.

SHIRL: Git that las' load out of here, Honeypot.

(Baxter goes.)

ROB: Better git our stuff.

(He runs upstairs for his saddle and bag. Shedevil crosses to get her bag.)

SHIRL: I'll help you tidy up.

BIG 8: Purely appreciate that.

(They go to get out cleaning materials. Rob returns with his gear.)

ROB: Big 8?

BIG 8: *(Turning.)* Yeah.

ROB: You got the spirit of the cowboy code, Big 8.

BIG 8: Uh-huh. *(He moves to embrace her. She forestalls him.)* Better say yer last words.

ROB: Huh?

BIG 8: Like Hoppy.

ROB: Oh, Jeez…holy moley… *(Goes and tosses his gear out the broken door.)* Darn-a-doodle, I almost forgot that. *(Turns.)* Lemme see. Ummm. Bad guy died. Good guy got the girl. Town's safe, an' justice triumphed. How's that?

BIG 8: Real good.

ROB: Guess me and the schoolmarm better mount up.

SHEDEVIL: Big 8?

BIG 8: Yeah.

SHEDEVIL: Y'all a bunch of schizoid murderin' misfits, an' you treated me bad as a stray dog while you done unspeakable horrors, but all in all I had a pretty good time.

BIG 8: Uh-huh.

SHEDEVIL: Thwack, kaboom.

BIG 8: Same to you, darlin'.

ROB: Let's mount up.

BIG 8: *(Rob and Shedevil start to go.)* Hey, Rob Bob?

ROB: Yes, ma'am.

BIG 8: Don't the hero carry his bride across the threshold?

ROB: Ain't that comin' in?

BIG 8: Well, you only got the goin' out.

ROB: Dang, I hadn't thought a that.

BIG 8: You almost did.

(Rob picks Shedevil up in his arms.)

ROB: All right now! Here we go. Ow!

BIG 8: What is it, darlin'?

ROB: Somethin' popped in my back.

BIG 8: Wouldn't be nuthin' serious.

SHEDEVIL: You drop me, you're toast.

ROB: Ow.

BIG 8: You carry her on out.

ROB: See you on down the trail. *(As he goes.)* Ow. Dang, that hurts. Ow. *(His voice disappears in the night.)* Dang. Oh my goodness. Ow. Shoot!

(Shirl and Big 8 watch them disappear into the world beyond.)

BIG 8: They're a pair, ain't they?

SHIRL: Did you pop that boy's back on purpose?

BIG 8: Oh, I don't know.

SHIRL: *(Eyes narrowed.)* What the hell you doin'?

BIG 8: What?

SHIRL: That girl absconded with your buckles.

BIG 8: I know.

SHIRL: I know you know.

BIG 8: Just a little weddin' present.

SHIRL: Uh-huh.

BIG 8: I got a big heart Shirl. *(Big 8 starts to clean. Shirl stares at her.)* You gonna take Baxter?

SHIRL: To the cleaners maybe.

BIG 8: Shirl?!

SHIRL: What he'll have in the police basement, hey, I'm goin' shoppin'.

BAXTER: *(Entering.)* I got him all in the cruiser.

SHIRL: You go along, sugar pie. I'm gonna help Sis tidy. *(He stands there.)* Baxter? *(He stands.)* What is it, Baxter?

BAXTER: I have forced my sweet beloved to dismember a human body, and with these hands I have carried slimy black plastic bags filled with dripping body parts, and now, by the dark of night, will stuff them in a basement cistern at the center of the temple of justice, and then, depraved, will go on livin' as part of the human community though I have become homicidal pond scum always seein' blood, blood, blood on my hands, branded forever with the mark of Cain, forsaken by my church and country, wanderin' like a wraith the secondary roads of Wyoming, giving out speeding tickets. The only upside is for the last three hours since I killed poor Jimmy, I been nonstop hard as a rock.

SHIRL: *(Pleased and amazed.)* Well, I'll be home real soon, Baxter.

BAXTER: The Lord works in mysterious ways.

SHIRL: You betcha. *(He raises a hand in benediction and exits.)* Hard day for you, Mama?

BIG 8: Seen better. Got its recompenses.

SHIRL: *(As they clean.)* Now what recompenses would those be, sister mine?
(Big 8 reaches in a drawer and tosses two rubber-banded stacks of bills onto the butcher block.) Well, goodness gracious.

BIG 8: You recall Black Dog come lookin' for his cocaine money?

SHIRL: How'd you git it, girl?

BIG 8: Oh, I found a spare minute to check her bag.

SHIRL: You cute ol' thing. She didn't notice, huh?

BIG 8: There was a lot goin' on.

SHIRL: Won't she miss it?

BIG 8: *(Picking up a cleaver.)* I don't believe she wants no further ado with us. Whatta ya' think?
(They smile and clean.)

SHIRL: How much would that be, sister mine?

BIG 8: Maybe nine thousand.

SHIRL: Six for the mortgage an' three for me?

BIG 8: I could see that.

SHIRL: *(Sticks out her hand.)* Sold American.
(They shake. From outside, we hear Rob's cry, "Hi yo, Silver, away!" Hoofbeats drum, moving away into silence.)

BIG 8: That boy is shameless!
(They clean.)

SHIRL: Did he hurt his back bad?

BIG 8: He did, yes.

SHIRL: Damn shame.

BIG 8: Damn shame. *(They clean.)* You think we're bad girls, Sis?

SHIRL: Littlebit, we're just doin' what we can.

BIG 8: Okay then.

SHIRL: You gonna miss the lovin'?

BIG 8: Gettin' harder to come by.

SHIRL: Damn truth.
(A beautiful young cowboy in full garb appears in the doorway.)

DONNIE: 'Scuse me.

(They see him.)

BIG 8: Thank you Jesus.

DONNIE: Woulda knocked but there's the lack of a door.

BIG 8: Uh-huh.

DONNIE: My name would be Memphis Donnie Pride.

BIG 8: Oh yeah. I believe I heard you're a pretty good roper?

DONNIE: *(Radiant smile.)* Ever onc't in a while.

BIG 8: Broke up, huh?

DONNIE: Doctors said I was flat done.

BIG 8: Doctors, huh?

DONNIE: Yes, ma'am.

BIG 8: Don't call me ma'am, Donnie Pride.

DONNIE: But you the legendary Big 8.

BIG 8: Gettin' more legendary by the minute.

DONNIE: Can you do 'er?

BIG 8: Cowboy, you take a seat on the porch. Little bit I'll be out to lay some hands on you.

DONNIE: Much obliged. I can't hardly wait.

(Tips his hat. Exits.)

SHIRL: He can't hardly wait.

(Shirl and Big 8 thrust their fists in the air, laughing. They take hands. The laughter grows.)

BLACK OUT

END OF PLAY

bobrauschenbergamerica
by Charles L. Mee

Copyright © 2001 by Charles L. Mee. All rights reserved. CAUTION: Professionals and amateurs are hereby warned that *bobrauschenbergamerica* is subject to a royalty. It is fully protected under the copyright laws of the United States of America and of all countries covered by the International Copyright Union (including the Dominion of Canada and the rest of the British Commonwealth), the Berne Convention, the Pan-American Copyright Convention and the Universal Copyright Convention, as well as all countries with which the United States has reciprocal copyright relations. All rights, including professional, amateur stage rights, motion picture, recitation, lecturing, public reading, radio broadcasting, television, video or sound recording, all other forms of mechanical or electronic reproduction, such as CD-ROM, CD-I, information storage and retrieval systems and photocopying, and the rights of translation into foreign languages, are strictly reserved. Particular emphasis is laid upon the matter of readings, permission for which must be secured from the Author's agent in writing.

ALL INQUIRIES CONCERNING RIGHTS, INCLUDING AMATEUR RIGHTS, SHOULD BE ADDRESSED TO: INTERNATIONAL CREATIVE MANAGEMENT, 40 W. 57th STREET, NEW YORK, NY 10019 ATTN: SAM COHN

BIOGRAPHY

Charles L. Mee. Among his plays are *Big Love* (24th Annual Humana Festival), *The Berlin Circle, Orestes, Vienna: Lusthaus, The Investigation of the Murder in El Salvador, Another Person is a Foreign Country* and *Time to Burn*. His plays have been performed in New York, Washington, Los Angeles and elsewhere in the United States, as well as in Venice, Vienna, Paris and other cities in Europe. Among his books are *Meeting at Potsdam, The Marshall Plan* and *The End of Order*. His books have been selections of the Book of the Month Club, the Literary Guild, and the History Book Club, and have been published in England, France, Germany, Italy, Argentina, Japan, Holland, Poland, Turkey, Yugoslavia, Israel and the United States. Mr. Mee's work is made possible by the support of Richard B. Fisher and Jeanne Donovan Fisher.

HUMANA FESTIVAL PRODUCTION

bobrauschenbergamerica was commissioned by Actors Theatre of Louisville and premiered at the Humana Festival of New American Plays in March 2001. It was directed by Anne Bogart with the following cast:

Bob's Mom	Kelly Maurer
Susan	Ellen Lauren
Phil's Girl	Akiko Aizawa
Phil the Trucker	Leon Pauli
Becker	J. Ed Araiza
Allen	Will Bond
Carl	Barney O'Hanlon
Wilson	Danyon Davis
Bob, The Pizza Boy	Gian-Murray Gianino
Girl	Jennifer Taher

and the following production staff:

Scenic/Costume Designer	James Schuette
Lighting Designer	Brian Scott
Sound Designer	Darron L. West
Properties Designer	Amahl Lovato
Stage Manager	Elizabeth Moreau
Assistant Stage Manager	Sarah Hodges
Dramaturg	Tanya Palmer
Assistant Dramaturg	Karen C. Petruska

CHARACTERS

BOB'S MOM
BECKER, THE FILTHY DERELICT
PHIL, THE TRUCKER
PHIL'S GIRL
SUSAN
WILSON
ALLEN
CARL
A 123-PIECE HIGH SCHOOL MARCHING BAND
BOB, THE PIZZA BOY

AUTHOR'S NOTE

The text for this piece was developed in a workshop with Tali Gai, Jane Comfort, Kathleen Turco-Lyon, Rebecca Brown, Reba Herman, Alec Duffy, Jacki Goldhammer, and Carolyn Clark Smith and incorporates texts from them as well as from Robert Rauschenberg, Fred Becker, Philip Morrison, Walt Whitman, William S. Burroughs, John Cage, Merce Cunningham, Allen Ginsberg, and Laurie Williams.

Charles L. Mee's work is made possible by the support of Richard B. Fisher and Jeanne Donovan Fisher.

Leon Pauli and Ellen Lauren in
bobrauschenbergamerica

25th Annual Humana Festival of New American Plays
Actors Theatre of Louisville, 2001
photo by Richard Trigg

bobrauschenbergamerica

An empty stage covered by a blank canvas. The actors come out to remove the canvas as music starts.

1 Title

A chicken slowly descends from the flies on a string.
It has a sign around its neck that says:
bobrauschenbergamerica

2 What I Like

A voiceover is heard while:

A roller skater bursts in with a big red umbrella.
The rest of the characters come out during the music, some with objects—the trucker has a bathtub on wheels with a light set in the mass of crunched steel where the showerhead should be, and maybe a One Way sign on the side of the tub. Susan has a stuffed deer on wheels, or maybe a goat with a tire around its stomach. Becker, the filthy, rag-dressed, disheveled, offhand derelict has a cardboard box. Phil's Girl pushes on a baby carriage with a stuffed chicken inside. Wilson has a house window on wheels. Allen crosses the stage carrying a ladder.

VOICEOVER: What I like to do is…
  I start with anything,
  a picture,
  these colors,

  I like these colors,

  or I might have an idea about something I'd like to try with a shoe,
  or maybe I just feel:
  happy.

Look,
everything overlaps doesn't it?

Is connected some kind of way.
Once you put it all together, it's just obvious.
I mean, tie a string to something, and
see where it takes you.
The biggest thing is
don't worry about it.
You're always gonna be moving somewhere so
don't worry about it.
See?
Start working when it's almost too late at night,
when your sense of efficiency is exhausted
and then just,
let it come on…

(The sign disappears and the characters exit as the voiceover ends.)

3 Bob's Mom

Bob's mom comes out onto the front porch.
She talks, while we hear crickets,
and while photos are projected behind her on the wall—
but her talk and the photos don't match up:

BOB'S MOM: That's Bob's first Birthday Party
on the back porch with the morning glories all in bloom
that's Butch East,
Johnnie East,
Susan East,
she just got arrested for drugs,
Billy Kraemer and Alex Cameron.

And that's Bob with Johnnie East in their canvas swimming pool
when they were about four
Johnnie popped that beach ball later that day
and I told Bob I wasn't buying another one.

252 CHARLES L. MEE

There's Bob with his dog Jab.
He used to feed him the cheese sandwiches I made the boys for lunch.
They're under the porch.

This is some kind of hut they made in the back yard
out of crates and branches and clothes.
You can see Bob's feet out the side.
That's Donna Kraemer trying to get in the back.

There are the boys outside Dobson's five & ten cent store.
They almost died blowing up those balloons—
they're six feet long.
It's Johnnie East, Bob and Tommy Hoffman.
The Port Arthur Independent ran this picture
on the front page of their second section for the Fourth of July.
Tommy Hoffman got meningitis and died.
That was a real sad day for all of us.

Art
art was not a part of our lives.

(*We hear a newspaper boy's bike bell. A newspaper is thrown onto the stage.
Bob's Mom picks it up, waves, and goes back inside.*)

4 Our Town

BECKER: Where I grew up
    you could walk to the end of the block
    and step right into the countryside
    field after field
    nobody owned this land so far as we knew.
    It had little lakes where we would cut down saplings
    and build lean-tos
    and camp out
    no grownups, just the kids, boys and girls
    we had no fear
    of anything.
    You could just go and go

you didn't know where you were headed
but you were a free person
you'd see where it was you'd been
after you came out of the woods at the end.

5 Setting Out

PHIL, THE TRUCKER: When I leave home at 5 AM,
    the Big Dipper is bright over my shoulder
    against the dark road we live on.
    And it's quiet.
    And if there's a moon
    it's still up and hovering
    over the little lake.
    The front range of hills is a dark silhouette in the background.
    In the evening ducks and geese are on the pond
    and the fish are standing on their tails.
    The quarry I load out of is surrounded by
    red monoliths of rock
    like sentinels
    with flocks of blackbirds perched on top.
    When the weather's hot the afternoon sky is blue,
    and it grows giant cumulus,
    which by evening go dark
    and shoot the most amazing sideways heli-arcs of fire.

(A bathing beauty, the trucker's girlfriend, enters sucking the tail end of a milkshake from a cup. Phil notices her.)

Everywhere I go there's something to see.
I don't know how I got so lucky.
But here I am.

(A girl on roller skates races across the stage.
Bob's Mom steps out onto her front porch, shaking out a dishtowel.

Faint music,
as though heard on a radio in a truck cab in the night,

or through the open window of a house in Kansas,
coming from another house, far distant across the field;
it could be the music of Ibrahim Ferrer,
or another country song.)

6 Falling in Love

Susan enters from the opposite side,
She sees Becker and he sees her. They stop.

SUSAN: So often we find
    we look at someone
    and
    we are disgusted.
BECKER: Oh, yes.
SUSAN: We think: here is a real dirtball
    and we think
    if we get too close
    we might catch something.
BECKER: Yes, we do.
SUSAN: And yet, as far as we know,
    we ourselves might be the contagious ones
    not knowing what it is we have
    but having it even so
    without knowing it.
BECKER: We never know.
SUSAN: Still, we think
    get this fellow away from me
    lock him up, put him away
    send him to an island
    you know, the island of the damned,
    the island of the rejects
    whatever
    just get him out of here.
    And yet, life twists and turns
    sometimes like lightning
    you don't know
    suddenly you've got cancer

and you are facing death
or in the least likely place
you see someone
and you fall in love
you look at the guy
and you think:
I don't think so
and yet there it is
you don't know why
your friends all say: are you crazy?
you love *him*?
but you love him so much
you just want to knock him down and kiss him.

(She runs at Becker,
knocks him down, and kisses him madly.)

7 The Triangle

Wilson enters.

WILSON: Hey, what the hell is going on here?
    Do you know who the hell you're kissing?
BECKER: No. No, I don't.
WILSON: This is my wife.
SUSAN: Wife?
WILSON: Fiancée.
SUSAN: Fiancée?
WILSON: My girlfriend.
    I mean, I thought we were going steady.
    What the hell is this?
    I walk/turn my back for one minute
    and you're taking up with someone else?
    What are you
    some sort of biological creature?
SUSAN: Yes. Yes, I am.
WILSON: I am from Chicago, Susan.
SUSAN: I know that, Wilson.

WILSON: So what do you think that means to me?
SUSAN: What?
WILSON: Kissing. What do you think that means?
SUSAN: I wouldn't have any idea.
WILSON: You see what's happened these days
    nobody can tell you what kissing means!
SUSAN: I can tell you what it means when I kiss you.
    It means goodbye.

(She walks out.)

8 Making Nice

> *A lone man, Allen, wearing shower cap and towel,*
> *enters and sings a song to smooth things over—*
> *The Inkspots' song: I don't want to set the world on fire—*
> *or something else to distract from the fight*
> *and get everyone's attention moving elsewhere—*
> *and the characters already on stage,*
> *Phil, Phil's Girl, Wilson and Becker the filthy derelict,*
> *sing backup for Allen. At some point in the song, Susan enters and joins in the*
> *song:*

> *I don't want to set the world on fire*
> *I don't want to set the world on fire*
> *I don't want to set the world on fire*
> *I don't want to set the world on fire*
> *I don't want to set the world on fire*
> *I don't want to set the world on fire*
> *I don't want to set the world on fire*
> *I don't want to set the world on fire*
> *I don't want to set the world on fire*

9 Another Lover

> *Another man, Carl, enters and dances to the song,*
> *and after Allen sings,*
> *while the music is still playing,*

Allen, the singer, joins Carl, the dancer,
so that they dance together.

Wilson takes over as soloist
when the lyrics pick up again.

(NOTE: as the piece goes on, there will be several relationships among the
characters contained in dialogue—but also all sorts of relationships are possi-
ble without dialogue, in bits of physical actions that occur on the side,
and in dances that suggest deeper, more lingering relationships.

At the end of the song, Carl and Allen exit together. During the following
scene, the rest of the characters gradually leave Phil and Phil's Girl alone in
the tub.)

10 The Bathing Beauty

PHIL, THE TRUCKER: I look at you and I think
    if it wouldn't be wrong
    I'd like to make love with you on a pool table.
PHIL'S GIRL: It wouldn't be wrong if you'd let me handcuff you to the pockets.
PHIL, THE TRUCKER: You could do that.
PHIL'S GIRL: What I think about is
    I'd like to have sex with you in the parking lot
    behind the Exxon station
    near that diner on the Malibu highway
    you know the one?
PHIL, THE TRUCKER: Near that road up into the canyon.
PHIL'S GIRL: That's the one.
PHIL, THE TRUCKER: That would be pretty public.
PHIL'S GIRL: I'd like to have the whole world see
    you want me so much
    you can't wait.
    I'd like to have the whole world see
    you're not ashamed of me.
PHIL, THE TRUCKER: Why would I be ashamed of you?
PHIL'S GIRL: I feel ashamed myself.
PHIL, THE TRUCKER: For what reason?

PHIL'S GIRL: Who knows?

Every fifteen minutes I feel ashamed of myself at least once.

And humiliated.

For no reason.

It just comes back to me over and over again.

Do you ever feel that way?

PHIL, THE TRUCKER: Every fifteen minutes I feel worried.

PHIL'S GIRL: Do you feel you want to hurt someone?

PHIL, THE TRUCKER: No.

PHIL'S GIRL: Do you feel you want to get even?

PHIL, THE TRUCKER: No.

PHIL'S GIRL: That's good.

Do you feel you want to bite something?

PHIL, THE TRUCKER: I don't think so.

Maybe I feel that.

PHIL'S GIRL: Do you feel you want to take off all your clothes?

PHIL, THE TRUCKER: No.

I usually don't feel that.

PHIL'S GIRL: Do you feel you want more money?

PHIL, THE TRUCKER: Oh, sure. Everybody feels that.

A VOICE CALLS OUT: Lunch is served!

(A big table and several chairs are brought out.)

VARIOUS PEOPLE SAY: Oh, thank god.

I'm famished!

Just in time!

I wasn't going to last another minute!

(Bob's Mom brings out a roast chicken. Chicken picnic lunch is served.
Everyone takes some food and sits in the chairs.)

11 Table Talk: The Stars

ALLEN: The way the stars are, with your naked eyes you can't see much.

SUSAN: Oh.

No. Unless you know a lot.

ALLEN: But even looking at the stars,
   I would rather say the night sky,
   you see two kinds of things…three or four kinds of things.
SUSAN: You see planets, you see stars, you see meteorites,
   you can see aircrafts…
   all these things…
ALLEN: so it's a great show
   the way the planets appear and dance around,
   we follow it all the time
   and we have on our bulletin boards in the back…
   and we have a chart of the whole thing,
   and people record that stuff…
   because we know these motions very well.
   It's the foundation probably of qualitative science.
SUSAN: The early work of people trying to understand…
ALLEN: first just day and night,
   then the seasons
   and then the stars and then the planets…
   there are different things that go back tens of thousands of years,
   older than written history.
SUSAN: Right.
ALLEN: There is a great deal more space than time, you know.
SUSAN: No.
ALLEN: Yes.
   And this is because the signals we can get
   all come in at the speed of light…
SUSAN: that's really fast.
ALLEN: Yes. And they cover a great distance.
   So it doesn't take them much time to cover a lot of distance—
   that's how you get more space than time in the universe.
SUSAN: Right.
   Right.

12 Table Talk: The Dispute

WILSON: How could you just suddenly: disappear?
SUSAN: I didn't.

WILSON: I thought you did.
　　And I thought you loved me.
SUSAN: Well, I do love you.

(The other characters exit.)

WILSON: Oh, yes, you love me,
　　but you don't love me in that way.
SUSAN: I never pretended to love you in that way.
WILSON: I can't go on in life
　　without being loved in that way.
SUSAN: A lot of people are never loved in that way.
WILSON: How can you tell
　　if you are really alive
　　if you're never loved in that way?
SUSAN: What do you mean: in that way?
WILSON: Unless I thought you were crazy for me
　　so crazy for me you couldn't stand it
　　you just had to kiss me
　　you just had to knock me down and kiss me
　　because you couldn't stand it
　　that you laughed at my jokes
　　or thought I was so cool
　　or like said really intelligent things that made you think
　　maybe not all of those things
　　but even just any one of them
　　just one of them
　　(Silence.)
　　You see what I mean, not even one.
SUSAN: I'm sorry.
WILSON: Why did you live with me, then?
SUSAN: I thought I loved you
　　but I guess I didn't know what love was.
　　I liked you in a way
　　not much
　　but in some ways
　　or at least in the ways I thought guys could be likeable
　　and the rest of it I thought maybe that's just

how guys are
and as time went on maybe it wouldn't matter so much
but then I find it does matter
I can't help myself
some stuff you do
I just can't get over it
and the stuff I liked:
that I thought you were a responsible person
and mature
solid and dependable
all those turned out not to be true at all
so what am I left with?

WILSON: It's not your fault.

SUSAN: No, it's not.

WILSON: Or maybe it is
that you weren't thinking very clearly
or being very focused when you made your choice
and a lot of people were depending on that choice being really clear
or at least I was

SUSAN: I know.
I'm sorry.

WILSON: Being sorry doesn't cut it somehow.
I know people always say they're sorry
and probably they are
and I don't think it means nothing
I'm sure it means something
and it's essential for people to feel it
and to say it
in order for life to go on at all
and yet
the truth is
it doesn't cut it.
I'm sorry: but it doesn't.

SUSAN: I'm sorry.

WILSON: Is that somehow now
supposed to cut it?

13 Table Talk: A Couple Seeks Advice

Everyone comes back on and starts clearing the table. Allen and Carl talk about their idea, both interrupting one another and talking simultaneously.

ALLEN: OK.

I would like to hear opinions or advice on my idea.

CARL: Well, our idea.

ALLEN: Our idea.

It's a business really.

CARL: A new business because...

ALLEN: because the catering business is not like a *big* business.

CARL: So a year ago we bought a small acreage

we thought: let's go into a real business for ourselves

have a small business

ALLEN: and we fixed up the chicken coop

CARL: and bought twenty broiler chicks to raise for our own butchering.

ALLEN: I have an ample enough coop to raise more chickens for butchering

and also some egg producers.

CARL: I like this idea because I've always wanted to do something with farming,

ALLEN: but we didn't inherit farmland,

CARL: which is usually how you get to be a farmer.

ALLEN: Well, anyway, how do you find your target market ?

CARL: Advertising would not be hard,

I have a good program on my computer to make flyers and

business cards,

ALLEN: but do we have to get a license to maybe sell to local restaurants?

CARL: Do we have to be monitored by the state since we'd be selling meat?

ALLEN: We just have the idea

and now we don't know what to do with it

CARL: and also we're nervous about failing

and Allen:

he's afraid if we go into the chicken business

he's going to end up looking like a chicken.

ALLEN: Well.

I mean, look at Frank Perdue.

CARL: What do you mean?

ALLEN: What do you mean, what do you mean?

CARL: You mean he looks like a chicken?

ALLEN: Well, look at him.

CARL: I don't think being a chicken farmer
is going to make you look like a chicken, Allen,
otherwise plumbers would look like pipes
carpenters would look like sawdust
the president of General Motors would look like a bumper.

ALLEN: Have you seen the president of General Motors?

(Allen and Carl storm off. Phil, Phil's Girl, Wilson, and Becker exit. Susan climbs into the bathtub. Bob's Mom is left on stage.)

14 Table Talk: Bob's Mom's Grandmother

Bob's Mom talking about family photos in album, a slide is projected behind her.

BOB'S MOM: When I was sixteen my grandmother had to be put into a home. My grandmother had terrorized my mother and uncle for so many years it was difficult to feel much in the way of empathy or compassion or love for her. But I related to her in one way. We shared a real passion for the color red. My grandmother's house was a museum. She collected cut Italian colored glass decanters and glasses. Each object uniquely shaped. Colors rich. I valued those objects deeply. I wanted to play with them, to make new shapes of them, to make new surfaces for them. I wanted to smash them and see what they looked like as heaps, to see how light played on their shattered surfaces. My grandmother always wore a large rectangular ruby pendant on a gold chain. I dreamed of having that one day. Of having that color. When my grandmother died I asked what became of the ruby. It turned out she had gone into the home years before and everything was sold at a yard sale. The objects she collected—beautiful objects—all discarded. Thrown out. No one wanted them. Cast off. I would have preferred to smash them against brick walls to see what they might have become.

Well, art was not a part of our lives.

(A girl skates through on roller skates. People drift back slowly and continue to clear away the food from the picnic.)

15 Guy Talk

Phil comes out with a checkerboard.
He sits down beside Susan and they start to play checkers.
As this scene goes on,
people drift to and from the table,
getting up to get something and then not coming back, going inside,
or getting up to get another drink for someone
and then not coming back,
some taking their plates or glasses with them
to continue eating and drinking wherever they stand.

And as the conversation continues,
the others may begin to engage in other activities—
Allen and Carl both bring out ironing boards and start to do some ironing in
the background;
Phil's Girl swings in a tire swing;
Becker the filthy derelict sets up housekeeping inside his box;
etc.

SUSAN: The woman next door
   is having an affair with an orchestra conductor in Cincinnati.
PHIL, THE TRUCKER: Does Cincinnati have an orchestra?
SUSAN: I guess it does.
PHIL, THE TRUCKER: Does her husband know?
SUSAN: He doesn't know.
   She just flies off to Cincinnati from time to time
   when her husband is away on business
   or the conductor comes to Denver.
PHIL, THE TRUCKER: How did they meet?
SUSAN: On an airplane.
PHIL, THE TRUCKER: What does she do?
SUSAN: I don't know.
   She flies around a lot.
PHIL, THE TRUCKER: Is she a stewardess?
SUSAN: Oh, right.
   She's a stewardess.
PHIL, THE TRUCKER: No wonder she can just go wherever she wants.

SUSAN: Right.

PHIL, THE TRUCKER: It's a perfect job if you want to have love affairs.

SUSAN: Right.

PHIL, THE TRUCKER: Do you think all stewardesses are having love affairs?

SUSAN: Well, most of them probably.

PHIL, THE TRUCKER: Why not?

SUSAN: Exactly.

PHIL, THE TRUCKER: Would you, if you were a stewardess?

SUSAN: Yes, I think I would.

PHIL, THE TRUCKER: So would I.

SUSAN: I have to pee.

PHIL, THE TRUCKER: What?

SUSAN: I have to pee.
Would you wait here?

PHIL, THE TRUCKER: Oh. Sure.

(She leaves;
everyone stops what they are doing,
turn to look, and just stand around waiting for her to come back;
we hear a flush from offstage;
finally she returns.)

SUSAN: Times have changed.

(Everyone else resumes what they were doing.)

PHIL, THE TRUCKER: Since when?

SUSAN: Since, oh, I don't know.

PHIL, THE TRUCKER: I don't think they have.

SUSAN: Of course they have.

PHIL, THE TRUCKER: Well, of course they have
in the sense that now you have electric lights and so forth
the internet
whatnot,
but otherwise I don't think times have changed.

SUSAN: I think they have.

PHIL, THE TRUCKER: Compared to what?

SUSAN: My grandmother.

PHIL, THE TRUCKER: You wouldn't know.

SUSAN: That's true.
I wouldn't know.
Maybe that's what changed.

But in Russia you know
they didn't have love affairs for years
all during the communists.

PHIL, THE TRUCKER: How do you know?

SUSAN: There was a study.
They didn't even have sex with their husbands and wives
not much.

PHIL, THE TRUCKER: Why not?

SUSAN: They didn't feel like it.

PHIL, THE TRUCKER: Are they having sex now?

SUSAN: Now! Well, sure. I suppose they are.
You know, things have changed in Russia.

16 Becker's Movie

Becker climbs out of his box, holding two old license plates, which he uses as the script. He casts the other people in the movie and they do the roles as well as being film crew and audience. The objects around them on the stage become props in the film. Bob's Mom watches from inside the house.

BECKER: OK. I have an idea for a movie.
I think this could be really great.

You will play Clem, the meteorologist
you will be the billionaire on his deathbed,
the roles are all marked for you in the script.

Ready?

CAST MEMBERS: *(Variously.)*
Sure.
OK.
Right.

BECKER: OK. Here it is:

This is a film about a conspiracy to blow up a train carrying nerve gas from the west coast to the east coast where it is supposed to be dumped into the Atlantic. Only one FBI man is alert to the danger and he cannot convince his superiors that a conspiracy exists. He is playing a hunch and sometimes he doubts the validity of his intuition. Minutes before countdown he has the evidence he needs.

OK.

The conspirators include a folksy meteorologist, an embittered homosexual, a Chinese cameraman, a Lesbian, a Mexican pistolero, a Negro castrated in his cradle by rat bites. The time and place for countdown depends of course on prevailing winds and the meteorologist is busy with continual calculations, weather maps, barometer and wind reads, telescopic observation of clouds and birds. There are also instruments of his own invention. He is contemptuous of weather reports.

ALLEN AS CLEM, THE METEOROLOGIST: Doesn't know a typhoon from a fart. You see that vulture up yonder? He can tell you more than a room full of weather maps and barometers. The birds know.

BECKER: The conspiracy is financed by a private inheritance. This sum was left to Clem the meteorologist by an eccentric billionaire perturbed by overpopulation, air and water pollution, and the destruction of wild life. Now there is a shot of the billionaire speaking on his deathbed.

CARL AS BILLIONAIRE ON HIS DEATHBED: Clem, swear to me by everything we both hold sacred that you will use every cent of that money to turn the clock back to 1899 when a silver dollar bought a good meal or a good piece of ass.

BECKER: Cut to conspirators headquarters in run-down 1920 bungalow. Audrey *(Becker indicates Susan)* the homosexual is looking through the Telstar. Inside the gate the last cylinders of nerve gas are being loaded into a train. The Telstar lingers lovingly on the ass of a young soldier who is bending over to pick up a cylinder of gas. Mr. Lee the Chinese cameraman takes over at the Telstar. Train doors shut and locked. A gum-chewing MP reading Sextoons presses a button. The train moves out.

ALLEN AS CLEM: You know I love this country. Only thing wrong with it is the folks living there.

BECKER: His face goes black with hate.

ALLEN AS CLEM: Mother loving stupid asses bible belt cuntsuckers.

BECKER: He smiles and turns to Audrey, Miss Longridge and the spade whose name is Jones.

(Phil's Girl becomes Miss Longridge, Wilson becomes Jones and Tio Mate.)

ALLEN AS CLEM: Now you're city folk. You never drank cool spring water on a summer afternoon. You never sat down to fried squirrel and jack salmon with black-eyed peas and wild raspberries. You never sank your hands in the soil and let it run through your fingers.

BECKER: He turns back to the map.

ALLEN AS CLEM: Yes, sir. We're going to lay down a mighty fine load of fertilizer.

BECKER: He sweeps his hand across the Middle West.

ALLEN AS CLEM: The trees will grow again, the bison will come back, the wild turkey and the deer.

SUSAN AS AUDREY: Other people are different from me, and I don't like them.

BECKER: Miss Longridge is looking at the nudes in Playboy. Tio Mate the Mexican pistolero is cleaning his Smith & Wesson tip-up 44. Jones is taking a fix.

Cut to FBI man pacing up and down in his office.

CARL AS ROGERS: I tell you I had a dream. I saw that train go up and that gas sweeping up the Eastern seaboard.

PHIL'S GIRL AS FALK: Are you going to tell the chief about your dream, Joe?

BECKER: *(ROGERS, picking up the phone.)*

CARL AS ROGERS: No, but I'm going to ask him for more agents.

BECKER: Cover story for the conspirators is that they are making a documentary film of America. Clem is the director, Lee the cameraman, Audrey the script writer, Miss Longridge the business manager and Tio Mate the studio guard. The film of course *is* a documentary of America.

In a deserted roadhouse Audrey rapes a young sailor at gunpoint while Lee impassively films the action.

AUDREY: OK. CUT! You can put your clothes on now. And now let's see how fast you can run.

BECKER: Sailor takes off like a rabbit and reaches the top of a hill fifty yards away. Tio Mate draws and aims and fires. Tio Mate can blast a vulture out of the air with his 44.

Miss Longridge rapes two female hitchhikers. And then, stark naked, she kills them with a baseball bat.

They stop at a filling station and honk. Nobody comes, so Jones gets out to fill the tank himself. At this moment, the owner of the filling station, a Nigger-killing lawman with six notches on his gun, comes out a side door.

PHIL,THE TRUCKER AS LAWMAN: Get away from that pump, boy.

WILSON AS JONES: Yassuh, boss.

(As Becker speaks the following lines, everyone tries to keep up. Chaos ensues.)

BECKER: Jones drenches the lawman with gasoline and sets him on fire.

Jones who is hooked on junk leaves a wake of dead druggists.

Audrey is restrained at gun point from mass rape of a Boy Scout troop.

Tio Mate shoots down an army helicopter.

Clem sounds a word of warning to his impetuous companions.

ALLEN AS CLEM: Such a thing as too much fun. We're leaving a trail like a herd of elephants.

BECKER: That's as far as I've gotten so far.
How do you like it?

(No one is sure how to respond.)

17 Line Dancing

Suddenly: a line dance.
At the end, it stops as suddenly as it began,
and everyone goes back to their normal lives. Phil's Girl crawls into the tub,
Becker climbs back into his box and watches the following scene. Everyone else
exits, except for Wilson and Susan, who are left onstage.

18 Crazy for You

WILSON: *(Confronting Susan.)* So
it turns out
you come to me
to be with me
and then
as soon as you feel reassured that I love you

you go back to your husband
and then if you talk to me on the phone
and I seem to be slipping away from you
if I seem anxious or uncertain
then you come back to me and make love with me
and stay with me
until you know you have me again
I can't help myself loving you
and then you go back to your husband again
so it turns out
the only way I can keep you is by making you feel anxious
keeping you on edge
making you feel I'm about to drop you
so the way to have you
is to reject you
and if I don't reject you
then I don't have you
we are in a relationship that is sick
where you show love by showing aversion
you show aversion by showing love
so that you live a backwards life
and the one person you want to love and cherish
and show how much you care
is the one person you will drive away by doing any of those things
how can we go on like this?
This is insane
this will make us both insane
this is how people go insane!

(He storms out.)

19 Dessert

Bob's Mom brings out a cake and
sets it down on the picnic table.
As this next scene goes along,
Susan starts to eat compulsively,
taking pieces of cake or cupcakes from the table—

at first absent-mindedly, at a normal cake-eating pace,
and then more and more compulsively,
until she is stuffing it into her mouth.

BECKER: I think I know how he feels myself.
I thought you cared for me, too.
SUSAN: I did care for you.
There was something about you
I don't even know what it was that just hit me
I couldn't help myself
but then it turns out
it was like a summer storm
it passed as quickly as it came
and then it was over.
BECKER: Maybe it wasn't over for me.
SUSAN: I'm sorry.
BECKER: I don't think you can just drop someone like that
and just say I'm sorry.
SUSAN: I didn't just say I'm sorry
I am sorry.
BECKER: This is why some people call women fickle.
SUSAN: I don't think it has anything to do with being fickle.
How it is for women:
Women feel what they feel when they feel it
and then when they don't feel it any more they don't feel it.

Unlike a man
who won't know what he feels when he feels it
and then later on
he'll realize how he felt
and so he'll talk himself into feeling it again
when he doesn't feel it
because he thinks he should be consistent about the positions he takes
and stick to them
so a man always thinks he feels things he doesn't feel
and so he never really knows how he feels at all.
BECKER: That could be true.

SUSAN: Of course it's true.
   Pretty soon
   you're going to thank god you had such a narrow escape
   you're going to feel lucky I dumped you.
BECKER: I'm never going to feel that.
SUSAN: Maybe not.
BECKER: I think you must be a sort of a tease
   or worse
   some kind of seducer and dumper kind of person
   who is just a loose cannon
   cutting a swath through men
   leaving them wrecked all around you
   what is that all about?
   (She speaks, with a mouth full of cake,
   eating as she speaks,
   with greater and greater animation as she goes on,
   till she is yelling through a mouth full of cake.)
SUSAN: Maybe that would be about something
   if it were in any way true
   but it is not in any way true
   I'm a person who is looking for true love
   like anyone else
   except the difference is
   I am trying not to be afraid of my feelings
   and censor things
   and lie and lie and lie all the time
   pretending I feel like this or that
   going with some guy because I couldn't be sure any more
   how I felt about him
   because he had some things I liked and other things I didn't
   and trying to talk myself into not caring about the things I cared about
   and caring about the things I didn't care about
   because I've done that a lot in the past
   so I am trying to let my feelings lead me through life
   And
   feelings are feelings
   they come and go.
   So probably I'm just as disoriented as you are

and left in the lurch
suddenly dropped
or thrown down the stairs
it's not as though this is not a struggle for me too
but the one thing you can be sure of is
if ever I am sure of how I feel
in a way that is the kind of feeling that I know will last
then when that time comes
if it so happens that I do tell you I love you
then you can be sure of it.

(Becker and Susan exit.)

20 Martinis

Music.

Phil's Girl brings out an immense piece of plastic sheeting
which she spreads out on the floor.
She takes a bottle of gin
and pours it out on the sheeting,
then she takes a bottle of vermouth
and waves it over the gin,
then she takes a bottle of olives and pours it out onto the gin;
she begins to slide forward on the gin,
licking it up with her tongue.
Phil enters in a bathing suit
and he joins her
sliding forward on his stomach
and licking up the martini.

Everyone enters and clears the stage.
A girl on roller skates rolls by.
The stage is empty.

21 Why does the chicken cross the stage?

A chicken crosses the stage—moving cautiously, stopping and looking around as he goes, scratching at the ground—maybe while we hear, as a voiceover, an astronaut talking to Houston base.

VOICEOVER FROM SPEAKERS: A man in a chicken suit crosses the stage.

(Silence, till the chicken is almost off the other side.)

Why does he cross the stage?

22 The Universe

Music begins to play. Characters arrive slowly, all of them moving as if walking on the moon. Allen emerges first, pushing a car door on wheels. Susan and Phil's Girl are cuddled up inside.
While:

A man (Wilson) practices his golf swing in slow motion and:

A young girl eats candy wrappers or dog biscuits to the awe of her peers while Allen speaks:

ALLEN: You think that you see what's present…but you don't, you never do…
All you can ever see is the past.
Look in the mirror,
you see a person in the mirror who is younger than you are…
because the light has to go from you to the mirror
and from the mirror to your eye.
So it leaves you, goes to the mirror
and comes back.
So whenever you see yourself,
you see yourself a little earlier.
It's actually unimportant. It's nanoseconds.
But the truth is:
all any human being can ever observe is the past.
You never see the present.

And everything you look at is younger than it is right now.
When you look at the universe,
you are looking at a universe that is billions of years younger.

(Allen and Susan drift off into space. Phil's Girl joins the golfer. Carl rides by on a bike. He climbs off the bike, and then laundry falls from above. Bob's Mom comes out and watches him.)

23 The Laundry Opera

Carl dives over and over again into a pile of laundry while we hear an operatic aria. After a while, Carl exits.

24 Clean Sweep

Becker the filthy derelict, as janitor with a push broom, crosses, sweeping up the laundry, while Bob's Mom speaks again, with slides projected behind her, but the photos don't match up:

BOB'S MOM: That's Bob and Freddie Martin
dressed up as The Lone Ranger and Hopalong Cassidy.
Look at them in their masks and cowboy hats,
with all those swords and guns and flashlights stuck in their belts.
Two tough little cowboys.
I don't think Hopalong ever wore a mask, actually.

This is Bob
and some kind of contraption he made in Boy Scouts
from hundreds of popsicle sticks.
You can see how he glued the sticks all straight
and organized at the bottom
and then where he got bored.
He started gluing the sticks every which a way
and adding feathers and bottle caps and twigs to it
so it looked like that on top.
He looks pretty pleased with himself,
but I don't think the Scoutmaster was.

Oh my Lord, that's Bob up on the roof
trying to fix his short wave radio antenna.
Just after I took that picture the antenna fell over
and touched the power line on the street.
He was smart enough to let go in time,
but the power blew up his radio and burned a hole in his desk.
I think he got more careful about things after that.

And here's Bob and Barbara Spangler
at Ethel Howell's Ballroom Dance Class end-of-the-year formal.
Barbara got the Most Polite Student Award that year.
I don't know why Bob didn't get one too.
He certainly was just as polite as she was.

25 The Galaxy

Allen enters with a ladder. He climbs to the top of the ladder and speaks.
During the scene, the other characters come out one by one and wave at him.
He appears to be waving back, but he exists in a different time and space,
and his gestures are linked to the images he is describing.

ALLEN: This connection between time and space is everything…and you can't
interpret or judge easily the way we can around here. That's why we're
not sure of many things because we have only one interpretation—the
way things look to us here on earth at one particular moment.

What we did: we thought it was, at that point, urgently necessary to do
that. But I don't know why that is. In any case, it all happened and it's
very hard to see how it could have gone otherwise.

But the place itself was fascinating, especially for a scientist engaged in the
work…

it was dangerous…it seemed very responsible, it demanded all our attention, and we worried a great deal about what was happening…

But, meanwhile, it was a beautiful place, a high mountain, 8,000 feet high,
fair weather in New Mexico, in the winter it snowed, in the summer it was

hot, never humid. The snow would cover the whole world in two feet of snow overnight and a week later it would be gone...no trace of it...

And when the snow was there you'd poke a hole, you'd look into it and you would see a deep blue color...because of the sky...the shadows are blue against it...for the same reason. The bright blue sky light...the bright blue sky light fills in the shadows and the shadows are intercepting the light from the sun itself. Just that little bright disc.

So behind it, in the shadow, like the earth's shadow, there's a kind of local light that has a blue tinge because the sky has not turned off. At night, the sky is turned off because the sun is what illuminates the sky, illuminates the earth and the sky, the sky is just there and we see the air in the shadow.

So it's the most beautiful place, Los Alamos... It was very grim, you knew the outcome couldn't work at all, that's what we all thought, but we weren't going to give it up.

(A newspaper boy's bell. Bob's Mom comes out to pick up the newspaper. The other characters come out to admire the stars.)

26 Square Dance

A country music song slams into the piece—
remember what country music does, how American it is, how it adds
automatically themes of love, betrayal, a hundred story lines enter the piece
with country music
a country music song
a country music song
a country music song
a country music song
a country music song
a country music song
a country music song
a country music song
a country music song

CARL : Square up everyone

(Music starts. Carl does a singing square dance call,
the old square dance standard:)

Four ladies to the center and back to the bar
four gents center with a right hand star
opposite ladies for an aleman thar
back up boys but not too far
throw in the clutch, put 'er in low
it's twice around that ring you go
on to the next for a do pass-o
and bring her on home as fast as you go
down in Arkansas on my knees
I thought I heard a chicken sneeze
I looked around here's what I saw
a bald headed maid with a pretty little taw

(The rest of the characters join in on the following verse.)

ALL: too old, too old
I'm too old to cut the mustard any more.

(The music cuts out into ecstatic mode—
The square dancers
do flat out clog-stomping
so that they seem to float in the air
and only occasionally it seems the heel of a boot stomps the floor
as they float in ecstasy.

As the music continues,
Wilson and Susan have an especially ecstatic duet.)

27 The Assassination

Carl is assassinated—several shots ring out and he drops dead. Allen catches
him and holds him. People stand around staring, then slowly go off, leaving
Allen, Carl and Phil onstage.

28 Chicken Jokes

Phil tells chicken jokes to distract from the solemnity.

PHIL: A chicken went into a library
and went up to the circulation desk
and said to the librarian:
Boooook!
Book! Book! Book!
So the librarian gave the chicken four books,
and the chicken left
and came back later that day,
put the four books down and said:
Book! Book!
So the librarian took back the first four books
and gave the chicken two new books
and the chicken left
and came back later the same day,
put down the two books and said:
Book! Book! Book!
So the librarian took back the two books
and gave the chicken three new books
and the chicken left.
But this time the librarian
followed the chicken out of the library
to see what it was doing with these books
since no one could read fast enough
to go through those nine books in a single day.
So the librarian followed the chicken down a dirt road
and right down a path through the woods
and came to a pond
where the chicken was handing the books
one by one
to a frog
who kept saying of one book after another:
Read it! Read it! Read it!

(Allen carefully places Carl down on the ground, and leaves.)

A chicken and an egg are lying in bed. The chicken is leaning against the headboard smoking a cigarette, with a satisfied smile on its face. The egg, looking a bit ticked off, grabs the sheet, rolls over, and says, "Well, I guess we finally answered THAT question!"

What do you call a chicken that wakes you up at the same time every morning?
An Alarm Cluck!

The sound it makes is tick tock a doodle do.

If you have deviled eggs, what you need is an eggsorcist.

Chickens are the hardest working animals. They work around the cluck.

Chicken soup is good for you. Unless you're a chicken!

When a chicken is crazy, it's referred to as a cuckoo cluck.

Why didn't the chicken look both ways before she crossed the road?

(Waits for the audience to answer.)

Because she was a dumb cluck!

(Phil exits.)

29 Welcome Speech

Carl, who has been lying on the stage dead, sits up and gives a speech welcoming everyone to an art opening, while we hear cement mixers, pounding, banging, clanking, sawing.

CARL: OK.
How we put the show together.
First, I want to welcome everyone

I'm glad you could all come tonight.
We don't often get to do a show like this
where we can just put on whatever we like
figure OK what the hell
lets just do whatever we feel like
and hope you'll enjoy it.
I often feel those of us who are in the museum world
are particularly blessed.
Because we get to explore our feelings
whatever they may be
that's a sort of freedom.
You know, that's how it is to deal with art
because art is made in the freedom of the imagination
with no rules
it's the only human activity like that
where it can do no one any harm
so it is possible to be completely free
and see what it may be that people think and feel
when they are completely free
in a way, what it is to be human when a human being is free
and so art lets us practice freedom
and helps us know what it is to be free
and so what it is to be human.

But, still, it often seems to me almost miraculous
how we can put things here in the museum
and ordinary folks
my mom and dad and my own neighbors
and I myself
will come to see things
sometimes things that I myself find completely incomprehensible
and really offensive
people will come to our museum
and think: oh, that's interesting
or, oh, that's stupid
but they don't really hold it against the show
they just move on and look at something else and think
oh that's cool.

And I wonder:
how do we get away with that?
And I think well, we are a free people
that's why
and we understand that
in a way maybe other people in the world don't
we like an adventure
often we might think
well, that's a piece of junk
but that's how this fellow sees the world
and there's a certain pleasure in seeing things from his point of view
we are a patient people
no matter what you hear people say
and a tolerant people
and a fearless, open people
that's how it is for us

I think that's how it is to be an American.

We're all unique.
It's a precious thing to compare ourselves to nothing else.
This is my working attitude.
I don't feel shame in my joy.

(He looks confused.)

I started out here knowing what I meant to say
and now I have to say
I don't know what I said.

But I'd just like to welcome you
and let you know
we're all glad to be here with you tonight
to share this with you
and we hope you have a swell evening.

30 General Applause

Canned applause and bravos from the audience at the 25th anniversary Cage concert at Carnegie Hall, which continues over the following scene:

31 Yard Sale

Bob's Mom comes out, puts something down, goes back inside.
A guy comes in, looks at something,
hands money to someone
and walks out with it,
and then others enter and do the same
while Phil speaks:

PHIL: On the way out of Albany
we stopped at Joe's Eat All You Want restaurant ($1.50).
Just for dessert Steve Paxton had five pieces of pie.
I asked the cashier on the way out:
how do you manage to keep this place in business?
Most people, she said rather sadly,
don't eat as much as you people.
Near the Grand Canyon
we found a lodge in a meadow surrounded by a forest
near the north rim of the canyon.
We were so comfortable there.
Fireplaces and good food.
Steak, salad, and Irish whiskey.
North of Seattle
we stopped at a place in the middle of the forest
that advertised homemade pies.
Some of us had two pieces.
Blackberry.
While we were there, some other customers came in
and ordered pie.
"I'm sorry: we don't have any more."

Eat
in any municipal, state or national park is my advice.

Build fires: broil steaks or chickens
roast vegetables in foil with butter, salt, and pepper.
Fill a large wooden bowl with salad greens you've collected.
Heavy cream, lime, salt, and mushroom catsup,
olive oil, lemon juice, chives (or shallots),
potato salad,
corn on the cob,
ice cream with chocolate sauce
red raspberries.
Ginger ale and beer.
Dark beer.
A big kettle full of chili.
Peanut butter.
Dill pickles.
Rare roast beef, mustard on the side
smoked salmon and cream cheese.
A sandwich of beef, ham, lettuce, tomato with Russian dressing.
Garlic.
Whenever anyone mentions they are going to put garlic in a dish
I always hope the cloves will be large.

(Phil exits.)

32 The Beating

Allen comes on carrying a square of astroturf, a garbage can, and a baseball bat. He sets the astroturf down carefully, places the garbage can on the astroturf, takes out two earplugs and puts them in his ears. He beats the garbage can with the baseball bat. He exits.

33 The Marching Band

A 123-piece local high school marching band enters, playing, and marches through the center of the piece and out again.

Everyone gathers to watch the parade.

Bob the pizza boy, a character we have not seen before,
enters from where the marching band exited with a pizza box in his hand.

BOB, THE PIZZA BOY : And yet, I think, nonetheless,
   forgiveness is possible.
SUSAN: You do.
BOB, THE PIZZA BOY: Well, sure.
   Really under any circumstances.

   Uh, primarily, uh, uh, the, uh, the…
   primarily the question is
   does man have the power to forgive himself.
   And he does.
   That's essentially it.
   I mean if you forgive yourself,
   and you absolve yourself of all, uh,
   of all wrongdoing in an incident,
   then you're forgiven.
   Who cares what other people think, because uh…
SUSAN: Was this a process you had to go through over a period of time?
   Did you have to think about it?
BOB, THE PIZZA BOY: Well, no.
   Not until I was reading the Aquarian gospel did I,
   did I strike upon,
   you know I had almost had ends meet because I had certain
   uh you know
   to-be-or-not-to-be reflections about of course what I did.
   And uh,
ALLEN: I'm sorry, what was that?
BOB, THE PIZZA BOY: Triple murder.
   Sister, husband. Sister, husband,
   and a nephew, my nephew.
   And uh, you know, uh, manic depressive.
CARL: Do you mind my asking what instruments did you use?
   What were the instruments?

BOB, THE PIZZA BOY: It was a knife.

It was a knife.

ALLEN: A knife?

BOB, THE PIZZA BOY: Yes.

ALLEN: So then, the three of them were all...

BOB, THE PIZZA BOY: Sssssss...

(Points to slitting his throat.)

like that.

WILSON: So, uh,

do you think that as time goes by,

this episode will just become part of your past,

or has it already...

BOB, THE PIZZA BOY: It has already become part of my past.

CARL: Has already become part of your past.

No sleepless nights? No...

BOB, THE PIZZA BOY: Oh, no. In the first three or four years there was a couple of nights where I would stay up thinking about how I did it, you know. And what they said...they told me later there were something like thirty stab wounds in my sister, but uh I remember distinctly I just cut her throat once.

(Becker offers him a chair. He sits, making himself at home.)

That was all, you know, and I don't know where the thirty stab wounds came from. So that might have been some kind of blackout thing. You know, I was trying to re- re- re- uh, re- uh, uh, resurrect the uh, the crime—my initial steps, etc. You know, and uh, and uh, I took, as a matter of fact, it came right out of the, I was starting the New Testament at the time, matter of fact I'm about the only person you'll ever meet that went to, to do a triple murder with a Bible in his, in his pocket, and, and, listening to a radio. I had delusions of grandeur with the radio. Uh, I had a red shirt on that was symbolic of, of some lines in Revelation, in the, in the New Testament. Uh I had a red motor...as a matter of fact, I think it was chapter six something, verses three, four, or five, or something where uh it was a man, it was a man. On a red horse. And, and, a man on a red horse came out, and uh, and uh uh, and he was given a knife, and unto him was given the power to kill and destroy. And I actually thought I was this person. And I thought that my red horse was this red Harley

Davidson I had. And I wore…it was just, you know, it was kind of a symbolic type of thing. And and and uh, you know, uh after the murders I thought the nephew was, was the, was a new devil or something, you know. This, this is pretty bizarre now that I think back on it. I thought he was a new devil and uh, uh. I mean basically I love my sister, there's no question about that. But at times my sister hadn't come through uh for me. You know and I was in another, one of these manic attacks. And uh, and uh, uh, uh, you know, uh, I was just uh, I was just you know, I mean I was fed up with all this you know one day they treat me good and then they tell all these other people that I was a maniac and watch out for me and etc. and like that. And uh, uh, so I went to them that night to tell them I was all in trouble again, you know, and could they put me up for the night, you know, and they told me to take a hike and uh so uh, believing that I had the power to kill, uh you know, that was that for them. You know. I mean when family turns you out, that's a real blow. You know. But uh, back to the original subject of forgiveness. If I forgive myself I'm forgiven. You know that's essentially the answer. I'm the captain of my own ship. I run my own ship. Nobody can crawl in my ship unless they get permission. I just *(He nods.)* "over there." You know. "I'm forgiven." You know. Ha-ha. You know. *(Laughs.)* It's as simple as that. You know. You're your own priest, you're your own leader, you're your own captain. You know. You run your own show, a lot of people know that.

Who ordered a pizza?

ALLEN: Oh.
SUSAN: A pizza.
ALLEN: I don't think anyone here ordered a pizza.
BOB, THE PIZZA BOY: Someone ordered a pizza.
    I don't go around picking up pizzas
    if nobody ordered one.
ALLEN: I think there's been some mistake.
BOB, THE PIZZA BOY: I think you are the one who is making a mistake
    if you think nobody
    is going to pay me for the fucking pizza.
    I paid for the pizza.
    You know: pizza
    is not returnable.

ALLEN: Right.
　I'll pay you for the pizza.
BOB, THE PIZZA BOY: Plain cheese.
ALLEN: Right.
　Here.
　Keep the change.
BOB, THE PIZZA BOY: *(Checking the money Allen has given him.)*
　Right.
　Thanks.
　Appreciate it.
　Which way did I come in?
　(The others all look at one another and then point in the same direction.)
ALLEN: Over there.
　Right out that way.
BOB, THE PIZZA BOY Right.
　Thanks again.

(He leaves. We hear a newspaper boy's bike bell. Bob's Mom comes out, takes the pizza, and goes back inside. Everyone follows her, except Allen, Carl and Phil's Girl.)

35 Lovers

ALLEN: You know
　I've been thinking about it
　and it turns out
　I love you.
CARL: You do?
ALLEN: Yes.
CARL: I didn't know that.
ALLEN: Neither did I
　but
　I look at you
　and I think you're good-natured.
CARL: Oh, good-natured.
ALLEN: Yes.
CARL: You do?
ALLEN: Yes, I really do.

And I think
if you think a person's agreeable and warmhearted
then I think there's something there you can't explain
that gives you real
delight.

CARL: Oh.

ALLEN: I find
you give delight to me.

CARL: Oh. Well.
That's what I'd hope for more than anything.

ALLEN: So would I.

CARL: And you're not sorry about it?

ALLEN: How do you mean?

CARL: That you find delight in someone
who doesn't seem to you in any other way
desirable
who doesn't perhaps have those qualities
that you can count on
for, you know, the solid, long-term kind of thing.

ALLEN: I would just take delight long-term.

CARL: Oh.
So would I.

(Bob's Mom comes out, Allen sees her and follows her back inside.)

36 Falling in Love

Carl begins to dance as he talks to Phil's Girl.

CARL: I think I fell in love with him
and I mean I fell in love with him like
the first time I saw him
I just couldn't stop looking at him
he was a soccer player
and I don't go to soccer games
and I don't like jocks
but I was there because a friend had taken me and bla bla bla never mind
but I was walking to our seats in the bleachers

and I saw him walking along the sidelines
and I just couldn't take my eyes off him
I was like a cartoon joke
I was looking at him and walking
and I could have walked right into a wall
and I think the reason I fell in love with him
is that he reminded me of a friend from high school
who reminded me of a guy I saw in a movie.

(Carl sits down beside Phil's Girl.)

37 Fidelity

PHIL'S GIRL: When I was nineteen
it seemed to me I shouldn't be tied down to one guy
I loved him
and when we were together we were just with each other
but if I went to Paris, for example,
I thought I should have love affairs because I was nineteen
and I thought he should, too,
and I told him I was having love affairs and he should, too,
and I wished he did
both because it would have made me feel less guilty
and also because I would have thought he wasn't such a nerd if he did
but he said he only cared for me
and it made me feel like such a bad person
that's definitely one of the reasons I broke up with him
and then, when we broke up,
he told me he had been having affairs with other women
and then that just tore it
after that, I just thought he was a jerk.

(Susan enters, bouncing a ping pong ball. Carl turns to Phil's Girl.)

CARL: Pizza?

(Phil's Girl nods. They both go into the house, leaving Susan outside.)

Wilson opens a window and sees Susan.

SUSAN: You know
    I've been thinking about it
    and it turns out
    I do love you.
WILSON: You do?
SUSAN: Yes.
WILSON: How could that be?
SUSAN: I look at you
    and I think you're sweet.
WILSON: Oh, sweet.
SUSAN: And good-natured.
WILSON: Good-natured.
SUSAN: Yes.
WILSON: You do?
SUSAN: Yes, I really do.
    And I think
    if you think a person's agreeable and warmhearted
    then I think there's something there you can't explain
    that gives you real
    delight.
WILSON: Oh.
SUSAN: I find
    you give delight to me.
WILSON: Oh. Well.
    That's what I'd hope for more than anything.
SUSAN: So would I.
WILSON: And you're not sorry about it?
SUSAN: How do you mean?
WILSON: That you find delight in someone
    who doesn't seem to you in any other way
    desirable
    who doesn't perhaps have those qualities
    that you can count on
    for, you know, the solid, long-term kind of thing.

SUSAN: I would just take delight long-term.

WILSON: Oh.

> (He runs downstairs and joins her outside.)

So would I.

39 The Waltz

> Music starts.
>
> Wilson and Susan do a beautiful Viennese waltz while Allen speaks:

ALLEN: Well, it depends on what you want to predict... I can predict the death of the sun quite accurately probably within ten to twenty percent... I don't think I'd be wrong by more than one billion years plus or minus. You can predict the positions of the planets hundreds of years into the future very accurately because we have studied vectors so much. But if you want to predict what's going to happen two years from now in Haiti you can't say very much—because the human system, that's a very complicated system.

> (Wilson and Susan continue to dance. Phil and Phil's Girl appear at the windows above them, and throw out ping pong balls like confetti. The music stops suddenly, they go inside.)

40 Whitman

> As Becker speaks, people wander out of the house and slowly clear the stage.

BECKER: O take my hand Walt Whitman!
Such gliding wonders! such sights and sounds!
Such join'd unended links, each hook'd to the next,
Each answering all, each sharing the earth with all.

What widens within you, Walt Whitman?
What waves and soils exuding?
What climes? what persons and cities are here?
Who are the infants, some playing, some slumbering?
Who are the girls? who are the married women?
Who are the groups of old men going slowly with their arms about each other's necks

What rivers are these? what forests and fruits are these?
What are the mountains call'd that rise so high in the mists?
What myriads of dwellings are they fill'd with dwellers?

What do you hear, Walt Whitman?
I hear the workman singing and the farmer's wife singing,
I hear in the distance the sounds of children and of animals early in the
day,
I hear the Spanish dance with castanets in the chestnut shade, to the
rebeck
and guitar,
I hear fierce French liberty songs,
I hear of the Italian boat-sculler the musical recitative of old poems....

What do you see, Walt Whitman?
Who are they you salute, and that one after another salute you?

I see a great round wonder rolling through space,
I see diminute farms, hamlets, ruins, graveyards, jails, factories, palaces,
hovels, huts of barbarians, tents of nomads upon the surface...
I see the tracks of the railroads of the earth...
I see the filaments of the news of the wars, deaths, losses, gains, passions,
of my race...
I see the site of the old empire of Assyria, and that of Persia, and that of
India...
I see the battlefields of the earth, grass grows upon them and blossoms
and
corn...
I see all the menials of the earth, laboring,
I see all the prisoners in the prisons,
I see the defective human bodies of the earth,
The blind, the deaf and dumb, idiots, hunchbacks, lunatics,
The pirates, thieves, betrayers, murderers, slave-makers of the earth,
The helpless infants, and the helpless old men and women.

I see the male and female everywhere,
I see the serene brotherhood of philosophs,
I see the constructiveness of my race,

I see the results of perseverance and industry of my race,
I see ranks, colors, barbarisms, civilizations, I go among them, I mix
 indiscriminately,
And I salute all the inhabitants of the earth.

(Becker exits.)

41 Bob

Late evening.
Do we hear an operatic aria faintly in the background?
A man singing a love solo.

BOB'S MOM: He was a sweet boy.
Of course, he loved his bicycle.
He would float for hours in the canal in an inner tube
and he built a go-cart out of wooden boxes.

We belonged to the Church of Christ
so of course there was
no drinking, no movies, no gambling
not even card-playing for fun,
no kissing before marriage,
no dancing.
You can be sure the Pleasure Pier on Lake Sabine,
which had a dance pavillion,
was definitely off limits.
Everything you did,
if it could possibly be interpreted as an indulgence,
was evil.
That's how it was then.

Everyone was poor those days.
We were a rural people so I knew how to sew.
I could arrange the paper patterns so close together on the fabric
I didn't waste a bit.

I scrubbed all the clothes on a washboard
I planted vegetables and canned them every year

and we raised chickens in the backyard for Sunday dinner.
We had linoleum on the floor in the kitchen.

He was a handsome boy
with a clear, fair complexion.
But he was not full of himself.
He was humble within himself,
and kind to everyone.

You knew he was going to go someplace,
you just didn't know *where*.

Isn't it something
how he can see the beauty in almost anything!

We were ordinary working people.
Art was not in our world.

(We hear a newspaper boy's bike bell.)

42 The Last Dance

Night time.
Stars in the sky.
Crickets.
The music of Ibrahim Ferrer (of Buena Vista Social Club fame). Bob's Mom
starts to dance. Becker the filthy derelict joins her. Eventually everyone else
enters and dances. They leave in couples. The last remaining couple is Bob's
Mom and Becker, and then he leaves.
Crickets.
Bob's Mom does a few moves alone on stage and enters her house.

43 The Final Moment

At the end of the piece: a man's voice says:
"OK!
That feels good to me."

END OF PLAY

Description Beggared; or the Allegory of WHITENESS
by Mac Wellman
music by Michael Roth

Copyright © 2000 by Mac Wellman. All rights reserved. CAUTION: Professionals and amateurs are hereby warned that *Description Beggared; or the Allegory of WHITE-NESS* is subject to a royalty. It is fully protected under the copyright laws of the United States of America and of all countries covered by the International Copyright Union (including the Dominion of Canada and the rest of the British Commonwealth), the Berne Convention, the Pan-American Copyright Convention and the Universal Copyright Convention, as well as all countries with which the United States has reciprocal copyright relations. All rights, including professional, amateur stage rights, motion picture, recitation, lecturing, public reading, radio broadcasting, television, video or sound recording, all other forms of mechanical or electronic reproduction, such as CD-ROM, CD-I, information storage and retrieval systems and photocopying, and the rights of translation into foreign languages, are strictly reserved. Particular emphasis is laid upon the matter of readings, permission for which must be secured from the Author's agent in writing.

ALL INQUIRIES CONCERNING RIGHTS, INCLUDING AMATEUR RIGHTS, SHOULD BE ADDRESSED TO: MITCH DOUGLAS, INTERNATIONAL CRE-ATIVE MANAGEMENT, 40 WEST 57TH STREET, NEW YORK, NY 10019.

FOR FURTHER INFORMATION REGARDING THE MUSIC, PLEASE CON-TACT THE COMPOSER C/O ROTHMUSIK@AOL.COM.

BIOGRAPHIES

Mac Wellman is the author of recent plays including *Cat's-Paw, Infrared, Fnu Lnu, The Sandalwood Box, Second-Hand Smoke, The Lesser Magoo* and *Girl Gone*. He also directed *I Don't Know Who He Was, and I Don't Know What He Said* as part of the four-month Mac Wellman Festival at House of Candles and elsewhere. He has received numerous honors, including both NEA and Guggenheim Fellowships. In 1990 he received an Obie (Best New American Play) for *Bad Penny, Terminal Hip* and *Crowbar*. In 1991 he received another Obie for *Sincerity Forever*. Four collections of his plays have been published: *The Bad Infinity* and *Cellophane: Plays* (both from PAJ/Johns Hopkins University Press), and *Two Plays* and *The Land Beyond the Forest* (both from Sun & Moon). Sun & Moon also published *A Shelf in Woop's Clothing*, his third collection of poetry, and two novels: *The Fortuneteller* (1991) and *Annie Salem* (1996). In 1997 he received a Lila Wallace-Reader's Digest Writer's Award. He currently teaches at Brooklyn College.

Michael Roth is a composer and sound designer whose work as a musician encompasses theatre, film, dance, and chamber music. Previous collaborations with Mac Wellman include *Terminal Hip, Bad Penny, tigertigertiger* (a musical for young people), *The Lesser Magoo,* and directing the premiere of *Albanian Softshoe*. He has been a resident artist and/or composer at the La Jolla Playhouse and South Coast Repertory (over seventy productions, including Daniel Sullivan's production of Donald Margulies' *Dinner With Friends,* also seen off-Broadway; Lee Blessing's *A Walk in the Woods,* also on Broadway and PBS; and Culture Clash's musical adaptation of *The Birds,* also seen at Berkeley Repertory). Collaborations with Randy Newman include the orchestrations for his *Faust,* editing two anthologies for Warner Brothers, and co-conceiving the music/theatre piece, *The Education of Randy Newman.* Other recent projects: collaborations with Kyle Donnelly, Richard Greenberg, Sharon Ott, Mark Rucker, Peter Sellars, Kate Whoriskey, Jeff Weiss, and many others, Des McAnuff's film *Bad Dates,* the independent feature *Holy Days,* Anne Bogart's *The Women,* collaborating with Carey Perloff and Tom Stoppard on the American premieres of *The Invention of Love* and *Indian Ink* at ACT in San Francisco, a new musical written with Garry Marshall, and his chamber opera, *Their Thought and Back Again* (for two singers, six dancers, and string quartet) available on CD via Rothmusik@aol.com.

HUMANA FESTIVAL PRODUCTION

Description Beggared; or the Allegory of WHITENESS was commissioned by Actors Theatre of Louisville with support from the National Endowment for the Arts. It premiered at the Humana Festival of New American Plays in March 2001. It was directed by Lisa Peterson with the following cast:

The Ring Family:

Cousin Julia	Adale O'Brien
Aunt Bianca	Anne O'Sullivan
Uncle Fraser	Edwin C. Owens
Moth	Eleanor Glockner
Louisa	Lia Aprile
The White Dwarf	Claire Anne Longest
Disputant	Lia Aprile
The Photographer	Nehal Joshi
Horn Girl	Emera Felice Krauss

Musicians:

Musician One (Vocals, Guitar, Bass, Keyboards)	Kelly Wilkinson
Musician Two (Violin, Trombone, Guitar, Vocals)	Peter Rhee
Musician Three (Percussion)	Richard Sisto
Musician Four (French Horn, Trumpet, Keyboards, Vocals)	Emera Felice Krauss
Musician Five (Bass, Vocals)	Nehal Joshi

and the following production staff:

Scenic Designer	Paul Owen
Costume Designer	Linda Roethke
Lighting Designer	Tony Penna
Sound Coordinator	Martin R. Desjardins
Properties Designer	Amahl Lovato
Stage Manager	Cat Domiano
Assistant Stage Manager	Debra Anne Freeman
Dramaturg	Amy Wegener
Assistant Dramaturg	Stephen Moulds
Casting	Bernard Telsey

CHARACTERS

 UNCLE FRASER...Fraser Outermost Ring₄, a damnable marplot
 AUNT BIANCA...a sort of human Blank, perhaps a parrot
 COUSIN JULIA...called "The Eraser" because of a wicked habit she has
 MOTH...an elegant older person
 LOUISA...something of a ninny (not really); she doubles as the
 DISPUTANT...who possesses
 Two ASSISTANTS
 A PHOTOGRAPHER
 MUSICIANS and
 THE WHITE DWARF

TIME AND PLACE

A vast, metaphysical Rhode Island. Late summer.

The turn of this century, or perhaps the last.

The floor is circular, a Malevich white-on-white target; time noodles around the here and now, whatever that may be.

Portions of this play have been adapted from "The White People" by Arthur Machen and from *The Ghost Sonata* by August Strindberg.

> Unto a life which I call natural I would
> gladly follow even a will-o-the-wisp
> through bogs and sloughs unimaginable,
> but no moon nor firefly has shown me
> the causeway to it. Nature is a personality
> so vast and universal that we have never
> seen one of her features.
>   —Thoreau, *Walking*

NOTE

The occasional appearance of an asterisk in the middle of a speech indicates that the next speech begins to overlap at that point. The overlapping speeches are all clearly marked in the text.

Anne O'Sullivan, Edwin C. Owens, Lia Aprile, and Adale O'Brien in
Description Beggared; or the Allegory of WHITENESS

25th Annual Humana Festival of New American Plays
Actors Theatre of Louisville, 2001
photo by Richard Trigg

Description Beggared; or the Allegory of WHITENESS

*Scene [**Steam**]: A party in a hypothetical Newport, Rhode Island; late summer; only something has gone wrong, radically wrong, during the taking of the annual family photograph; present are The Marplot (Uncle Fraser), Aunt Bianca and Cousin Julia (The Eraser), Moth and Louisa (the one they call The Ninny); and Musicians. And a very frustrated Photographer, standing next to an enormous silver-plate camera. Everyone is gossiping (at the same time) animatedly about everyone else [for cues, see Appendix]; there is a lot of bad jazz. Abruptly the bad jazz stops.*

THE PHOTOGRAPHER: *(In horror.)*
Cousin Julia The Eraser.

HORN GIRL: They don't call her The Grand Parade for nothing.
(Bad jazz starts up once more.)

JULIA: *(In a rage.)*
Whited sepulchers. Whited hypocrites
and creatures of the blench. Blenched
and two-faced, the whole bloody lot.* We
get together once a blue moon, once a
decade, once a century, once a millennium,
and you see the incredible result. Chaos.
A horrid, nasty scene. A picture of the
most appalling kind. A model of indecorous

outrage and unhinged incivility. Injured
merit run amuck.

Observe The Marplot there. Fraser is so filled
with swarthy venom he must disrupt this,
this most innocent of occasions.

Can he hear me? No, of course not. Too
wrapped up in his own foul rancor,
a whirlwind of a man. A local disturbance
posing as one of us. A hypothetical
human.

BIANCA: And I was doing nothing harmful;
and I was doing nothing of the kind;
and I was merely minding my own business
when the two of them, yes, the two
of them swept down upon me
like the spider; yes, very much the spider.

(She makes the spider.)

The two of them, with their eight legs
arranged just so. The two of them, yes

*(Creeping sideways in
her idea of spidery motion,
her long red tongue lolling.)*

*(She stops; looks over her
shoulder to see if Fraser
is noticing her; he is not;
reprise.)*

And* I was doing nothing harmful, etc.

FRASER: Can you believe it?* I am surrounded by
maniacs and idiots. It is hard to say
which is worse, the maniacs or the idiots.
It is hard to say which is worse, the
mania of the maniacs, or the idiocy of the
idiots. For if there is one thing I
cannot abide it is the mania of maniacs;

for if there is something I hate even more
than that it is the idiocy of idiots.
And the worst...

(He rages silently.)

And the worst is the idiocy of bad jazz,
and the noise of these infernal idiots and maniacs,
idiots and maniacs as you see arrayed all about me.
Me! Arrayed all about in a way that I find...
Arranged in obsequious propinquity. Arranged
in a way cunningly contrived to inflict the
maximal insult upon the auditory person of my
personhood.

*(He dances a jig of
insult.
Reprise.)*

MOTH: I am the only soft one; I am the only
soft one, even though I am not covered
with fur. Yes, not with fur.

I am the only soft one; I am the only
soft one, because I am covered with
feathers. Yes, with feathers. Not with fur.

Yes.

Yes. The others are not covered with feathers.

Yes. With fur, look at them. Fur.

Yes. And I should have stayed home.
Yes, I should have stayed, and rested
quietly behind the floral screen, in my
very own room.

Yes, behind the floral screen, where I love to sit
in the darkness reading the geometrical writings
of Isaac Ring Barlow, our ancestor. Yes and yes,

I should have stayed at home, behind the
floral screen, in my own little room, eating

a prickled bloatfish,

there,

in suburban Kama-Loka, where I grew up.
Curious.

*(She smiles and shows
her good teeth.)*

JULIA: **Curious**

BIANCA: **Curious**

LOUISA: **Curious**

JULIA: When we were young, we girls sang a
song about Fraser. I shall sing it now:

> **Curious the man**
> **who has time to fiddle**
> **hack upon a can**
> **but not to riddle**
> **the heart of man, nor his piddle;**
> **Curious the man**
> **who has time to fiddle.**
> **Curious**

(Reprise by Bianca and Moth, as a round.)

ALL: **Whether boy or girl;**
whether top or swirling
curiosity.
O black black black curiosity.
O black black black black
hearted curiosity.

LOUISA: **Curious the man**
who has time to fiddle
hack upon a corn
but not to riddle...

Er,

(Poor Moth faints in horror.)

All this is my fault, I suppose, and, er...

It is true that I am a ninny though my name
is not that, er...

It is Louisa; but I am called "Ninny" because
as a child, I visited with some distant relatives,
strange white people from the deep, interior regions
of Rhode Island's vast wasteland
and was told many wondrous things, er...

well, I suppose it comes down to that:
I told my parents how...how impressed
I was by those strange people, not to
mention their whiteness which was of an extraordinary
kind;

*(All stop to hear what she is
about to confess:)*

and, well, I said to them, my parents, I mean,
er...

I want to be one of them when I grow up.

*(All turn slowly to regard her
with cold condescension.)*

(Pause.)

But when I think of running off to join them I get shivers up and down
my spine, like I used to when Uncle Fraser talked about "that certain gentleman" he once met at the Astor, or of the silver-tipped claw of a kind of
rooster*, "the White Flaw" he received from that strange man in return
for a favor of some kind he would not specify.

FRASER: Shut up, silly girl. I told you we were never to talk of such things in
front of strangers.

LOUISA: But they're all family, Uncle Fraser.

FRASER: Nothing more strange than family, if you ask me. Especially the
damned Ring family.

(All look away.)

LOUISA: So, I guess, well, I guess you could say
I was a real big disappointment.

(The Marplot breaks out of the
freeze and begins a confidential
talk to some of the members of the
audience.)

FRASER: Can you believe it? Can you? Well, I can't.
Because actually it is quite beyond whatever
we mean when we call something "unbelievable."
Such a pretty girl, and so stupid. Yes,
so profoundly stupid that her stupidity
possesses a pallor that is almost…

(He considers the question
of what might constitute
an apt comparison.)

…that is almost godly; in other words,
a whiteness that simply beggars description.
And all this must be the outcome of some genetic
predisposition or some ancient curse laid upon
our tribe by…

(A glimmer of insight.)

Who knows? By some other tribe of equally
ancient, but heathenish morons…

(A more substantial glimmer.)

I am referring to those ancient and heathenish
ones who occupied the place even before us.

(A pause for reflection.)

If indeed the place could be said to have been
occupied at that remote time, because it is clear
that in the absence of our occupation the place
can hardly be thought of as a place, place *qua* place.

A place actual, that is.

No, for in our absence a place cannot
be said to constitute a place, only an
emptiness.

A noplace.

A primeval wasteland, devoid…

*(He illustrates what it is
he is attempting to convey with
a motion of hand and arm.)*

*(Pause. He does this again,
it was so much fun;)*

(However;)

*(clearly such gestures are not
The Marplot's long suit, and so
he gives it up.)*

*(Seeing him apparently conclude
his remarks, the Musicians start
up their machines again, and we
hear more Bad Jazz.)*

Stop…stop…stop* that hideous din.

JULIA: Oh Fraser, do put a lid on it, will you?

*(She steps forth, imperiously;
a magnificent specimen.)*

*(Louisa in particular is impressed
by her aristocratic bearing:)*

LOUISA: This is a cousin—not of the moron variety—
but of another, equally drastic: Cousin Julia,
Cousin Julia, called The Eraser because her visits
tend to be accompanied by an unexpected removal,
so that these visits are much feared by the rest
of the family; er,

Cousin Julia has just returned from a trip
to Jerusalem, where she has become a…a
jewel.

FRASER: A monstrous carbuncle, one might say.

JULIA: Just who am I? you ask and since you pose that
    question I shall give you a fit reply. I am The
    Grand Parade, and that is the whole of it. That
    is also why I am universally feared and respected.

    Yes, I am she who guarantees when
    a way is found that it be the right way
    because what good would a way possibly
    be if it were not the correct way? The splendor
    of my being shall illuminate all these matters
    until the time comes.

LOUISA: Er,

JULIA: Please do not interrupt.

    Yes, my dear, The Grand Parade must run,
    run and run her course till what has been
    implied has taken on manifestation, a local
    habitation, and borne the shame of such.

LOUISA: No, I was merely going to point out, however
    weakly and without conviction, that it has
    begun snowing. Even though it is still September.

(A pregnant pause, as it has indeed
begun to snow.)

(We hear, very quietly, the
Siegfried Idyll;*)*

(Or is the music emanating from
some far stranger, metaphysical
domain?)

(All are deeply concerned about
this question,)

(but none of them wishes anyone
else to be aware of his or her
concern.)

(An Aryan pause.)

FRASER: It *is* snowing, of course. What of it?

BIANCA: May I go back to the cupboard now?

JULIA: Yes, Lady Blank, you may go back to your damnable
cupboard. Only see that you behave.

BIANCA: Only the tiniest peek, I promise.

JULIA: Only the tiniest.

*(Scene begins to fade out
strangely.)*

MOTH: And so, at the turn of the century, we all
assembled in this place, to greet the new
century, and yes, the new millennium, yes,
only somehow we got it dreadfully wrong.

JULIA: Radically wrong, one might say.
Drastically wrong.

(The Marplot turns away from them.)

(All turn to him.)

(An accusatory silence.)

(From depths of his remoteness:)

FRASER: Yes, yes. I know what you are thinking.
You are thinking it is Uncle Fraser's fault.

It is a problem I have with the black art, yes,
the black art of photography. And that problem
revolves with a regular orbicularity about
an unassailable truth: namely, that the
photographer's devilish craft involves the
complete effacement and wiping out of the
human soul. This process can be gradual
or instantaneous, depending on the relative
thickness or thinness of the spiritual entity
in question.

*(He casts a significant glance at
The Ninny, who looks down
abashedly.)*

I of course have suspected this all my life,
but did not arrive at a finished conclusion
until I had secured my fortune, and by implication
the fortune of the entire clan, with that old
enterprise in the depths…of the depths of the
Telegu Archipelago.

(All the women do something strange.)

Yes, yes. You scoff at things foreign. Strange
gods and the like. But after we signed
documents with the presiding fugleman in
Frontenac Bay, all went according to our
whitened way.

(A pale-faced pause.)

Deep, deep truths I learned from my hetman
there, Baga and his catchild, Squeech. Deep,
deep things.

*(A strange, slow and dark
music breaks out.)*

At the rituals we…we participated in,
as full equals, I might add…

(As Baga:)

**WHATAMDISFER? WHATAMDEMFER?
WHATAMDOSFER? WHATAMYAMFER?**
Or, more correctly:

**WHAT AM DIS FOR? Holy holy holy.
WHAT AM DEM FOR? Lordy lordy lordy.
WHAT AM DOS FOR? Allalu, allalu, allalu.
WHAT AM YAM FOR? Blory, blory, blory.**

(The Musicians take up the chant, quietly.)

And, thus, even among the indigenous dwellers
of that remote region, the central questions revolve
just as they do for us; with, one might say, as
equal and perfect an orbicularity: Who am I?
What am I here for? Who are they? What are they
here for?

(Music ends.)

Baga and his catchild, Squeech. These were the first
to clarify the matter for me; the whiting out of the
oft photographed human soul.

JULIA: All this feels rather arcane and superfluous, Fraser,
given the difficulty of assembling the family. All
at one time. All at any one place, that is.

FRASER: I am resolved in my decision.

JULIA: You have marred the occasion.

FRASER: The occasion be damned.

*(The Photographer, who has been standing idly by,
rages and chews on the brim of his hat.)*

JULIA: The camera is prepared; the photographer has been
standing idly by; we shall be forced to proceed
without you.

FRASER: I, the photographer be damned.

LOUISA: Er,

(Another white pause.)

(Aunt Bianca abruptly sits down.)

(Cousin Julia signals to the Musicians.)

JULIA: Aunt Blank, will you lead us in a few verses of the
originary document?

(Aunt Bianca brightens, gets up.)

BIANCA: The family hymn?

JULIA: Yes, my dear. That will do. After all, it is Founder's Day and Founder's Day it shall be all day long, despite the black mood of Kaiser Fraser here.

(The Musicians do their best as Bianca begins, uncertainly:)

BIANCA: **Mine eyes have seen the something of the coming of the Lord; he is something something something with his terrible swift sword...**

(The song dissipates as it becomes apparent that neither Bianca nor the Musicians know what they are doing.)

(The scene piffles out.)

(All leave except The Marplot and The Ninny.)

FRASER: Have they all gone?

LOUISA: Not quite.

(And in fact: Julia and Bianca are intently observing from just offstage, in the audience.)

(Elsewhere, Moth observes both the observers and observed, herself unseen.)

FRASER: They have ruined me, Louisa, with their wicked wicked obsession with establishing a visual record of all events, even the most seeming innocent.

LOUISA: I don't know what to say.

———

BIANCA: What are they saying?

JULIA: How can I hear if you're always yapping?

BIANCA: I think* they are talking about how you
turned Mother into an insect by an act of partial
erasure.

———

FRASER: Well, they know what to say, Louisa. And
what they are saying they are saying
about you and me; some of it about you and
the greater part no doubt about me, and
all of it revolting.

LOUISA: They mean well enough, Uncle Fraser.
They can't help being who they are, vague
and insubstantial. Fraught with the intangible.
These qualities go with the terrain of their
awful whiteness.

———

MOTH: I think all of this is very silly. I think
all of this is so very silly, so silly I am going to
tell you all a little story about the olden days
when the vast metropolis of Newport had
not been dreamt of. Long before our
ancestors had discovered the principle,
long hidden, of certain, wonderful flea circuses
far away in the Telegu Islands, and came
shortly thereafter to corner the market
here. Long before Fraser, who was just a
young boy (I think it was this Fraser),
who had not yet developed such a malign and
flinty dislike of all things associated
with mechanical flea circuses and other
miniature, wind-up automata. A profound
hatred of all miniatures, be they natural,
or artificial.

Long before Grandfather Lockhart
stood up during a performance of the
Ninth Symphony at the Crystal Pavilion

and took the bullet meant for Governor
Gormley, a big, bald, whitish sort of man,
and was declared a hero in his abrupt
deconstruction.

———

LOUISA: She's talking about imaginary things again,
Uncle Fraser. Decompression. Shadow
dances on the Neman River in old
Byelorussia. White Russia. Lovemaking
under a pontoon bridge on Decoration Day.

FRASER: She has changed into one of them.

LOUISA: What?

FRASER: A lepidopteran.

MOTH: Long before that, indeed. Long before Cousin Julia
The Eraser erased the last two letters from
my good maternal appellative and spat them out
at poor little infant Louisa Outermost...

LOUISA: Er,

FRASER: What is it?

LOUISA: Er. I said "Er."

FRASER: Be quiet then.

LOUISA: It has started to snow again.

MOTH: And long before my own Great Uncle, Tom Blank,
exhibited his device at the World's Fair
in Providence, the Rhode Island White-tailed
Dioptrical Silver-Plate, in whose shimmer
shimmer even the Negro and his Negress might take
in the radiant whiteness of his and her eternal
Christian soul.

———

JULIA: What are they talking about now?

BIANCA: Something about going to the cemetery.
　　　Putting up a monument to the Bishop.
　　　He wrote books, I think.

JULIA: Who wrote books?

BIANCA: The Bishop. He collected things too. They tell me
　　　he was a bug man.

JULIA: What?

BIANCA: He had these pieces of cork with needles in
　　　them, and he catches bugs and sticks them
　　　on. We don't understand these things but
　　　it's true, just the same. Can I go to the kitchen
　　　and look at the Chiffonnier?

———

(Something strange happens.)

(All stop whatever they are doing; and)

(missing a beat,
try to figure out, privately,
what has gone awry;
they attempt to do this
without being detected.)

JULIA: What did you say?

BIANCA: I forget, something about wanting to go
　　　back to the kitchen.

JULIA: And just what would you be up to, if
　　　you should do that?

BIANCA: Well...ah...

JULIA: Yes.

BIANCA: Well, since Lady Moth seems to be preoccupied
　　　with a fit of fantastical reminiscence, I shall
　　　maybe, at any rate, I might...ah...

JULIA: Yes. I think I know.

BIANCA: If you think you know, why do you ask me?

JULIA: I am hoping, dear Bianca, that I have misjudged your intentions.

BIANCA: Well, I thought with all these temporarious disturbances, what with everyone acting like the white mouse trapped within the tikum-tokum of an originary Diophantine Challenge Box...

The original model came only in alabaster and Mother of Pearl. Even the brilliant porches of Newport were not so brilliant, but...dear me...I have quite lost the thread of my idea.

JULIA: That is because you are being evasive.

BIANCA: Was I really?

JULIA: Yes you were.

BIANCA: Funny, I was not aware of being evasive.

JULIA: That is not a justification.

BIANCA: Do you think my lost thread of thought requires a justification?

JULIA: There is a justification, or the implication of one floating about in the fluid suspension of your consciousness, my dear. Just asking to be rubbed out.

BIANCA: My word, Julia. You make it sound like we are bobbing for apples.

JULIA: —

BIANCA:—

———

*(The Musicians mutter in their corner,
their hushed voices strange, barely
human. They sound like rodents.)*

MUSICIAN ONE: They call him The Marplot because he's a grump.

MUSICIAN TWO: They call him something like that, I suppose.

MUSICIAN THREE: He hates us. He hates the music we make.

MUSICIAN TWO: He is rich. And large, and white. He can get angry
at whomever he will.

MUSICIAN ONE: He hates us because he is one of us.

MUSICIAN THREE: You don't say? Say, he and that ninny niece
of his are making faces at us.

(Indeed, they are. Quite ugly faces.)

MUSICIAN FOUR: He is a hateful grump. And a grouch.

MUSICIAN ONE: What is a grouch?

MUSICIAN FOUR: Similar to the grump, but worse.
Worse as rat is to mouse.

MUSICIAN TWO: Worse.

MUSICIAN THREE: Yes, much worse.

*(Ruminative pause. Musician Two
scratches his hump [he has a hump].)*

MUSICIAN ONE: Then why have we been hired to play
music here?

MUSICIAN FIVE: His wicked cousin, the one they call The
Grand Parade has arranged the whole business.
My surmise is that, in a previous life, he
was an inventor of music boxes and mechanical
flea circuses himself* …but I cannot be
entirely sure…

FRASER: What are you saying, my good man? What
idiotic calumny are you giving voice to?

You have laid siege to my wits with
this expensive, idiotic noise.

JULIA: Music, it is called, Fraser. Please desist
from this outrageous behavior. They are
only doing as they have been commissioned.

FRASER: Noise, noise, noise.

(The Musicians start up in a fury.)

(He dances his angry jig.)

Expensive noise then.

A stench in the ear.

(The Musicians sing:)

MUSICIANS: **Description is the beggar**
rolling up the floor
cutting up the carpet
upon which the Devil poured

bleach of his depiction.
whirling like a djinn,
pure description beggared
White as sin.

White as sin; white as sin;
whirling like a djinn
whirling like a djinn.
White as sin; white as sin
white as description beggared.

ALL: **Description is the beggar**
rolling up the floor
cutting up the carpet
upon which the Devil poured

bleach of his depiction.
whirling like a djinn,
pure description beggared
White as sin.

(All begin to whirl, their
white clothes like monstrous blooms
rotating around them.)

MUSICIANS: **In the white squall**
of the metaphysical ocean.
In the white squall
of the metaphysical ocean.

ALL: **White as sin; white as sin;**
whirling like a djinn
whirling like a djinn.
White as sin; white as sin
white as description beggared.
White as sin; white as sin;
whirling like a djinn
whirling like a djinn.

———

(Music stops suddenly—as a mean
and petty practical joke of the
Musicians. They hide a cackle.)

(All the others look somewhat embarrassed.)

(In this awkward moment, Moth
chooses to start up her story
again:)

MOTH: …and long before that; and long before that even,
and before the time we celebrate on Founder's Day
and before, yes, even before the signing of the
originary document and the preliminary description;
and before even the first voyage of our brave
ancestor to the Isthmus of Telegu…and the
station at Whydah, along the bleached, bone-white
sands of Dahomey;

and before the invention of the Rhode Island
Silver-Plate Dioptrical Flea Circus, and all

the various types of music box:
those of ivory and those of horn;
those of the right, and those of the left brain;
those of the angel who is the wandering
    albatross, and those of the imp Obsidian
    whose weight forces the fulcrum up,
    whose weight forces the fulcrum down;

and before even the naming of names;
of Leucoblast and Leucorrhea;
of Leucocyte and Leucocytosis;
of Leucoderma and Saint Leukemia;

of all things so turned and so leprous
    they outwhite oblivion; for

*(Softly; all the Women join
in the song, as this is a ritual
from the olden days;
all conventional lights dim;
but black light comes in.)*

WOMEN: **In every town, there is a white girl;**
There is a white girl
whiter than the rest,
whiter than the rest.
Whiter than snow, whiter
than corn tassel, whiter than
wheat flowing in the evening breeze;
whiter than the air we breathe;

(A fluffy white silencio.)

Whiteness is the color of what
want is. So whiteness is want;
what we all want, not knowing.
Not knowing.

(A choral reprise.)

In every town, there is a white girl
there is a white girl
whiter than

the rest;
whiter than
the rest;
whiter than the air we breathe;
whiter than the air we breathe;
breathe.
Breathe.

MOTH: *(Once more.)*
   And I thought I was that girl.* I was, I confess,
   that girl.

FRASER: I should have stayed at home, Louisa.

LOUISA: Oh, Uncle Fraser, cool it, will you?
   Dear Moth is entitled to her imaginary
   raptures.

FRASER: All this resembles nothing so much
   as a Sikkimese hangover.

JULIA: Don't like it, Fraser, when the hens come
   home to roost?

FRASER: Witchetty, all of it. Witchetty. Witchetty.
   Witchetty.

LOUISA: What's "Witchetty"?

JULIA: What in the name of Great Aunty Dahlia
   do you mean?

   (Aunt Bianca brightens.)

   (A music of ominous footfalls.)

   *(A transcendental music lifts
   our souls.)*

   (Pause.)

BIANCA: I was just getting around to that.

LOUISA: "Witchetty." What's it mean?

FRASER: How the devil should I know?

*(A strange, little Man enters. This
is The White Dwarf. All freeze
except The Marplot, who is the only
one to see him.)*

*(The White Dwarf, like the others,
is dressed entirely in white
except for a red fez with a
black tassel.)*

*(This is the only scenic color
in the play [well, almost].)*

*(The White Dwarf mutters to himself
angrily. We do not hear much of what
he says.)*

———

*(He limps over to an audience member
[a shill]; grabs that person's program;
bites it and growls; rips the program
into pieces; stomps on the pieces, and
rolls around on the stage scratching at
them with his hind feet, rather like
a nasty housecat with her prey.)*

(The Marplot watches all this in horror.)

(A Dwarfish pause.)

*(Suddenly The White Dwarf catches sight
of The Marplot, gets to his feet, and
begins to mutter again. We hear only
the following amidst his demented garble
and cackling.)*

THE WHITE DWARF: "Witchetty"! Witchetty, ha. It's all one big Polo
Bear bottom. One big white torpedo. An obsessional
white horde, ha!

*(Now he begins taking flash pictures
of Fraser with his instant Kodak.)*

*(The latter grimaces in the agony of
unwilling exposure;)*

*(but The White Dwarf continues, briefly,
examining each photo before discarding
it with gleeful contempt;)*

*(The White Dwarf moons
The Marplot, who thereupon faints.)*

*(Before exiting, he places his visiting
card in The Marplot's open mouth.)*

———

*(A stuffed Zebra, on wheels, appears just
at the lip of the stage. Greeting this
with delight, The White Dwarf carefully
places his camera on the stage, where it
shall remain for the rest of the play,
lit by a pin-light.)*

(Pause.)

(The transcendental music stills.)

*(The White Dwarf hobbles off, with the
Zebra [his trophy] in tow.)*

*(The Musicians are the first to snap
out of it, and begin to play in a
more soothing vein—but still their
old Bad Jazz.)*

———

BIANCA: I said. I was just getting around to that.

JULIA: Getting around to what?

*(The Ninny spies The Marplot stretched
out at her feet, and lets out a short
but energetic scream.)*

(Lights back to normal.)

*(All focus on him; Moth alone
smiles because, with all her years
and wisdom, she finds the scene
amusing;)*

*(Louisa leans over to remove from
Fraser's open mouth the visiting card
which The White Dwarf has placed
there. She reads:)*

LOUISA: Parking lot of the Wal-Mart on Route 7.
Near the dumpster. At the back of the
abandoned Weiss Mechanical-Musical Flea
Circus Factory. This Tuesday. Four p.m.
Be there. The Dwarf will lead you on
from there. White Whiskey John, Assistant
to the Disputant.

*(The Marplot has come to his senses,
but is still groggy;)*

(turns to Moth, almost tearful.)

JULIA: Disputant? We shall have no disputes
during the holiday. Fraser, what does
this mean?

LOUISA: I'm sure there is a rational explanation,
Cousin Julia.

BIANCA: Moth, what can this mean? Whatever can this
mean?

LOUISA: White Whiskey John?

MOTH: It's a kind of shrike.

(All look at Moth with surprise.)

BIANCA: And what I was going to suggest is that we
call it a day, since the photographer seems
to have disappeared.

(All look at Julia, who feigns innocence.)

And Fraser has suffered from a stroke or other
moral lapse;

and the musicians, or whatever they are,
have assumed a dark and gloomy aspect,
probably because they are waiting to be
paid; and they shall not be paid;

And they shall not be paid
   because there is no money to pay them with;

(The music stops.)

And they shall not be paid,
   because they are dark and witchetty, and
   possibly in league with the Adversary;

And they shall not be paid,
   because given the family structure, it is
   unclear who among us holds the authority
   and controls the purse strings governing
   the writing of checks;

And they shall not be paid,
   because their music is of a disturbing kind,
   and lacks the melodious harmoniousness which
   above all the family fancies on these occasions,
   such as Founder's Day, or the Day of the Signing
   of the Originary Document; or on

White-Handed Goose Day; or
Woonsocket Day; or
Gravity Feed Day; or
Moon Dead Dog Day; or
Anna Innermost Ring Day; or
on Prickled Bloatfish Day…or…

JULIA: You are not making any sense, Bianca.

BIANCA: That is because I wish to return to my little room,
   and hide behind my little floral screen…

JULIA: We all wish to return to our little rooms, and we
   all wish to hide behind our little floral screens,

but all the rest of us have the internal fortitude
and the willpower to resist that temptation.

BIANCA: I know, I know, I know.

*(Pause. Something happens
in the vicinity of The Marplot's
nose.)*

*(Something connected to the
idea of butterflies.)*

*(Suddenly Fraser sits bolt
upright. Perhaps he is
aware of the possibility
of The White Dwarf's return.)*

JULIA: In fact, Bianca. In fact you are resorting
to your old bad habits.

BIANCA: Julia, how can you say that? In what way
can I be said to be resorting to my old
bad habits?

JULIA: You know.

BIANCA: I do not know.

JULIA: Yes you do.

BIANCA: No I don't.

(A standoffish pause.)

JULIA: Yes you do.

BIANCA: No I don't.

JULIA: You know.

BIANCA: I do not.

LOUISA: Er,

JULIA: Shut up, you feeble-minded white-handed tree-mouse.

BIANCA: Just because I would like to tip-toe into the kitchen
and out the back way…

JULIA: Yes?

BIANCA: Out the back way, and down the steps that
lead to the other place;

(Universal fear at the mere mention.)

The other place, you call the Gaming Room *(Fraser)*;
and you *(Louisa)*
call the Montessori Bughouse Underfloor Area;
and you *(Moth)*
call the Highborn Muskrat Hideaway;
and you *(Musicians)*
call the Take-After Take-Out Taj Mahal;
and you, Julia,
call the White-Haired White Leather White Tie;
but is, in fact, only the antique cupboard,
or chiffonnier, that was Great Aunt Dahlia's.

JULIA: And is now her final resting place.

BIANCA: I only want a teensy peek. Teensiest of the
teensy.

JULIA: It is a low, depraved wish on your
part, Bianca. Ancestor worship must
aspire to more elegant expression in our
contemporary Rhode Island, dear.

LOUISA: Er,

JULIA: Shut up, you hideous white crappie.

(Shock.)

*(The Grand Parade gestures to the
Musicians, who begin to play
more or less morally affirming music—)*

Whited sepulchers. Whited hypocrites and...
and creatures of the blench. Blenched and...
two-faced, the whole bloody lot. Great Aunt
Dahlia has entered into the phase of her
long and rich existence we denominate
as her Egyptian Alabaster years; not

quite among the living; not quite among
the dead. So;

Bianca,

when we disturb her profound meditation
upon the higher things, transubstantiation and
the transmigration of the human soul, we
threaten her delicate equipoise. For good reason
she has returned to the enameled sanctuary of
her treasured chiffonnier, most treasured of all
the family heirlooms we possess;

Before her it belonged to Lydia Lockhart; and
before her to Anastasia, perhaps better known
    as the natural daughter of Mr. French Church;
and before that to Gloria Defiance Ring; and
before that to Philippa Outermost Ring; and
before that to Augusta Outermost Ring; and
in the beginning, before the signing of the originary
    document, and before the framing of the preliminary
    question, and the opening of the field and the
    closing of the old Weiss factory across Route 7
    and before the establishment of Founder's Day
    which is also known in the local parlance
    as Prickled Bloatfish Day; and before the
    framing of the other question, the eternal one...

(In a whisper:)

The one we dare not think too much about...

(A thoughtful pause.)

to Louisa Outermost Ring, for whom our
    silly little Louisa was named, named
    with the misguided hope that names truly
    are fates, as the philosopher Pseudo-Mennipus
    opined, and not mere slank appellatives.

LOUISA: But I thought Aunty Dahlia was dead.

JULIA: Aunty Dahlia will be dead, silly, if Bianca continues to
    disrupt her dream time flat line.

BIANCA: So I am to have nothing for my trouble?

JULIA: What trouble is that, Bianca?

BIANCA: The trouble of driving here, all the way from my little room in suburban Kama-Loka.

JULIA: That is not such a far place. I drove all the way from Paris, France.

MOTH: Disaster, disaster, disaster.

JULIA: --

BIANCA: --

LOUISA: Er,

JULIA: Be quiet please.

LOUISA: Er,

JULIA: Please.

LOUISA: Er, I was only going to point out that it has begun to stop snowing.

(All look about, as if to confirm or contradict this assertion.)

JULIA: It has begun to do no such thing.

(Indeed, The Grand Parade is, on this occasion, quite correct.)

MOTH: Disaster, disaster, disaster.

(Aunt Bianca lies down on the stage, and thrashes both hands and feet in total postverbal frustration.)

(One of the Musicians grows bold [the first];)

(All glare at him disapprovingly; he loses his nerve;)

*(Bianca rages once more; his
nerve returns;)*

*(he approaches very close to Julia's
chin.)*

MUSICIAN ONE: We will be paid.

JULIA: I beg your pardon?

MUSICIAN ONE: We have played some music, some pretty
darn good music and we will be* paid.

MUSICIAN THREE: Yes. It is only right that, as god-fearing
taxpayers, that we be paid.

JULIA: Go whistle for it then.

*(All turn their backs on the poor
Musicians;)*

*(save Moth who has put on her
snow shoes and trudged out;
and Fraser who is studying
the card lately placed in his
mouth by The White Dwarf;)*

*(Ambivalent as ever, Louisa
does not know what to do,
nor with whom to sympathize
so she counts imaginary
rabbits as they hop on her knee.)*

*(After a stingy pause, Musician One
signals to Musician Four who
thereupon sings a song:)*

MUSICIANS: **I am in an economic hell;
bell, do not ring for me
bell, do not ring for me
bell, do not ring for me**

**I am in an economic hell;
because I am not
because I am not at all…**

And I have lost my whiteness.
Have lost thereby,
Lost my rightness, it's true.

MUSICIANS AND LOUISA: **Oh hell, what a hell. Oh, what a hell.**
Oh, rabbit of loss
Oh, rabbit of loss
I am in an economic hell

ALL: **Bell**
tell me what to do.
Bell
tell me what to do.
Bell
tell me what to do.

(Humiliated, The Grand Parade opens
her ratty little clutch purse,
produces a coin; bites it;
regrets biting as the taste is foul;)

(pauses;)

(and tosses the coin over her
shoulder; the Musicians let the
coin fall where it may; pause;)

(then Musician Two signals Musician One
who recovers the coin and pockets it.)

————

(Bianca and Julia slip out
as Musician Two signals once more
to Musician One who begins to
sing:)

MUSICIAN ONE: **Beautiful girl, you are so fair***…

(The Marplot angrily and quite suddenly
interjects:)

FRASER: And just what the hell am I supposed to do
about this idiotic invitation?

LOUISA: Er, I suppose you might want to take
  the bull by the Melanesian antlers,
  cross the road, as the message indicates
  and see what lies on the other side.

  *(He considers this option;
  reconsiders.)*

FRASER: Storm's approaching white out.

LOUISA: Then you'd best stay at home.

FRASER: Stay at home is what I should have
  done in the first place, Louisa.

  *(Dresses for the storm and
  vanishes into the storm like
  the white-tailed deer.)*

  *(No one knows what to do
  for a second.)*

  *(Louisa smiles fetchingly at the
  Musicians who smile back.)*

  *(Musician One begins to sing
  once more:)*

MUSICIAN ONE: **Beautiful girl, you are so fair
  I am made deaf, whiter than air;
  and I shall fall down
  I shall fall down
  I shall fall down like the
  moon.**

  **One bite of your blanch,
  a strand of your hair
  collides with my habit, whiter than air;
  and I shall fall down
  I shall fall down
  I shall fall down like the moon.**

ALL: **And I shall fall down like the
  moon.**

MUSICIAN TWO: **Blond beyond belief, and**
wrecked upon a reef
of disbelief;

MUSICIAN ONE: **alive in whiteness**
ultimate whiteness.

ALL: **Whiteness alchemical;**
and metaphysical.

Beautiful girl, you are so fair
I am made deaf, whiter than air;
and I shall fall down
I shall fall down

MUSICIAN ONE: **I shall fall down like the moon.**

———

(Lights dim as the storm
whitens.)

(We catch sight of The Marplot
trudging along in the direction
of the highway, and the abandoned
Musical-Mechanical Flea Circus
Factory where his fateful
appointment is shortly to
occur.)

FRASER: Witchetty. All of it, witchetty. What a hell
of a local disturbance is mankind...

(We see Moth high up
in a dormer window.)

MOTH: Disaster, disaster, disaster.

(The First Scene peters out
like the last of the white sand
in the hourglass.)

*First Entr'acte [**Sleet**]: The Marplot staggers through the storm, as if on a treadmill. He passes the ghostly white mansions of Astors and Vanderbilts; he mutters to himself.*

FRASER: Damn that crowd at the White Horse Tavern…

Damnable flea circuses.

God Damned Wanton-Lyman-Hazard House.

Witchetty. All of it vile and witchetty.

Damnable Samuel Whitehorse Museum.

Astors and Vanderbilts be damned, the whole lot. Arrivistes and social climbers, all of 'em.

Isaac Bell? Phooh! I knew Isaac Bell when he was shucking shellfish at a third-rate clam-shack down by the pier.

Damnable music-boxes. Witchetty and damnable, the whole shebang.

(Far above, on the metaphysical plane and surrounded by fluffy white clouds are Julia, Bianca, Louisa and Moth; they look down on Fraser's progress with transcendental benignity—and softly sing, as before:)

WOMEN: **Mine eyes have seen the something
of the coming of the Lord;
he is something something something
with his terrible swift sword.**

(All fades to white.)

*Scene [**Snowy**]: The vast interior of the abandoned factory. Eerie light from a skylight high above. A very very long table with a chair at each end. At the far end of this is the Disputant, cloaked in silvery whiteness (though shadowy) and barely visible. Two Assistants hover nearby and whisper in the Disputant's ear. Light silvery laughter rises from time to time, barely audible and barely human. The Marplot enters and stands near the empty chair; he can only just make out the distant figure for all the gloom. A silvery pause.*

FRASER: And so?

DISPUTANT: Your name is Fraser Outermost Ring4?

FRASER: And so? What of it?

DISPUTANT: Answer the question.

FRASER: What question was that?

DISPUTANT: Must I repeat myself, Mister Ring?

FRASER: Why have I been summoned to this place?

DISPUTANT: You are the fourth Ring to bear the family
     name of Ring?

FRASER: Why should I discuss my family name with you?

DISPUTANT: And so? I might just as well reply, "And so?"
     and then that leads us, in perfect circularity,
     back to the beginning.

     (A circular pause.)

FRASER: And so? What of it? What do you want from me?

DISPUTANT: Maybe the whole point is that there is no issue
     to any of it.

FRASER: There is no point to any of WHAT? What the hell
     are you driving at?

     *(The distant figures consult
     and whisper. Light, silvery
     laughter.)*

*(Fraser takes off his coat and
drapes it carefully over the
back of the chair.)*

(He scratches his head.)

(He sits down upon the chair.)

DISPUTANT: Why do you think you have been summoned here?

FRASER: Have I been summoned here? I believe I came
of my own free will.

DISPUTANT: Do you imagine you are whiter than the rest?

FRASER: Of course I am whiter than the rest.
All the Outermost Rings are whiter
than the rest. What the devil does that
have to do with the price of tea in Telegu?

(Silvery laugh.)

DISPUTANT: Quite the wit.

FRASER: Runs in the family, on my mother's side at least.

DISPUTANT: Quite the wit. Wit. From *Witan* in Old English:
to know. Are you the knower, Mister Fraser
Outermost Ring?

FRASER: I misspoke: Wit does not run in the family.
Rather it runs from the family—idiots and
maniacs the whole bloody lot.

DISPUTANT: Strawberry.

FRASER: *(Clearly shaken.)*
What?

DISPUTANT: Was that not the name?

FRASER: I have no idea what you're talking about.

DISPUTANT: Strawberry. As in strawberry blond—your nickname
as a youth in the remote, wild outer reaches of North
West Rhode Island some three thousand miles away,
where you and your young accomplices made balls out of

the blubber of the white seal and toyed with the bleached
skull of the Telegu white stork.

FRASER: And so? What is the point of this?

Well, what if I did? What of it?

(A silvery pause.)

DISPUTANT: Is there not hell to pay? Hell, Fraser, hell?

CHORUS OF FIGURES: **Shake shake shake**
Shake the Devil off
Shake the Devil off
in the name of Jesus.* *[X7]*

DISPUTANT: And did you not play Taji in the school play;
Taji, lost in the mindless pursuit of Yillah?
Lovely, yellowhaired Yillah, she who was
whiter than the rest?

FRASER: The part was a minor one.

DISPUTANT: Could you speak closer to the machine,
Strawberry?

FRASER: The part was a minor one. The play of no
significance. I have forgotten the whole matter
till this very moment.

DISPUTANT: Your various selves seem to have a way
of sliding away from the central axis.

FRASER: That is natural, is it not? I see nothing
wrong with that.

DISPUTANT: Others in the family call you The Marplot
because you have a way of spoiling their
plans, Strawberry.

FRASER: Their plans are often silly, silly ones. Plans
deserving of spoliation. And who in the
name of Roger Williams are you?

DISPUTANT: I am your Disputant.

FRASER: My what?* What is the name of hell is that?

DISPUTANT: You heard me, Strawberry. I am your Disputant,
and you have been summoned to this place
to answer for some actions undertaken in
your name, by you and your other selves
and selflings—as the Millennium draws
nigh.

(The Marplot laughs.)

In particular, you are accused of disrupting
the fundamental plan;

as proposed in the Originary Document;

as a response to the Preliminary Question, and
the opening of the field, and other cognate
selves and selflings relative to that question.

(He is stunned.)

In fact the whole family of Ring is responsible;
is responsible for these actions; actions which
have over the course of time beggared description,
and which have caused the heavenly dome of whitest heaven
to be

*(The Disputant and her
Assistants,)*

(Each & every one,)

*(make a motion,
ever so slightly,
of the hand.)*

To become smutched, to become as smutched
as the black orchid Taji brought to Yillah
in that high school play, foolishly thinking
that by so doing he would win her love.

Black as the teeth of the inhabitants of
Tsalal.

(He reaches the boiling point.)

FRASER: What does this have to do with me? I have
always been an exception to the white rule
of the Ring family.

DISPUTANT: You are one of the central rings; the last, in fact,
of a long succession of Rings; you are, therefore,
a critical link in that deplorable argument.

FRASER: And precisely what argument would that be?

DISPUTANT: Enough of this back-pedaling. You know
perfectly well what I am talking about.

FRASER: Damnation. I had nothing whatsoever to do
with the evils you have alluded to. The
lunacy of the Ring family has nothing to do
with me. Why hound me? It is senseless.
Why not pursue your savage vendetta
against all the others? Cousin Julia, for
instance, the one they call The Eraser;
the one who calls herself The Grand Parade?
Cousin Julia the Eraser so called because
of her strange ability to cause people and
things to vanish. Whole epochs of the family
chronicle caused to disappear under the insidious
rub a dub dub of her India rubber eraser.
Most of the chronicle from the time of Fraser₁
and Fraser₂ reduced to powder, mere pulverized
rubber. Similarly, my own childhood, the time
of my own father, Fraser₃ has become, through her
doing, a horrid, white blank or blot. An empty page
in an old old book, once hallowed, now hollow.
Hollow through the vile praxis of Cousin Julia.

(The Disputant and her Assistants
move about and make a noise
like crumpled paper.)

Er, her visits are seldom. It is duly recorded:
Her visits are seldom, but much feared because
they are so terrible.

(Pensive. Grasping for straws.)

Just now she has returned from a trip to
Jerusalem, where she has become a jewel.
Can you imagine?

As if we needed jewels after the vast fortune
I made lately in Durango, yes, in the uranium
mines at Durango; and somewhat earlier at
Telegu...

*(His mind grows dim
with hollow time.)*

Yes, at the Isthmus of Telegu, where my
father's friend, Isidor—Isidor Weiss—
first devised the Weiss Semi-Pneumatic
Musical Flea Circus in...

DISPUTANT: That was fifty-four years before your
birth, Fraser.

FRASER: *(Sputtering, confused.)*
Well, what of it?

DISPUTANT: You have confused your self with other
semi-erased fingers of your pseudo-group.

*(Holds up her hand, sheathed
delicately in a white glove.
She moves her fingers ever so
slightly.)*

FRASER: What in the name of Babbalanja is that? A
pseudo-group?

DISPUTANT: Identical selves—out of time they form a pure
group, white on white so to speak, of identical,
yet separate beings. I am speaking of Fraser the
first, Fraser the second, Fraser the third, and you:

Fraser the fourth. In it, time that is, they
fool eye and mind by an apparent difference that
both IS and is NOT the case.

(High above, near the skylight
a white rag flutters.)

(All look up.
We hear the winter wind
blow, blow whitely.)

(A dreadful pause.)

FRASER: Are you saying I am not who I am?

DISPUTANT: In this particular instance, you have
confused your doing, the doing of
Fraser₄ with those of your ancestor,
Fraser₁.

(The Marplot is stunned.)

(He looks out: can this be?)

You have confused Late Capitalism with
the dawn of the Wealth of Nations;
mediocrity with accomplishment;
parasitical decline with the miracle
of appearance.

(Sudden realization.)

FRASER: Oh, now I see.

(Quietly.)

My own failings, modest though they be, are
to be confounded with those of my forebears.

DISPUTANT: The others and selflings of your pseudo-group,
Strawberry.

(Light and silvery laughter.)

FRASER: I wish you would not use that…that turn
of phrase.

DISPUTANT: And why not, Strawberry?

(He lowers his head.)

FRASER: It is just that it reminds me of so many
things I would just as soon forget.

DISPUTANT: Like that clandestine meeting, with a certain
gentleman, at the Astor?

FRASER: The encounter happened by chance, I swear.

DISPUTANT: The bargain sworn on that day, or rather…

(With grim determination.)

…late in the witching hours of that day,
did not happen by chance.

FRASER: The version you recount is not the correct version.

DISPUTANT: It is the version as recorded by you, in the
diary you kept for that year, and it is
in no way ambiguous. Your agreement
with that certain gentleman

(A Whitish pause.)

Specifies in great detail…

*(Assistants snap their fingers
seven times.)*

*(Fraser moves from one foot
to the other.)*

*(He has forgotten, thus, that
he is standing.)*

…the intended terms of the arrangement.

*(The white rag in the skylight
is ruffled, lightly—whitely.)*

FRASER: You have been speaking with Bianca, my
country cousin—the young ninny's aunt.

(Silence. Pause. Silence.)

Bianca, Bianca. Tsk, tsk.

*(A hissing from the distant
Assistants.)*

She was so, so pretty so long ago.
Her eyes the color of the deep ice we
sawed in massive cubes and hauled
up from White Wolf Lake.

(He titters again, despite himself.)

Bianca we used to call Aunt Blank. You
might say she was totally erased by
Julia and became a radical. A lot of us
Rings were radicals in those days. But
then the bubble grew in swollen ... in
swollen wonderment, and we all grew
richer even than the Rings who worked
for it. Yes, richer by far.

*(He whistles in the bubble
of his wonderment,)*

(intensely white.)

And so radical Aunt Blank went off to
gay Paree, much to the shame of the
family and became at first a photograph
(Can you imagine?); and then, and then:
and became a rhododendron;
and became a speck of hoarfrost;
and became a hangnail;
and became a doorstop;
and became a great white peach louse;
and became a whited sepulcher;
and BECAME A PARROT.

THE ASSISTANTS: **Shake shake shake
Shake shake shake**

Shake shake shake
Shake the Devil off
Shake the Devil off
in the name of Jesus. *[X3]*

*(He acts as if he had done nothing
unusual.)*

DISPUTANT: But we have strayed from the mark.

FRASER: Indeed, we have. For the worst crime of all
also came about as a result of Julia's
penchant for the systematic removal of
all traces. For concealed within that penchant
lay the even deeper obsession, common to all
us Rings, Innermost and Outermost alike,
to go back to the starting point with a
series of...with a series of searching
questions.

And thus to initiate an interrogation,
in the simplest of language, but an
interrogation nevertheless. A drastic
interrogation.

Simple terms. Drastic interrogation.

Much like this one, in fact.

DISPUTANT: And? And so?

FRASER: And the long and short of it was that
before Julia had quite gotten the hang
of it all (these two impulses being
in direct contradiction), she had
accidentally erased the last two
letters of her mother's good
name, and so transformed her from
a Mother into a Moth.

DISPUTANT: And what did she do with the two letters
she had removed from her Mother's good
name?

FRASER: Trick question. But I was prepared for it.

*(He prepares himself further
to reply; and replies:)*

Thereupon she accidentally sneezed, and in
so doing accidentally obliterated poor
little Louisa's wits and replaced her
adolescent speech faculty with a single,
odd vocalization.

DISPUTANT: And what was that vocalization?

FRASER: Er,

*(All three Figures lean
forward, as if mishearing.)*

ALL THREE: Beg your pardon?

FRASER: Er. The letters E and R. Er. The fragments
of our own dear Moth's former matriarchal
appellative. Er.

(Amused by a peculiar thought.)

At least we were able to keep the two
errant letters in the family.

(Suddenly sarcastic.)

So that
We Outermost Rings are able, despite
all Bianca's slanders and Julia's
erasures, to perpetuate the miracle
of appearance, even amidst the sham
of the contemporary and likewise
the parasitical decline of our kind
in the debacle of Late Capitalism
you have so astutely alluded to.
The miracle of appearance and the
riddle of amazement. Yes, these
remain to our credit. White out!
Bull's-eye! White out!

*(He gestures stiffly,
but triumphantly;)*

*(just like Uncle Adolf
in the railway car
outside gay Paree.)*

ALL THREE OF HIS TORMENTORS: Bull's-eye! Ha!

(He is caught off guard by this.)

DISPUTANT: All this lies as far afield of the mark,

ALL THREE: Strawberry;

DISPUTANT: All of this lies as far afield of the mark
as the silver-tipped claw of the White Flaw

(Pausing for effect.)

A kind of rooster you will* recall

ASSISTANTS: Aw…aw…aw…

(They flap arms as wings.)

DISPUTANT: …that was given to you, in the Ivory Room
of the Astor, by that certain gentleman,
oh, oh, oh, so long ago.

Do you recall that silver-tipped claw?

(He is suddenly frightened by the snare.)

FRASER: That was not me. That was my great grandfather,
the primal Fraser, Kaiser Fraser, whose wicked ways
we in the family have long since amended;

amended, indeed and made up for, in various
noble ways…

DISPUTANT: Made up for? How can what is fixed in
the past be so easily "made up" for?

FRASER: Over the years we have given to the poor,
and mentally impaired; we have rewired the

chronically dislocated and restored the
oh so endangered...

ASSISTANTS: And rare. And rare. And* rare.

FRASER: endangered Sweet Ratfish to his
native habitat in the vast, oily
cypress bog region of Lower Rhode Island;
especially near Lake White Choler where
year-round the mists hang heavy in
the spidery Spanish moss and sawgrass;

*(Pause to see if his tack
has taken; it has not.)*

established foundations and institutions for
the better class of Arts and Letters, those
tending toward the spiritual and moral correction
of the stained and blenched American soul;
I am referring to the Outermost Ring and
Plantation of Providence Foundation, and
her cousin at White Fin Harbor, The Prickled
Bloatfish Institute which is devoted to the,
ah,

reintroduction, ah,

*(Clearly doesn't know what
he is talking about.)*

...of all that glides, monstrous and half-seen;
of all that rests there, submerged and
opalescent. Deep, deep at the bottom of the sea.

(Desperate. Sings, badly:)

**And has suffered a sea-change
into something rich and strange.**

(This does not placate anyone.)

And then there's this INSANE dwarf following
me around, following me taking pictures...

(An odd ritual begins:)

(All are locked into
the mechanism.)

ALL THREE: And did the Long White Man give you
the coconut?

FRASER: For the coconut brings good luck; yes, yes,
he did. In sooth.

ALL THREE: If you have the gift of ivory,
you will be very lucky.

FRASER: I was not worthy, but I was given
the gift of ivory. Yes, yes, I was.
In sooth.

————

ALL THREE: And did the Long White Man make the
fairies dance by moonlight,

DISPUTANT: Strawberry?

FRASER: Er,

DISPUTANT: And? So?

FRASER: *(With great difficulty.)*
He said: "I shall teach you how to knead
the white triangular cake of St. Wolof";
and he did.

ALL THREE: And he did.

FRASER: He said: "I shall make for you white witches
sensible of the stroke of the white elder
at seven miles"; and he did.

ALL THREE: And he did.

FRASER: *(Finally broken.)*
Yes, he did.

(A sudden quiet.)

*(We hear the snowy wind
high above, in the eaves.)*

(The three Women above [Bianca,
Julia and Moth] sing a
wordless hymn of thanks.)

DISPUTANT: *(Quietly.)*
So, you do admit.

FRASER: Yes, it is all true.

DISPUTANT: All of it?

FRASER: Yes. All of it.

DISPUTANT: You admit this all? All of your own free
will?

FRASER: Er,

DISPUTANT: All of your own free will? Under no
compulsion?

FRASER: Under no compulsion. Yes.

DISPUTANT: And you admit you bartered away what is
most precious in an evilish compact
with that certain gentleman...

FRASER: ...at the Ivory Room of the Astor, yes.
But I never received that damned silver-tipped claw,
the claw I was promised, no, all I received in return
was a wooden nickel...

(The wordless hymn ceases.)

(An innocent afterthought.)

At the time I imagined there was a great future
in wooden nickels. How was I to know?
Skip it.

DISPUTANT: And to hide your crimes you confined poor
Great Aunty Dahlia to her treasured chiffonnier;
and banished poor Bianca—with her stutter—
to exile in gay Paree, knowing full well
she was doomed to become, through a sordid
series of transformations, to become a PARROT;

(He is shaken.)

and gave to Cousin Julia, the one you contemptuously term "The Eraser"...

(He writhes in the grip of remorse.)

...and gave to her, her first seemingly innocent Kodak Instamatic, knowing full well what might, given her proclivity for scratching or rubbing out, what might be the outcome?

(He accepts the whitest of white judgements upon his white soul.)

(His expiation begins; sobbing, etc.)

FRASER: ---

(A slow white out begins.)

BIANCA, JULIA, MOTH, AND ASSISTANTS:
And what will you say to the White Zebra?

ASSISTANTS: **And what will you say to the White Zebra?**
What will you say to him?
What will you say to the White Zebra?
White as sin.

What will you say to the White Zebra?
What will you say to the White Zebra?
What will you say to the White Zebra?
What will you say to the
to the White Zebra?

(Fade to White.)

*The Second Entr'acte [**Hoarfrost**]: The Marplot trudges back to the Big House from his meeting with the Disputant at the abandoned factory. There, The Marplot encounters the stuffed Zebra from earlier. He looks at the Zebra. The Zebra looks at him. Next to the Zebra there is an old stone bench. Slowly the heavy snowfall is covering everything.*

(Pause.)

(Silence.)

(Pause.)

(He stands for a long time looking, looking at the Zebra.)

(He has never seen a Zebra in real life before, and this Zebra is a mighty fine one.)

FRASER: Wow.

ZEBRA: —

(The Zebra is the most beautiful creature The Marplot has ever seen.)

(A joyous and brindled pause, after which The Marplot claps his hands;)

FRASER: Wow.

(He waddles through the thick snow, and sits down on the little stone bench, next to the Zebra.)

ZEBRA: —

FRASER: That's okay. That's okay. I understand.

I would like to tell you a story, a true
story from my youth. Owing to an accident
of history and the foolhardiness of youth
I ended up a volunteer with the American

Brigade of the Finnish Army in the Winter
War of 1939. I was wholly innocent, at
the time, of the darker implications
of the project, and we were stationed at
Viipuri in the Karelian Isthmus…

*(The Marplot's story is lost in
the story of the winter storm.)*

(All fades to whitest opalescence.)

*Scene [**Icicle**]: Back in the Big House. The fury of the storm has abated, and as the scene begins we see, through the windows, a marvelous sunset. Moth, Julia and Bianca are snapping the palest of wax beans and Louisa, seated facing her across the room, shells cranberry beans, mirroring the former. It is a good deal quieter than it ought. The White Dwarf is lurking, lurking somewhere unseen.*

LOUISA: Will Uncle Fraser be home for supper?

MOTH: No, Louisa. He will not.

LOUISA: Why not?

Has he decided to return to his mountain
fastness at White Jaw? on the Yukon?
in the remote crag regions of Northwest
Rhode Island? Has he?

*(Moth looks at The Ninny
queerly and stops snapping
beans.)*

*(The White Dwarf enters and
narrates some of the stage directions
which follow.)*

(Something odd happens.)

*(The smiling faces of the
Musicians appear in the
window;)*

(they unsmile;)

(they disappear.)

MOTH: Louisa.

JULIA: Louisa.

BIANCA: Louisa.

LOUISA: Er, did I say or do something wrong?

(Moth looks away.)

(Moth begins snapping beans.)

JULIA: Devil raise a hump upon that damnable Marplot,
    that Kaiser Fraser...

BIANCA: *(As a parrot.)*
    Kaiser Fraser.

LOUISA: Er,

(An ivory pause.)

THE WHITE DWARF: Something happens somewhere.

Someone does something;
only it turns out to be a
naughty something;

so it must be effaced;

so it must be done all over
again

this something is a thought
thing—

this something is a thought
thing—

so it must be done over and
over till someone (whoever)
has got it right.

(This happens.)

*(This happens, and all the time
Moth remains stiff in her chair)*

(snapping beans;)

*(and The Ninny remains motionless
in her chair.)*

The Ninny devises an imaginary world
in her head;

a world of white water and
alabaster beaches, glowing
under a white star.

White water crowfoot and white
water lilies abound;

this world is called "Whizzbang"
and she is happy here.

*(The Musicians enter, one playing
the violin. The other sings:)*

MUSICIANS: **Poor Louisa, poor Louisa,**
why are we doing so poorly?
Why are we doing so poorly?
The bugs and the bats are alive,
bright eyes ablaze in the halls
in the walls of the halls
of "The White Rose," your home.

LOUISA: Sorry. I was someplace else. For a moment.

MOTH: Well, he's had a very serious accident, and he
won't be coming back.

LOUISA: Won't be coming back? Uncle Fraser?

BIANCA: No. He won't be coming back.

JULIA: Not ever.

(The song continues:)

MUSICIANS: **Poor Louisa,**
why are we doing so poorly?
Why are we doing so poorly?
The big, blank, bucket-faced moon, oh,
the moon has risen early,
for you, just for you, riding a wire
The moon's high wire

For Louisa, poor Louisa.
Louisa Outermost Ring;

**It's for you alone we sing,
we sing...**

(All stop suddenly.)

(Pause. Silence. Pause.)

(All begin again; ghostly quiet.)

**Hold on, Hold on,
Poor Louisa,
why are we doing so poorly...**

LOUISA: Because...

MOTH: --

LOUISA: Why can't he come home again?

MOTH: Because.

LOUISA: Because why? Because why not?

JULIA: Because he did not know how to reply.

LOUISA: Did not know how to reply to WHAT?

BIANCA: To the White Zebra of course.

*(This simply baffles The Ninny,
just as you would expect.)*

*(She sighs, goes back to her
cranberry beans.)*

MOTH: You see, Louisa, he was not able to finish
the story he was telling and that story was the
most telling of all.

LOUISA: All this is my fault, I suppose, er.

MOTH: Silly ninny. Confine yourself to the
shelling of cranberry beans, while dear
old Moth confines herself to the
telling of a true tale.

Owing to an accident of history, and the
foolhardiness of youth, Fraser$_2$ ended up

a volunteer with the American Brigade of the
Finnish Army in the Winter War of 1939. Young
Fraser was wholly innocent, at the time, of the
darker implications of the project, and was
promptly stationed at Viipuri, in the Karelian
Isthmus.

Young Fraser, like many in those days, believed
what he had been told: that the Soviet Union
must be stopped in her aggression against
tiny Finland, a truth as apparent to him as
the fact that Stalingrad had been named for
Lenin.

He and a young colleague, Truesdale, came to
be posted on a low bluff, near the outermost ring
of Viipuri, with an ancient Maxim gun from the Great
War, seven crates of rusty ammunition, and a firing
radius of forty-five degrees. The Finns deposited these
young Americans here thinking the main Russian
thrust would come well to the South. Foolish Finns.

Well.

*(As she applies some Gum
Arabic to her whitish gums)*

*(Louisa once more
counts imaginary rabbits
as they hop on her knee.)*

For several hours, the two discussed boyish
things such as Fraser's shocking escape
from the altar at the rehearsal of his
wedding to young Dinah Morgan, a relation
to the great magnate of Hartford—and ever
after a source of embarrassment to the family.

Do you think, do you think, Clyde, for
that was Truesdale's Christian name, that I
did the right thing or was I a cad; or
was I a cad to do the right thing? Or

was I not a cad even though the thing
was not the right thing? Or was the
act both wrong and right and hence
undecidable, and therefore was I not
in fact both a cad and not a cad?

LOUISA: ——

MOTH: Truesdale ended the conversation
and incidentally, their friendship
forever, with the rude insult:
Why Fraser, you strike me simply
as a passive-aggressive hostile fuck!

As it began to darken and glower;
as it began to darken and glower and to
snow rather heavily.

An uncomfortable few minutes passed
with this reply hanging heavily
in the air.

But just at this moment

Fraser happened to catch sight of something rising
slowly out of the snow, at the far end of the
snowy field. A snowy figure, in fact.

(She adjusts the working of her
teeth and gums.)

And then another, and then another, and another.
Slowly arising like squat, appalling snowmen
from the snowfield, each indistinguishable in hue
from the field itself; each figure arising then
slowly, very slowly trudging towards the two lads.
What is that? quipped Fraser. Damned if I know,
responded his fellow;

but

what it was, was the Russian Winter Army, yes,
advancing slowly but inexorably across the

snowy field and through the snowy haze.
Young Fraser watched in astonishment, and
so did young Truesdale.

Slowly trudging across the snowy field
of frightening angles and incalculable
vortices.

At three hundred meters Fraser and Truesdale
opened fire, raking the open field from one side
to the other, rat-a-tat-tat, rat-a-tat-tat;
For a time Fraser would fire and Truesdale
would feed the long belt of cartridges; then
Truesdale would fire and Fraser would feed. Oh,
the advancing snowmen would fall silently
one after another, and be buried in the mounting
drifts of snow. Be buried as more and more
snowmen rose behind them in the white mists
beyond, near the edge of the white wood.

All day this went on: the two young boys slowly
raking their forty-five degrees of angle, filling the
snowy vortices of that nameless place with a
death more breathtakingly beautiful than any
Christmas scene. Time passed even as

Time seemed to stop.

And no more snowmen came. All were dead
And for another few minutes the snow fell
and quietly buried all signs of the...
fateful action...
I am not sure how you would denominate
such an event.

LOUISA: *(By now listening closely.)*
A massacre, I would say.

MOTH: I was just thinking the same thing, Louisa.
A massacre. Yes, I suppose I would call it that.

(Pause for reflection.)

The two young men never spoke of this incident; nor ever exchanged a
word. Ever again. I must go now
and check on poor Great Aunty Dahlia. You too
like Fraser and the rest are new to the secrets
of this house, for Great Aunty Dahlia grows unquiet
unless I apply whitening unguents to the creases
and folds of her indescribable pallor. Even now
I can hear the hinges of her cupboard creaking,
creaking ever so slightly.

(She gets up with her bucket
of beans, turns out a light
and is gone.)

(Louisa slowly stands and goes
to the window.)

(Julia and Bianca smile at Louisa,
and go out, gravely.)

(Moth returns,
for one last twist of the knife.)

MOTH: The white identity, his father Fraser₃ used to say,
is a burden born of successive false effigies.
A row of object zeroes.

(She disappears, leaving poor
Louisa alone.)

(Something happens somewhere.)

(Louisa stands and speaks, all
without the slightest pause:)

LOUISA: The sky was gray, like that day in the
Karelian Isthmus, but there was a white
gleam behind, and from where I was
sitting I could look down on the town
of Newport, and it was still and quiet
and white, like a picture.

I remembered that it was on that hill
that Moth (or someone very much like her,

maybe even older and more white) taught
me to play an old game called "Whizzbang"
in which one had to dance, and wind in
and out of a pattern in the grass, and
then when one had danced and turned long
enough the other person asks you questions,
and you can't help answering whether you
want to or not, and whatever you are told
to do you feel you have to do it. This
person said there used to be a lot of games
like that that some people knew of, and
there was one by which people could be
turned into anything you liked and an old
man her great-grandmother had seen had known
a girl who had been turned into a large
snake. And there was another very ancient
game of dancing and winding and turning,
by which you can take a person out of
himself and hide him away as long as you
like, and his body went walking about
quite empty without any sense in it.

(Suddenly thoughtful.)

This was before we Outermost Rings
discovered, quite accidentally, you could
do the same thing by photography.

*(Suddenly pensive, in her
white way.)*

But I came to that hill because I had been
talked to by the terrible White Zebra, and
I wanted to think of what had happened
the day before, and of the secrets
of the woods. From the place where I was
sitting I could see beyond the town, into
the opening I had found, the opening in
the field, the opening leading to the
question standing at the beginning of things,

where a little brook had let me into an
unknown country. And I pretended I was
following the brook over again and I went
all the way through into my mind.* And
at last I found the wood, and crept into it .
under the bushes, and then in the dusk I saw
something that made me feel as if I were
filled with fire,

*(Violin plays the tune from
"Whiter than the Rest";)*

*(Everyone, except for Fraser,
troops out for the family photograph,
which is now possible.)*

as if I wanted to dance and sing and
fly up into the air, because I was
changed and wonderful. But what I saw
was that I had not changed at all,
and had not grown old...

*(The jubilant Photographer sets
up the antique camera.)*

...And I wondered again and again
how such things could happen and
again how Uncle Fraser's rage against
depiction had so totally backfired
and whether Moth's stories were
really true, because in the daytime
in the open air everything seemed
quite different from what it was
at night, when I was quite frightened,
and thought I was to be burned alive.

*(The bright magnesium flash
of the camera ignites
a slow)*

(fade to [can it be?] black;)

*(A sort of white blackout
[in blacklight to emphasize
the terrible pallor of their
clothes].)*

*(In which we hear the entire
cast sing:)*

ALL: **Description is the Beggar
rolling up the floor
cutting up the carpet
upon which...**

LOUISA: A white witch, I hope.

(We see her teeth are quite pointed.)

ALL: **Upon which the Devil poured
bleach of his depiction
whirling like a djinn.**

**Pure description beggared
white as sin**

**White as sin; white as sin;
Whirling like a djinn
Whirling like a djinn.
White as sin; white as sin.
White as description beggared.**

**In the white squall
of the metaphysical ocean.
In the white squall
of the metaphysical ocean.**

**White as sin; white as sin
White as sin; white as sin
White as sin; white as sin.**

———

*(All begin
to whirl
their
white
clothes
like
monstrous
blooms.)*

(Slow fade to white.)

END OF PLAY

APPENDIX
Cues from the Actors Theatre of Louisville production

At the beginning of the play, Julia, Bianca, Fraser, and Moth each begin to speak simultaneously their opening speeches (before the beginning of "Curious is the Man"). Certain cues, mapped out below, cause everyone to stop for a moment while an individual is brought into focus. One ground rule: during simultaneous speech, if anyone reaches the conclusion of his or her monologue, they begin again.

(The play begins with simultaneous speech.)

JULIA: *(In a rage.)*
Whited sepulchers. Whited hypocrites
and creatures of the blench. Blenched
and two-faced, the whole bloody lot.

(When Julia finishes this sentence, everyone freezes except for her. She continues solo:)

JULIA: We get together once a blue moon, once a
decade, once a century, once a millennium,
and you see the incredible result. Chaos.

(Resume simultaneous speech. Julia continues from this point in her monologue, while everyone else resets to the beginning of their monologues.)

(When Julia finishes the sentence, "Injured merit run amuck," everyone freezes except for her. She continues solo:)

JULIA: Observe the Marplot there. Fraser is so filled
with swarthy venom he must disrupt this,
this most innocent of occasions.

Can he hear me? No, of course not. Too
wrapped up in his own foul rancor,
a whirlwind of a man. A local disturbance
posing as one of us. A hypothetical
human.

(Julia freezes. Moth begins solo:)

MOTH: I am the only soft one; I am the only
   soft one, because I am covered with
   feathers. Yes, with feathers. Not with fur.

   With fur, look at them. Fur.

   (Moth freezes. Bianca begins solo:)

BIANCA: and I was merely minding my own business
   when the two of them, yes, the two
   of them swept down upon me
   like the spider; yes, very much the spider.

   (Resume simultaneous speech. Julia resets to the beginning of her monologue. Moth and Bianca both continue from where they had left off in their solo moments. Fraser begins to speak, amidst everyone else, the text which follows:)

FRASER: It is hard to say which is worse, the
   mania of the maniacs, or the idiocy of the
   idiots. For if there is one thing I
   cannot abide it is the mania of the maniacs;
   for if there is something I hate even more
   than that it is the idiocy of idiots.
   And the worst...

   (At this point in Fraser's speech, everyone freezes except for him. Fraser continues solo:)

FRASER: And the worst is the idiocy of bad jazz,
   and the noise of these infernal idiots and maniacs,
   idiots and maniacs as you see arrayed all about me.
   Me!

   (Resume simultaneous speech. Everyone, including Fraser, continues from where they had left off.)

   (When Fraser finishes the sentence, "Arranged in a way cunningly contrived to inflict the maximal insult upon the auditory person of my personhood," everyone freezes except for Moth. Moth begins solo:)

MOTH: I should have stayed at home, behind the
   floral screen, in my own little room, eating
   a prickled bloatfish,

there,

in suburban Kama-Loka, where I grew up.
Curious.

(The song "Curious is the Man" has begun.)

JULIA: **Curious.**

BIANCA: **Curious.**

LOUISA: **Curious.**

(The text resumes with Julia's line, "When we were young, we girls sang a song about Fraser...")

Heaven and Hell (On Earth): A Divine Comedy

A comic anthology by
Robert Alexander, Jenny Lyn Bader,
Elizabeth Dewberry, Deborah Lynn
Frockt, Rebecca Gilman, Keith Glover,
Hilly Hicks, Jr., Karen Hines, Michael
Kassin, Melanie Marnich, Jane Martin,
William Mastrosimone, Guillermo
Reyes, Sarah Schulman, Richard Strand,
Alice Tuan, and Elizabeth Wong

Copyright © 2001 by Actors Theatre of Louisville. All rights reserved. CAUTION: Professionals and amateurs are hereby warned that *Heaven and Hell (On Earth): A Divine Comedy* is subject to a royalty. It is fully protected under the copyright laws of the United States of America and of all countries covered by the International Copyright Union (including the Dominion of Canada and the rest of the British Commonwealth), the Berne Convention, the Pan-American Copyright Convention and the Universal Copyright Convention, as well as all countries with which the United States has reciprocal copyright relations. All rights, including professional, amateur stage rights, motion picture, recitation, lecturing, public reading, radio broadcasting, television, video or sound recording, all other forms of mechanical or electronic reproduction, such as CD-ROM, CD-I, information storage and retrieval systems and photocopying, and the rights of translation into foreign languages, are strictly reserved. Particular emphasis is laid upon the matter of readings, permission for which must be secured from the Authors' agent in writing.

ALL INQUIRIES CONCERNING RIGHTS, INCLUDING AMATEUR RIGHTS, SHOULD BE ADDRESSED TO: DRAMATISTS PLAY SERVICE, INC., 440 PARK AVENUE SOUTH, NEW YORK, NY 10016.

Heaven and Hell (On Earth):
A Divine Comedy

Heaven and Hell: whether we envision them as actual places or states of mind, these extreme realms—with their contrasting promises of ecstasy or misery—have fueled both the literary and the popular imagination for centuries. But what might the idea of Heaven and Hell look like to young people as they attempt to navigate their lives circa 2001? Putting a contemporary spin on an eternal obsession, Actors Theatre of Louisville posed this question to an array of devilishly talented playwrights, each of whom contributed a scene or monologue to this unique collaboration. The result is *Heaven and Hell (On Earth): A Divine Comedy*, a collection of surprising, diverse impressions generated around a single thematic spark.

This experiment—which brings together myriad voices to create a single theatrical event—began by suggesting provocative thematic territory and inviting playwrights to invent the characters and their varied dilemmas. The project was devised for twenty-two young actors, the members of Actors Theatre of Louisville's 2000-2001 Apprentice Company (who performed in the 2001 Humana Festival premiere), but the play could easily be performed by a smaller ensemble of actors.

In this comic anthology, the diversity of voices, identities, and points of view are integral both to the play's moment-to-moment pleasures and its cumulative impact. As the characters reveal their own experiences of vice and virtue, salvation and damnation, we see them grappling with everything from finances to relationships to the loss of youth itself. And for these witty playwrights, contemporary heavens and hells, like good and evil, are interconnected concepts—because here on earth, experience is complex, shifting, and always a matter of our own perception.

—*Amy Wegener*

BIOGRAPHIES

Robert Alexander's plays include *Servant of The People; A Preface To The Alien Garden; Gravity Pulls at the Speed of Darkness; Bulletproof Hearts; Hatemachine; The Last Orbit of Billy Mars; Will He Bop or Will He Drop?; Moon in Gemini; The Hourglass; Air Guitar;* and *I Ain't Yo' Uncle* (published by Dramatic Publishing Company). His works have been produced or workshopped by Negro Ensemble Company, The Kennedy Center, Los Angeles Theatre Center, Hartford Stage Company, Jomandi Productions, St. Louis Black Repertory Company, Lorraine Hansberry Theatre, Crossroads Theatre, Mark Taper Forum, Trinity Repertory, San Diego Repertory, Woolly Mammoth, Arena Players, and Karamu House. He holds an M.F.A. in Playwriting from the University of Iowa, where he was a Patricia Roberts Harris Fellow. Formerly a NEA/TCG resident playwright at Jomandi in Atlanta, he is currently playwright-in-residence at Woolly Mammoth in Washington, D.C. through a residency from TCG and the Pew Charitable Trusts' National Theatre Artist Residency Program. He is a member of The Dramatists Guild.

Jenny Lyn Bader's plays have been produced at Center Stage, Pulse Ensemble, Lincoln Center Theater Directors Lab, New York International Fringe Festival ("Best of the Fringe" selection), HERE, John Montgomery Theatre, and other venues. Her play *Manhattan Casanova* won the Edith Oliver Award at the National Playwrights Conference at the Eugene O'Neill Theatre Center. Her work has been anthologized in *Next: Young American Writers on The New Generation* (Norton) and other collections. Ms. Bader wrote the internet serial drama *Watercooler* (MSN) and frequently contributes to *The New York Times*. She co-authored *He Meant, She Meant* (Warner). She is a graduate of Harvard and a member of The Dramatists Guild.

Elizabeth Dewberry most recently premiered *Happy Mug* in Wintermezzo, the 2000 Apprentice/Intern Showcase at Actors Theatre of Louisville. She premiered her first short play, *Head On*, at the 1995 Humana Festival and her first full-length play, *Flesh and Blood*, at the 1996 Humana Festival. *Who's On Top*, a ten-minute play, premiered in the 1999 Summer Apprentice/Intern Showcase at ATL. Her second full-length play, *Four Joans and a Fire-Eater*, premiered at Swine Palace Theatre in the fall of 1999. She is also the author of two novels, *Many Things Have Happened Since He Died* (published by Doubleday, 1990 and Vintage Contemporaries, 1992) and *Break the Heart of Me* (Nan A. Talese/Doubleday, 1994). Ms. Dewberry holds a Ph.D. in twentieth century American literature from Emory University and a B.S. in English from Vanderbilt. She lives in Lamont, Florida, with her husband, author Robert Olen Butler.

Deborah Lynn Frockt's work has been seen at Actors Theatre of Louisville, Alabama Shakespeare Festival, Alliance Theatre, Playhouse in the Square and Seattle Children's Theatre, among others. *The Book of Ruth* was the recipient of an AT&T Onstage award. *When I Grow Up, I'm Gonna Get Some Big Words*—adapted from the writings of the Civil Rights Movement—recently premiered to critical acclaim in Seattle. She has worked on many new plays as a dramaturg at ATL and Seattle Children's Theatre. She is the editor of *Seattle Children's Theatre: Six Plays Volume II*. A Louisville native who now resides with her family in Seattle, Ms. Frockt is a graduate of Stanford University and the University of London.

Rebecca Gilman's plays include *Spinning into Butter, Boy Gets Girl* and *The Glory of Living*. Her plays have been produced at Actors Theatre of Louisville, The Goodman Theatre, Lincoln Center Theater, Royal Court Theatre, Manhattan Theatre Club, Seattle Repertory, St. Louis Repertory, Alliance Theatre, and Mixed Blood Theatre, as well as other theatres around the country and abroad. She is the recipient of the Prince Prize for commissioning original work; the Roger L. Stevens Award from the Kennedy Center Fund for New American Plays; the Evening Standard Award for Most Promising Playwright; and an Illinois Arts Council playwriting fellowship. A native of Alabama, Ms. Gilman lives in Chicago.

Keith Glover recently adapted/directed *Golden Boy* for Long Wharf Theatre, and his new play, *Dark Paradise* (Rosenthal Award), premiered at Cincinnati Playhouse, under his direction. *Thunder Knocking on the Door* (Osborne Award), commissioned/produced by Alabama Shakespeare Festival, was subsequently produced at Yale Repertory, Dallas Theatre Center, Baltimore Center Stage, Northlight Theatre, A Contemporary Theatre, San Jose Repertory, The Guthrie, Meadowbrook Theatre, Arena Stage, Cincinnati Playhouse, Great Lakes Theatre Festival, Old Globe, and GeVa. *Dancing on Moonlight* was produced off-Broadway by New York Shakespeare Festival; *Coming Of The Hurricane* (finalist for Osborne Award, runner-up for Theodore Award Prize) premiered at Denver Center, and was produced at Arena Stage and Crossroads Theatre Company. Mr. Glover directed productions of his play *In Walks Ed*

(Rosenthal Award, Pulitzer nomination) at Cincinnati Playhouse and Long Wharf Theatre, as well as productions of *Thunder* at Northlight, Arena Stage (Helen Hayes nomination), Cincinnati Playhouse, Great Lakes Theatre Festival, Old Globe and GeVa. He is a member of New Dramatists and The Dramatists Guild.

Hilly Hicks, Jr. is the author of *A Hole in the Dark*, which recently premiered in Atlanta, and opened in the spring of 2001 at City Theatre in Pittsburgh. His newest play, *The Home Life of Polar Bears*, was originally developed at New York Theatre Workshop and at the July 2000 National Playwrights Conference in Connecticut, and was further developed at Mark Taper Forum's New Work Festival 2000. Mr. Hicks was part of Manhattan Theatre Club's reading series, 6@6: Discovering the Next Generation. His other plays include *The Trophy Room* and *Racolla's Wedding*. He is the recipient of a Van Lier Playwriting Fellowship from New York Theatre Workshop and a commission from South Coast Repertory. He is a member of Drama Dept.

Karen Hines Chicago-born, Toronto-bred, Karen Hines is an award-winning writer and performer. Her two solo shows, *Oh, baby* and *Pochsy's Lips* (ATL Flying Solo Festival '94) have toured across North America. The third, *Head Movements of a Long-Haired Girl*, is currently in development. She also wrote and co-composed *Hello...Hello (A Romantic Satire)* which was a finalist for Canada's coveted Chalmers Award for playwriting. Karen is the director of the Canadian horror clown duo Mump & Smoot (most recently at Yale Repertory). She was a writer and performer with Toronto's Second City and has appeared extensively in television and film, including Ken Finkleman's cult hits *Newsroom* (PBS), and *Married Life* (Comedy Central), for which her performance recieved a CableAce nomination. Recent favorite projects include John Cameron Mitchell's *Hedwig and the Angry Inch* as well as Finkleman's upcoming series *Foreign Objects*.

Michael Kassin This is Mr. Kassin's second trip to the Humana Festival. *Today A Little Extra* was produced in the 1980 Humana Festival and subsequently Off-Broadway at the American Jewish Theater, and was published in *Best Short Plays* and *Baker's Plays*. Another full-length, *Brother Champ*, was produced at the Mixed Blood Theater and selected for the National Playwrights Conference before receiving an award-winning production at the West Coast Ensemble in Los Angeles. His most recent full-length, *The Shroud*, was produced by the West Coast Ensemble in 1999. As a screenwriter, Mr. Kassin has written for New Line Cinema and Tri-Vanguard Pictures. His greatest achievement, however, is his marriage to Beverly Miller, in 1999.

Melanie Marnich is the author of the plays *Blur, Quake, Beautiful Again, Tallgrass Gothic*, and *Season*. *Blur* was included in New York's Public Theater's New Work Now Festival, the U.S. West Festival of New Plays, and premiered at the Manhattan Theatre Club in April 2001. *Quake* was selected for the Fall 2000 A.S.K. International Writers Exchange held at London's Royal Court Theatre, and was produced in the 2001 Humana Festival of New American Plays at Actors Theatre of Louisville. Major awards include two Samuel Goldwyn writing awards, two Jerome Fellowships, a McKnight Advancement Grant, inclusion in Lincoln Center's American Living Room Festival, and the Francesca Primus Prize. Ms. Marnich earned her M.F.A. in playwriting from the University of California, San Diego. She now lives in Minneapolis. She is a member of The Dramatists Guild and of the Playwrights' Center.

Jane Martin returns to ATL with her latest play following the premiere of *Anton in Show Business* at the 24th Humana Festival, which won the American Theatre Critics Association Award for Best New Play of 2000. Ms. Martin, a Kentuckian, first came to national attention for *Talking With*, a collection of monologues premiering in the 1982 Humana Festival. Since its New York premiere at the Manhattan Theatre Club in 1982, *Talking With* has been performed around the world, winning the Best Foreign Play of the Year award in Germany from *Theater Heute* magazine. Ms. Martin's *Keely and Du*, which premiered in the 1993 Humana Festival, was nominated for the Pulitzer Prize in drama and won the American Theatre Critics Association Award for Best New Play in 1996. Her other work includes: *Mr. Bundy* (1998 Humana Festival), *Jack and Jill* (1996 Humana Festival), *Middle-Aged White Guys* (1995 Humana Festival), *Cementville* (1991 Humana Festival) and *Vital Signs* (1990 Humana Festival). Ms. Martin's work has been translated into Spanish, French, German, Dutch, Russian and several other languages.

William Mastrosimone, a resident of Titusville, New Jersey, debuted with *The Woolgatherer* (1992 L.A. Drama Critics Award for Best Play), followed by *Extremities*, which premiered at Actors Theatre of Louisville in the 1981 Humana Festival (New York Outer Critics Circle Award for Best Play 1982-83, John Gassner Award for Playwriting) and later became a feature film.

Nanawatai! opened in Norway, later becoming the film *The Beast* (1988 Roxanne T. Mueller Award for Best Film, Cleveland International Film Festival). *Sinatra* received a 1992 Golden Globe Award for Best Mini-Series while *The Burning Season* received an Emmy nomination, a Humanitas and an Environmental Media Award (1995). Other films include *With Honors* and *Escobar* (HBO). Other plays include *Tamer of Horses* (1987 L.A. NAACP Award for Best Play), *A Tantalizing* (1982 Humana Festival) *Shivaree* (Warner Communications Award), *A Stone Carver, The Undoing* (1984 Humana Festival), *Sunshine, Cat's Paw, Burning Desire* and *Benedict Arnold.* He holds an M.F.A. from Rutgers University's Mason Gross School of Arts, and is a 1989 recipient of the New Jersey Governor's Walt Whitman Award for Writing and an Honorary Doctorate of Humane Letters from Rider College.

Guillermo Reyes The Chilean-born author's plays include *Chilean Holiday, Men on the Verge of a His-Panic Breakdown, Deporting the Divas, Miss Consuelo, The Seductions of Johnny Diego,* and *Mother Lolita,* among others. *Chilean Holiday* was produced at Actors Theatre of Louisville, and published in *Humana Festival '96: The Complete Plays* (Smith and Kraus). *Men on the Verge* won Theater's L.A.'s Ovation Award for Best World Premiere Play and Best Production 1994, and has since played across the country including New York City where it also won the 1996 Emerging Playwright Award and received an Off-Broadway production by Urban Stages at the 47th Street Playhouse. *Deporting the Divas* premiered at Celebration Theater of L.A. and won a 1996 Drama-Logue Award for Playwriting for its Bay Area premiere at Theatre Rhinoceros. Mr. Reyes won the 1997 National Hispanic Playwrights Contest with *A Southern Christmas,* and the Nosotros Theater of Los Angeles' 1998 Playwriting Award with the comedy, *The Hispanick Zone.* A brand new play, *Mother Lolita,* recently opened Off-Broadway in New York City, produced by Urban Stages in November 2000, and *Sirena, Queen of the Tango* is being produced by Celebration Theater and Theater Rhinoceros in their current seasons. Reyes received his Masters Degree in Playwriting from the University of California, San Diego. He is currently Assistant Professor of Theater at Arizona State University in Tempe and head of the playwriting program. He is a member of The Dramatists Guild.

Sarah Schulman is the author of eight novels including: *The Child* (forthcoming), *Shimmer* (Avon, 1998), *Rat Bohemia* (Dutton, 1995—Ferro/Grumley award for Lesbian Fiction, Finalist—Prix de Rome), *Empathy* (Dutton, 1992), and two nonfiction books: *Stagestruck: Theatre, AIDS and the Marketing of Gay America* (Duke University Press, 1998—American Library Association Gay/Lesbian Nonfiction Award), and *My American History: Lesbian and Gay Life During the Reagan/Bush Years* (Routledge 1994—Gustavus Meyer Award for Work on Tolerance). She was a 1984 Fulbright Fellow in Judaic Studies. She is currently developing six plays including: *The Child* (workshop at Trinity Repertory Company in February, 2001 directed by Craig Lucas, workshop at Strassberg Studio of LA, directed by Moisés Kaufman); *Correct Usage and Common Errors* (reading at Playwrights Horizons directed by Michael Greif); and *Carson McCullers* (Sundance Theater Lab, 2000). Ms. Schulman is also collaborating on a musical, *Shimmer*, based on her novel.

Richard Strand is the author of *The Bug* and *The Death of Zukasky*, both of which premiered at the Humana Festival. Other plays by Mr. Strand have premiered at Steppenwolf Theatre and Victory Gardens Theater in Chicago, The O'Neill Festival in Connecticut, GeVa Theatre, The Cricket Theatre in Minneapolis and Zena Group in New York. His plays are published by Heinemann, Samuel French, and Dramatists Play Service. Mr. Strand lives in Glendale, California and teaches theater at Mt. San Antonio College. He is a member of The Dramatists Guild.

Alice Tuan is this year's emerging artist recipient of both the Richard E. Sherwood Award through Los Angeles' Mark Taper Forum, and the Colbert Award for Excellence through New York's Downtown Arts Project. Productions include *Last of the Suns* (Berkeley Repertory Theatre), *Ikebana* (East West Players), and *Some Asians* (Perishable Theater). Performances include *New Culture for a New Country* (En Garde Arts) and *Sprawl* (with Rachel Hauck at the Actor's Gang). Ms. Tuan recently finished a residency at East West Players through the NEA/TCG Playwright Residency Program where she assembled the "Turn Asian America Inside Out" Conference/Performance to find new spaces to think about Asian America. She is also the Resident Playwright at the Los Angeles Theater Center through the Los Angeles Cultural Affairs Dept. Upcoming projects include *Hit* (a Public Theater commission), the adaptation of Middleton's *The Roaring Girle* (through the Foundtry Theater) and *The 2050 Project* (with New World Theater). Recent productions include *Ajax (por nobody)* at The Flea, *Coastline* (virtual hypertext theater) at ASK's Common Ground Festival and *mALL* at Cypress College.

Elizabeth Wong is the winner of the Kennedy Center's David Mark Cohen Award for *China Doll*, which will be produced by Chay Yew at Northeast Asian American Theatre in Seattle, and was recently featured at Arena Stage in Washington, D.C. as part of the inaugural "Downstairs" reading series for new American plays. *Letters to a Student Revolutionary* was produced Off-Broadway by Pan Asian Repertory Theatre, East/West Players in Los Angeles, Northwest Asian American Theatre in Seattle, Brecht Festival in Tokyo and Singapore Arts Festival. Other productions include *Kimchee & Chitlins* at Chicago's Victory Gardens Theater and West Coast Ensemble in Los Angeles; *Prometheus* and *Amazing Adventures of the Marvelous Monkey King*, both commissioned and produced by Denver Center Theatre Company; *Boyd & Oskar*, commissioned and produced by Ed Stern and Cincinnati Playhouse in the Park; and *Let the Big Dog Eat*, commissioned and produced by ATL. Upcoming projects include *The Happy Prince*, an opera for children commissioned by the Kennedy Center for the Performing Arts, and *Legend of Miao Shan* for Honolulu Theatre For Youth. She holds an M.F.A. from New York University's Tisch School of the Arts. She is a member of The Dramatists Guild, UASSITEJ, PEN West, and Writers Guild West. Currently, she teaches at the University of Southern California, Santa Barbara. She was a Disney Writers Fellow and winner of the Petersen Emerging Playwrights Award. Her television credits include ABC's *All-American Girl.*

HUMANA FESTIVAL PRODUCTION

Heaven and Hell (On Earth): A Divine Comedy was commissioned by Actors Theatre of Louisville and premiered at the Humana Festival of New American Plays in March 2001. It was directed by Sullivan Canaday White and Meredith McDonough with the following cast:

The Victimless Crime. . . . . Maesie Speer
by Deborah Lynn Frockt

Saints at the Rave. . . . . Matt Ryan Whitesel (Roommate),
by Guillermo Reyes   Gian-Murray Gianino (Saint)

Coco Puffs . . . . Misty Dawn Jordan (Coco)
by Alice Tuan

Just Hold Me . . . . Brad Abner (Randy),
by William Mastrosimone   Jessica Browne-White (Michelle)

Robin. . . . . Star Xaviera Little (Robin)
by Sarah Schulman

i-*kissandtell* . . . . Travis Horseman
by Michael Kassin

Virtual Virtue. . . . . . . Andrew Jackson (Todd), Pauline Yasuda (Ella)
by Elizabeth Dewberry

Young Man Praying . . . . Nehal Joshi (Young Man)
by Karen Hines

Capitalism 101 . . . . Peter Stone (Matt), Atticus Rowe (Chris)
by Rebecca Gilman

White Elephants. . . . . Nastaran Ahmadi (Giselle)
by Jane Martin

Swirling with Merlin. . . . . Breton Nicholson
by Keith Glover

Worldness . . . . Shoshona Currier (Viv),
by Jenny Lyn Bader   Rebecca Brooksher (Suzanne)

RIOT Grrrrl GUITAR. . . . . Lia Aprile
by Robert Alexander

Note to Self. . . . . Joey Williamson (Tommy),
by Hilly Hicks, Jr.   Emera Felice Krauss (Constance)

Rosa's Eulogy. . . . . Jennifer Taher (Jeanne)
by Richard Strand

Badass of The RIP Eternal. . . . . Alex Finch (Thrasher)
by Elizabeth Wong

and the following production staff:

Scenic Designer . . . . Paul Owen
Costume Designer . . . . Kevin McLeod
Lighting Designer . . . . Tony Penna
Sound Designer . . . . Jason A Tratta with Martin R. Desjardins
Properties Designer . . . . Doc Manning
Stage Manager. . . . . John Armstrong
Assistant Stage Manager . . . . Erin Tatge
Dramaturgs . . . . Amy Wegener, Tanya Palmer, and
                                           Michael Bigelow Dixon
Assistant Dramaturg . . . . Karen C. Petruska

The cast of
Heaven and Hell (On Earth): A Divine Comedy

25th Annual Humana Festival of New American Plays
Actors Theatre of Louisville, 2001
photo by Richard Trigg

Heaven and Hell (On Earth): A Divine Comedy

The Victimless Crime
by Deborah Lynn Frockt

A twenty-something-looking woman, wearing retro chic circa 1976, is arranging an absolutely stunning bouquet of long-stemmed roses in every color. They are romantic but not clichéd.

So I never meant for it to go this far.

One day I'm having drinks right at the beginning of everything. I mean I was at that singular moment when it was all just about to begin. And the next…it's Eternal Rest *Cemetery* calling to push plots. Who knew that being in your thirties—your relatively early thirties—was enough to change your goddamn demographic group? Who in their right-thinking American mind would want that?

But I've always had this face. *(She gestures in a showy way to her face.)* This going to be carded until I'm fifty-seven and a half face. So I'm thirty…ish. Why couldn't I be twenty-nine? *(She thinks.)* Twenty-eight. At twenty-seven, I return to that singular moment. It's all just beginning. And eternal rest? I'll never need it.

So six months ago, I reincarnated myself as a twenty-six-year-old dot.commer. (What else would you come back as?) Would maturity have gotten me options? Would the truth have allowed me to play Ping-Pong at the office and enjoy team building on the face of a rock? Could I reasonably wear these, *(She indicates her retro chic clothes.)* not acquired from thrift stores but actual vintage duds from my very own Brady years? Would I have this man…man-boy…boy…as my steady?

Would I have this boy just a cubicle away at my beck and call? This great-looking, at that singular moment, it's all just about to begin, hot, naïve, rock-climbing, on his way up, young young…really young…gonna be a grown-up one day but not too soon…would I have this man…born in our nation's bicentennial year…suggesting that we grow old together?

    (She regards the flowers.)

I think not.

Saints at the Rave
by Guillermo Reyes

THE ROOMMATE: Nineteen-year-old student in Catholic college, stuffy.
ST. AUGUSTINE OF HIPPO: His roommate, also in his late teens, and a party
animal.

A college dorm, modern times. The Roommate enters and sees St. Augustine
sleeping on the couch.

ROOMMATE: Alright, get up.

SAINT: Huh?

ROOMMATE: Your bags are ready, and the Carmelite nuns have agreed to put you up until you can be sent back to—to, you know, the fourth century or wherever it is you belong.

SAINT: Oh? Huh?

ROOMMATE: I'm sorry, St. Augustine, but this exchange program just isn't working out anymore. Your behavior's been lewd, gross and a bit too Ancient Rome for my taste. I was expecting a lot more from you and…well, have you anything to say for yourself? ?

SAINT: *(Burping.)* Arrrgh!

ROOMMATE: Oh, that's good, that's really good. Maybe it's my fault. I thought you'd be good at least for research.

SAINT: To you, I was just research?

ROOMMATE: Well, frankly, yes, but—wait, why am I feeling apologetic? You're the one who stayed up all night at the rave doing mushrooms— or was it ecstasy? Don't answer that! I really wish you would just pick up and go now, and consider this exchange a bad experiment in inter- century activities.

SAINT: You didn't specify.

ROOMMATE: What?

SAINT: Dude, when you asked for St. Augustine of Hippo, you didn't specify the older, wiser scholar. They sent you the young debaucherer instead! You can order St. Augustine in all of life's passages.

ROOMMATE: Spare me the Gail Sheehy analysis. Your bags are packed.

SAINT: Well…geez…man, oh, man, I'm sorry—

ROOMMATE: No need to apologize. I fooled myself. I forgot that besides being a saint, you were also a man.

SAINT: "Man." You say it with such disdain.

ROOMMATE: No, no, somebody's got to gangbang the sorority girls—

SAINT: You say that with disdain, too.

ROOMMATE: After all, this is a Catholic college. I thought I'd left all that teenage excess behind in high school, but no, this lack of discipline among my contemporaries, it's quite overwhelming! You should go now!

SAINT: Alright, I will!

ROOMMATE: Wait! I mean no—just go, go!

SAINT: I am—

ROOMMATE: Wait! *(Roommate starts to cry.)*

SAINT: Now, what's this?

ROOMMATE: Never you mind.

SAINT: Say it.

ROOMMATE: When you first came, you were like a brother, you know.

SAINT: Yeh?

ROOMMATE: You explained the Manichean heresy so well, I got an A in that exam. I've never had a brother, you know, nor a sister, nor anybody who could be wiser than I am.

SAINT: It's good to have a saint around, yeh.

ROOMMATE: I thought so.

SAINT: You wanna go raid the pear orchard?

ROOMMATE: What? Now why do you do that?

SAINT: I don't know, it's a prank, builds comradeship amongst pranksters.

ROOMMATE: As President of Catholic Youth, I'm deeply offended by your behavior.

SAINT: Well, you know what, Mr. President of Catholic Youth? I'm a little tired myself of you cloaking yourself in my religion, the one I helped define, to judge me! Me! I reached my state of beatitude the hard way, dude! I had to struggle with lust, and gluttony and—you know the other deadly sins—

ROOMMATE: You mean you don't know the seven deadly si—

SAINT: I said don't judge me!

I didn't become the saint without struggling with those sins in the fourth century the way you are in the twenty-first.

ROOMMATE: I've done well against sin!

SAINT: The point is you wanted me to be an example and I only ended up a man who has to undergo his life's passages like any other. I'm sorry if you don't want me around—I could have used your help.

ROOMMATE: My help?

SAINT: Sure, I never had anybody to confide in either.

Somebody to help me steer away from sin, you know.

ROOMMATE: This is the vulnerable stage of your life passage, isn't it?

SAINT: The most vulnerable.

ROOMMATE: We could pray for you, I suppose.

SAINT: That, too, but how about learning to just…listen.

ROOMMATE: To you? I mean…alright, alright, I see…you need a friend.

SAINT: Good, you're helping me, see? Helping me steer away from sin which is something St. Augustine really needed at this age.

ROOMMATE: Well…I suppose I can do that, but don't push your luck—

SAINT: If I misbehave, if I fall into temptation, I'm sure you'll be there to remind me.

ROOMMATE: Would you also take your socks and put them in the laundry basket or something?

SAINT: Sure. We could go do laundry, and then make some of that hangover soup—

ROOMMATE: Too first century, just take Tylenol.

We could go to dinner though—

SAINT: The steak house—

ROOMMATE: Alright, the steak house—

SAINT: I know some Puerto Rican girls who work there who are dyyyying to meet you—

ROOMMATE: No allusions to Mick Jagger please—

SAINT: Sorry!

ROOMMATE: We'll buy you Gregorian chants. You'll see, Saint Augustine, I'll help you steer away from sin.

SAINT: Sure you will. Brothers?

ROOMMATE: Alright…brothers.

Coco Puffs
by Alice Tuan

Coco holds a smoke. She frantically checks her pockets.

COCO:

Excuse me.

Excuse me.

Excuse me, do you have a light?

Excuse me, um, might you have a light?

(No luck with any of it.)

I don't smoke. Not usually. I really don't. Well, not for two weeks now. I used to, I mean I was...a...smoker...but I stopped. I didn't quit. I stopped. Cuz quit is just too, it's too *definite* a word. Quit is altogether, where stop is just, well you know pause. Although...

Excuse me...

Although when you think about it, smoking is the most active form of pause. You're doing something while you're not doing anything. And it isn't as obvious as eating...cuz eating...and I don't want to eat, but I'm starved...that's why I started...and now I've stopped I have.

(She looks at the cigarette, eventually sniffing it...longing for it.)

It's intermission. It's intermission at the theater. And if it weren't for Carmen, I wouldn't be standing here contemplating breaking the stopping...I hate theater. I really do. A really bad play is just so hard to shake. My thought is that theater has the elasticity to bring new and complicated populations to the stage. That's what I always thought theater provided the culture. And these days I'm tired of the same white lens telling the lame story of non-white people...why don't we ever follow the grocer home?

But I love Carmen...she's my best friend...it's unconditional, though I have my opinions...and sometimes, you can't tell the truth cuz...But of all the brilliant things she is, she...wants...to...*act*. And Carmen is...I mean...Her person is really fabulous, but get her on stage and she stiffens into a cardboard cutout. And so she ends up...in these horrible plays...that I have to support her in...these plays that proliferate dead culture…one of the worst sins in my eyes…now that the smoke has lifted…

Excuse me.

(No luck with the light. She finds matches in her inside pocket. She holds both up.)

Get through it Coco get through it.

(She inaudibly and continuously chants to get through it, 'Coco, get through it,' as she slowly rolls the tip of the cig back and forth in her fingers, the tobacco sprinkling on the ground. She puts the matches back in her pocket.)

OK, Coco. Act Two.

Just Hold Me
by William Mastrosimone

Darkness. Contemporary love song. Lights up on two folding chairs, side by side, facing audience. Randy driving slowly, looking for something on his right. He finds what he's looking for. Enter Michelle in a dark raincoat. She gets in the car. They embrace.

RANDY: I've waited so long for this night.

MICHELLE: Just go.

RANDY: You smell nice.

MICHELLE: I shaped pillows under a blanket in case my mom takes a peek in my room.

RANDY: Everything will be fine.

MICHELLE: You just went through a stop sign.

RANDY: Did I?

MICHELLE: With your lights off.

RANDY: Oh. What is that you're wearing?

MICHELLE: Why am I so nervous?

RANDY: Maybe it's good nervous.

MICHELLE: No nervous is good nervous.

RANDY: What's to be nervous about? Got protection. Our favorite wine.

MICHELLE: I hate myself when I lie to my parents.

RANDY: It's not lying. It's protecting them from harsh realities.

MICHELLE: They're so good to me. Where are we going?

RANDY: I know a good place to park.

MICHELLE: I just got a very bad feeling.

RANDY: Michelle, we've been through this already.

MICHELLE: I know.

RANDY: This is our special night.

MICHELLE: I just wonder if we shouldn't wait.

RANDY: Wait for what?

MICHELLE: I don't know.

RANDY: Another guy?

MICHELLE: I want it to feel right.

RANDY: Tell me something.

MICHELLE: I think I'd like to know you better.

RANDY: There's nothing more to know.

MICHELLE: I hope that's not true.

RANDY: I'm an open book. Know what this book says, sweetheart? I just wanna be close to you.

MICHELLE: I want that too.

RANDY: So what's the problem?

MICHELLE: Why can't we just hang out?

RANDY: You can't do this.

MICHELLE: Do what?

RANDY: Get somebody's hopes up and then—

MICHELLE: I think you're going too fast.

RANDY: The pedal.

MICHELLE: This is too fast.

RANDY: The pedal's stuck.

MICHELLE: *(Reaching for ignition.)* Turn it off!

RANDY: *(Pushing her away.)* No! Then the steering locks up!

MICHELLE: Watch out—the car!

RANDY: I know! Lift the pedal!

MICHELLE: How?

RANDY: Just lift it!

MICHELLE: It won't.

RANDY: Try!

MICHELLE: It's stuck! You're gonna rear-end that car!

RANDY: Can't pass on a curve!

MICHELLE: Pass on the right! *(As he steers that way.)* No! Parked car!
(He turns the other way.)

RANDY: Was that a cop car?

MICHELLE: Don't know. Ditch the wine.
(She tosses bag out the window.)

RANDY: No! Idiot!

MICHELLE: Tree!

RANDY: Oh God!

MICHELLE: That was so close!

RANDY: Put on your seatbelt.

MICHELLE: I knew something bad would happen.

RANDY: Oh shut your stupid mouth.

MICHELLE: Mailbox, moron!

RANDY: Unavoidable, shithead!

MICHELLE: You can't drive for shit. Turn there.

RANDY: Where?

MICHELLE: Turn turn turn!

RANDY: In a field?

MICHELLE: There's nothing to collide with in a field, jerk.

(He turns and they bounce violently in their seats.)

RANDY: There goes the suspension.

MICHELLE: Oh, big loss.

RANDY: My dad is gonna kill me.

MICHELLE: So will mine if I go home dead.

RANDY: Where's this go?

MICHELLE: Just make big circles till we run out of gas.

RANDY: That could be hours!

MICHELLE: Death could be even longer!

RANDY: Stop yelling in my ear!

MICHELLE: How I ever let you talk me into this.

RANDY: Oh, virtuous you corrupted by evil me.

MICHELLE: What the—?

RANDY: Mud. Deep mud.

(The car comes to a stop. Randy turns the car off. They both lay back and sigh. Exhausted.)

MICHELLE: We're alive.

RANDY: My heart won't stop.

MICHELLE: Mine too.

RANDY: We were up to seventy-five.

MICHELLE: Eighty-five.

RANDY: Whatever.

MICHELLE: It's very dark here.

RANDY: Ever see so many stars?

MICHELLE: What now?

RANDY: I'll think of something.

MICHELLE: Shut up.

RANDY: My protection was in the bag with the wine anyway.

MICHELLE: Really?

RANDY: You don't have to be so happy about it.

MICHELLE: Just hold me.

(Beat. Lights fade.)

Robin
by Sarah Schulman

ROBIN: My brother and I were sitting in the park talking about how like when you want pants, they're all beige. Like when you have to buy something, and everybody has to, they only let you make boring choices, I mean all the possibilities are wrong. Beige or khaki is not a choice. Then he said "But what can you do?" so suddenly I had this great idea that maybe all shops should cease. Instead each of us would think of what we wanted, tell the computer, charge it. The computer would then order it from production plants in Kansas or the Democratic Republic of Congo and keep the profit. They wouldn't have to stock inventory so they wouldn't be pre-choosing our choices. I know this idea would intrigue everybody because they would have to rely on their imaginations to understand what they would like. They would have to project an image, instead of cathect with a displayed object. So, I started dreaming up stuff, like boxes of dried boysenberries and goat milk soufflé, reversible cars, instant intimidation machines, automatic sneaker scrubbers and see-through jock straps.

So my brother and I started talking over my father, and how I imagined he could be. I thought of him being interested in me, so that I could find protection. I mean, protection is a father who will stand up for you, right? My father was beige. But what was great was that my brother has an imagination when it comes to feelings, so he is a brother of human loyalty, not a brother of family currency. Even though my father couldn't get over what the neighbors think, my brother and I had that benchtime in the park, where everyone could see us. And we were sitting there watching four hundred khaki couples walk by with their little babies in jogging strollers. All of the mothers were over thirty but dressed like fifteen-year-olds. All of the fathers had these pained expressions of possibility under wraps. The kids all had these yuppie names like Cornelius or Theadora. Names that would grow up to become Republican Supermodels. You know, beige. It was pathetic and that's why I'll never be part of it, and my brother said that that was OK with him. He saved me.

i-kissandtell
by Michael Kassin

An eighteen-year-old boots up his laptop. Looks at the audience.

I been in college two weeks. And I *rule*, man! *(Beat.)*
I met her last night. At this party? Off-campus? She's—like—Heather
Graham—on the cover of *Gear?* And *she's staring at me.*
"Is that real?" she says.
She points to the Go-Go White Sox pin on my chest.
"The pin. That's from '59, right?"
"Yeah," I say. "From the '59 World Series. Last time the Sox ruled. A gift
from my *padre.*"
So she starts naming the entire starting infield of the '59 Go-Go White
Sox—Nellie, Sherm, Big Klu.
Her fave is Luis Aparicio. Little Louie? I mean, the woman *knows...*
Then she takes the Sox pin off my chest. Puts it on hers.
"I'm Julie." She says.
'Mick.'
"South Sider."
'Me too.'
"Let's go," she says.
Back at *her* room. Her suite mates are out. "Till Monday." I check out
her baseball card collection—Gift from her dad...Check out her iMac,
Sony camcorder, and iMovie edit software...
Check out the bird of paradise tattoo over her left breast...
And then
I check it *all* out, dudes...
Morning. Back here to the crib—E-mail? Yes! Oh yes!
(He looks closer at the E-mail.)
This is not from her.
(Reading out loud.)
"Little Louie:
I'm Sandy. Julie's suite mate? Just caught Your Night With Julie. She
recorded it. Showed us. File attached.
Wow. Little Louie. You should be in the Guinness Book of Records.
For miniatures."
(Beat. He looks up at the audience. The mask drops. He's a hurt little boy.)
You think I'll get my Sox pin back?

Virtual Virtue
by Elizabeth Dewberry

ELLA: Twenty-something, dressed to impress corporate America.
TODD: Twenty-something, wearing jeans and a T-shirt with a cartoon character or something similarly unreal on it.

We are in Ella and Todd's apartment. As the lights come up, Ella finishes reading, or rereading, a short stack of pages from a computer printer. She looks impatiently at her watch or a clock. She's mad. Todd enters.

TODD: Hey, what's up.
(Sensing her mood.)
What?
(Ella holds up the papers.)
TODD: *(Feigning innocence.)* What?
ELLA: *(Deadpan, reading from the papers.)* Big'n'hard—
(She looks up at him.) I presume that's you?
TODD: Not at the moment.
ELLA: *(Rolling her eyes, then reading again, alternating between imitations of Angelbaby and Todd.)* Big'n'hard, I dreamed about you last night… What'd you dream, Angelbaby?… We were on the beach and I was wearing this little sarong skirt with no panties and you untied—
TODD: Oh good grief.
ELLA: Sweetie, "good grief" is what Charlie Brown says when Lucy yanks his football out from under him.
TODD: It's an expression.
(He shrugs: what's the big deal?)
ELLA: Right. As in, "My boyfriend, Big'n'hard, is cheating on me with some computer bimbo named Angelbaby. Oh good grief!"
TODD: *(Incredulous.)* I'm not cheating on you. That's not who I am.
ELLA: I'm your girlfriend. I'm not Angelbaby. You're having cybersex with Angelbaby. Ergo, you're cheating on me.
TODD: Cybersex is not sex.
ELLA: Well, in the words of Bill Clinton, I guess that depends on what your definition of "is" is.

TODD: Don't do this, Ella.

ELLA: Don't tell me what to do.

TODD: I'm asking you not to turn self-righteous and sarcastic on me. Honey, she doesn't even know my name. We're not real to each other. For all I know, she's a three-hundred-pound man.

ELLA: *(Sarcastically.)* Oh! I see! And I mean this non-sarcastically: what you're saying is that not knowing who she is makes having sex with her okay!

TODD: That is not what I said.

ELLA: You know what bothers me the most? Aside from the fact that you're having this little affair at all—

TODD: Would you stop acting like you don't even know me? I am not a lying cheat.

ELLA: The detail that really gets to me? She can't spell! You have this…whatever-you-want-to-call-it…that only exists in writing, and she spells "fetish" with two T's. It's just…ick. What do you see in this person?

TODD: Nothing. Come on, you're the only one whose spelling *means* anything to me. I don't even notice other women's spelling.

ELLA: You really do think this is funny, don't you? *(She's more hurt than mad now, and he puts his arms around her to comfort her.)*

TODD: Hey, I'm sorry. But Angelbaby is…she's like a character in a novel. I don't get jealous when you read romance novels.

ELLA: I don't read romance novels. But if I did, I wouldn't expect my "characters" to dream about me undressing them, and I wouldn't—

TODD: Okay, it's more like…an interactive novel. I'm a fictional character too.

ELLA: I wouldn't come up with a stupid name for myself like…Wet'n'Juicy—

TODD: Not for several months.

ELLA: And I wouldn't promise to make my "characters'" dreams come true.

TODD: It's a game.

ELLA: And you and Angelbaby are merely players in it!

TODD: Right!

ELLA: Todd, at the risk of sounding like a responsible adult, it's *wrong*.

TODD: Unlike being angry, resentful, smug, and self-pitying, not to mention no fun anymore?

ELLA: That's what you see in her?

(Todd gestures: what?)

ELLA: She doesn't ask you for a commitment, doesn't tell you to put the toilet seat down, doesn't need you to deal with her feelings when you hurt her?

TODD: I told you. All I see in her is that she's not real.

(Beat.)

ELLA: Well, I can't compete with that.

TODD: Why would you want to?

ELLA: Todd, how could you not know why I wouldn't want to, unless you *do* know, and you want me to want to?

TODD: What?

ELLA: I don't want to compete with a lover who's not real because I *am*, moods and zits and all, and my feelings for you are real. I love you. But you also irritate the hell out of me, and I can't just turn you off, and I can't stand it when I feel like you're turning *me* off.

(Beat. She grabs her purse, goes to the door.)

I'm going for a walk.

TODD: Don't you dare walk out that door.

ELLA: Don't you dare dare me not to.

TODD: You're not playing fair.

ELLA: I'm not playing.

TODD: Look, I may not be the world's easiest person to live with, but neither are you. So I went on the Internet to have a little fun. But I'm still here.

(She shakes her head: that's not enough. She puts her hand on the doorknob and waits with her back to him for him to stop her.)

TODD: I could have done this with a real woman, but I didn't. Because of you.

(Pause.)

ELLA: *(Without looking at him.)* Then you're a fool.

(She exits. He watches the door close behind her as he flips on the computer. It hums its start-up refrain as he sits down in front of it. He smiles and relaxes, turns off the lights, and lets the world disappear when he hears...)

COMPUTER'S HUMANOID FEMALE VOICE: Welcome. You've got mail.

TODD: *(Typing as he talks.)* Hi Angelbaby. It's me, uh, Big'n'hard. My real name is Todd.

Young Man Praying
by Karen Hines

A young man in Calvin Klein button-fly boxers kneels in prayer. He is moon-lit. He speaks swiftly. Italicized lines are whispered.

YOUNG MAN: Every morning, I step into the shower, exfoliate my flesh, and weep for the dead cells I will never see again.
My heart is sore, I have no peace.
I drink a glass of orange juice made from oranges enhanced with genes from the bones of small monkeys—for a higher concentration of calcium.
My heart is sore, I have no peace.
And though I want to pray to You...I cannot remember Your name.
(Deep breath out, as though to control a sudden cramp.)
I grab my keys, and slide into my car: the new "Ford Impatience." *Darkness is everywhere.* I speed downtown, park in the shadow of a bank and remind myself: "These are my saving years." *Darkness is everywhere.* A girl comes up to me, and I think she's trying to ask for directions, but there's something weird about her voice, and something very wrong with her skin...and then I realize: she is old.
If I ever got old I would just die.
I grab a tazo chai tea with soy milk laced with ginkgo biloba and living cells of bovine udders, and I breeze into work. *The world is my oyster, I shall not want.* Everybody's wearing clothes that seem serious but are actually about having a sense of humour. And all day long we work tirelessly, shunning lunch, renouncing all coffee breaks, because we believe the future is now—it just hasn't happened yet. *The world is our oyster, we shall not want.*
Still I want to pray to You, and still I cannot remember Your name.
(Very deep breath out, as though provoked by a deeper cramp.)
Six o'clock I'll have drinks with my girlfriend: pretty girl; the kind of girl who's in tune with what people are starting to articulate about the new century. *Her heart is sore, she has no peace.* In the orange light of the Lava Lounge she will bat her obsidian lashes and effuse about the disarming of genes that trigger senescence and death. *Darkness is everywhere.* I'll ask her

if she'd like another black vodka on ice. She will touch my thigh, bite the lobe of my ear and moan: "I just want to live long enough to be young and beautiful forever."

Every night I kiss the pulse in her throat, and deceive her fine mind to sleep, the way she likes. *"The world is your oyster, you shall not want."* Then I sneak out here to this faux wrought-iron balcony where every night, from the chasmic shadows of these faux marble condos I send my voice up. Flying out past buildings and hills.

Do I want an answer?

Or an echo?

Please forgive me:

I'm great with faces…

But I can't quite remember your—

(Very deep, quick exhalation/moan/groan as though provoked by stabbing pain.)

Capitalism 101
by Rebecca Gilman

At rise: A park bench. Matt and Chris, both in their mid-twenties, both in baggy shorts and T-shirts, are taking off their Rollerblades and putting on street shoes. They are in mid-conversation.

MATT: I don't know. You get in these dilemmas and then it really forces you to look inside yourself and ask yourself, you know, what kind of person am I exactly? I've always thought I was a generous person. I mean, if I saw some guy right now passed out on this park bench, I'd slip him a buck. Or if I saw he wasn't breathing, I'd give him CPR even though he'd probably be drunk and puke all in my mouth—

CHRIS: Jesus.

MATT: It happens.

CHRIS: I'm sure.

MATT: But also, I look at our numbers, and I think to myself, if not now, when? I mean, they're *my* stock options? Right? Everyone, including me, busted ass for three years, that's why we did so well in the IPO. So why shouldn't I cash in?

CHRIS: What's stopping you?

MATT: I don't know. I just think now, for me to cash in now, would be a total betrayal.

CHRIS: How's that?

MATT: Well, these guys I work with, we've been working together for three years, busting ass for three years. I mean, we hung in there. A lot of other people bailed and went with other companies. Hell, *I* was tempted to bail. I get other job offers every day practically. I have a rare skill set, you know. I write code and you can't do shit without code.

CHRIS: I know.

MATT: But we hung in there because we're warriors. We've been in the trenches for three years. And I can't betray my fellow warriors.

CHRIS: Yeah.

MATT: But then, sometimes I think if I stay in the trenches, I'll explode.

CHRIS: With just, the sheer intensity of it all?

MATT: No. With just the fact that I'm working eighty hours a week. Last month, we put in so many hours I had to sleep in my office. On the floor. I was practically living on Mountain Dew and Pop Tarts and between you and me, I was rank. I smelled something one day, I thought somebody was eating a Limburger and onion sandwich, then I realized it was my own B.O.

CHRIS: Jesus.

MATT: It's okay though. I have a vision of the future.

CHRIS: So you work eighty hours a week? Seriously? Because I thought all this time you were lying. Trying to avoid me. I thought you had a skanky computer geek girlfriend, or a coke habit, or something.

MATT: No. I've been working. Practically every weekend. For the past three years.

CHRIS: Man.

MATT: But we're definitely rewarded for the overtime. I mean the perks are amazing. Every Friday night they bring in a keg and like, fifty pizzas and then we get free soda, free snacks, free dry cleaning, free car washes. There's a rec room with a pool table and free pinball and Lady Pac Man. The perks are amazing.

CHRIS: That is amazing.

MATT: I know.

CHRIS: When I work overtime all I get is time and a half.

MATT: Yeah. Well...

CHRIS: Different scenario.

MATT: Different scenario.

(Beat.)

So how's it going?

CHRIS: Fine. You know. Telemarketing.

MATT: Right.

CHRIS: This week we're doing a homeowner's survey. "Have you ever considered the benefits of aluminum or split-concrete siding? On a scale of one to five with one being poor and five being excellent, how would you rate your home's exterior in terms of durability? In terms of attractiveness?"

MATT: No offense, but that sounds awful.

CHRIS: No offense back, but your job sounds worse.

MATT: What?

CHRIS: Seriously. It sounds hellish. I mean, when's the last time you got laid?

MATT: Look, I'm gonna cash in my stock options and retire at forty and live on a yacht and sit around all day sipping cognac and listening to Mitch Miller on the hi-fi.

CHRIS: That's your vision of the future?

MATT: Yeah, and you're gonna be forty and eating Vienna sausages out of a can and walking around in flip-flops, drunk on peach schnapps.

CHRIS: *(Considers.)* Excellent.

(Beat.)

Look, do me a favor: don't wait till you're forty. Do it now.

MATT: It'd be a betrayal.

CHRIS: Who's betraying who here? I mean, put aside your stock options and the free Lady Pac Man for half a second, and figure it out. You get paid for a forty-hour week, right?

MATT: That's not the issue.

CHRIS: It's not?

MATT: No.

CHRIS: How much do you make an hour? If you work an eighty-hour week?

MATT: That's not the issue.

CHRIS: I can figure it out.

MATT: I already figured it out. Okay?

(Small beat.)

Twelve bucks an hour. But that's not the issue.

CHRIS: Twelve bucks an hour? That's exactly what I make. And I don't have a rare skill set.

(Small beat.)

Look, it's not like my job is great or anything. It's not. It sucks. But it doesn't suck like, I-don't-have-a-life-and-I-haven't-gotten-laid-in-three-years-and-even-if-I-met-a-girl-who-wasn't-a-skank-she-wouldn't-sleep-with-me-anyway-because-I-smell-like-a-Limburger-and-onion-sandwich. It's just mildly purgatorial. There's fluorescent lighting and the only thing left in the Coke machine at the end of the week is Diet Squirt. But I also get to go home at five o'clock and once I get there, I don't think about my job.

MATT: I'm a warrior.

CHRIS: You're a schmuck. I mean seriously, you're getting screwed. Ask yourself this: on a scale of one to five, with one being only a technical penetration of your anus, and five being an actual exploration of your upper colon, how far are you taking it up the ass?

MATT: I am not taking it up the ass.

CHRIS: Okay then. What are you gonna do if the stock market crashes?

(Pause.)

MATT: You know, if there was a bum passed out on this bench I would totally give him CPR.

CHRIS: I know you would. But letting a guy die on a bench because you don't want his puke in your mouth is not on the same ethical plane as taking home the money you earned.

(Small beat.)

Matt. It is not selfish of you to want to have the money you earned for yourself.

MATT: I don't know.

CHRIS: Matt.

(Reaches into his backpack and pulls out a cell phone.)

Call your broker.

White Elephants
by Jane Martin

GISELLE: Good morning, and to all our cherubim and seraphim inductees, we would like to welcome you to Republican Heaven. If you'll all just flap over here and hover for a minute or two, I'll give you the introductory. First of all, you'll be pleased to know liberals don't go to heaven; it's music we want around here—not whining. You may have noticed there are no black people here; that's not racism—that's interior design. Actually, we do have African Americans, but anyone who is black and Republican has to be so crazy we keep them in a separate space. This isn't about Apartheid; this is about mental health. After the period of acclimatization, many of you will become guardian angels. This means you look after people on earth who make more than $250,000 annually. They'll be up here with us eventually, and we don't want them damaged or scratched. Obviously, most harpists come from high-income families, plus seeing as we're here together for eternity, we prefer you've gone to cotillion. And, as we say here in Heaven, it's about manners, manners, manners. Dress code: ties for the gentlemen; ankle-length skirts for the ladies. Please socialize, but remember our house rules: no free needle exchange; no condoms (angels practice abstinence); and definitely no abortion. Pick up your tax rebates on the table to the left and, remember, your heirs will not be paying estate taxes. Hey, if this isn't Heaven, what the hell is, huh? You'll notice the banners, the ice cream cake, the party poppers—that's just our endless preparations for Strom and Jesse. All right, seraphim and cherubim, let's mingle, fox-trot, dove hunt and swap stories about Tuscany. One final thought about our timing and good fortune—you don't have to be down there during a Republican presidency. Joking.

Swirling with Merlin
by Keith Glover

I had him in my pocket, but I didn't keep him there for long. Why? 'Cause, I don't have the strength of my convictions. I used to know myself. All things that pertained to my status quo. I was a rock. I liked my coffee black, my sugar sweet and my women tall and with their own apartments. When the census takers knocked on my door I answered. When the Jehovah's Witnesses rang my bell on Sundays, I let the doorbell ring until they went away. Why? Because that's how you live. But then he came along, things changed. Him: Merlin. Beside my bed chewing on a piece of bread because that's what they do. I was quick enough to grab him with a dirty sock. "Let me go," he said. Why should I? "Because I am here to save the world. Make the world a better place with your help of course. You my friend can be instrumental in bringing heaven to the earth." Oh really? I threw him in the toilet. Listen, I said, I have lived in this apartment for the last four years. In the summer it's hot in the winter it's cold and besides I'm months behind in my rent. I long for the touch of human kindness but have been denied it. I need a break. Now if you want to serve me, I'll let you go. "I can't save the world and serve you as well," he said. Then you must choose. Serve me and live or serve the world and die. I moved my hand over to the lever. "I can't believe you are taking this position," he shouted at me. It's the only one I know. I have greeted the world with a smile and still I received nothing back. "But you can change that. Let me fulfill my mission and things will change for you and for everyone else." Promise. "I give you my word." As a what? "As what I am, Merlin the Great." I closed the lid because I'd been lied to all my life and why should I believe anything different. Let the world take care of itself was the last thing he heard as I flushed.

Worldness
by Jenny Lyn Bader

A jail visitation room. Viv sits behind the glass, waiting. Suzanne enters and sits across from her. She opens the speaking panel so Viv can hear her. She stares at Viv.

SUZANNE: Oh lord. Look at you. *(She weeps. Her cell phone rings.)* Hold on. Hi. Could you stop forwarding my calls please? I'm dealing with a friend's personal emergency? *(Viv looks at Suzanne.)* Thanks. *(Hangs up.)* Sorry. This has been the day from hell. How are you?

VIV: I'm. Loving. Centered. You know, considering…this. *(Beat.)* I need your help with the bail. *(Suzanne nods, and stares at Viv across the glass.)*

SUZANNE: Why did you do it?

VIV: I wanted to—spread hope? To remind the world *of* the world and of Worldness. *(Beat.)* And I guess I've always wanted to stage a protest.

SUZANNE: Couldn't you have staged a normal protest? With people holding signs and shouting things?

VIV: This seemed like the best way to send the message.

SUZANNE: *(Skeptical.)* To move into a tree.

VIV: *(Nods.)* And I read a magazine article about this girl who moved into a tree in California, Julie Butterfly, and—

SUZANNE: Julia Butterfly Hill was not…close with anyone in the lumber business, as far as I know. Did you remember, during this tree-sit of yours, that I work in the lumber business?

VIV: It may've crossed my mind. *(Beat.)* How's Mom?

SUZANNE: She's a little upset. First you don't go into the family business—and now you go—sit in it.

VIV: I love Mom. Does she know how much I love the tree?

SUZANNE: Everyone in the Pacific Northwest knows how much you love the tree. You've got concerned citizens writing hate mail, religious activists saying logging is a sin. And you've even inspired a group of little girls to sit in trees in their backyards in your honor!

VIV: Really? I think it's so hard for kids to find someone to look up to. Or to have faith in any—You know, when we were little… *(She trails off.)*

SUZANNE: *(Irked.)* What? When we were little what?

VIV: *(Shakes her head.)* Nothing.

SUZANNE: When we were little, animals and plants loved you. Just like now. But I got along better than you with all of our relatives, living and dead. Always. You resent me. And this whole thing has not been for nature or the planet. It's been against me. And your phone call would never have been to me, except that you need money.

VIV: No! The phone call was...

SUZANNE: What about the money Grandpa left us? I invested mine. It's doubled.

VIV: I—

SUZANNE: Knowing you, you gave yours to those—tree people. Because you think that they are your family. And I will tell you now, I am your family. And they are tree people!

VIV: *(Genuinely upset.)* But Suzy I think of you as a tree person. Even when you cut them down. You're part of what I want to save. I wish I could save you.

SUZANNE: I wish I could save you! But you have to stop sitting in that tree. And get your friends out too.

VIV: What friends?

SUZANNE: You moved out, five of your friends moved in, with their own video cameras. You didn't see it on TV?

VIV: My friends were on TV? How great. Oh, not great. You're upset. You want me to...*(Realizes:)* Wait, I can't get them out if they have cameras! It would be taped! How ridiculous would I look?

SUZANNE: You? Have you considered how ridiculous I look?

VIV: No.

SUZANNE: I can just imagine my business school reunion now. "So, did you make your first hundred million by cashing out on your stock options?"—"No, I tried to make a living chopping down a few trees but I couldn't even do that because my sister was sitting in one of them!"

VIV: Angel. You shouldn't worry about what those people think...

SUZANNE: "And now to top it off, I have to bail her out of jail!"

VIV: Actually, if it makes you feel better, that money that Grandpa left us, I invested mine too.

SUZANNE: You did?

VIV: In a stock.

SUZANNE: Which stock?

VIV: Borzon.

SUZANNE: *(Stunned.)* You invested in an oil company?

VIV: I asked about environmentally responsible investing but the broker said that's for people with more money than I have.

SUZANNE: *(Moved.)* Viv, you had money in the bull market!

VIV: I'm selling it today. I just wanted to see if you would help me. If you would even visit. I miss you.

SUZANNE: Oh Viv. I thought you just wanted me... *(Interrupts herself:)* You really wanted to see me? *(Viv nods.)* But—you shouldn't sell Borzon now! It's a growth stock.

VIV: I realize that, but...

SUZANNE: Strategically, I'd advise you against it. Let me pay your bail. I want to.

VIV: *(Thrilled.)* You do? Oh thank you Suzy! *(Beat.)* I was going to say before, when we were little, you used to be my hero.

SUZANNE: Oh yeah? Who's your hero now?

VIV: I don't have one.

(Suzanne nods in recognition.)

SUZANNE: *(Beat.)* You know what? You're better off.

RIOT Grrrrl GUITAR
by Robert Alexander

Lights discover Nadine, strumming a battered guitar that is missing a couple of strings. She can't play, but there is something sweet and sincere in her. There is a certain musicality in her lack of musicality.

NADINE: I hope. I hope. I hope, hope hope I hope like Bob fucking Hope, I hope hope hope I learn how to play this thing and appear on MTV, so you can hear me sing. I'm Nadine, Nadine the Beauty Queen. Born in hell, but raised in New Orleans by my singer single mom, a former Beauty Queen. She got herself locked in and knocked up in the backseat of a Chevy by the homecoming queen. I mean homecoming king, king, king, king—a jerk jerk jerk who thought he was the second coming of Steve McQueen. He played a mean mean mean guitar and made all the girls scream scream scream scream. He made them cream, cream, cream, cream. He lured them to his backseat and he made them scream and cream and scream some more. I scream for Ice Cream, ya know what I mean? My mom screamed and creamed and screamed, "Sing, sing sing a simple song for your supper boy, you played with my heart like it was a toy."

Well, this is for you Mom! I hope, I hope, I hope hope hope I one day learn how to play this thing and appear on MTV, so you can hear me sing, "Fuck you Dad! Dad! Dad! This is your daughter, Dad and I'm stark-raving mad, you spineless worthless sperm donor, oooh you make me mad. Well I famous now. How do you like dem apples? FUCK YOU DAD!! Look at me. Look at me! Look at your fucking TV. I'm on your fucking TV, while your fat ass is spreading like cheese spread all over that fucking couch like cheese wiz on a fucking cracker Mr. Potatohead, you worthless spermazoid. You cockroach. I am so fucking famous I scare myself sometimes. I'm so fucking famous I don't need you now." I hope like hell I learn to play this thing and show up on yo' TV screen, so I can scream, "FUCK YOU DAD!!" To me, that would be heaven.

Note To Self
by Hilly Hicks, Jr.

TOMMY McCRACKEN: Twenty-two, fresh out of school, new to the professional world and completely overwhelmed by it. He wears a suit, but still manages to look utterly boyish.

CONSTANCE WINTER: Twenty-six, ordinarily bright-eyed and cheery, her disposition is gradually being overtaken by a sense of dread. She is primly dressed, perhaps a little scuffed around the edges.

TIME AND PLACE: Here and now.

Lights rise on a second-rate one-man accounting firm. Tommy sits at a desk. A small clock and a bowl of fortune cookies are on the desk. He looks at the door, checks the clock, shakes it to make sure it's working and looks back to the door. Constance knocks and enters. Tommy stands, too eager, smiling to cover his pique.

TOMMY: You must be my two o'clock! *(Beat.)* At least you *used* to be. Three hours and forty-eight minutes ago. Before I started imagining bad things happening to you.

CONSTANCE: *(Confused.)* I—I'm here to see my accountant, Marvin McCracken.

TOMMY: Not that I *wanted* bad things to happen to you. It's just that the thought of you being pushed in front of a speeding subway train would've meant your blowing off our appointment was an act of God and not something *I* fucked up. *(Beat, disappointed.)* Promptness is a sign of respect. Why don't you respect me? Is it because I cried uncontrollably when we spoke on the phone yesterday? Well, you said some very hurtful things and I can't just bottle up all my feelings. That might make me neurotic! You weren't going to leave me, were you? Have my ex-clients been talking to you?

CONSTANCE: *(Completely baffled.)* Well, no. I don't even know—

TOMMY: Fine. Don't tell me. It's not like I don't know what they're saying about me. Well, tell me this, if their money is so "heinously mismanaged," where'd they get the cash to build a letter bomb? Anyway. Let's get down to business, shall we, Hazel? Hazel. That's a pretty name. It's nice to finally be able to put a face to the shrill voice. Now, you're probably a little concerned that arithmetic bugs the hell out of me, right? Well, Hazel, math has nothing to do with why I completely screwed up your checking account last week…

CONSTANCE: Um, I'm not Hazel. My name is Constance Winter. I—I don't have an appointment.

TOMMY: Uh-huh. I see. So what you're saying is that bitch Hazel left me for another accountant. Just like all those other BACKSTABBING DESERTERS! WELL, THEY CAN ALL EAT SHIT AND DIE! DIE, MOTHERFUCKERS, DIE!!! *(Then calmly writing on a yellow Post-It note.)* Note to self: get professional help.

(He picks up a briefcase covered with Post-It notes, finds some space and sticks the new note on.)

CONSTANCE: Who are you? Where is Marvin?

TOMMY: I'm Tommy, Marvin's son. I'm handling all his clients from now on. *(Beat.)* My dad passed away last month.

CONSTANCE: Oh, no! I'm sorry. How did it happen?

TOMMY: I'm not sure, but according to my mom, she came home and found Dad in the tub with one of his clients…and the toaster. Which is strange since he was allergic to wheat.

CONSTANCE: Oh, my God. I'm so—I'm terribly sorry. Maybe I should go—

TOMMY: No! Don't go! Please! You know, you're my last client.

CONSTANCE: I was just going to ask Marvin about—

TOMMY: Ask *me!* Let *me* help. Then you can vouch for me. You can tell all my ex-clients they can trust me.

CONSTANCE: *Should* I trust you?

TOMMY: Absolutely. 'Cause if you don't I'll sink into a vortex of financial ruin.

CONSTANCE: Well… *(Pause, hands him a letter.)* I got this from the IRS.

TOMMY: Ooh, a letter. A letter with lots of bold print and capital letters. Those IRS guys are such drama queens.

CONSTANCE: I've never owed back taxes before. I always thought that was for rich people. You know, people with Lifestyles. *(Beat.)* I'm an assistant librarian, for God's sake. Even if I could *afford* a Lifestyle, I couldn't fit it in my apartment!

TOMMY: I should get your file.

(Tommy begins going through the desk drawers.)

CONSTANCE: I just have so many other people to worry about: the utility people, the credit card people, the student loan-sharks… My *landlord*. When

I got home from work today there was an eviction notice on my door! *(Breath.)* So, I came to ask Marvin for money. For bus fare. I'm getting out of town. I'm scared.

TOMMY: Maybe you've got demons. I do.

CONSTANCE: But I'm a good person. I go to church. I take pity on pitiful people. Like the man who sleeps and pees in front of my building. I give him a little change coming and going. I'm a beacon for the pitiful people in this dark city. But where's *my* beacon? I feel so cheated. *(Beat.)* Marvin promised I wouldn't have to worry about money. He *owes* me. *You* owe me. *Somebody* owes me. Right now. The bus leaves soon.

TOMMY: Hold on a sec, will ya? Gimme a chance to find your file. Just…sit. *(Beat.)* Please? Have a fortune cookie. An ex-client gave them to me. I'll work this whole thing out.

CONSTANCE: Well. *(Long beat.)* I guess I can wait a minute or two.

(Constance sits, takes a cookie and breaks it open. She reads her fortune.)

CONSTANCE: "It's all your fault." What kind of fortune is this?

TOMMY: Lemme see that… What's this doing in there? Gee, Constance. I'm sorry about that. Take another one.

(She does.)

CONSTANCE: "I hate you."

TOMMY: Oh, my God!

(He takes the fortune from her, reading it. She takes another one.)

CONSTANCE: "You're the worst accountant ever."

TOMMY: That fucking bitch! God I hate my ex-clients. *(Beat.)* If I were you I'd spit that cookie out.

(She does so.)

CONSTANCE: I need that money, Tommy. That eviction notice made me so mad, I just…*(A heavy breath.)* I packed a few things and ran out of the building. And I tripped over that man who sleeps and pisses in the doorway. And it made me so mad, I…I kicked him! I didn't mean to, but before I knew it I kicked him again. Oh, it was terrible! I told him he was a filthy, stinky, pockmark on my building. And I kicked him again and I ran. I didn't look back. But I could swear I heard…I thought I heard him behind me, running after me. I was afraid he'd catch me and…and…

TOMMY: Don't…go.

CONSTANCE: I'm going to disappear, Tommy. I'm already disappearing.

TOMMY: Look! I found your file! *(Blows a thick layer of dust from file.)* I guess it's been a while…*(Reading a note stuck to file.)* "Note to self: Send Miss

Winter her dividend check from bank. Big money. Send immediately."
(Awkward beat.) I'll pop that right in the mail.

(There is an insistent knock at the door. A pause.)

CONSTANCE: Please don't answer it.

(Another knock. Louder. Constance and Tommy stare at each other, unable to move.)

CONSTANCE: Please don't…

(Another knock. Quite loud, thunderous and insistent. A pause.)

Rosa's Eulogy
by Richard Strand

Jeanne stands over a cardboard box which she has surrounded with lit votive candles. Occasionally she will fondly stroke the contents of that box.

JEANNE: Dear Lord, I am here before you to honor this cat, who I don't actually know but who I found in the street outside my apartment where some bastard hit her with his car and then just left her for carrion. I call her Rosa because, because, I don't know her real name and I like the name Rosa. What do we know about Rosa? We know that she is one of your creations and, therefore, precious. We know, in fact, that she was more worthy in your eyes than the bastard who probably got her as a kitten because she was cute but didn't take even a second to consider that getting a cat is a lifelong responsibility so he just tossed her out of his car onto Foothill Boulevard when he got bored with her where the chances of her surviving even two days are about nil because—Foothill Boulevard, for Christ's sake—that's a busy street and if she's not hit by a car she's going to get sick or eaten by a coyote—whatever—what we know is that Rosa is going to heaven and the bastard who called himself her owner is going…

(Jeanne stops herself.)

Sorry. Sorry. Not my decision. That's up to you, of course. Sorry. Didn't mean to overstep.

(Jeanne returns to her eulogy.)

Even though I never met Rosa when she was alive, I can tell—anyone could tell just looking at her lifeless corpse—that she was a Maine Coon, which is one of the most beautiful breeds of cat that you ever thought to place on this earth. Well, you know, you gave breeders the gift of scientific insight so they could create the Maine Coon breed, but still, your fingerprints are all over this. We know Rosa was a Maine Coon by the striped tail and the distinctive dark patches over her eyes and the nose which, well, um, seems a little longer than would be considered show quality…

(Jeanne looks closer at Rosa.)

Okay, she's probably not a pure bred Maine Coon, but she is clearly…

(Jeanne takes another close look at Rosa.)

Holy cripe, she's a raccoon. What the hell am I doing petting a raccoon?
Eoo. Eoo.
(Jeanne is wiping her hands on her pants.)
Sorry.
(Jeanne blows out a candle.)
Sorry.
(Jeanne blows out another candle.)
Didn't mean to bother you over a raccoon.
(Jeanne blows out another candle.)
Oh, man. Gotta wash my hands. Sorry, God. Sorry. Go back to whatever
you were doing. I'll take care of the raccoon.
(Jeanne blows out the remaining candles.)
Toss this in the dumpster. Sorry, Lord. Sorry.

Badass of The RIP Eternal
by Elizabeth Wong

THRASHER: A guy in his twenties, with a well-used Sims Lester-Kasai skateboard with rat bone wheels.

THRASHER: It's totally whacked man. Sucks, bigtime. First Phil, then Reuben, now Curtis. Curtis was the biggest rip-dog, flowin' and slashin' like Jackie Chan. Dude was kung fu on a Sims Lester-Kasai board with rat bone wheels. Dude was not afraid to slam hard and pay gravity tax. Broke his nose, collarbone, tailbone, arm, leg, finger, finger, finger. Cracked his skull on Mister Concrete one too many. He goes, "Bro, the more you break it, the easier it gets." Dude was sooooo right. Just last week, I did this sweet fingerflip to a late 180, missed the transfer bigtime, heard this sick pop. Like the bone is sticking out, and I'm freaking. Curtis goes, "Dude, tighten your nuts. Your trucks are loose." On the way to the hospital, I tightened my bushings. Dude gave prime advice. Also thanks to Curtis, we got busted like six times. We'd knock on a door, pretend to be Acme pool cleaners, drain the pool, skate until the clueless owners figured out we were like totally bogus. Dude was like crazy extreme. Sure, he coulda gone pro, but he wasn't buyin'. I'd go, "Dude, money." He go, "Dude, it's not about money." I go, "It's not?" He'd go, "It's not about tricks. It's not about the rush." He goes, "It's about rewriting the rules of physics. It's about going where no man has gone before. We're space explorers, gravity defying, nonnegotiable." Oh yeah, no denying Curtis was here. That night, we weaseled our way into Wiggy's. Dude was rockin' the house. Jammin' on a backside grind. All of a sudden, his deck splits. He keeps going. Left foot, on one half. Right foot, on the other. It's a miracle. Then he goes for broke. Dude falls, slides down the transition, and just lays there. We all thought he was goofin'. I'm waitin' for Curtis to flash me one of his big dumb-ass grins. But Dude just laid there. I yell, "Call 911." Fuck. Dude died righteous, pulled an awesome air disaster on a broken board. Two feet. Two pieces. Airborne. Total commitment until his head hit. Oh yeah. Right now, I know, Curtis, you are ripping your way across heaven. Doing fakie five-o to fakie kickflip off God's eternal grind bar. When I bite the big one, I'm gonna do it listening to your music, bro.

(Music from the Black-eyed Peas or Sevendust or Mos Def or Blink 182 cuts into the darkness.)

Oh yeah. Badass outlaw, thrasher of the new millennium! Rip on, Curtis! Rip on!

(Thrasher thrusts his board skyward! Howling!)

Heaven and Hell (On Earth):
A Divine Comedy

Additional Monologues

Red Popcorn by Robert Alexander
Gone Goth by Melanie Marnich
Barefoot Woman in a Red Dress by Jane Martin
The Way Down and *The Millennium Fallacy* by Richard Strand

Red Popcorn
by Robert Alexander

Lights discover Jenny wearing an orange jumpsuit, property of the Alameda County youth detention center a.k.a. Juvie Hall.

JENNY: Sometimes I wish I was dead. If I was dead…maybe the voices would stop. *(Beat.)* Sometimes I feel I'm already dead, so I cut myself just to remind myself—I'm alive. The sharp blade of the knife piercing my skin reminds me—I'm alive. The sight, the taste, the warm sticky wet feel of my blood always reminds me I'm still alive. I'm not dead—yet. *(Beat.)*

I don't know why I did it. Maybe it was the pot. Maybe it was the booze. Maybe it was Satan himself who got my panties wet. Maybe it was the thought of killing something, anything that got my panties knotted in a wet clot as I grabbed the cat by its tail and stuffed it into the microwave…and the kitty the pretty little white kitty just looked at me all meek, never suspecting a thing as I closed the door to the microwave…as I closed the door to her electronic coffin and I turned on the juice full blast thinking what if the Nazis had microwave ovens instead of gas—could they have been more efficient…could they have been more efficient? And I just fell on my ass laughing, rolling on the kitchen floor stoned out of my fucking mind listening to the pretty little kitty squeal as her guts popped open like a bag of red popcorn and I could smell the tempting smell of cooking flesh and I knew I had the munchies cause it smelled so good. The smell of death never smelled so good. *(Beat.)*

I was too stoned to get up off the floor. So, I just sat there…I just sat there waiting in the kitchen for my dad to come home with his newest girlfriend…but he never came. *(Beat.)*

Which is better? Microwave or gas? Which is better? Pop Secret or Orville Redenbacher's? Is Orville Redenbacher Jewish? Would you think I was a freak if I told you I had the munchies now for some hot buttered popcorn sprinkled with some red cayenne pepper? Would you think I was a freak if I told you I ate that cat that night and it kinda sorta tasted like chicken? Only better.

(Lights slowly fade on Jenny.)

Gone Goth
by Melanie Marnich

About 4:30 a.m. At a bus stop in an American town.

Emily X., a young woman in her early twenties, nervously waits for the bus. She smokes a cigarette held in a very long cigarette holder.

She's dressed head-to-toe in layers and folds of (mostly) black. Black dress, black scarf, black opera gloves, black pointy boots. There may be accents of red and black velvet, Goth jewelry (a cross or two)... She wears very white make-up covering her entire face, dark lipstick, dramatic eyes. Jet-black long hair. A Goth geisha.

Her rat Edgar sits on her shoulder.

EMILY: I was diagnosed with a severe allergy to the sun the same week Goth came to town. Talk about timing. UV rays hit my skin and I'm nothing but blisters. Five minutes and it's third degree burns. Goth was God's gift to me. Besides, if you can only be out after sundown, it totally messes with your parents' attempts at a curfew. The white make-up thing worked out well. My dad mixes it at his paint store. He's cool.
(She takes a dramatic drag from her dramatic cigarette and stays nervous.)
I am waiting for a bus. There is nothing sadder than a Goth on a bus. But my car died and I have to get home before the sun comes up or I'm toast. Usually I'd find some kind of irony in this, but not this time. This is a disaster even by my standards.
(She scratches at her chest.)
Sorry. Ow. My nipple ring's infected.
I work the graveyard shift at a suicide prevention hotline—which I operate more like my own personal recruiting station. It's cool there because they let me bring my rat Edgar. As in Allan Poe. We've been together for eight months now, which is like seventeen years in rat years, and—
(Edgar drops from her shoulder and lands with a thud.)
Edgar?
(She pokes at him with her toe.)

Oh Edgar.

(She bends down to pick him up. As she straightens up, she notices the sun on the horizon.)

Oh oh. Sun. There. Oh God. Here it comes. Any Goth worth her velvet would go down fighting. YOU WANT A PIECE OF THIS?

(She starts wiping off her make-up with the rat. She's having a face-to-face confrontation with the sun.)

COME AND GET ME YOU FREAK!! COME ON! GIMME ALL YOU GOT!!!

(Gold sunlight hits her feet and works its way up her body to her face. She grimaces. Waits. Nothing. No pain. No blisters. The light illuminates her now bare face, which is young and sweet. She peels off her gloves and holds out her bare arms. Nothing happens.)

(She tosses Edgar over her shoulder and holds out her bare arms.)

No blisters. No pain. A miracle. Look at that. Look at that.

(She takes off her wig, revealing her own hair.)

Look at me.

Barefoot Woman in a Red Dress
by Jane Martin

A young woman in a red dress on a bare stage with bare feet. As the lights come up, she stands, looking at her feet. A moment. She looks up and sees the audience.

CLAIRE: Oh.

You're looking at me.

I'm going to do my dance for you now.

(She does. And very nicely too. She obviously has had training. It's simple and elegant. As she dances, she speaks.)

You've probably noticed I'm naked.

Some of you are imagining me with clothes on.

Whatever.

We can do what we want here.

Till we run out.

(She dances for a moment in silence. Then, still dancing, speaks again.)

As you see…

It's flat all the way to the horizon.

And empty.

No Danish furniture or geologic formations.

No flicks.

No sex.

No shopping.

Those who dance, dance separately.

We have only what we can do and what we know.

Which is pretty scary.

The big finish.

(She dances beautifully. She finishes.)

That's the end of my dance.

(Silence.)

Now I just stand here.

(She does.)

I don't know any poetry.

My singing was the despair of the Midwest.

I play field hockey. But there's no equipment.
I don't do imitations.
(Silence.)
Thank God you're just other people who don't know what to do.
And not an audience.
Imagine having to watch me for eternity.
And vice versa.
(A pause.)
Even at these prices.
Especially naked.
Now, there's something that gets old.
If I had known I would be thrown back on my own resources, I would
have become a more interesting person.
Learned an instrument.
As it is, I think I'll lie down.
(She does.)
The hardest thing is…
We don't have to sleep
Or eat.
We can watch each other.
(She watches the audience carefully.)
Please don't take this the wrong way, but
you're not particularly worth watching.
We all should have worked on it.
(She lies still, looking back at her feet. Then she looks up.)
I wonder what made me think I was a self?
Probably the SAT's.
(Silence.)
I really can't tell if I'm being punished or beatified.
(A pause.)
I know one thing.
It's not
eternal
rest.

What I think is

We're fucked.

The Way Down
by Richard Strand

Danny is suspended in mid-air. All we see is Danny—and the blackness that surrounds him. There is nothing rushed about his musing.

DANNY: It's funny. I don't think my life is passing before my eyes. But it does feel like time has slowed. A lot. And, and, it seems like, like, there is a certain clarity to my thinking now. I've never had clarity of thinking before. It's fun. Let's see, I was about two hundred feet up when I jumped which, at a rate of thirty-two point two feet per second means I should hit the ground in roughly three seconds with a couple milliseconds to spare. And, yet, it feels like I got all the time in the world. Only, of course, I don't. I wonder if jumping was such a good idea.

(Pause.)

Clearly, if I was going to give this a second thought, I should have done that a second ago. Only, I don't know, falling so slowly, and with this newfound clarity of thought, I gotta ask myself, Was this the best choice I could have made? I mean, for example, before I go killing myself, maybe I should have explored a few less precipitous options. Like, like, oh, here's one: Maybe I should have thrown a rock at a police car.

(Pause.)

Why did that come to mind? I guess that would sort of get 'em back for hassling me all the time and, at the same time, what could they do to me? I'm going to kill myself anyway. Oh, Oh, Idiot, I coulda hung myself in jail after they picked me up for throwing the rock at their car! That would get 'em in no end of trouble. Or, or, I coulda taken Mom's wallet and run up her credit cards. Then when she says, "You are grounded for a year, young man," I could hang myself in my room. The guilt trip I'd be laying on her. Man! Not to mention sticking her with three hundred and sixty-four days left on my grounding which she could never collect on. I coulda bought a Les Paul guitar on Mom's credit card, thrown the rock, and stolen a car and still had plenty of time to jump off a building or hang myself or…

(Danny thinks.)

...I coulda moved out of Mom's house. I coulda got my own place. Why didn't that one occur to me? 'Cause I didn't have clarity of thought in that house. Damn it. Damn it. Hell of a time to be coming up with options. Hell of a time to figure out that life is, well you know, might be, worth, I don't know, living. Shit. This kinda sucks.

(Danny thinks some more.)

Okay, you know what? I don't think more than a second has gone by. I still got time. Plenty of time. I still got two seconds to figure out some way of not dying. Two seconds. Practically an eternity. And I'm thinking very clearly right now. Anything is possible.

(Danny continues to think as the lights fade to black.)

The Millennium Fallacy
by Richard Strand

Adrian sits on a cot, in front of a video camera which she has mounted on a tripod. She holds a glass of something. She speaks to the camera.

ADRIAN: Hello. My name is Adrian. You probably heard about my dend who fried last year in …Oh, dammit. Damn. Do over. Do over.

(Adrian rewinds the tape. She starts again.)

Hello. My name is Adrian. You probably heard about my friend who died last year in Rancho Santa Fe. He was one of the guys who thought the millennium would bring a spaceship in the trail of a comet close enough to the earth that they could beam aboard by poisoning themselves. Okay, how many things were wrong with that plan? Like God has spaceships. Like if God did have a spaceship, he'd fly behind a comet. I'm so sure. Only, only, okay, I don't mean to be making fun of my friend. Does it sound like I'm making fun of him?

(Pause.)

Okay, here's the thing. You know, my friend died and I don't want to make light of that. You know, he did what he thought he was supposed to do. He did what he thought was best. And I tried to talk him out of it. I'm like, "God doesn't have spaceships," and he's all like, "How do you know God doesn't have spaceships," and we're back and forth like that. Really, I didn't think he'd do it. I didn't think any of 'em would do it. Because, here's the really big thing: The year two thousand is not the millennium. Because there's no year zero. And everybody knows that two thousand and one is the millennium—you know my friend knew that—everybody knew that—but just because people started counting wrong he figures God was counting wrong too. Like God wouldn't know his own son's birthday. Yeah, right. I'm sure. Well, I know when the millennium is. And it wasn't last year. It's this year. It's now. It's right now.

(Adrian drinks the contents of her glass. She lies down on her cot. She places a gauze handkerchief over her face.)

Merry Christmas.

(Adrian goes to sleep.)

The Phone Plays

The Phone Plays

The Phone Play has quickly become a tradition at the Humana Festival, where audience members dare to eavesdrop on several three-minute plays played over payphones in the lobby. Now in its third year, this new and innovative form has sparked creations by some of America's leading playwrights, and given us a chance to listen in on conversations we might never have had a chance to hear.

This year, we added a new twist. Artistic Director Marc Masterson invited five small, adventurous theatre companies from across the country that are dedicated to producing new work to give us an earful of the most exciting voices they have to offer. The results are as diverse as the companies themselves. Some wildly comic, others deadly serious, these plays offer us a rare glimpse into the future of American Theatre.

—Tanya Palmer

Subliminable
by Greg Allen

Copyright © 2001 by Greg Allen. All rights reserved. CAUTION: Professionals and amateurs are hereby warned that *Subliminable* is subject to a royalty. It is fully protected under the copyright laws of the United States of America and of all countries covered by the International Copyright Union (including the Dominion of Canada and the rest of the British Commonwealth), the Berne Convention, the Pan-American Copyright Convention and the Universal Copyright Convention, as well as all countries with which the United States has reciprocal copyright relations. All rights, including professional, amateur stage rights, motion picture, recitation, lecturing, public reading, radio broadcasting, television, video or sound recording, all other forms of mechanical or electronic reproduction, such as CD-ROM, CD-I, information storage and retrieval systems and photocopying, and the rights of translation into foreign languages, are strictly reserved. Particular emphasis is laid upon the matter of readings, permission for which must be secured from the Author's agent in writing.

ALL INQUIRIES CONCERNING RIGHTS, INCLUDING AMATEUR RIGHTS, SHOULD BE ADDRESSED TO: THE NEO-FUTURISTS, 5153 N. ASHLAND, CHICAGO, IL 60640.

BIOGRAPHY

Greg Allen is the founder and Artistic Director of the Chicago-based Neo-Futurists and creator of *Too Much Light Makes The Baby Go Blind (30 Plays in 60 Minutes)*. He has written, directed, and performed more than five hundred original plays for the show over the course of its unstoppable thirteen-year run. His full-length productions with The Neo-Futurists include *K.*, his award-winning adaption of Kafka's *The Trial*, *Crime and Punishment: A (mis) Guided Environmental Tour With Literary Pretensions* and *Boxing Joseph Cornell* (both with Connor Kalista), and *The Complete Lost Works Of Samuel Beckett As Found In An Envelope (partially burned) In A Dustbin In Paris Labeled "Never to be performed. Never. Ever. EVER! Or I'll Sue! I'LL SUE FROM THE GRAVE!!!* (with Theatre Oobleck). His most recent script, *Jokes And Their Relation To The Unconscious (a comedy to end all comedy)*, just completed its extended, sold-out run at The Neo-Futurarium, and will be filmed by a Seattle-based company for DVD release in the fall of 2000.

THE NEO-FUTURISTS

The Chicago based Neo-Futurists started their unique history with the ongoing twelve-year hit *Too Much Light Makes the Baby Go Blind (30 Plays in 60 Minutes)*. In addition to premiering new work every week, this theatrical collective has toured nationally and continues to present award-winning, experimental work in their space above a funeral home, The Neo-Futurarium.

HUMANA FESTIVAL PRODUCTION

Subliminable premiered at the Humana Festival of New American Plays in February of 2001 and was produced in association with The Neo-Futurists. It was written, directed and performed by Greg Allen.

Subliminable

The voice is conspiratorial, quick, and persuasive.

VOICE: Hello there. Listen to my voice. Focus on my voice. There may be a lot of distraction around you so its incredibly important that you focus on my every word, my every syllable, my every intonation. You are not the first to receive this message, nor will you be the last. However, how you respond to this message may determine the success or failure of the rest of your day, possibly the rest of your life, and certainly the rest of this play.

Try not to look too conspicuous. Try not to look too inconspicuous. Don't look around! Try not to look around. Stare straight ahead. Focus on the handset why don't you? Relax. Just relax. Breathe. Take a moment to just breathe.

Good.

Not everyone knows what I am about to tell you. Some do, some don't, some have not acted upon it. Their loss. Try to remain calm. Try to remain focused. Breathe. Here we go:

I am going to give you a message. I am going to give you a very specific message which you will need to learn. It will seem to be a rather innocuous message, but when used in a particular way it will have a significant effect.

I must warn you that the message should not be used indiscriminately. It is very important that you only use the message with the utmost discretion and care. You must only pass on the message to a single person whom you have chosen specifically for a specific reason, but we'll get to that later. First the message. It is quite simple. You say: "Have you listened to the phone plays? They're over there. *I* think you should listen to the one called *Subliminable*." That's it. Three simple sentences. I'll say it again. "Have you listened to the phone plays? They're over there. *I* think you should listen to the one called *Subliminable*."

Now it's time to learn the message. Repeat after me. "Have you listened to the phone plays?" (Try not to move your lips, someone may be watching you.) Again. "Have you listened to the phone plays?"… "They're over there."… (You might want to point for that.) "They're over *there*."… "*I* think you should listen to the one called *Subliminable*."… Think you got it? Now together with me. "Have you listened to the phone plays? They're over there. *I* think you should try the one called *Subliminable*." Good job.

Did you notice how I emphasized the "*I*" each time? This is not an accident. Implicating *your*self and emphasizing *your* choice is perhaps the most important part of the message. You see, who *you* decide to give the message to is the *crux* of the message.

Now stop focusing on the handset and slowly turn around and start scanning the room. Look around you and see who else is here. Now find someone who, for one reason or another, intrigues you. Someone whom you do not know, but someone whom you feel is somehow special…to you. You may just like their eyes, or their hair, or their nose. You may just want to speak to this person. You may just want to meet this person. You may just want to sleep with this person. All you know is that you desire to connect with this person. This is the chosen person in the crowd whom you desire to connect with the most. This is the person to whom you will give the message.

You may now be realizing, if you are listening to this phone play at the bequest of some stranger who came up and directed you here, why that person chose you. They are probably watching you right now. This may be flattering. This maybe exciting. This may creep you out to no end.

But now, of course, it's *your* turn. You can act on your own personal desires. You can now pass the message on to whomever you wish. And, since that stranger is probably watching you, you might want to pass it on to somebody else while they watch. And then I'm sure, they'll get the message—so to speak. On the other hand, you might want to pass the message right back to them. But if you do, don't hold me responsible for what happens next.

The most important thing is that you do it now. It all rests on your shoulders. This is your chance to take a little risk. "Have you listened to the phone plays? They're over there. *I* think you should try the one called *Subliminable*." These simple words could lead you on an exciting, unknown adventure. Or just help make somebody's day. But I suppose some of you will just choose to hang up and walk away and watch some-body else do it. Or wait to see if someone passes the message on to you. But what will you say to them then—having already heard it?

So do it now. "Have you listened to the phone plays? They're over there. *I* think you should listen to the one called *Subliminable*." Go ahead. Don't be scared. Take a risk. Good luck.

END OF PLAY

Hype-R-Connectivity
by Andy Bayiates

Copyright © 2001 by Andy Bayiates. All rights reserved. CAUTION: Professionals and amateurs are hereby warned that *Hype-R-Connectivity* is subject to a royalty. It is fully protected under the copyright laws of the United States of America and of all countries covered by the International Copyright Union (including the Dominion of Canada and the rest of the British Commonwealth), the Berne Convention, the Pan-American Copyright Convention and the Universal Copyright Convention, as well as all countries with which the United States has reciprocal copyright relations. All rights, including professional, amateur stage rights, motion picture, recitation, lecturing, public reading, radio broadcasting, television, video or sound recording, all other forms of mechanical or electronic reproduction, such as CD-ROM, CD-I, information storage and retrieval systems and photocopying, and the rights of translation into foreign languages, are strictly reserved. Particular emphasis is laid upon the matter of readings, permission for which must be secured from the Author's agent in writing.

ALL INQUIRIES CONCERNING RIGHTS, INCLUDING AMATEUR RIGHTS, SHOULD BE ADDRESSED TO: THE NEO-FUTURISTS, 5153 N. ASHLAND, CHICAGO, IL 60640.

BIOGRAPHY

Andy Bayiates recently mounted his solo piece, *SubliMania* at the Neo-Futurarium in Chicago, where he writes and performs weekly in the thirteen-year-running subcultural institution *Too Much Light Makes The Baby Go Blind (30 Plays in 60 Minutes)*. He has been a Neo-Futurist since 1999, performing also in *The Unfinished Works of Sir Linear Scribble* and *Jokes and Their Relation to the Unconscious*. Before moving to Chicago, his work in Massachusetts included performances at the Gloucester Stage Company, Mobius, The Comedy Studio, ArtSpace and The Boston Center for the Arts. His plays, *Leaving Mr. Wonderful* (1998), *Is It Physics or Lousy Luck That Turns Everything To Crap?* (1998) and *Toying With Bobby* (1999) were produced at the AmeriCulture Arts Festival. *Waging Minimum War* (1999), a co-written play, was produced at the Boston Center for the Arts and *Salvation, Thy Name is Woman* (1999) was produced at the City Playhouse in Los Angeles.

HUMANA FESTIVAL PRODUCTION

Hype-R-Connectivity premiered at the Humana Festival of New American Plays in February of 2001 in association with The Neo-Futurists. It was written, directed and performed by Andy Bayiates.

Hype-R-Connectivity

A cheery recorded voice which never takes a breath is heard in characteristic stops and starts.

RECORDED VOICE: Welcome to the Hyper-Connectivity Customer Care Menu. Your attention is important to us. Please hold while we connect you to our menu.

(Blaring elevator music for two or three seconds.)

Thank you for holding. Please listen to our Hyper-Connectivity menu carefully before making your selection.

If you wish to hear a comedy, please press one now.

If you wish to hear a tragedy, please press two now.

If you wish to hear a barbed comedy, a dark comedy, a tragicomedy or a political satire, please press three now.

For all other genres, please press four or stay on the line to speak with one of our genre representatives.

If you would like this play to end, please hang up and extricate yourself from this listening station immediately.

I'm sorry. We did not detect a recognizable selection. Please try again—

I'm sorry. We did not detect a recognizable selection.

Please try again—

I'm sorry. We did not detect a recognizable selection. Please hold while we connect you to our help menu.

(Blaring music again.)

Welcome to our Hyper-Connectivity help menu. An easy navigation through our Great Fun Interactive Tele-Com-Portal is one of our highest priorities. In order that we may assist you more efficiently, please listen to our Hyper-Connectivity help menu carefully before making your selection.

(Voice much louder.)

If you are having difficulty hearing our menu selections, please press one now.

(Back to normal volume.)

Tu ne comprendes pas l'anglais? Press two now.

If you have a rotary phone, or you have been pressing numbers and you believe your dial pad is not registering, please press four now, or stay on the line for further assistance.

(Blaring music.)

Thank you for holding. A customer care representative will be with you shortly.

(Blaring music.)

Your attention is important to us. Please stay on the line.

(Blaring music interrupts with a ringing phone, a hopeful pickup...a short silence.)

Your call has been transferred. Please hold.

(Blaring music.)

In order that we may meet your needs more efficiently, you have been transferred to a voice-activated customer care menu. Before you speak with one of our representatives, please make a selection from the following menu, using your own voice.

If you have a rotary phone, please say the word "one," now.

If your dial pad is malfunctioning, please say the word "two" now, or hang up and dial your phone company.

If neither of these selections is appropriate and you would like to speak directly with one of our customer care representatives, please say the word "three" or stay on the line for further assistance.

Your call has been transferred.

(Blaring music, twice as long as before.)

Due to heavy call volume, we estimate you will spend more than nineteen minutes waiting for our next available representative. It is our recommendation that you call us back at another time.

If you do wish to hold to speak to one of our representatives, bearing in mind it will take more than twenty-three minutes to do so, please press "one" now.

If you wish to call us back at another time, please hang up now, or stay on the line until we disconnect you.

(Blaring music.)

You will be disconnected shortly.

(Blaring music.)

Your attention is important to us.

(Blaring music, more hopeful ringing, a click, a pause...)

Thank you for your patience. Please hold.

(More music.)

You will be disconnected shortly.

(Music, stop, click, silence...)

Good-bye.

END OF PLAY

Call Waiting
by Rachel Claff

Copyright © 2001 by Rachel Claff. All rights reserved. CAUTION: Professionals and amateurs are hereby warned that *Call Waiting* is subject to a royalty. It is fully protected under the copyright laws of the United States of America and of all countries covered by the International Copyright Union (including the Dominion of Canada and the rest of the British Commonwealth), the Berne Convention, the Pan-American Copyright Convention and the Universal Copyright Convention, as well as all countries with which the United States has reciprocal copyright relations. All rights, including professional, amateur stage rights, motion picture, recitation, lecturing, public reading, radio broadcasting, television, video or sound recording, all other forms of mechanical or electronic reproduction, such as CD-ROM, CD-I, information storage and retrieval systems and photocopying, and the rights of translation into foreign languages, are strictly reserved. Particular emphasis is laid upon the matter of readings, permission for which must be secured from the Author's agent in writing.

ALL INQUIRIES CONCERNING RIGHTS, INCLUDING AMATEUR RIGHTS, SHOULD BE ADDRESSED TO:THE NEO-FUTURISTS, 5153 N. ASHLAND, CHICAGO, IL 60640.

BIOGRAPHY

Rachel Claff has been performing and writing with the Neo-Futurists in Chicago, Illinois since October 1996. Since her debut, she has written over 200 original short plays for *Too Much Light Makes the Baby Go Blind (30 plays in 60 minutes)*. Her most recent Neo-Futurist work, *Curious Beautiful* (co-written and devised with partner Connor Kalista) was named one of the Best Shows of 2000 (*Chicago Sun-Times*) and Most Transcendent Show of 2000 (*Chicago Tribune*). She is also the author of two Neo-Futurist solo performance pieces: *Spit it Out* (1997) and *Why2K* (1999). Her full-length play, *Press Release*, won the 1995 New England New Playwrights Contest and was a finalist in Boston's Clauder Competition (1995). Other credits include work with Chicago's Shakespeare Repertory (*Hamlet, The Merry Wives of Windsor*), the Goodman Theatre (*Arcadia*), Open Door Theater Company and Bailiwick Repertory. Ms. Claff is a 1995 graduate of Oberlin College and attended the National Theater Institute in Waterford, Connecticut in 1994.

HUMANA FESTIVAL PRODUCTION

Call Waiting premiered at the Humana Festival of New American Plays in February of 2001 in association with The Neo-Futurists. It was written, directed and performed by Rachel Claff.

Call Waiting

Sound of an off-the-hook telephone buzz, faint. Added sound of busy signal, faint and slightly slowed. Added sound of faint clicking of a telephone being replaced and lifted from its cradle. This forms the underscore for the female voice, which speaks in rhythm to the sounds.

VOICE: i know you won't call
    but its all about waiting
    to want you
    to reach me
    to teach me the sound of your voice
    i'm forgetting you   letting you
    slip
    out of range

    it seems strange
    that two people so greedy for touching each other
    so needy to know how to say the word lover
    so skilled in the language
    of lips hands and eyes
    it's surprising
    to struggle for words
    and to listen to silences
    turning against me
    immense and untold
    and unfolding like maps
    of an enemy land

    in the flat of your hand
    i could pour my life story
    you'd heard it before
    still
    you listened with care

"if i let you keep this
i know you can't hurt me"
i said
"now i know that
it's going somewhere"

what i didn't count on
was distance
hissing through wires
and missing you
kissing
it disconnects me

rejects me

and forges your name
at the end of each half-hearted letter
"it's better
this way"

but which way is that?

can you give me directions?
can you show me a street sign
or line me up facing the sun
or the moon?

or just call me

soon

(Sound of clicking drops out. Sound of busy-signal drops out. Only the buzz of the phone line for a few beats. Then silence.)

END OF PLAY

Message Sent
by Sterling Houston

Copyright © 2001 by Sterling Houston. All rights reserved. CAUTION: Professionals and amateurs are hereby warned that *Message Sent* is subject to a royalty. It is fully protected under the copyright laws of the United States of America and of all countries covered by the International Copyright Union (including the Dominion of Canada and the rest of the British Commonwealth), the Berne Convention, the Pan-American Copyright Convention and the Universal Copyright Convention, as well as all countries with which the United States has reciprocal copyright relations. All rights, including professional, amateur stage rights, motion picture, recitation, lecturing, public reading, radio broadcasting, television, video or sound recording, all other forms of mechanical or electronic reproduction, such as CD-ROM, CD-I, information storage and retrieval systems and photocopying, and the rights of translation into foreign languages, are strictly reserved. Particular emphasis is laid upon the matter of readings, permission for which must be secured from the Author's agent in writing.

ALL INQUIRIES CONCERNING RIGHTS, INCLUDING AMATEUR RIGHTS, SHOULD BE ADDRESSED TO: JUMP-START PERFORMANCE COMPANY, 108 BLUE STAR, SAN ANTONIO, TX 78204.

BIOGRAPHY

Sterling Houston is Artistic Director and Writer-In-Residence for Jump-Start Performance Company. During his thirty-year career in theater as an actor, composer and playwright, he has worked with Charles Ludlam, Sam Shepard, Maya Angelou and George C. Wolfe. Houston has premiered twenty plays since 1988. He is the recipient of numerous awards and grants including commissioning grants from Mid-American Arts Alliance, National Endowment for the Arts, The Texas Commission on the Arts, The Rockefeller Foundation, and Art Matters, Inc. His plays have been presented throughout Texas and regionally at Judson Poet's Theater, NYC, Victory Gardens Theater in Chicago, Cleveland Public Theater and the Phoenix Theater in Indianapolis. His first book of fiction, the novella *Le Griffon*, was published in 2000 by Pecan Grove Press.

JUMP-START PERFORMANCE COMPANY

Jump-Start Performance Company of San Antonio has produced or presented five hundred original works since it was founded in 1985 and has reached an audience of over a quarter million people. Taking a special interest in community outreach and education, Jump-Start Performance Company sponsors several programs that bring theatre to the community at such venues as homeless shelters, juvenile detention facilities, and a variety of public and private schools.

HUMANA FESTIVAL PRODUCTION

Message Sent premiered at the Humana Festival of New American Plays in February of 2001 in association with Jump-Start Performance Company. It was directed by Steve Bailey with the following cast:

Nurse . . . . Debbie Basham-Burns
Male Friend. . . . . Steve Bailey
Sister. . . . . Lisa Suarez
Jonathan . . . . Paul Bonin-Rodriguez

and with the following production staff:

Sound/Music. . . . . Felice Garcia

Message Sent

AUTOMATED VOICE: You have eight new messages in you mailbox. First message, Friday, 6:30 AM. *(BEEP)*

NURSE: *(Cool professional concern.)* Hello, this is the Hospice service calling. Your friend Jonathan has gone into a coma and you are on a list of people we need to call. Please call here or leave a message at Dr. Moore's answering service as soon as you get this. Thanks. God Bless. *(BEEP)*

AUTOMATED VOICE: Second message, Friday, 10:05 AM. *(BEEP)*

MALE FRIEND: *(With forced good cheer.)* Hey dude, are you there? Where the hell are you? Listen, Jon is going fast—call me when you get this, we really need you now. Even though we knew what was coming, now that it's here, well, you know it's a whole different ball game. You were always the strongest one, dude, that is, next to Jon. God I hope you get this. Anyway, we'll see you soon. *(BEEP)*

AUTOMATED VOICE: Third message, Friday, 2:24 PM. *(BEEP)*

SISTER: *(With controlled alarm.)* Hey. Are you still out of town? Pick-up if you're back... shit! Listen this is your sister as if you didn't know. I had a long visit with Jon a few days ago. Before he...He seemed really scared. I tried to soothe him but he couldn't stop crying. It was pretty awful. He kept talking about Paris and trying to apologize for something. He misses you. I didn't get it, maybe it was just the meds but it was real tough. Anyway, please—please call us, babe. I don't think he's gonna last much longer.

AUTOMATED VOICE: Fourth message, Saturday, 9:45 AM. *(BEEP)*

NURSE: This is Dr. Moore's office calling, we wanted to let you know that we're taking Jonathan back to his home, as he requested. He's regained consciousness and is as stable as can be expected. Give a call back when you get this, or come by after noon today, if you can. Have a nice day. *(BEEP)*

AUTOMATED VOICE: Fifth message, Saturday, 3:00 PM. *(BEEP)*

MALE FRIEND: *(With suppressed rage.)* God, aren't you home yet? I'm getting real tired of this... Look, we need Jonathan's phone book to make calls and none of us can find it. So you know where it is? The one he brought back from hospice was all out of date, most of the numbers are disconnected or the people are all dead. It's too weird. Christ! Where are you? Will this ever end? Call me, goddammit, OK? I love you. *(BEEP)*

AUTOMATED VOICE: Sixth message, Saturday, 7:35 PM. *(BEEP)*

SISTER: *(Distraught, on the verge of breaking.)* Hey, it's me again. Uh, he's dying. I helped him home but he...he didn't seem to recognize it. Kept asking me, "Is this my room?" "Yeah, honey," I told him, "just like you left it." I told him. He said, "No really, is this my room?" It was strange. He looks sorta bad, but he keeps asking about Paris and where you are and when can he go. Where are you? The hospice worker says this is probably it. Call me. *(BEEP)*

AUTOMATED VOICE: Seventh message, Sunday, 5:01 PM. *(BEEP)*

NURSE: *(Cool and calm.)* This is Dr. Moore's office. I'm sorry to have to inform you that your friend Jonathan was pronounced dead at three minutes after nine this morning. His remains, as per his wishes, will be cremated this afternoon. You have our deepest sympathy. Please have a nice day. *(BEEP)*

AUTOMATED VOICE: Eighth message, today, 12:02 AM. *(BEEP)*

JONATHAN: *(Scratchy hollow voice.)* Hey honey...it's me. It's Jon. It's cold here. I can see without my glasses. I tried to wait for you...I'm sorry. For everything. But I—well, you know...don't you? Can you take my ashes to Paris? Someday. If you feel like it. I feel you with me, even though you were stranded. I...God, it's beautiful here...there's music. Can you hear it? What is that...music? *(BEEP)*

AUTOMATED VOICE: There are no more messages in your mailbox. Thank you for calling.

END OF PLAY

Owls
by Erin Courtney

Copyright © 2001 by Erin Courtney. All rights reserved. CAUTION: Professionals and amateurs are hereby warned that *Owls* is subject to a royalty. It is fully protected under the copyright laws of the United States of America and of all countries covered by the International Copyright Union (including the Dominion of Canada and the rest of the British Commonwealth), the Berne Convention, the Pan-American Copyright Convention and the Universal Copyright Convention, as well as all countries with which the United States has reciprocal copyright relations. All rights, including professional, amateur stage rights, motion picture, recitation, lecturing, public reading, radio broadcasting, television, video or sound recording, all other forms of mechanical or electronic reproduction, such as CD-ROM, CD-I, information storage and retrieval systems and photocopying, and the rights of translation into foreign languages, are strictly reserved. Particular emphasis is laid upon the matter of readings, permission for which must be secured from the Author's agent in writing.

ALL INQUIRIES CONCERNING RIGHTS, INCLUDING AMATEUR RIGHTS, SHOULD BE ADDRESSED TO: CLUBBED THUMB, 312 EAST 23RD ST #4B, NEW YORK, NY 10010.

BIOGRAPHY

Erin Courtney has been an affiliated artist with Clubbed Thumb for five years. Clubbed Thumb has produced three of her plays: *Pricked, Summer Play,* and *Downwinders.* Her play *Mother's Couch* was produced by the Flea Theater in New York City and her ten-minue play *A Brilliant Fast* was produced by Lightening Ensemble at the Soho Theatre in London. Ms. Courtney earned her B.A. in Art from Brown University and she is currently working towards her graduate degree in playwriting from Brooklyn College. She is a recipient of a Mac Dowell fellowship and a New York State Council of the Arts grant. Ms. Courtney has taught art and playwriting in the New York City public schools through the Guggenheim Museum, and she has been an adjunct faculty member at Brooklyn College and Cooper Union.

CLUBBED THUMB

Founded in New York in 1996, Clubbed Thumb has produced over thirty plays by living American writers, many of which have been presented as part of Summerworks, their annual festival of new plays. Clubbed Thumb has premiered the works of such writers as Charles L. Mee, Jr., Carson Kreitzer, Karl Gajdusek, and Erin Courtney, and produced two new plays by Mac Wellman in the 1998 Mac Wellman Festival.

HUMANA FESTIVAL PRODUCTION

Owls premiered at the Humana Festival of New American Plays in February of 2001 in association with Clubbed Thumb. It was directed by Pam MacKinnon with the following cast:

Female Voice . . . . Colleen Werthman
Male Voice. . . . . Dan Illian

and with the following production staff:

Sound Designer . . . . Mark Huang

Owls

FEMALE VOICE: I'm surrounded by owls.

MALE VOICE: How many?

FEMALE VOICE: Wait. I'll hold the phone up so you can hear them everywhere. *(Silence.)* Isn't it amazing?

MALE VOICE: How many are there?

FEMALE VOICE: Hundreds. Fifty. Their eyes are peeping out of trees.

MALE VOICE: What state are you in?

FEMALE VOICE: I'm lying on the ground just looking up at the stars.

MALE VOICE: Your mother wants to know your exact coordinates.

FEMALE VOICE: Just below Orion's belt.

MALE VOICE: In case we need to send a search party for you. HA HA. *(Cell phone static.)* Are you there?

FEMALE VOICE: The owls are swooping and crying.

MALE VOICE: What?

FEMALE VOICE: They're swooping down.

MALE VOICE: Can you hear me?

(Static clears.)

FEMALE VOICE: It's quiet now. They've stopped.

MALE VOICE: We want to see you.

FEMALE VOICE: Do you think Mom will let me back in?

MALE VOICE: Come home. *(Pause.)* Is it cold out there?

FEMALE VOICE: I'm wearing thermals and I've got a fire going.

MALE VOICE: You're missing a lot of good T.V.

FEMALE VOICE: I've got books.

MALE VOICE: And owls.

FEMALE VOICE: There's a llama here, too. There's two of them. I weave their wool during the daylight hours.

MALE VOICE: You? Weave?

FEMALE VOICE: I do. It's a farm and this is how I help out. There's a pond here too and a willow tree. And here comes a pig. You should see it. It is an ugly P.I.G.

MALE VOICE: It doesn't sound like you are outside. I don't hear anything.

(The sound of a toilet flushing.)

FEMALE VOICE: Oh!

MALE VOICE: Where are you? A Walmart? Which Walmart? I'll come get you.

FEMALE VOICE: I'm in the great outdoors.

MALE VOICE: Which Walmart?

FEMALE VOICE: I'll say goodnight to the stars for you. And to the pig and the llamas and the thousands of owls.

MALE VOICE: Don't hang up. I'll come get you. Don't hang up.

FEMALE VOICE: They all say goodnight Dad. Goodnight Dad.

MALE VOICE: Don't go.

(The sound of a phone disconnecting.)

END OF PLAY

Somebody Call 911
by Jennifer L. Nelson

Copyright © 2001 by Jennifer L. Nelson. All rights reserved. CAUTION: Professionals and amateurs are hereby warned that *Somebody Call 911* is subject to a royalty. It is fully protected under the copyright laws of the United States of America and of all countries covered by the International Copyright Union (including the Dominion of Canada and the rest of the British Commonwealth), the Berne Convention, the Pan-American Copyright Convention and the Universal Copyright Convention, as well as all countries with which the United States has reciprocal copyright relations. All rights, including professional, amateur stage rights, motion picture, recitation, lecturing, public reading, radio broadcasting, television, video or sound recording, all other forms of mechanical or electronic reproduction, such as CD-ROM, CD-I, information storage and retrieval systems and photocopying, and the rights of translation into foreign languages, are strictly reserved. Particular emphasis is laid upon the matter of readings, permission for which must be secured from the Author's agent in writing.

ALL INQUIRIES CONCERNING RIGHTS, INCLUDING AMATEUR RIGHTS, SHOULD BE ADDRESSED TO: AFRICAN CONTINUUM THEATRE COMPANY, 3523 12TH STREET NE, SECOND FLOOR, WASHINGTON, DC 20017-2545.

BIOGRAPHY

Jennifer L. Nelson is the Artistic Director of the African Continuum Theatre Company. She is the former the Artistic Director of the Everyday Theatre Company and Associate Artistic Director of the Living Stage Theatre Company, the community outreach program for Arena Stage. She has worked for twenty-eight years as an actress, arts administrator, director and playwright. She has been the recipient of such awards as the Mayor's Award for Excellence in Artistic Discipline, the Charles McArthur/Helen Hayes Award for Most Outstanding New Play, and two Larry Writers Awards. She is also currently an adjunct faculty member of George Washington University. Other plays by Ms. Nelson include *A Mile in My Shoes, No Harm Done, Torn from the Headlines, Hubert & Charlie* and several short plays.

AFRICAN CONTINUUM THEATRE COMPANY

Originally founded in 1990, the African Continuum Theatre Company (ACTCo) of Washington D.C. has quickly established a reputation for bold new work, placing emphasis on reflecting the African and African-American experience. ACTCo has premiered several new plays and collaborated with other companies on various projects including experimentations in hip-hop theatre. They have won numerous honors in recognition of their social and artistic contributions.

HUMANA FESTIVAL PRODUCTION

Somebody Call 911 premiered at the Humana Festival of New American Plays in February of 2001 in association with African Continuum Theatre Company. It was directed by Jennifer L. Nelson with the following cast:

Cassandra . . . . Deidra LaWan Starnes
Jerome . . . . KenYatta Rogers
Global Messaging Service. . . . . Jennifer L. Nelson

Somebody Call 911 was recorded at WPFW-FM Pacifica Radio with the following production staff:

Sound Engineer . . . . Bob Daughtry

Somebody Call 911

Sound of answering service picking up.

MACHINE VOICE: Welcome to Global Power Voice Messaging Service. Please hold while the party you have dialed is located.

JEROME: *(Young African-American male voice on answering machine.)* Yo. Bow-wow-wow. The big dawg is out so he can't come to the phone right now. Leave them numbers after the beep and somebody will get back to you soon as I can. Peace. Out. Oh yeah, in the future if you don't want to hear this message, press star.

CASSANDRA: *(A distraught young African-American female. In the background is the sound of a very young infant crying.)* Jerome, I know you're home. Pick up the phone. Come on, Boo, pick up the phone. Please? Look, I know you're there 'cause I just seen Big Mac drive by and I know you don't go nowhere with out him watching your back. *(Pause. We hear the girl breathing and the baby crying.)* Aright aright, if that's the way you want to play it, that's the way it's gon be. You ain't all that, no how, Jerome Delonte Brown. Only reason I'm calling you is to tell you to come get your son.

JEROME: Yo, Cassandra, I thought I told you to stop calling me. Why you trying to carry me like this?

CASSANDRA: Un-hunh. I knew you was home and I ain't trying to carry nobody. You was supposed to pick RayQuon up from my mother on Thursday but you ain't never show up and she missed her appointment to get her nails did, sitting here waiting on your sorry behind.

JEROME: Man, you know you mother and I can't be in the same room together. She always act like she got a beef with me.

CASSANDRA: So? I don't want to hear all that. That's your son. Now Mama say she won't stay with him when you supposed to be doing it and I can't get out the house at all. And you know I can't be up in this apartment all day long by myself. I'm too young to let a baby tie me down. *(Sound of crying gets louder.)* Shut up, boy! What I tell you about crying all the time? *(The sound of a slap, followed by louder crying.)* Shut up!

JEROME: Damn. Don't be hitting my son.

CASSANDRA: What else I'm gonna do? This boy cry all the time. I think he retarded or some kind of not normal, always want somebody to hold him or something. Listen to this... *(Baby crying.)* I'm telling you, Jerome, you need to come over here and get this baby now.

JEROME: Damn Cassandra, I told you I can't. Why don't you call that social worker lady and leave me the fuck alone.

CASSANDRA: Hell no. Every time I see her she talking about foster care and adoption. Shit. Don't nobody want to hear that. It's your turn. You 'sposed to take care of him half the time, that's what you said you was going do, now you need to get your narrow ass over here and do it. *(Hang up click.)* Jerome? Oh no you did-int. I know you did not hang up on me. Jerome? *(Redial; answering service picks up.)*

MACHINE VOICE: Welcome to Global Power Voice Messaging... *(star tone)*

CASSANDRA: *(Now in tears.)* I cannot believe you hung up on me! This is not fair. Alls I'm trying to do is go back to school this month so I can graduate with the rest of the ninth grade. *(Baby's crying is now desperate.)* Goddam it, boy, shut up! Shut up! *(Sound of two slaps.)* Look, I can't take this. I got to get outta here. You can come get this baby when you ready. I'll leave the door unlocked. I got to get outta here.

(Sound of door slamming, then crying resumes.)

MACHINE VOICE: Thank you for using Global Power Voice Messaging Service. To send your message, press pound now.

(Crying continues. Dial tone.)

END OF PLAY

Click
by Brighde Mullins

Copyright © 2001 by Brighde Mullins. All rights reserved. CAUTION: Professionals and amateurs are hereby warned that *Click* is subject to a royalty. It is fully protected under the copyright laws of the United States of America and of all countries covered by the International Copyright Union (including the Dominion of Canada and the rest of the British Commonwealth), the Berne Convention, the Pan-American Copyright Convention and the Universal Copyright Convention, as well as all countries with which the United States has reciprocal copyright relations. All rights, including professional, amateur stage rights, motion picture, recitation, lecturing, public reading, radio broadcasting, television, video or sound recording, all other forms of mechanical or electronic reproduction, such as CD-ROM, CD-I, information storage and retrieval systems and photocopying, and the rights of translation into foreign languages, are strictly reserved. Particular emphasis is laid upon the matter of readings, permission for which must be secured from the Author's agent in writing.

ALL INQUIRIES CONCERNING RIGHTS, INCLUDING AMATEUR RIGHTS, SHOULD BE ADDRESSED TO: CHARLES KOPELMAN, DOUGLAS & KOPELMAN ARTISTS, INC., 393 WEST 49TH STREET, SUITE 5G, NEW YORK, NY 10019.

BIOGRAPHY

Brighde Mullins' plays include *Dominant Looking Males* (NYU's Tisch School of the Arts, directed by Marc Wing-Davey); *Fire Eater* (The Actors Centre, London, directed by Marc Wing-Davey; New York Stage and Film, directed by Maria Mileaf); *Topographical Eden* (The Magic Theatre, San Francisco, winner, Jane Chambers Award). Residencies and workshops include Mabou Mines, Lincoln Center Director's Lab, Harvard's Institute on Art and Civic Dialogue, Hartford Stage, The Public, and New York Theatre Workshop, where she is a Usual Suspect. Her poems appear in many journals and in *The Best of the Best American Poetry 1984-94* edited by Harold Bloom. Mullins was raised in Las Vegas, Nevada, and studies at UNLV, Yale, and the Iowa Writers Workshop. She divides her time between San Francisco, where she teaches college, and New York, where she works at an art museum.

THICK DESCRIPTION THEATRE COMPANY

Located in San Francisco, California, Thick Description has premiered new plays by American authors Suzan-Lori Parks, David Greenspan, Oliver Mayer, Han Ong and more during its seven-year production history. In 1997, Thick Description was featured in *American Theatre* for the importance of their experimental work.

HUMANA FESTIVAL PRODUCTION

Click premiered at the Humana Festival of New American Plays in February of 2001 in association with Thick Description Theatre Company. It was directed by Tony Kelly with the following cast:

Woman . . . . Amy Resnick
Man . . . . Warren David Keith

Click

MAN: What are you doing?

WOMAN: Doing?

MAN: While you're talking to me. I hear something. What are you doing?

WOMAN: What does it sound like?

MAN: Click—click—click.

WOMAN: Oh—that click?—it's the window blind in a breeze. A slight breeze—it's me unsnapping my tortoise shell barrette—I clipped and unclipped it. It's my Italian lighter lighting up my last blonde gauloise. It's some cheap Christmas trash tinselling its way down the street. It's my birthstone ring hitting the floor. It's a bird's beak tapping, it's morse code, it's an urgent message we can't decipher but need to know, it's the deadbolt on the back-door, it's the heater snicking into action, it's the clock stuck on One, One, One, it's a glitch on the wires, it's the loose jawbone that clicks in my head from where I took a fall on the ice last winter.

It's my nailclipper.

MAN: I'm really sick of your metaphors.

WOMAN: You used to like my turns of phrase.

MAN: That was before I started re-hab.

WOMAN: Recovery takes the Poetry out of Things, huh?

MAN: At a nickel a minute from a payphone in a drafty corridor, yeah. I'd say so. Yeah. It's all just words.

WOMAN: That's all we have right now, isn't it? You're two thousand miles away and we're reduced to Words, Right?

MAN: Yeah. I guess so.

WOMAN: So the corridor is drafty.

MAN: Yeah.

WOMAN: What color are the walls?

MAN: Green.

WOMAN: Make me see the green.

MAN: Greenish.

WOMAN: A brown green or a yellow green?

MAN: Cocktail olive green. Drab green. Military green.

WOMAN: Windows?

MAN: One up high. Too small for a body to crawl through.

WOMAN: Describe it.

MAN: High. And sideways. And there are tables, and old mouldy armchairs, they give off a smell like sweat and urine—or maybe it's like old cheese—

WOMAN: Brie?

MAN: Cheddar—sharp and sickly—and there are magazines, lots of them. Piles of old *National Geographics*. And God all of this and talking to you and "this is like" and "this is like." Nothing is Like Anything except that I could use something like a drink.

(Sound in: click.)

MAN: There's that click again. Are you opening a beer?

WOMAN: *(Momentary pause.)* I'm opening a SODA.

MAN: You're drinking beer! You're drinking beer while I'm calling you from rehab?

WOMAN: I understand how very difficult this is for you, and I'm talking to you and I'm trying to be supportive. I would never drink a beer while talking to you. *(Pause.)* It's a lite beer. It's practically a soda.

MAN: A lite beer? I have to go.

WOMAN: Wait. That was a Metaphor— *(Sound in: Click. Dead Wire.)* Hullo—

END OF PLAY